Childhood Temporary Separation
Long-term Effects of W   Var 2

J.S.M. Rusby

DISSERTATION.COM

Boca Raton

Childhood Temporary Separation:
Long-term Effects of Wartime Evacuation in World War 2

Copyright © 2005 J.S.M. Rusby
All rights reserved.

Dissertation.com
Boca Raton, Florida
USA • 2008

ISBN-10: 1-59942-657-9
ISBN-13: 978-1-59942-657-0

Childhood Temporary Separation: Long-term effects of wartime Evacuation in World War 2

James Stuart Musgrave Rusby

Thesis submitted in fulfilment of the requirements for the degree of
Doctor of Philosophy in the University of London

Department of Psychology
Birkbeck College
2005

Abstract

This study investigates possible links between temporary separation from parents in childhood due to evacuation in World War 2 and later psychological development and adult relationships. The conclusions from an earlier qualitative pilot study had suggested that the developmental outcome of evacuation was perceived by those involved as lying on a continuum, at one extreme the experience was 'life-enhancing' and at the other it had left an 'emotional legacy' depending on an individual's experience. This present lifespan survey using self report questionnaires and involving 900 respondents from the county of Kent confirmed these perceptions and examined whether they were reflected by measures of mental health, marital history and adult attachment. The methodology employed univariate and multivariate analyses, including causal structural models of depression for both sexes, and involved both childhood and life-course mediating variables.

In terms of mental health highly significant associations were found for the evacuation experience variables of Age at Evacuation and Care Received with the Incidence of Depression, Clinical Anxiety and Factor 2, Self-criticism, of the Depressive Experiences Questionnaire (Blatt et al., 1976), all in the predicted sense. Females were found to be particularly vulnerable to Clinical Anxiety if evacuated at 10-12 years with an incidence of 18%, accompanied by a high level of Self-criticism. Structural path models for the onset of depression confirmed that females not only had higher levels of Factor 1, Dependency, but were more vulnerable to these levels. Divorce rates were also highly associated with these same evacuation variables and multiple divorce rates for both sexes fell from 10%, if evacuated at 4-6 years, to 0% for those evacuated at 13-15 years. Adult attachment style measured by the self-report Relationship Questionnaire (Bartholomew & Horowitz, 1991) was also affected, with a fall in the Fearful style from 25% to 7% with increasing age at evacuation. Overall there was a tendency for male respondents to move to the Dismissive and females to the Fearful styles when secure attachment was lost.

It is believed that such a lifespan development study, based on an 'experiment in nature' and involving an ageing cohort, has potential value in influencing future policy in the fields of mental health and social care.

This survey is dedicated to Diana - who inspired me with her story

to Vigdis - who provided encouragement
and support over many years

to 'Bonnie' - who ensured I got two good walks a day
to drive the cobwebs away

and to all those 'evacuees' who generously shared their
experiences and feelings with me and are the heart of this work

Acknowledgements

My thanks go to a number of people who have encouraged and supported me as well as providing practical and technical help in this project.

Stephen Frosh was kind enough to supervise the 4th-year BSc. psychology final year research project which became the pilot study which preceded this PhD survey and Stephen Davies of the Princess Alexandra Hospital at Harlow gave me great encouragement after I had completed the pilot study and also assessed the draft questionnaire for the main survey. My thanks go to Sydney Blatt of Yale University who kindly agreed to provide me with a copy of the Depressive Experiences Questionnaire and the item factor coefficients required for the scale analysis. Caroline Kelly kindly volunteered to be my first supervisor and gave me valuable guidance before disappearing to do more vital things like adding to her growing family. Paul Barber always took a kindly interest in my slow progress and was instrumental in encouraging me to sample the delights of structural equation modelling; Chris Fife-Schaw of Surrey University was responsible for attempting to inaugurate me into the mysteries of this black art, but I do not hold him responsible for the output! I would also like to thank Greta Cason in the Birkbeck office for coping with the delivery of the many completed questionnaires. My thanks also to Antonia Bifulco and Stephen Davies in their capacity as my examiners and for the many valuable recommendations they made.

Above all, though, I owe a great debt of gratitude to Fiona Tasker, who stayed by me as my supervisor over eight years, and who was always available to hear my woes and did so much to encourage and guide me and to try to keep me on the straight and narrow scientific path. Thank you Fiona.

The author gratefully acknowledges the financial support provided by the University of London Central Research Fund in the production of the questionnaire for this survey.

This study was carried out solely by the named author.

Contents   Page

Abstract   2

Acknowledgements   4

Chapter 1 The Evacuation - history and experience   23

    1.1 Introduction   23

    1.2 The evacuation scheme and its implementation 23

    1.3 Experience of the evacuation   25

Chapter 2 Research studies and theoretical considerations   29

    2.1 Introduction   29

    2.2 Research studies related to the long-term effects of evacuation or childhood separation   30

    2.3 Theoretical considerations regarding the choice of outcome variables   35

        2.3.1 Respondent's perceptions of the effect of their evacuation experience on their development and adult lives   35

        2.3.2 The evacuation experience and adult mental health   37

        2.3.3 The evacuation experience and marital history   41

        2.3.4 The evacuation experience and adult attachment   45

    2.4 Summary of the research aims   50

Chapter 3 Methodology   53

    3.1 Samples and Procedures   53

        3.1.1 Characteristics of the evacuation experience   55

	Page
3.2 Measures	57
3.2.1 The Questionnaire	57
3.2.2 The chosen variables	59
3.2.2.1 Upbringing variables	59
3.2.2.2 Evacuation variables	60
3.2.2.3 War-related variables	61
3.2.2.4 Life-course variables	62
3.2.2.5 Outcome variables - Perceptions	63
3.2.2.6 Outcome variables - Mental Health	67
3.2.2.7 Outcome variables - Marital History	69
3.2.2.8 Outcome variables - Adult Attachment	70
3.3 Statistical procedures	74
3.3.1 Univariate statistics	75
3.3.2 Multivariate statistics	76
3.4 Layout of results chapters and summary of key hypotheses	77

Chapter 4 The evacuation experience and respondents' perceptions of its influences on their development and adult lives — 80

4.1 Introduction	80
4.2 Respondents' perceptions of the evacuation experience and its influence on their development and adult lives	80
4.2.1 Analysis	80
4.2.2 Results	80
4.3 Conclusions	86

Chapter 5 Mental Health — 88

5.1 Introduction	88
5.2 Long-term effects of evacuation on mental health	89
5.2.1 Analysis	89

		Page
5.2.2 Results		90
5.2.2.1 Overall effect of the Incidence of evacuation and Gender as a function of the outcome variables of Mental health		90
5.2.2.2 Evacuation Experience variables and Gender as a function of the outcome variables of Mental health		94
5.2.2.2.1 Incidence of Depression		96
5.2.2.2.2 Incidence of Clinical Anxiety		99
5.2.2.2.3 Mean score for Factor 1 - Dependency		100
5.2.2.2.4 Mean score for Factor 2 - Self-criticism		102
5.2.2.2.5 Mean score for Morbidity symptoms		104
5.2.2.2.6 Age at evacuation		105
5.2.2.2.7 Care received during evacuation		106
5.2.2.2.8 Period away, Frequency of parental visits and Number of billets		107
5.2.3 Summary		108
5.2.4 Discussion		109
5.3 Long-term effects of upbringing on mental health		113
5.3.1 Analysis		113
5.3.2 Results		114
5.3.2.1 Nurture		115
5.3.2.2 Divorce or Separation of parents		119
5.3.2.3 Death of a parent		119
5.3.2.4 Parental Class		120
5.3.3 Summary		121
5.3.4 Discussion		121
5.4 Long-term effect of the quality of nurture in upbringing and care received during evacuation on adult mental health		124
5.4.1 Analysis		124
5.4.2 Results		124
5.4.2.1 Incidence of Depression		125
5.4.2.2 Mean score for Factor 1 - Dependency		127

	Page
5.4.2.3 Mean score for Factor 2 - Self-criticism	128
5.4.2.4 Mean score for Morbidity symptoms	129
5.4.3 Summary	131
5.4.4 Discussion	131
5.5 Long-term effect of bombing and of father's absence due to war	132
5.5.1 Analysis	133
5.5.2 Results	133
5.5.2.1 Absence of Father	135
5.5.2.2 Effect of Bombing	135
5.5.3 Summary	136
5.5.4 Discussion	136
5.6 Effect of occupational class, educational level and life crises on the mental health of respondents	138
5.6.1 Analysis	138
5.6.2 Results	138
5.6.2.1 Occupational Class	140
5.6.2.2 Educational level	141
5.6.2.3 Life Crises	141
5.6.3 Summary	144
5.6.4 Discussion	144
5.7 Testing the validity of a model structure linking the major input variables of evacuation and upbringing to the Incidence of Depression	145
5.7.1 Analysis	145
5.7.2 Results	148
5.7.2.1 Female structural path model to Depression	151
5.7.2.2 Male structural path model to Depression	154

	Page
5.7.3 Summary	157
5.7.4 Discussion	158
5.8 General conclusions regarding mental health	160

Chapter 6 Marital History — 167

6.1 Introduction — 167

6.2 Long-term effects of evacuation on marital history — 167

6.2.1 Analysis — 168

6.2.2 Results — 168

6.2.2.1 Overall effect of the incidence of evacuation and gender on the outcome variables of marital health — 170

6.2.2.2 Outcome variables of Marital History as function of the Evacuation Experience variables and of Gender — 170

6.2.2.2.1 Age at evacuation — 171
6.2.2.2.2 Care received — 172
6.2.2.2.3 Period Away — 172
6.2.2.2.4 Frequency of parental visits — 173
6.2.2.2.5 Number of billets — 173

6.2.3 Summary — 173

6.2.4 Discussion — 173

6.3 Long-term effect of upbringing on marital history — 174

6.3.1 Analysis — 175

6.3.2 Results — 175

6.3.2.1 Nurture — 176

6.3.2.2 Divorce of parents — 176

6.3.2.3 Death of parents — 176

6.3.2.4 Parental Class — 177

6.3.3 Summary — 177

		Page
6.3.4 Discussion		177
6.4 Long-term effect of the quality of home nurture and care received during evacuation on the marital history of respondents		178
6.4.1 Analysis		178
6.4.2 Results		178
6.4.3 Discussion		180
6.5 Long-term effects of fathers' absence due to war service and of bombing on the marital history of respondents		180
6.5.1 Analysis		180
6.5.2 Results		181
6.5.3 Discussion		182
6.6 Relationship between occupational class and education level on the marital history of respondents		182
6.6.1 Analysis		182
6.6.2 Results		183
6.6.3 Conclusions		184
6.7 Predicting divorce through multiple regression models		184
6.7.1 Analysis		184
6.7.2 Results		185
6.7.3 Discussion		186
6.8 General conclusions regarding marital history		
Chapter 7 Adult Attachment		189
7.1 Introduction		189
7.2 Long-term effects of evacuation on adult attachment		190
7.2.1 Analysis		190
7.2.2 Results		190

7.2.2.1 Overall effect of gender	191
7.2.2.1.1 On the relationship between adult attachment styles and Depression, Morbidity and DEQ Dependency as a function of gender	191
7.2.2.2 Overall effect of evacuation	193
7.2.2.3 Outcome variables of Adult Attachment as a function of the Evacuation Experience variables and of gender	194
7.2.2.3.1 Age at evacuation	196
7.2.2.3.2 Care received during evacuation	201
7.2.2.3.3 Period away	202
7.2.2.3.4 Frequency of parental visits	203
7.2.2.3.5 Number of billets	204
7.2.3 Summary	204
7.2.4 Discussion	205
7.3 Long-term effect of upbringing on adult attachment	206
7.3.1 Analysis	207
7.3.2 Results	207
7.3.2.1 Nurture	208
7.3.2.2 Divorce or separation of parents	212
7.3.2.3 Death of parents	212
7.3.2.4 Parental class	212
7.3.3 Summary	212
7.3.4 Discussion	213
7.4 Long-term effect of the quality of home upbringing and care received during evacuation on adult attachment	214
7.4.1 Analysis	214
7.4.2 Results	214
7.4.3 Summary	218
7.4.4 Discussion	218
7.5 Long-term effects of fathers' absence due to war service and of bombing on the incidence of adult attachment	219

	Page
7.5.1 Analysis	219
7.5.2 Results	220
7.5.2.1 Fathers' absence	221
7.5.2.2 Effect of bombing	221
7.5.3 Summary	221
7.5.4 Discussion	221
7.6 The relationship between Occupational Class, Education level and Life Crises on adult attachment style	222
7.6.1 Analysis	222
7.6.2 Results	222
7.6.2.1 Occupational Class	223
7.6.2.2 Education level	224
7.6.2.3 Life Crises	224
7.6.3 Summary	224
7.6.4 Discussion	225
7.7 General conclusions regarding adult attachment	226
Chapter 8 Final conclusions of the study	230
8.1 Strengths and limitations of the survey	230
8.2 Major conclusions of the overall study	232
8.2.1 Respondents' perceptions of the effect of their evacuation experience on their development and adult lives	233
8.2.2 The effect of respondents' evacuation experience on their mental health in adulthood	234
8.2.3 The effect of respondents' evacuation experience on their marital history	238
8.2.4 The effect of respondents' evacuation experience on their adult attachment style	240

	Page
8.3 Recommendations for future work and Food for thought	243
8.3.1 Recommendations for future work	243
8.3.2 Food for thought	245
Appendix 1 Summary of the project report: *Wartime evacuation: A pilot study of some effects using grounded theory* (Rusby, 1995)	248
Appendix 2 Example of the note sent to secretaries of school associations in Kent for their use	252
Appendix 3 Research Questionnaire: *A Survey of the lives of War Children from Kent*	253
References	274

List of Tables

Page

Chapter 3

Table 3.1	(a) Occupational class distribution of the recruited sample compared to that of the population of Kent (b) Educational level of the recruited sample	55
Table 3.2	Categories of Occupational class, Educational level and Life-crises employed in the statistical analyses	62
Table 3.3	Critical events in a respondent's life which qualify as a Life crisis in terms of the statistical analysis	63
Table 3.4	Evacuation input categories with their most important properties and dimensions	65
Table 3.5	Scales used in the analysis to measure seven components of the general perception of the influence of the evacuation experience on respondents' development and lives	66
Table 3.6	Seven morbidity symptoms selected for the mental health analysis	67
Table 3.7	Coding as a function of marital status for the statistical analyses	69
Table 3.8	Statements formulated by Bartholomew & Horowitz for use in their Relationship Questionnaire	72
Table 3.9	Structural and analytical advantages of SEM over multiple regression analysis	77
Table 3.10	Summary of the hypotheses given in Chapter 2 relating to the evacuation experience	78

Chapter 4

Table 4.1	Respondents' perception of the effect of their evacuation experience on their development and adult lives as a function of the Evacuation Experience variables	81

Chapter 5

Table 5.1	Outcome variables for mental health as a function of gender on the occurrence of evacuation and the overall sample	91
Table 5.2	Incidence of Depression as a function of three conditions based on the upper (>75%) and lower (<25%) quartiles of each distribution	93
Table 5.3	Outcome variables for mental health as a function of gender and the Evacuation Experience variables	95

		Page
Table 5.4	Summary of the main results for the long-term effects of evacuation on mental health	108
Table 5.5	Comments made on the quality of care received by those female respondents who were evacuated at 10-12 years of age and suffered clinical anxiety in adulthood	111
Table 5.6	Outcome variables for mental health as a function of gender and childhood upbringing	115
Table 5.7	Summary of the main results for the long-term effects of upbringing in childhood on adult mental health	121
Table 5.8	The 8 items of the DEQ scale which load most strongly onto Factor 2, Self-criticism, of the DEQ scale, from the items listed in Section 10 of the questionnaire in Appendix 3	122
Table 5.9	Outcome variables for mental health as a function of gender, the quality of childhood upbringing and the care received during evacuation	125
Table 5.10	Summary of the results for the effect of quality of upbringing and care received in evacuation on adult mental health	131
Table 5.11	Outcome variables for mental health as a function of gender, the absence of a father due to war service and of bombing	134
Table 5.12	Summary of the results for the long-term effect of fathers' absence due to the war and of bombing	136
Table 5.13	Outcome variables for mental health as a function of gender, occupational class, education level and life crises	139
Table 5.14	Summary of the results for the effect of occupational class, educational level and life crises on the mental health of respondents	143
Table 5.15	Measured variables selected for use in the SEM analysis	147
Table 5.16	Summary of an examination of the structural path models for evacuated female and male respondents	157

Chapter 6

Table 6.1	Outcome variables for marital history as a function of gender on the overall sample and on the occurrence of evacuation	169
Table 6.2	Outcome variables for marital history as a function of gender and the evacuation experience variables	170

		Page
Table 6.3	Summary of the main results for the long-term effects of evacuation on the marital history of respondents	173
Table 6.4	Outcome variables for marital history as a function of gender and four input variables of childhood upbringing	175
Table 6.5	Summary of the results for the long-term effects of upbringing on the marital history of respondents	177
Table 6.6	Outcome variables for marital history of respondents as a function of gender, the quality of nurture and the care received during evacuation	179
Table 6.7	Outcome variables for the marital history of respondents as a function of gender, bombing and the absence of a father due to war service	181
Table 6.8	Outcome variables for the marital history of respondents as a function of gender, occupational class and education level	183
Table 6.9	Multiple linear regression analyses predicting the history of divorce for female respondents	185

Chapter 7

Table 7.1	Outcome variables for adult attachment as a function of gender on the overall sample and on the occurrence of evacuation	191
Table 7.2	Outcome variables for adult attachment as a function of gender and of the evacuation experience variables	195
Table 7.3	Summary of the main results for the long-term effects of evacuation on adult attachment	204
Table 7.4	Pearson bivariate correlation coefficients between Self-criticism and the four adult Attachment Style ratings	206
Table 7.5	Outcome variables for adult attachment as a function of gender and the four input variables of childhood upbringing	208
Table 7.6	Summary of the main results for the long-term effects of upbringing on adult attachment	213
Table 7.7	Outcome variables for adult attachment as a function of gender, the quality of childhood nurture and the care received during evacuation	215
Table 7.8	Summary of the main results for the long-term effects of the quality of home nurture and care received during evacuation on adult attachment	218
Table 7.9	Outcome variables for adult attachment as a function of gender, bombing and the absence of father due to war service	220

	Page
Table 7.10 Summary of the results for the long-term effect of a father's absence due to war service and to bombing on adult attachment style	221
Table 7.11 Outcome variables for adult attchment as a function of gender, occupational class, education level and life crises	223
Table 7.12 Summary of the results for the relationship between Occupational Class, Education level and Life Crises on attachment style	225

Appendix 1

Table A1.1 Summary of 16 interviewees evacuation details	249
Table A1.2 Input conditions on a dimension scale contributing to a perceived positive or negative outcome of th e evacuation experience	251

List of Figures

    Page

Chapter 2

Figure 2.1   Respondent's pathway through life, with the main input and mediating   51
variables and those outcome variables selected for the analysis

Chapter 3

Figure 3.1   Mean period of evacuation in years as a function of sex and the age   55
when first evacuated

Figure 3.2   Mean number of visits made during the total evacuation period as a   56
function of sex and the age when first evacuated

Figure 3.3   Mean number of foster billets as a function of age when first evacuated   57

Figure 3.4   Bartholomew and Horowitz model of adult attachment   71

Chapter 4

Figure 4.1   Mean scores for respondents' Perceptions of the effect that the   83
evacuation experience had on their development and lives, as a
function of their Age when first evacuated and their gender

Figure 4.2   Mean score for respondents' Perceptions of the effect that the   84
evacuation experience has on their development and adult lives,
as a function of the Care received during evacuation and gender

Figure 4.3   Mean score for CONFIDENCE, +/- 1 standard deviation, as a   86
function of Age in years when first evacuated

Figure 4.4   Mean score for CONFIDENCE, +/- 1 standard deviation, as a   86
a function of Care received during evacuation

Chapter 5

Figure 5.1   Respondents' pathway through life, with the input and mediating   88
variables and the mental health outcome variables selected for analysis
in this chapter

Figure 5.2   Incidence of Depression as a function of Age when first evacuated   97

Figure 5.3   Incidence of Depression as a function of Care received during   98
evacuation

Figure 5.4   Incidence of Clinical Anxiety as a function of Age when first evacuated   99

		Page
Figure 5.5	Incidence of Clinical Anxiety as a function of Care received during evacuation	100
Figure 5.6	Mean score for Dependency as a function of Care received during evacuation	101
Figure 5.7	Mean score for Dependency as a function of the Number of billets occupied by respondents	101
Figure 5.8	Mean score for Self-criticism as a function of Age when first evacuated	102
Figure 5.9	Mean score for Self-criticism as a function of Care received during evacuation	103
Figure 5.10	Mean score for Self-criticism as function of length of evacuation period in years	103
Figure 5.11	Mean score for Morbidity symptoms as a function of Care received during evacuation	104
Figure 5.12	Percentage of respondents emotionally abused as a function of age at the start of evacuation	107
Figure 5.13	Mean Self-criticism score as a function of the period away for each of the Age at evacuation groups	107
Figure 5.14	Incidence of Depression as a function of nurture received in upbringing	116
Figure 5.15	Incidence of Clinical Anxiety as a function of nurture received in upbringing	116
Figure 5.16	Mean score for Self-criticism as a function of nurture received in upbringing	117
Figure 5.17	Mean score for Morbidity symptoms as a function of nurture received in upbringing	118
Figure 5.18	Incidence of Depression as a function of the divorce or separation of parents in childhood	118
Figure 5.19	Mean score for morbidity symptoms as a function of the divorce or separation of parents in childhood	119
Figure 5.20	Incidence of Depression as a function of Death of a parent in childhood	120
Figure 5.21	Incidence of Depression for female respondents as a function of Nurture received during upbringing and Care received in evacuation	126

		Page
Figure 5.22	Mean score for Dependency as a function of Nurture received during upbringing and Care received in evacuation, plotted separately by gender	128
Figure 5.23	Mean score for Self-criticism as a function of Nurture received during upbringing and Care received in evacuation, plotted separately by gender	129
Figure 5.24	Mean score for Morbidity symptoms as a a function of Nurture received during upbringing and Care received in evacuation, plotted separately by gender	130
Figure 5.25	Incidence of Depression as a function of the Bombing of home or neighbourhood while the respondent was away from home	135
Figure 5.26	Incidence of Clinical Anxiety as a function of the Bombing of home or neighbourhood while the respondent was away from home	136
Figure 5.27	Incidence of Depression as a function of the Occupational Class of respondents	140
Figure 5.28	Mean score for Morbidity symptoms as a a function of the Occupational Class of respondents	141
Figure 5.29	Incidence of Depression as a function of a respondent suffering one or more stressful life events in adulthood	142
Figure 5.30	Mean score of Self-criticism as a function of a respondent suffering one or more stressful life events in adulthood	142
Figure 5.31	Mean score for Morbidity symptoms as a function of a respondent suffering one or more stressful life events	143
Figure 5.32	Hypothesised path structure to Depression based on the univariate and bivariate results	146
Figure 5.33	Final structural path model to Depression for females who were evacuated. Standardised coefficients displayed	149
Figure 5.34	Final structural path model to Depression for males who were evacuated. Standardised coefficients displayed	150

Chapter 6

| Figure 6.1 | Respondents' pathway through life, with the main input and mediating variables and the Marital history outcomes variables to be considered in this chapter | 167 |

		Page
Figure 6.2	Incidence of respondents who have been divorced as a function of their age when first evacuated	172
Figure 6.3	Percentage of respondents who have experienced multiple divorces, as a function of age when first evacuated	174
Figure 6.4	Divorce rate of respondents as a function of the quality of nurture received at home	176
Figure 6.5	Percentage of female respondents who have been divorced as a function of the care received during evacuation for the two levels in the quality of home nurture	179

Chapter 7

Figure 7.1	Respondents' pathway through life, with the main input and mediating variables and the adult attachment outcome variables to be considered in this chapter	190
Figure 7.2	Incidence of depression as a function of Attachment style	192
Figure 7.3	Mean score for Morbidity symptoms as a function of Attachment style	192
Figure 7.4	Incidence of high DEQ Dependency scores (>0) as a function of Attachment style	193
Figure 7.5	Attachment style as a percentage of respondents evacuated or not evacuated	194
Figure 7.6	Incidence of Secure adult attachment category as function of Age when first evacuated	197
Figure 7.7	Incidence of Dismissing adult attachment category as a function of age when first evacuated	198
Figure 7.8	Incidence of Fearful adult attachment category as a function of age when first evacuated	199
Figure 7.9	Attachment style as a percentage of each sample as a function of age when first evacuated	200
Figure 7.10	Attachment style as a percentage of each sample for those male respondents evacuated between 7-12 years of age and those not evacuated	200
Figure 7.11	Incidence of Secure adult attachment category as a function of the Care received during evacuation	201

	Page
Figure 7.12 Incidence of Fearful adult attachment category as a function of Care received during evacuation	202
Figure 7.13 Incidence of Secure adult attachment category as a function of the number of visits made by parents per year	203
Figure 7.14 Incidence of Fearful adult attachment category as a function of the number of visits made by parents per year	204
Figure 7.15 Incidence of Secure adult attachment category as a function of the quality of nurture received during upbringing	209
Figure 7.16 Incidence of Dismissing adult attachment category as function of the quality of nurture received during upbringing	209
Figure 7.17 Incidence of Fearful adult atttachment category as a function of the quality of nurture received during upbringing	210
Figure 7.18 Attachment style as a percentage of each sample as function of the quality of nurture received in upbringing	211
Figure 7.19 Incidence of Secure adult attachment category for female respondents as a function of home nurture and the care received during evacuation	241
Figure 7.20 Incidence of Secure adult attachment category for male respondents as a function of home nurture and the care received during evacuation	216
Figure 7.21 Incidence of Fearful adult attachment category for female respondents as a function of the quality of home nurture and the care received during evacuation	218
Figure 7.22 Attachment as a percentage of the male sample as a function of Occupational Class	224

Chapter 1 The Evacuation - history and experience

1.1 Introduction

This quantitative study into the long-term effects of childhood separation from parents is based on the experience of some 900 respondents from Kent who were evacuated to the West Country and South Wales during 1939-45 in the Second World War. None of them were evacuated privately or with their mothers and their individual circumstances and experiences varied greatly in terms of their age when first evacuated, the period they were away from home and the care they received. Little has been written about the possible long-term effects of such a childhood diaspora, which is surprising considering not only the innate sociological importance of the subject but also its relevance to developmental psychology in that it allows an examination to be made of a naturally occurring sample who experienced separation from their parents in childhood under a range of circumstances. As Wolf (1945) says in her review of the literature of that period: 'History has here made a cruel psychological experiment on a large scale' (p.389).

In this introductory chapter we will look briefly at the history of the evacuation scheme and how it was experienced, particularly by those who took part in a pilot study for this present research (Rusby, 1995). In Chapter 2 we will discuss the results of this pilot study, which used grounded theory analysis of oral histories, and consider how these results might relate to developmental theories in psychology and the overall implications for the quantitative study detailed in this thesis.

1.2 The evacuation scheme and its implementation

The evacuation of children in World War 2 was a large-scale scheme for the evacuation of mainly unaccompanied children from largely urban and industrial areas of Britain where the Government believed they were likely to be at risk from aerial attack in the event of war with Germany. Although some preparatory work had been carried out in 1937 the main planning for such an eventuality began in May 1938 when the prime organising committee, the Sub-committee for Evacuation of the Imperial Defence Committee, met in the House of Commons under the chairmanship of Sir John Anderson. Their terms of reference were 'to examine the problem of the transfer of persons from areas which might be exposed to continuous air attack and to recommend plans for the purpose' (Titmus, 1950, p.32). One of the first things implemented was a large-scale survey in potential reception areas of the amount of surplus accommodation that was available and whether householders were willing to receive unaccompanied children or their teachers. This was carried out by over 100,000 volunteers throughout the country known as 'visitors'. This information was tabulated by the local councils and then forwarded via the county councils to the Ministry of Health. By the end of July 1938 the Anderson Committee report had been completed and the Home Secretary presented the main points to Parliament. These were that evacuation should be compulsory, accommodation should be mainly in private houses, under powers of compulsory billetting if needed, and that unaccompanied children would be in school groups under the charge of their teachers. All children under five years were to be accompanied. Due to Government concerns on secrecy the report was not available for publication and discussion until the end of October, leaving some ten months before the outbreak of war in September 1939. During this period, as Parsons (1998) reports little was done to take account of the possible social and human problems which were likely to arise in such a complex and huge undertaking. He comments critically that:

'these recommendations came from a bureaucratic procedure which ostensibly ignored the feelings of the individuals concerned, both in the evacuated areas and the designated reception areas, relied on the unquestioning cooperation of teachers without whom the scheme would have collapsed before it was instigated, and thought fit to create a billeting scheme which required no expert supervision and monitoring from outside agencies both before and during the evacuation process. The latter responsibility was very much left to the teachers'. (Parsons, 1998, p.59).

It is also made plain in Parsons' account that local councils were very hard-pressed to find suitable accommodation for the designated numbers of children allocated by the Ministry to their area. Many householders objected to the prospect of having urban children in their homes, believing them to be dirty, poorly nourished and likely carriers of disease. Fortunately others took a more generous and sanguine view. Billeting officers were appointed by the councils, recruited directly from local folk, to oversee the accommodation and wellbeing of children and teachers, and to report back to the local Welfare Officer in cases of poor care or hardship.

Three days before the outbreak of war with Germany the evacuation plan was put into operation. In the short period from the 1st to the 3rd of September 1939 trains from all over Britain carried 3 million children away from their homes in urban and industrial areas. Just under a million of these children were moved, with their teachers, from Greater London to reception areas, mainly in Dorset, Wiltshire, the West Country and South Wales. In terms of logistics the operation was efficiently handled, although many of the children were in a poor state by the time they arrived at their appointed destinations. What followed was etched into many of their memories, and relates to the title of Parsons' (1998) social history of the evacuation, entitled *I'll take that one*. In most cases the children were taken to a village or church hall where their potential foster parents were gathered and they were then picked out by them in an arbitrary manner and conveyed to their foster homes.

Following this initial movement of children, the subsequent lack of significant enemy action meant a 'drift back home' began, so that by early December 1939 some 30% of children had returned to the Greater London region (Titmuss, 1950). Mainly through Government intervention this movement was reversed in the summer of 1940, after the defeat of the British army in France but more particularly because of concern over the increasing bombing campaign by the Luftwaffe. Again in 1941, when the German air strategy was redirected to target civilian populations, there was a further imperative to move children back to those regions believed to be less affected by bombing. This was not always successful in that many children from Kent reported that they experienced enemy action in South Devon and South Wales during their evacuation period. Finally there was a further movement of children in the summer of 1944 when the flying bomb, or V1, menace was at its height. This especially affected Kent since the county lay in the direct line between the launch sites near the channel coast and London. This tended to keep many children from Kent away from their homes rather longer than those from other parts of Britain. However, by the end of 1944 most children from London and the Home Counties had returned home as the allied armies overran the V1 and V2 launch sites in the Channel region.

1.3 Experience of the evacuation

As would be expected the stories recounted by those who were evacuated are extremely varied. For many, especially those who left home at a young age, the time of separation could be a time of loneliness and insecurity, but for those in their teenage years it could be a time of exciting and valuable new experiences which they believed contributed significantly to their development. Many books of reminiscences have been written by former evacuees, as well as articles for local newspapers and for the Newsletter of the Evacuation Reunion Association edited by James Roffey (see for example: Wicks, 1988, *No time to say goodbye*; Richardson, 1990, *Children in retreat*; Hayward, 1997, *Children into exile*). Almost all such accounts were written many years after the war and most appeared from about 1990 onwards when those who had been evacuated felt it to be 'all right' to talk and write about the experiences and emotions which had for so long been ignored and possibly denied. It seemed as if 50 years had to pass before either those involved, or the general public or the 'authorities' were able to look honestly at these recollections.

From the published accounts the experiences of those evacuated from Kent seem, in general, to have been no different from those of other evacuees throughout the country. Most travelled by train, with their school and teachers, to the West Country or South Wales. Like the others from Greater London they too suffered the trauma of arbitrary selection by their 'hostess' or foster parent and many found the change in home background, culture and class very alien, for example the 'chapel culture' of South Wales. Some returned after a relatively short period due to the lack of enemy action, usually to be evacuated again later as the bombing started, while some stayed away for periods of up to 5 years.

Perhaps the best way to illustrate their varied experiences and reactions is to give some extracts from the transcriptions of the 16 respondents interviewed from my Pilot Study Rusby, 1995), which is due to be described more fully in the next chapter as it relates to the theoretical base of this quantitative study.

The care and kindness these 16 children received varied widely and this is evident from the following short extracts:

> 'I can remember - she was ever so kind to us. She would take us down to the beach and let us play - and she would sit there reading - that was great. Perhaps she always wanted little girls. I don't know!' (MS -female)

And after JN's foster mother had soundly berated his headmaster for daring to cane him!:

> '... she really *did* look after me (emotionally affected) - so much so that I used to go back there after the war for holidays...' (JN - male).

But there was the other extreme when JN was placed in another billet:

> '...we had our meals in the scullery - that was our living quarters... We had to prepare supper, sandwiches and some cocoa, for the mother and her two children... We would be allowed a glass of cold milk or water and the crusts we had cut off...'

And NF's foster parent, a headmistress, told her mother on her one and only visit to see her two daughters:

> 'I chose them because they were good, clean looking gels ... Now that you have seen them you do not need to see them again - do you?' (NF - female).

Often there was a sharp contrast between their own home background, class or culture and that of their foster parents:

> 'And so we moved to a cottage about 3 miles out, in a village ... thatched cottage, soil lavatory outside, one tap, oil lamps... He was out of work and we lived on his poached rabbits and vegetables from the garden ... it was that terrible winter (1940) ... it was bitterly cold and I don't think we washed ...' (DG - female).

Or the impression made on FC:

> '... she taught us to embroider, she taught us to knit ... I mean they were lovely people ... they came to my wedding and those of my daughters' ... but they were upper crust, and my old Dad said 'You went there at the right time' ... the runners all embroidered ... but *bathroom* and the loo *inside...*'

A number of the Kent interviewees had certain potentially harmful experiences, relating to physical, sexual or emotional abuse. Here are three examples:

> 'And in a matter of days, I would say - it could have been weeks, the oldest son came back home from Borstal (prison for young offenders). He was no better when he came back than when he went in, in my view. He used to knock us about, including his own brothers and sisters. There was no father in the house... ' (JN - male)

> 'We would be allowed to go out and play in the fields and that. And I can remember, a 'so-called' uncle of the family starting to molest me and I clicked on right away, although I was very innocent, 'that shouldn't be happening' - and I couldn't wait to get away ...' (CG - female)

> 'In at least two (billets) they were very strange in religious terms ... they were Nonconformist religions I was involved with. One was Apostolic chapel, where some very strange things happened - so there was a very strange religious background ... one of the billets had a woman who had a young daughter that was younger than me - and she bitterly resented me being in that house, and made it clear throughout. Another billet was an old lady with a spinster daughter and they could not cope with someone like me in the house. They also made

it absolutely clear that this was something they resented (quietly said). (JT, - male, who had 7 billets).

However, for some it was a very positive experience which they believe contributed significantly to their development:

> 'I am very fond of Wales and of mountains too. We used to go up into the hills, the village sort of backed onto a mountain and we used to go up there on every opportunity ... I was of an age, 14 or thereabouts, when I was looking for a bit of independence and that gave me independence. I was just away with my mates - as it were - and my parents sent me two or three shillings a week, and there was money in my pocket and it was a great time ...' (WC - male).

> '... and when I became a shipwright ... within 5 years I was a supervisor - I was the youngest supervisor in Sheerness Dockyard. And from then on I just climbed and climbed - I did very well for myself! ... I am certain it gave me more confidence by being evacuated and meeting other people ...' (FR - male).

> 'I think it was the contrast - such a complete contrast. I mean, our home in Croydon - we were right on the main road, with the factory next door ... then suddenly going to this house which had huge vases with beautiful copper beech leaves in them ... the only thing I had to do was knit for the soldiers, wind bandages - and do my piano practice, Miss C insisted on that ... I had to sing beside her while she played sometimes. Many years afterwards my Mum did tell me she would have liked to have adopted me ... And then my husband and I had gone out shopping one afternoon (1962) and we came home and the man next door said you've had a visitor, a funny little old lady with a bright red hat' ...And I cried and I cried and I cried because I had missed her ... That's right I gained from it, I gained from it - I do. I just wish that she was alive now so I could tell her...'
> (PE - female).

These extracts may help to give some idea of the varied experiences that these children enjoyed, or endured, during a time of separation from their parents. Both the frequency of parental visits, the total time away and the number of billets occupied varied greatly. In this sample of 16 children a few hardly saw their parents while others were visited regularly. The total period away ranged from 3 months to over 5 years and the number of billets occupied from 1 to 15. Their primary and secondary education invariably suffered. Many were of the age to sit scholarship examinations for grammar schools so that their preparatory study and the arrangements for the exam were affected, particularly as the evacuees' schools had to share premises and facilities with the local schools on a 'box and cox' basis.

For many the return to their families and home environment was not easy; during an important period of their development they had lived quite a different life, often with scant contact with home and parents. Some adjusted well, but others, particularly the older children, had as PE said, 'grown up too fast'. One of the most poignant accounts of the return home came from FC, who had been well looked after in a middle class home (see above quotation) and here expresses the shame she felt on her return:

> 'I shall never forget the day I returned to my mother's house. I suppose it was the first time I ever felt ashamed of myself and my thoughts ... I went through the house - Oh! (started to cry) ... I was ashamed - it was so poor ... and my mother said 'how do you like being home now?' ...because we had this love we didn't notice we didn't have things.' (FC - female).

Extracts such as these from the Pilot Study led to the generation of a range of themes, both positive and negative in outlook, which helped to define an overall picture of the effects of evacuation and which have contributed to the subsequent design of this quantitative study (Rusby, 1995). In the next chapter these results and those of other research surveys will be examined in the light of related work in the field of the long-term effects of childhood history, and how these considerations led to the selection of outcome variables.

Chapter 2 Research studies and theoretical considerations

2.1 Introduction

A considerable amount of research was carried out by a wide range of psychologists and psychiatrists in the first years of the Second World War on the effects of the evacuation on children. Unfortunately much of this work lacks overall homogeneity and rigour in the scientific sense so that is difficult to evaluate and compare results and to determine their significance in statistical terms. Wolf (1945) has listed some 200 references from the academic literature of this period from 1939 to 1943 and gives examples of the contradictory nature of many of the authors' findings, mainly due to the difficulty of comparing 'like with like'. There is also a lack of adequate control groups so it is difficult to interpret the relative significance of the incidence of say, 'neuroticism', given between those children who were or were not evacuated.

Perhaps the best known work of this early period is that of Freud and Burlingham (1944), initially at the Hampstead Nurseries, and later in Chelmsford, and that of Isaacs et al. (1941) who edited *The Cambridge Evacuation Survey*, which includes input from Bowlby and Fairbarn amongst others. Unfortunately these two reports are not directly comparable. Freud and Burlingham based their report on observations of 103 children under 5 years of age at their residential nursery near Chelmsford between 1940 to 1942; many of these children having been orphaned by the bombing in London. Isaacs et al. based their report on the observations of untrained billeting officers, known as 'visitors', and on essays written by 650 children of school age fostered in homes in Cambridge in 1940 and who had been evacuated from Central London. If a comparison is, however, tentatively drawn between these two sets of children then Wolf (1945) believes 'that the extent of neurosis formation caused by evacuation is relatively low considering the deep trauma we would have expected separation from parents to constitute' (p.396). Both reports stated that successful adaptation to the billeting situation depended critically on a previously stable home relationship and that those children with a 'friendly outgoing nature' stood the best chance of adaptation. Those with poor mental health, or boys of the overactive, aggressive type were least likely to adapt. Freud and Burlingham found that separation due to evacuation to be far more distressing for pre-school children than the effect of bombing from which they were being protected. They recommended a gradual separation rather then a sudden traumatic break for young children, in the hope that this would lessen the danger of a later rejection reaction toward their parents. Isaacs et al. found that the presence of siblings in the same billet and frequent visits from parents made for greater happiness. They also believed that 'misfits' could often have been avoided by billeting the more lively children in families with younger foster parents and other children, and the more withdrawn children in homes with older foster parents and no other children. Many children returned within the first year of the war and they found that this was usually due to anxiousness or loneliness of the parents and/or children, or parent's dissatisfaction with the foster home or to parent's poverty, i.e. the cost of billeting, clothes, visits etc. None of these children were followed up, and this seems to have been the norm for the wartime studies.

Burt (1940; 1941; 1943) carried out a series of surveys based on 'systematic enquiries' made among evacuated children and found 25% of evacuated children to have some form of neurotic symptoms, but believed 17% of these had been present before evacuation took place. The most common symptom was enuresis. From an analysis of cases of 'maladjustment' to billeting he recommended more care be taken in the matching of children to suitable foster parents, better preparations be made prior to the arrival of evacuees, that improved recreational facilities be provided and that suitably trained social workers be introduced.

Wolf (1945) concludes that by eliminating those studies which lack care and rigour it would be safe to say that the percentages of neurotic disorders in evacuated children was between 25% and 44%, and that a third of these children either acquired or suffered an increase in their neurosis due to evacuation alone. Wolf finds that the specific factors which may have influenced this neurosis are again discussed in the literature in what she calls a 'most contradictory fashion'. This particularly applies to the influence of age at evacuation, which she believes to be of the greatest theoretical importance. The divergence of views amongst authors on this topic is such that there cannot be said to be any agreed form of association demonstrated between the age at which parental separation took place and the incidence of neurotic symptoms. However, there is general agreement that evacuation, rather than bombing, had the more serious effect on the mental health of children.

Although such wartime studies may have done little to further our theoretical understanding of those factors which are most significant in affecting the adaptability and mental health of such evacuated children they did contribute in a more general and practical way to the debate on the inadequacies of social and health care in the community as it related to children. Organisations such as the Fabian Society (see Padley & Cole, 1940) and the Women's Group on Public Welfare (1943) helped to bring these inadequacies to the attention of the post-war government and so the studies were influential in the provision and content of the much improved social services and health care plans which were enacted after the war. This is particularly the case for the Children Act of 1948, with its concern for the careful selection of foster parents and the supervision of children in foster homes and in residential care. The Children Act of 1989 built on this base, and gave a greater emphasis to the importance of parental contact and, whenever possible, the preference for children to remain in their own homes but under the supervision of social services.

2.2 Research studies related to the long-term effects of evacuation or childhood separation

By comparison with the considerable corpus of surveys and research work carried out during the war the period since has been remarkable sparse. A few papers and further surveys did appear until about 1949, mainly through clinical examinations of war-damaged children seen by psychiatrists and psychologists at child guidance clinics. The most thorough of these was made by Carey-Trefzer

(1949) who carried out an investigation to determine how many children attending the child guidance clinic at the Hospital for Sick Children in Great Ormond Street, London, showed neurotic symptoms caused, or aggravated, by war experiences. For the period from 1942 to 1946 she examined the patient records of 1203 children and found a total of 212, or 17%, had suffered war-related symptoms. These war-related cases were contacted and the young people attended with their mothers for a follow-up interview in which they were re-examined and any relevant school and other clinic reports obtained. Although she found that enemy action due to air-raids was associated with the greatest number of reactions, some 55% of the 212 children being affected, she found that the effects of evacuation, although less in number, some 33%, nevertheless created deeper and more persisting neuroses or symptoms of disturbed behaviour. Children evacuated under 5 years of age suffered the most severe damage, followed by children who were of a nervous disposition before evacuation. The most frequent symptom was a change in behaviour, followed by anxiety and fears, particularly after bombing. She said that psychomatic reactions appeared about equally often after either evacuation or bombing. Any delinquency found consisted of small-time thieving and any such incidences were all related to evacuation rather than bombing and appeared to be associated with feelings of rejection. This conclusion is in agreement with that of Bowlby (1946) who found in his analysis of 44 young people who were habitual thieves that 17 of these had suffered separations in excess of six months from their mothers during their first five years of life, whilst only two, non-thieving; controls had suffered similar separations, a statistically significant result. Carey-Trefzer summarises the negative human context of the evacuation experience for both child and parents in the following words:

> 'we find that as well as the separation from their home - the unsuitability of some foster homes, guilt over having left their parents in danger, jealousy of siblings who remained at home and anxiety over the dangers which threatened their parents - (all) added to the emotional difficulties created by evacuation. The climax was often only reached when these children came back home, deeply disturbed and insecure. They then were rejected by parents, who could not understand why their previously 'nice' child had become such a monster' (p543).

It might have been expected that in these first years after the war there would have been a number of reports from the Ministry of Health examining the lessons to be learnt from the implementation of the evacuation scheme, particularly as it affected the emotional and physical security and well-being of the children and relating this to any potential long-term effects. In fact, a search through the Department of Health Library archives, with the assistance of librarian Janet Cockayne, only elicited one report: Ministry of Health Report 1948, entitled *Children and the British Government Evacuation Scheme*. This was a thirteen-page factual summary of the arrangements made and the numbers of children moved. There was no mention of an analysis of any concerns about the evacuees welfare or the psychological or social lessons which might be drawn from this immense demographic experiment. It would seem that only the Titmus (1950) report, *Problems of Social Policy*, published by the Home Office, attempted to address such concerns, although it had a much wider social remit for the improved welfare of all families and children in post-war Britain.

It was not until the 1980's that any studies were made which included any reference to the possible long-term effects into adulthood of the wartime evacuation of children in World War Two, and these few studies related to multiple causes of separation including childhood illness, parental death or illness and marital discord, as well as separation caused by wartime evacuation (Tennant et al.,1980; Tennant et al., 1982; Birtchnell & Kennard, 1984). The original work of Tennant et al. in 1980 did not distinguish between these causes, but the later paper in 1982 did do so. They assessed any possible association between childhood separation experiences and adult depression, anxiety and general morbidity on a random population of 800 subjects recruited in South London. Separations, as defined above, were categorised in three age groups, 0-4, 5-10, and 11-15 years. Any periods of evacuation greater than one week were included but most lasted several months. Interviewers used the Present State Examination (PSE; Wing et al., 1974) to assess psychiatric disorder, demographic data and information about parental deaths and parent-child separations. The survey included a control group that had not experienced any such separations in the study period, i.e. from birth to 15 years of age. They found that childhood separations occurring up to 5 years of age bore no significant relation to depression, anxiety or general morbidity. From 5-10 years of age separations caused by parental illness and marital discord were significantly related to general morbidity, and in the latter instance were more likely to cause depression rather than anxiety. From the age of 11-15 years only separations due to parental illness were of significance, and in association with general morbidity only. None of the results related to separation by war evacuation reached significance although those evacuated when aged 0-4 years had nearly twice the incidence of depression than controls. All these results were obtained via chi-square tests by a comparison with the control sample incidences but some cell sizes were small so that expected cell sizes fell below the generally accepted limit of 5 expected occurrences. Tennant et al. say that their findings were not readily comparable with other work on childhood separation experiences mainly because most of the previous work was directly concerned with the effect on children (see Rutter, 1972) whereas they were concerned with long-term effects in adulthood. They also comment briefly on another community study in the same part of London by Brown and Harris (1978), in which loss by separation or parental death were not differentiated, but again, this work is not directly comparable.

Birtchnell and Kennard (1984) conducted a survey of 128 women, aged 40-49 years, in London which did differentiate between the causes of loss or separation. These women had either lost their mothers by death, or they had been separated from them by evacuation or other reasons, all before they reached 11 years. Control data on a further 69 non-affected participants were included, and all were asked to complete the Middlesex Hospital Questionnaire, plus a self-rating depression scale and the MMPI dependency scale. For all the groups increased levels in the depression scale were associated with lower parental social class (SES) and for those who had experienced separation depression was also related to the quality of replacement care, either with foster families or in children homes. A poor outcome for evacuated children was also associated with having a poor relationship with their natural mother. They concluded that poor parent-child relationships were more damaging than a break in the continuity of care.

Prior to the start of this present study the only work which is specifically concerned with the long-term effects of evacuation per se came from Finland, a country which also suffered the traumas of World War Two. Some 75,000 children were evacuated from the eastern region of Finland to Sweden during the Finno-Russian War between 1939-45. Some of these children remained in Sweden after the war, many of whom had been adopted by their Swedish foster parents, while others returned at various stages to Finland. Although the numbers involved were much less than in the British evacuation this event has given rise to academic observations on the possible long-term somatic and psychological effects of this childhood separation. In the only quantitative study Räsänen (1992) has analysed the physical and mental health of 379 respondents who had been evacuated to Sweden from Kuopio county in the east of Finland and compared these results with a control group of 144 respondents who had remained in Kuopio. She found that there was no significant difference in the physical state of health between the two groups, except that the control group had a significantly increased incidence of cardiovascular problems. She believes this may be due to the better nutrition enjoyed by those evacuated to Sweden, particularly as Kuopio has the highest incidences of such disorders in Finland. In terms of psychological symptoms related to mental health those evacuated suffered a significantly increased incidence of anxiety, self-condemnation, fears and obsessive thoughts as defined by the Present State Examination (PSE) (Wing et al., 1974). There were no significant effects in the other direction. Twenty three per cent of those evacuated had suffered from depression in their adult life compared to 16% of controls, but this difference was not found to be significant. Cross tabulations were used in examining possible relationships between the age at separation, duration of the evacuation period, and the numbers of respondents having permanent illness or mental health disorders but no significant effects were found. Räsänen says that the results regarding age at separation are unreliable due to the small cell sizes; however no details are given of the contingency tables or of the chi-square tests involved. With these overall results she concludes that the Swedish foster parents must have been protective and caring, but unfortunately there is no self-report data on this nor on the quality of family nurture which both groups received during their upbringing in Kuopio.

Serenius (1995, 1996) has commented critically on this research, based on her own experience and that of fellow members of the Riksforbundet Finske Krigsbarn (Finnish Warchild Society). She says that there is a need for a more subtle and deeper approach if the underlying feelings and emotions of those evacuated are to be discerned and believes that the PSE questionnaire developed for formal psychiatric examinations is of limited value in this respect. Her own difficulties, and that of many of her fellow evacuees, in finding a secure identity and 'wholeness' in adult life is, she believes, related to the separation experience they suffered in childhood. She cites mental health problems, high divorce rates, obesity and drug misuse etc. as indicators of this lack of integration, and comments on the great therapeutic value of the meetings of the Swedish and Finnish warchild societies in allowing repressed feelings of childhood to emerge. This is something James Roffey (1997), founder of the Evacuees Reunion Association in Britain, would confirm. Work by Lagnebro (1994) for her doctoral thesis at Umeå University in Sweden, in which she interviewed 58 individuals who had been evacuated and then had settled in northern Sweden in adulthood, generally supports Serenius's concerns regarding the possible outcome of such a childhood experience. In discussions at Umeå with the present author (Lagnebro, 2002) she also confirmed her conclusion that the effects of such childhood separation were most severe in her sample for those evacuated at a very young age, and who would not have been able, initially, to speak Swedish.

While we need to be suitably cautious about generalising from both Serenius' experiential paper and Lagnebro's thesis, their general conclusions taken together do conflict with those of Räsänen who found little evidence for the effects of the evacuation experience. The present author believes this difference may be partly explained by the fact that Räsänen conducted her research in Finland primarily on those who had been reunited with their parents, whereas both Serenius and Lagnebro were concerned with those who had either been adopted by Swedish parents or who had remained in Sweden after the war. There is of course also the difference in methodology to take into account. When making a statistical comparison between those evacuated and those who stayed at home in Kuopio it should also be remembered that the home lives of Räsänen's control group were very directly affected by the continuing fighting between Finland and Russia on the Kuopio/Karelian front from 1940 to 1944. These factors make it difficult to come to any general conclusions on the long-term effects of wartime evacuation from the Finnish studies.

Since 1997, when the design of the present study had been completed, two theses have been written which relate to possible long term psychological effects of the Second World War. The most relevant of these is a quantitative study by Foster (2000) which compared a group of 169 former evacuees with a control group of 43 respondents who were children during the war but were not evacuated. Regression analysis was used to investigate the effect of certain predictor variables based on the evacuation experience with the outcome variables of adult attachment, measured by the Hazan and Shaver (1987) Relationship Questionnaire, and that of psychological well-being, based on the General Health Questionnaire (Goldberg, 1978). Foster found that attachment style mediated a relationship between childhood evacuation and present psychological well-being, such that former evacuees were more likely to have insecure attachment styles and lower levels of psychological wellbeing; she also found that the quality of home parenting moderated this relationship. In terms of the details of the evacuation experience only age at evacuation was predictive of attachment style, with younger evacuees being at a greater risk of insecure attachment, but no details were given on how this might vary with age in developmental terms or with gender. No effects were found for the length of period away, number of billets, presence of siblings or frequency of parental contact.

The second recent thesis examined the effect of war experiences, including that of evacuation and air raids, on those who were children in World War 2 (Waugh, 2001). Three hundred and forty one respondents completed self-report questionnaires on evacuation, war-related experiences and the childhood care they received, and the possible effects of these on their adult attachment styles and psychological health were examined by regression analysis, using the same measures as Foster. Waugh found that war experience due to enemy action was significantly related to psychological morbidity, mediated by symptoms of post-traumatic stress disorder (PTSD) as measured by the Impact of Event Scale (IES). Analysis also showed that evacuees were significantly more at risk of being abused, in terms of emotional or sexual abuse or neglect, than non-evacuees, but no significant relationship was found between evacuation and attachment style. She comments on the fact that Foster (2000) found a weak but significant relationship between evacuation and attachment styles and believes this difference between their results may be because the association found by Foster was actually being mediated by abuse, i.e. poor care received during evacuation, although this information had not been specifically measured. She goes on to argue that it may not be the fact of family separation that affected security of attachment but rather how these children were treated when they were evacuated. Apart from the quality of care received no other details of the evacuation experience are included in the analysis.

From an examination of the above limited number of research studies in Britain and Finland prior to 1997, when this present research project was started, it was not possible to clearly define with any certainty either the relevant variables of the evacuation experience or the pertinent outcome variables of adulthood, let alone the associations which might exist between them in terms of any long-term emotional or developmental effects. Since the main aim of this present study is to test for such associations and to model their structure, a pilot study (Rusby, 1995) was first undertaken to try and gain a better understanding of the most relevant predictor and outcome variables before embarking on a quantitative study. The main conclusions from this study are included in the following section which also discusses theoretical considerations with regard to the choice of outcome variables. A more detailed summary of the pilot study is given in Appendix 1.

2.3 Theoretical considerations regarding the choice of outcome variables

In the following five subsections the theoretical considerations underlying the selected outcome variables will be discussed, starting with respondents own perceptions of any long-term effects from their evacuation experience.

2.3.1 Respondents' perceptions of the effect of their evacuation experience on their development and adult lives

In Appendix 1 are summarised some of the findings from the grounded theory analysis of the pilot study (Rusby, 1995) and emphasis was placed on the contrast between those who had found the experience generally life-enhancing and those who believed their subsequent development and adult lives had been negatively affected.

Of the 16 participants interviewed in the pilot study five believed their experiences were beneficial (Mrs FC, Mrs PE, Mr FR, Mr WC and Mr RN - see Table A1.1). They were all well cared for and enjoyed a constructive change in culture, coming as they did from poor urban backgrounds. Each of them had had a secure family upbringing and in all cases a connection with parents was maintained. All were over 10 years of age at evacuation, and the longest evacuation period was just over one year. These conditions are believed to have contributed to an experience which, after a lapse of 50 years, they could look back on and say;

- it altered my outlook on life' (Mrs JA)

- 'it was a great time for us ... my Dad used to say 'it was the making of you and your sister'....' (Mrs FC)

- 'it brought me out' (Mr FR)

- 'I gained from it...I just wish she was alive now so I could tell her...' (Mrs PE).

By contrast four participants believed that they had been negatively affected emotionally and in developmental terms by aspects of their evacuation experience (Mrs DG, Mrs CG, Mr JN and Mr JT - see Table A1.1). All had evacuation periods in excess of 2 3/4 years and had multiple billets, the majority of which provided indifferent or poor care. All suffered a 'loss of attachment' to their parents and had difficulty in 'fitting back' after the evacuation period. During evacuation it appeared that all four were dependent on a stratagem used by those evacuated for long periods, and labelled 'Covering-up' in the analysis. This survival mechanism included 'repressed feelings', misunderstandings', 'repressed anger', avoidance of problems and 'chameleon-like' behaviour. The following quotations from their transcriptions may help to illustrate some of their feelings:

'... there is a solitariness about us - ' (Mrs DG)

'... the unfinished business...the need to put a name to the chapter' (Mrs DG)

'... but what they see is the veneer I had to acquire to cover the emotional aspects of my life...but I'm tearing myself to pieces and bleeding to death inside...' (Mr JN)

'... there is even less of an emotional link (with mother) than between myself and my
last foster mother' (Mr JN)

'... People find me arrogant, aggressive, not suffering fools gladly...and that aspect of me may well have been influenced by those early experiences...' (Mr JT)

'... there was no one to run to, hold on to my Mum, nothing like that - you see I just couldn't get rid of it - and that was awful...' (Mrs CG)

It should be emphasised that the hypothesis suggested here that a period of separation from the security of a family can be perceived as a positive gain for development, or, at the other extreme, an emotional legacy through life, depending on a range of input conditions or variables, has emerged inductively from a qualitative study of only 16 individuals. However, this apparent dichotomy in their attributions to the experience is reflected in many accounts within the newsletter of the Evacuees Reunion Association and in anthologies containing individuals' stories of evacuation (see Parsons, 1998; Richardson, 1990; Wicks, 1988; Hayward. 1996). In this present quantitative study it is planned to statistically test some of these perceptions or attributions as a function of the input variables of evacuation, such as age at evacuation, period away, frequency of parental visits and the number of billets occupied. These results can then be compared and contrasted with the adult outcomes of these same respondents using standardised measures of mental health, marital history and attachment relationships.

2.3.2 The evacuation experience and adult mental health

The review in Section 2.2 found few studies related directly to the long-term effects of evacuation, and such studies as there are do not systematically explore the possible association between the details of the evacuation experience and the subsequent mental health of participants in adult life. There is, however, a large body of work from the past thirty years which has been concerned with childhood adverse experiences in the family and their effect on their subsequent psychological well-being. This includes childhood separation or loss due to parental death, illness or divorce and its possible association with affective disorders in adulthood such as unipolar depression and clinical anxiety. Although the 'loss' being considered is rather different in form and possible effect from the loss due to temporary separation experienced by those evacuated, nevertheless both may involve a loss of parental attachment and so in terms of attachment theory they may be expected to lead to comparable long-term effects.

This body of work has provided evidence that such childhood adversity may be implicated as antecedents in adult affective disorders, including depression, although the levels of significance found have been small and the majority of studies have female participants only (Brown & Harris, 1978; Roy, 1978; Brown et al., 1986; Harris et al., 1986; Faravelli et al., 1986; Bifulco et al., 1987; Kessler et al., 1997; Furukawa et al., 1999; Takeuchi et al., 2002; Infrasca, 2003). However some studies do not support significant associations between childhood adversities and adult depression (Birtchnell, 1970; Perris et al., 1986; Zahner & Murphy, 1989). This apparent inconsistency tends to be explained in recent literature by the need to consider the adverse consequences of parental loss or separation rather than just the loss itself, and that although there is no consistent evidence that parental death is a significant risk factor for later depression there is evidence that separations, particularly those occurring in the context of family discord, do contribute to adult depression (Brown et al., 1986; Tennant, 1988; Quinton, 1989; Amato & Keith 1991; Parker, 1992). As Furukawa et al. (1999) emphasize such differences in the literature are likely to be exacerbated also by variations in the definition of 'loss' employed and also by differences in the populations surveyed, particularly in terms of socioeconomic status and culture. There is also the important question of childhood age at which the loss or separation occurs and the availability or otherwise of any wider family support available at that time. Faravelli et al. (1986) emphasise the importance of matching childhood age, social class and age of parents, both for patients and controls. Most of the reported studies employ patients who have attended clinics after receiving treatment for major depression and are then asked to recall the occurrence of certain listed adversities in their childhood. There is some concern in the literature about their ability to do this effectively and it is possible that these abilities may differ from healthy controls in this respect (Faravelli et al., 1986). Such an approach may also preclude assessing all the factors from their childhood history which could have had an influence on their affective state, including the degree of any parental neglect or conflict involved.

Perhaps the studies which have done most to unravel the strands linking childhood adversity and trauma to adult disorders have been those conducted by the Royal Holloway College team since the 1970's under George Brown's original initiative (Brown & Harris, 1978; Brown et al., 1986; Bifulco et al., 1987; Harris et al., 1990, Bifulco et al., 1992 and Bifulco & Moran, 1998). The work is based on four studies involving, in total, about 800 women from South London who were interviewed and the transcriptions independently rated. This included one study of 100 women, each of whom had a sister who was also interviewed, and was designed to examine the level of shared childhood experiences and the corroboration which existed in their individual, retrospective accounts of family history. The degree of corroboration was found to be high for the incidence of the various forms of adversity examined in the studies: Childhood neglect, physical or sexual or psychological abuse, and parental loss and parental conflict.

Although the main concern in these Royal Holloway studies was with the long-term effect of childhood neglect and abuse in its various forms, the team did investigate the relationship between childhood parental loss by separation on adult depression (Brown et al., 1986). In the 1986 study they examined a group of 255 women who had been separated from their mothers in childhood, some of whom had experienced a depressive episode and the remainder who were free of depression. Their main finding was that those who had been depressed had a significantly different experience of the quality of care after the loss from those who had not suffered from depression. Depressed women were more likely to have been sent away to institutions, or to live with rejecting relatives, because their fathers were not able to care for them at home. By contrast the non-depressed group were more likely to have described a continuity of emotional care following maternal separation. In a further study (Harris et al., 1990) they found that the loss of a mother in childhood, either through death or by separation for a year or more, was associated with a doubling in the rate of adult depression from 14 to 28%, but this significant effect was only found when the family history had included neglect and/or abuse. From this they concluded that it was the neglect and abuse components which increased the risk of adult disorder rather than the loss itself. These results have some resonance with the conclusions reported by Rutter & Smith (1995) who found that in the case of poverty this alone does not lead to depressive risk, but does so in conjunction with neglect and abuse in an individual's childhood history. In their analysis of the effects of parental loss Harris et al. (1990) make an important distinction between those who lost their parents by death or separation, a distinction which could have some relevance to this present study. They found that those women who had been older than 6 years when they had lost their mother by death rather than by separation were less at risk of depression in adulthood and they explain this by suggesting that they would have been more likely to have benefitted from the care provided by a committed mother and so be 'inoculated by earlier adequate care' (p.323). However they go on to say that this does not explain the high risk they found for those who lost their mother by death before the age of 6 years irrespective of the subsequent level of care received. They suggest that children of such a young age may have particular problems mourning their loss due to the relative immaturity of their cognitive development; in terms of attachment theory this would be interpreted as a loss of attachment. Bemporad and Romano (1993) have conducted a review of seventeen studies related to the level of dysfunction in childhood histories of unipolar depressives and have come to a similar conclusion: That childhood maltreatment was more strongly correlated with adult depression than was childhood separation and loss, that is the long-term pathogenic effect of such parental loss was largely determined by the quality of the subsequent care received.

Paul Amato has also been in the forefront of investigations into the long-term effects of childhood loss, particularly through divorce, and like the Royal Holloway team has helped to unravel some of the apparent inconsistencies which have been found (Amato, 1988; Amato, 1991; Amato & Booth, 1997; Amato, 2001). In Amato (1991) he says that both public and scientific concern had been raised over the consequences of parental absence for children's development and well-being as a result of the dramatic rise in divorce in the United States over the past three decades. In his summary of previous work he says the evidence is clear that parental divorce is negatively associated with later psychological well-being, but that it is equivocal in relation to parental death. There is also continuing uncertainty about the relative effects for men and women and for different ethnic groups and cultures (Kulka & Weingarten, 1979; Glenn and Kramer, 1985; Amato & Keith, 1991). Amato & Keith's (1991) survey is based on the National Survey of Families and Households (NSFH) containing a data set of over 10,000 respondents from a wide range of backgrounds. Because of this sample size the authors were able to address some of the previous inconsistencies in the effects of race/ethnicity and gender. Unfortunately their analyses do not include the age at which parental loss or separation occurred. In the regression analysis carried out the dependent variable Depression was based on 10 items from the Centre of Epidemiological Studies Depression Scale (CES-D) (Radloff, 1977). From this regression analysis Amato & Keith found that all causes of parental absence, defined as death of a parent, divorce or 'other causes', were associated with an increase in depression for African Americans whereas for Hispanics no such associations were found. In the case of White respondents he found associations for the effects of divorce and 'other separations' but not for the loss of a parent by death. Amato & Keith suggest that the lack of any association between parental loss and adult depression for Hispanics could be due to the closely knit extended family providing a 'protective' factor. In the case of African Americans the relatively strong association of depression with parental loss could be affected by the residence patterns found in inner-city estates. The study did not find a significant interaction between parental absence and gender and he concludes that, considering all the evidence, 'the best conclusion is that family disruption during childhood has long-term consequences for the subjective well-being of both men and women' (p.553).

In 2001 Amato completed a review study to update that of Amato & Keith (1991) with an analysis of 67 studies published in the 1990's (Amato, 2001). He found that compared to children with continuously married parents those children with divorced parents continued to score significantly lower on measures of psychological well-being and social relationships during their development. Amato comments that notwithstanding the use of more sophisticated multivariate analyses during this decade, which would tend to reduce the magnitude of effects, studies in the 1990s actually yielded an increase in these magnitudes. This increase occurred in spite of the growth of school-based interventions, parenting classes for divorcing parents and divorce mediation. He believes this may partly be explained by the increasing gap in economic well-being between children with single parents and those with married parents.

Alternative theoretical concepts have been invoked to explain the above connections, although they are sometimes unstated. These are that the psychopathological effects being detected are primarily due to the family as an agent of socialisation, i.e. in which attachment theory, cognitive psychology and social learning theory play their part, or that they are primarily due to the concepts of behaviour genetics. This latent difference has become particularly evident in the last few years with the increasing interest in genetics and the advent of more sophisticated methodology based on twin studies. Recent work such as the Virginia Twin Study (Eaves et al., 1997) and the Non-shared Environment and Adolescent Development (NEAD) project (Reiss et al., 1995), both in the United States, have shown that the biological, or genetic, component of the total variance between certain childhood adversity and later affective disorders is higher than previously considered. Reiss et al. found that the only psychological disorder of childhood with a near neglible genetic variance component is believed to be that of separation anxiety for males at 0-19%, whereas girls were found to be biologically more affected at 31-74%, something which is of direct relevance to this present study.

In an endeavour to clarify the issues Fonagy (2003) has produced a comprehensive and important review paper which draws attention to the limitations of the methodologies of the twin studies employed and which he also believes have partially confounded genetic similarity with environmental influence. However he does believe that genetic and environmental effects do combine to produce a phenotype for an individual or group, but that their effects cannot be simply 'added' or 'subtracted' in terms of their contribution to the overall variance of a measure of social relationships or pathological disorder. He says his main objection as a clinician, however, to the validity of such genetically-based data would not be methodological or conceptual but rather pragmatic. Genetic effects may well be indirect as well as direct and even a high genetic loading for a certain psychopathological risk may be found to be environmentally mediated. Fonagy believes that this interaction is not 'objective', it is the child's experience of the environment that counts and this is a function of appraisal - the manner in which the environment is experienced will act as a filter in the expression of genotype into phenotype. He says 'this is where the role of parenting is central for genetic research, particularly in terms of attachment theory which is concerned with the interactions of multiple layers of representations in generating developmental outcomes; data from genetics calls for exactly such sophistication in understanding the way genes may or may not be expressed in particular individuals' (p.222). Fonagy believes that the interaction of genetics and the environment, i.e. whether or not specific environmental factors trigger the expression of a gene, may depend not only on the nature of those factors but also on the way the child experiences them, which in turn may be a function of attachment and other intrapsychic experiences. This level of sophistication is likely to be very relevant in this present analysis where genetic effects, the quality of childhood attachment and the details of the separation experience are all likely to be components which bear on the long-term psychological well-being of a respondent.

Although much of the research reviewed here is not directly applicable to an examination of a temporary 'loss' of a parent by evacuation it nevertheless has highlighted a number of factors which need to be incorporated in the analysis. The first is that the long-term effects for the mental health of respondents is likely to be dependent not only on the details of the evacuation experience - as the pilot study suggested - but also on the quality of upbringing and the subsequent care received. For it is clear from the literature that it is not so much the act of parental separation per se which may be associated with the occurrence of affective disorders but rather the context in which it occurs. Secondly a number of authors have suggested that the age at which separation takes place is likely to be of particular importance, with those individuals aged less than 6 years being at a greater risk of later disorders through cognitive immaturity leading to a loss of attachment. Thirdly that there is a need to consider the genetic or biological component in any multivariate analysis undertaken, not that this can be entered as data, but this should be allowed for when interpreting the results, particularly as a function of gender. It will also be important to include life-course variables such as occupational class and marital history as well as those stressors which may be the immediate precursors of affective disorders.

So the research question being asked here is: Are there any significant associations between the input variables relating to an individual's evacuation experience and his or her adult mental health, and if so how are these mediated by life-course variables? The key hypothesis proposed is that the prime associations with mental health will be due to the age at which evacuation took place and the care received, and that such associations will be mediated by the quality of home background and significant life events such as loss or disability of a partner or dependent.

2.3.3. The evacuation experience and marital history

The inclusion of marital history as an outcome variable in this study is largely based on the stories of those who were evacuated, including the work of Lagnebro (1994, 2002) and Serenius (1995, 1996) which suggested that those who had been evacuated were at risk of marital disruption. Such an hypothesis is also in agreement with the 'emotional legacy' category which arose from the pilot study which relates to the long-term psychological well-being of those evacuated. However there is little to be found in the psychological literature which is directly related to the effect of childhood separation on marital instability. There is, however, a large body of work mainly in the sociological literature over the past thirty years which is concerned with the intergenerational transmission of divorce.

Although little has been done to examine in detail the effect of the diverse components of childhood history on divorce, the case for the generational association between the occurrence of parental divorce and offspring divorce has been substantiated by many workers in the field (Bumpass & Sweet, 1972; Pope & Mueller, 1976; Teachman, 1982; Bumpass et al., 1991; Amato, 1996; O'Connor et al., 1999; Diekmann & Engelhardt, 1999; Wolfinger, 1999; Teachman, 2002). However even after this relatively long period of research it has not been found possible to clearly define the mechanisms which mediate this effect. As Teachman (2002) says: 'Overall the picture that emerges from prior research is murky. This lack of clarity is the result of using different measurement strategies, data bases and statistical procedures. However the available results suggest that family statuses and transitions other than parental divorce may be related to the risk of offspring marital disruption' (p.719). This last sentence may be seen as an implied criticism that the majority of workers have simply used the dichotomy ' parents divorced/not divorced' as the input variable of interest. The problem of clearly defining which mechanisms are at work and relating these to the inherent diversity of family history in this field is a daunting one, and bears on the practical difficulties of designing more sophisticated studies and the accumulation of the necessary specialised data.

In their first paper in 1976 Pope and Mueller postulated five mechanisms or 'rationales' to explain this intergenerational effect:

1. The 'personality' rationale posits 'deficient' personality characteristics in the offspring,
2. The 'social control' rationale posits reduced control over the child on the part of family and kin network,
3. The 'role model' rationale posits the inappropriateness of sex-role learning by the child.
4. The 'economic' rationale posits reduced income and leads to downward family mobility, and
5. The 'permissive attitudes' rationale posits tolerant attitudes toward divorce learned by the child.

Following this early work, Amato (1996) developed a model based on Levinger's (1976) theory of divorce for summarising and outlining the mechanisms through which parental divorce is presumed to affect marital instability. The model postulates only three mediating mechanisms: patterns of interpersonal behaviour, life course and socioeconomic variables, and commitment and attitude towards divorce. Effectively the first mechanism subsumes the first three rationales of Pope and Mueller. Teachman (2002) believes that each of these three mediating mechanisms has been shown to be linked to the risk of marital dissolution and that taken together they can explain part, if not all, of the increased risk of offspring divorce associated with parental divorce (Pope & Mueller, 1976; Glenn & Kramer, 1987; Amato, 1996; O'Connor et al., 1999; Diekmann & Engelhardt, 1999). But Teachman is concerned that the emphasis placed on the occurrence or non-occurrence of divorce has diverted attention away from other dimensions of family histories which are important to consider, such as the different 'childhood living arrangements' following parental divorce. It is this aspect of the body of the research which has some, modest, bearing on the present survey, although the number of relevant studies are few. They will now be considered.

Pope and Mueller (1976) used data from five surveys in the United States to examine the intergenerational transmission of divorce with over 30,000 respondents available, using divorce data from those brought up by parents in stable marriages as a statistical base. Although the main finding was that there was a greater percentage transmission effect for those from childhood homes disrupted by divorce or separation rather than by parental death, the large sample also allowed an investigation of the effects of a range of 'childhood living arrangements' following marriage dissolution and the significance of the role model rationale. They found that respondents of both sexes were at the greatest risk of divorce if they had been separated from either of their parents following parental divorce and that if they did live with one parent then the greater risk was for those living with their mothers. From these results Pope and Mueller concluded that the role model rationale was not as well supported as the economic rationale. They say that they were not surprised to find that the transmission effects detected were small, in that parental disruption is only a rough indication of the theoretically meaningful categories or rationales which are believed to contribute to the intergenerational effect. No attempt was made to look into any psychological concepts which might contribute to the personality rationale. In this context attachment theory may well help to explain the relatively high risk suffered by those children who were not cared for by either parent following divorce. It would also have been valuable to have included age at separation or divorce as a factor. However, Pope and Mueller do predict that 'further research will show that there is no direct causal effect of parental disruption on the child's marital stability; all of the effect is mediated or transmitted through intervening factors identified for each of these rationales' (p.60).

O'Connor et al. (1999) have examined the intergenerational transmission of divorce by obtaining predictive and outcome data from over 8000 mothers in the United Kingdom with an average age of 28 years. They found by regression analysis that respondents were significantly more likely to have suffered divorce if their own parents had divorced, but also if there had been parental marital conflict or if home care had been poor. These findings are largely in agreement with earlier work by Amato (1996) who conducted a prospective study over a period of 12 years with a mixed gender sample of over 1000 respondents in the United States. Like O'Connor et al. he found that parental divorce was associated with an increased risk of offspring divorce and that the largest share of this effect was mediated by interpersonal behaviour problems. Both these studies, with their different approaches, have found that the occurrence of parental divorce is directly associated with offspring divorce but that there are also important family and relationship components which contribute to this prediction.

Dickmann and Engelhardt (1999) have carried out an extensive sociological study of the intergenerational effect of divorce using data gathered from some 7000 individuals interviewed in the German Family Survey (Alt, 1991). From this large data source they were able to examine by regression analysis the effects of parental divorce, loss of a father and loss of both parents on the risk of divorce. They were also able to subdivide the sample into those born before and after 1945. They found that the risk of divorce was greatest for those whose parents divorced or who had lost both parents, usually as the result of allied action in the war. They found no difference in the risk between those from intact two-parent families and those who had lost one parent, so long as the parental loss occurred after the age of five. Their conclusions were that the intergenerational effects were predominantly due to the social inheritance of divorce based on pessimistic attitudes towards marriage and the family and deficiencies in role-learning caused by more frequent and perhaps aggressive styles of conflict resolution. There was no direct consideration given to the quality of family emotional support and the role of attachment in the processing and interpretation of social experience, which Fonagy (2003) believes reflects an individual's ability to function in close personal relationships.

As mentioned earlier Teachman (2002) maintains that the emphasis on the intergenerational transmission of divorce has diverted attention away from other dimensions of family histories, or as she puts it 'living arrangements', which may be linked to divorce. In order to investigate this she selected a sub-sample from the Survey of Family Growth (National Centre for Health Statistics, 1998), which has recorded data relating to the life history of 10,800 women between the ages of 15-44 years residing in the United States. The sub-sample is of those 4900 married women whose first marriages were contracted between 1970 and 1989. Because of the comprehensive detail included in the survey it was possible for Teachmen to study the relative risk of divorce compared to those from families with intact marriages as a function of a wide range of childhood living arrangements using regression analysis. These included those not raised by their mothers, possibly a category which comes closer than any other found in the literature to the present study's interest in the possible long-term effect of childhood separation on marital history. She found that the relative risk was greater for this category than for those whose childhood included parental divorce. Both effects were significant, with a 70% and 53% increase respectively in the likelihood of divorce. Again unfortunately the analysis did not include the age at separation. She ends the paper by concluding: '... The results presented in this article indicate that it is not just parental divorce that is linked to the risk of subsequent divorce. Rather, it appears that time spent away from both biological parents, for any number of reasons, is associated with a set of circumstances that are linked to an increased risk of divorce. This finding draws attention to the diversity of the life course experiences of children and the impact that these experiences have on relatively long-term outcomes'. (p.728).

Although it is true that the body of research summarised here does not relate directly to the subject of this present study there is evidence that the attendant changes in living arrangements following divorce, and the effect these have on child security and behaviour, do play a part in the intergenerational transmission of divorce. From this it is reasonable to enquire whether a temporary separation from both parents as a result of evacuation may be linked to subsequent marital instability, particularly for those of a young age at the time of separation.

So the general research question asked in this study is: Are there long term associations between temporary childhood separation and marital disruption? From the above review of the literature, and the largely anecdotal accounts and studies related to the effects of evacuation, the hypothesis put forward here is that there will be associations but that these will be of a complex nature, dependent on age at evacuation, care received and the degree to which parental attachments have been lost, all mediated by life course variables.

2.3.4 The evacuation experience and adult attachment

The fourth outcome variable which will be employed in the analysis is a measure defining secure and insecure attachment styles which will be used to determine if there are any significant associations between the evacuation experience of respondents and their adult pattern of relationships.

Attachment theory owes its origins to the work of John Bowlby, which he based partly on his experience of children separated from their parents in World War 2 and also on his clinical work at the Tavistock Clinic and later his survey for the World Health Organisation (WHO) on the effect of maternal deprivation. His official report for the WHO was also published in a popular form under the title *Child Care and the Growth of Love* (Bowlby, 1953) which sold 450,000 copies in the English edition alone. In 1963 he left the Tavistock Clinic and became a part-time member of the Medical Research Council and during the period from 1964 to 1979 he was able to formulate his theory of attachment based on his earlier studies of maternal deprivation and the ethological work of Tinbergen (1951) and Lorenz (1952). Holmes (1993) comments that at this time Bowlby believed the time was ripe for a unification of psychoanalytic concepts with those of ethology, which would lead to a rich vein of research. It was during this period that he wrote his trilogy on attachment and loss (Bowlby, 1969, 1973, 1980).

Possibly the earliest paper in which Bowlby dissociates himself from contemporary Freudian theory on maternal attachment and loss is in his review of separation anxiety (Bowlby, 1961). Unlike Freud (1905) with his initial theory of transformed libido, or Rank (1924) with that of birth-trauma anxiety, or Klein (1934) with her emphasis on physiological needs, Bowlby saw attachment between a mother and infant as a psychological bond. In this paper he deliberately ascribes separation anxiety to be part of a primary instinctual response to any rupture in this bond and one which can also be observed in certain classes of animals and which can be related to grief and mourning. The work of Lorenz (1952) had shown that certain avian species demonstrated bonding without feeding and that of Harlow (1958) with rhesus monkeys demonstrated feeding without bonding. So Bowlby postulated an attachment system independent of physiological needs, thus adopting a biological approach, and one at odds with prevailing psychoanalytic theory. It was based on an inherited need for infants and small children to stay close to their mothers and to signal separation if they are to remain safe from predation. This is a formulation which lies close to that considered by Freud in his later work, after what Bowlby describes as Freud's somewhat confused musing over the problem of separation anxiety in his book *Inhibitions, Symptoms and Anxiety* (Freud, 1926). Bowlby (1961) charmingly acknowledges this meeting of minds when he says this 'permits me to entertain the agreeable idea that towards the end of his life Freud was searching after a formulation not very different from that advanced here' (p.257). Bowlby also says that Freud finally clarifies what Bowlby believes to be the true relatedness of *separation anxiety*, *mourning* and *defence*, something Freud admits in the book he had been previously confused about. Now Freud sees the sequence clearly when he says: 'Anxiety is the reaction to the danger of loss of object, the pain of mourning a reaction to the actual loss, and defences protect the ego against instinctual demands which threaten to overwhelm it and can occur all too readily in the absence of the object' (p.164).

Bowlby did not believe that such a formulation meant that monotropism was absolute, but that attachment usually relates to a single figure which is most often the mother but does not preclude other close figures. These early thoughts were developed by Bowlby and led to the concept of an 'attachment behavioural system' that he believed functions to regulate infant safety in the environments in which we originally evolved. Such a system, by providing a secure base, also allows for a degree of exploration as an aid to development in the knowledge that such a haven exists (Ainsworth, 1982).

Following this initial phase in the development of attachment theory by Bowlby, Ainsworth took the lead in the second, operational phase with her naturalistic observations of infant-mother interactions in homes in Kampala, Uganda and then in Baltimore (Ainsworth, 1967, 1978). This work led to the development of the laboratory-based Strange Situation procedure which made use of an infant's responses to two very brief separations from, and a final reunion with, a given parent. In the short intervening period a stranger enters the room twice. Surprisingly, she found that the responses of the infants were not uniform in regard to attachment and exploratory behaviour. Ainsworth had expected to demonstrate the near universality of infant attachment behaviour in response to natural clues to danger as envisaged by Bowlby. She anticipated that these clues would lead to infant crying at least by the time of the second separation and to a rapid approach with the mother upon reunion. Once reunited it was assumed that the mother's presence would provide sufficient security to permit the infant to return to play. While a majority of infants in the initial sessions behaved as expected and were later named *secure*, some showed little or no distress at being left alone in the unfamiliar environment and avoided the mother on her return. They behaved like toddlers who had reached the stage of detachment in response to major separations, as described by Robertson & Bowlby (1952). These infants, called *avoidant*, seemed to Ainsworth to be responding to this stressful situation by repressing expressions of both anxiety and anger. Finally a minority of infants were too distressed to engage in exploration or play in the strange situation even when the mother was present. Termed *resistant/ambivalent* they seemed preoccupied with the mother throughout the procedure and yet too angry and/or distressed to take comfort in her return (Main, 2001). Ainsworth and her colleagues also found that these forms of attachment were predictable from the mother's sensitivity or otherwise to the infant's behavioural signals when observed in the home.

Following this operational development in the study of attachment the third phase opened with a move to the level of representation. The major figures in the field, including Bowlby (1969), Bretherton and Waters (1985), and Main, Kaplan and Cassidy (1985) give credit to the Robertsons' research based on the childhood film series they devised and directed which demonstrated such a level of representation. As Main (2001) says:

> 'Whereas Ainsworth had shown that repeated rejection of attachment behaviour on the part of a mother could lead an infant to avoid her in stressful situations, the Robertsons' films on the effects of separation demonstrated that toddlers who in all likelihood had never previously been significantly rejected could also come to avoid mothers on the basis of changes in mental or emotional processes taking place in the absence of interaction' (p.1058).

Main was particularly struck by the film 'Thomas' in which a 2-year old who had previously enjoyed an harmonious relationship with his mother was several times presented with her photograph during an extended foster-care placement. Over this period his attitude to the photograph changed, initially fondling it he later in the period backed away from it and then at the end of the separation period turned away from it with an anxious expression. Main makes the point that since a photograph cannot *behave* it cannot be said to have elicited Thomas' changing reaction; the gradual development of avoidance must have included aspects of change in their *imagined* relationship.

Bowlby maintained that this idea of an attachment relationship, rather than a simple behavioural mechanism for maintaining proximity, was established by the third birthday and persists on through life (Holmes, 1993). At this stage the child can begin to think of parents as separate people and attachment theory merges into a general theory about relationships and how they may be maintained. A key concept here is that of Bowlby's *internal working model*, one which describes the internal world of psychoanalysis but is formulated in practical terms. This assumes that the child builds up a set of models of the self and others, based on repeated patterns of interactive experience. These are used to predict and relate to the world. As Holmes says:

> A securely attached child will store an internal working model of a responsive, loving, reliable care-giver, and of a self that is worthy of love and attention and will bring these assumptions to bear on all other relationships. Conversely, an insecurely attached child may view the world as a dangerous place in which other people are to be treated with caution, and sees himself as ineffective and unworthy of love (p.78).

Bowlby and others believed that these assumptions are relatively stable and enduring and that those built up in the early years of life are particularly persistent and may not easily be modified by subsequent experience. He believes it is through such internal working models that the young person's style of attachment and dependency remain active throughout the life cycle, contributing to the different stages of an individual's development and psychological health. If true, such a 'life-time' concept should be in evidence when a longitudinal comparison is made between infants tested in the Strange Situation and when interviewed as young children and in adulthood. Work by Main, Kaplan and Cassidy (1985) and others found that differences in the Strange Situation behaviour did predict corresponding responses in the same children six years later following a range of tests based on parent-child separations (Strange & Main, 1985; Kaplan, 1987; Main and Cassidy, 1988). Furthermore studies have shown that a similar significant relationship holds between response to the Strange Situation procedure and that found twenty years later using the Adult Attachment Interview (AAI) developed by George, Kaplan & Main in 1984 (Beckwith et al., 1999; Waters et al., 2000a; Hamilton, 2000; Weinfield et al., 2000). However Main (2001) warns that these results are mainly from low-risk samples with middle-class backgrounds and there is evidence that when traumatic events intervened between infancy and late adolescence no such associations were found. So she concludes with Bowlby (1969) that despite the overall predictability between early strange situation behaviour and later representation processes attachment security may not be always fixed or fully determined in infancy. As Waters et al. say,

> 'One of the cornerstones of Bowlby's theory is that attachment-related expectations and working models remain open to revision in the light of changes in the availability and responsiveness of secure base figures. That is, attachment theory predicts both stability under ordinary circumstances and change when negative life events occur which effect caretaker behaviour'. (Waters et al., 2000a, p.685).

On this basis it is reasonable to suppose that a temporary separation from parents in young childhood could lead to a change in attachment and that this may be associated with a level of insecure attachment in adulthood. But it also raises the question: How does such a possible change in security depend on the details of the separation? This would include the age at which separation took place, the care received during fostering, the time period involved and the level of contact between parents and child during the period of separation. Or more generally what proportion of the variance in adult attachment can be accounted for by the details of such separation experiences?

Although no systematic work has been reported which tries to answer these particular questions it is worth looking at the longitudinal studies referred to above since these have helped to clarify the mechanisms of stability and change in attachment representations from infancy to early adulthood.

The three longitudinal studies of Waters et al. (2000a). Hamilton (2000) and Weinfield et al. (2000) have all examined the degree of consistency in attachment between infancy and early adulthood using three different survey samples. They all employed the Strange Situation procedure to test one-year old infants and followed this up by rating them in early adulthood by means of the Adult Attachment Interview (AAI). Two of the studies involved predominantly middle-class conventional families with a low risk of negative life events, while the third, Weinfield et al.(2000), selected a sample from a population of mainly non-conventional and disadvantaged families with a high risk of poor developmental outcomes. Although participant numbers in all three analyses were low it was possible for Waters et al. (2000b) to conclude that these studies had demonstrated both the coherence of individual development in attachment security and the fact that any changes in security is meaningfully related to one or more negative changes in the family environment. Such negative life events included loss of a parent, parental divorce, life-threatening illness of a parent or child, parental psychiatric disorder and physical or sexual abuse by a family member. This conclusion is in agreement with both Bowlby's original hypothesis (1973, 1980) and the beliefs of Vaughn & Egeland (1979) and Ainsworth (1982) and others that attachment theory presupposes both stability and change, and that change occurs when existing beliefs about significant others and relationships are under assault.

Although it was not possible in these studies to delineate which negative events were most deleterious, nor was any attempt made to investigate the effect of age at which such events occurred on the change in security, nevertheless they are valuable in the context of the present study. They have demonstrated the stability of attachment security over a developmental period of 20 years and that any changes in this security can be attributed to changes in the family environment. This present, retrospective study involves a natural experiment and seeks to do something similar over a much longer time period. The 'negative life events' are variable periods of parental separation which occur at a range of ages and under differing regimes of foster care. In addition it will be possible to test for frequency of parental visits and the effects of multiple billets.

Unfortunately although no systematic work has been found which bears directly on how the details of childhood separation experiences may effect adult attachment, the studies of Robertson (1953) and Maccoby (1980) have shown that such separations in childhood are likely to be most distressing between the ages of 6 months and 3 years, when children are unable to hold an image of the absent parent or understand the concept of a limited separation period. The quality of the substitute care has also been found to be important, as Freud and Burlingham (1944) have shown in their report of their work in the Hampstead Nurseries during World War 2. So this present study does provide an opportunity, through the wartime evacuation of children, to determine if there is any association between the details of that evacuation experience and the security of adult relationships expressed through their adult attachment styles some 55 years later.

The research question asked in this present study is: Is temporary separation from a parent due to wartime evacuation associated in any way with adult attachment security assessed some 55 years later? From the above theoretical and empirical review the hypothesis is tentatively advanced that such associations will exist but will be dependent on any individual's experience of the evacuation in terms of age, care received and the degree to which parental attachment is maintained or lost, as well as the modifying and mediating effects of the early family environment and later life events.

2.4 Summary of the research aims

The research aims of this study have been implicitly given at the end of each of the previous four sections in which the underlying theoretical and empirical evidence for each of the outcome variables selected was discussed. In this short final section these aims and the consequent research questions will be summarised.

The first research aims relate to respondents *perceptions*, where the conclusions of the qualitative pilot study undertaken led to the hypothesis that a period of separation from the security of a family due to evacuation can be perceived as a positive gain for development, or, at the other extreme, an emotional legacy throughout a respondent's life, depending on an individual's particular evacuation experience. So in this context the first aim of the present, quantitative study is to evaluate this hypothesis by statistically testing some of these perceptions or attributions as a function of certain input variables of evacuation, such as age at evacuation, care received, period away and the degree of parental contact maintained. This then leads on to the second aim which is to compare and contrast these results, based on such perceptions, with the adult performance of respondents using outcome measures of mental health, marital history and adult attachment. So the research questions being asked are:

> 1a. Can the wide range in the *perceptions* of the long term developmental effects of temporary childhood separation due to evacuation be explained in terms of an individual's experience, particularly in terms of age at evacuation, care received and the degree of parental contact maintained?

And following on from this:

> 1b. Do outcome *measures* of mental health, marital history and adult attachment support and confirm these range of *perceptions*?

The second category of research aims is rather broader in scope, making use of this World War 2 evacuation event to study, in the form of a natural experiment, the ways in which the occurrence of temporary childhood separation may be directly, and also indirectly associated with the same outcome variables. Theoretical arguments and empirical evidence assessed in this chapter make it clear that, although direct research on the long-term effects of childhood separation per se is minimal, there is support from research in related fields that it is primarily the context surrounding parental loss or separation in childhood, rather than the event itself, which predisposes children to later developmental problems or disorders, and that these associations may be mediated by certain life-course variables. This conclusion applies equally to the investigation of those childhood antecedents associated with either affective disorders, or the occurrence of divorce or insecurity in adult attachment terms. The research question being asked here is:

2. In what way are respondents' mental health, marital history and adult attachment style associated with their evacuation experience and family upbringing, and how are these associations mediated by life course variables and events?

These research questions will be addressed through the use of both univariate and multivariate analyses based on the model shown below in Figure 2.1, illustrating a respondent's pathway through life.

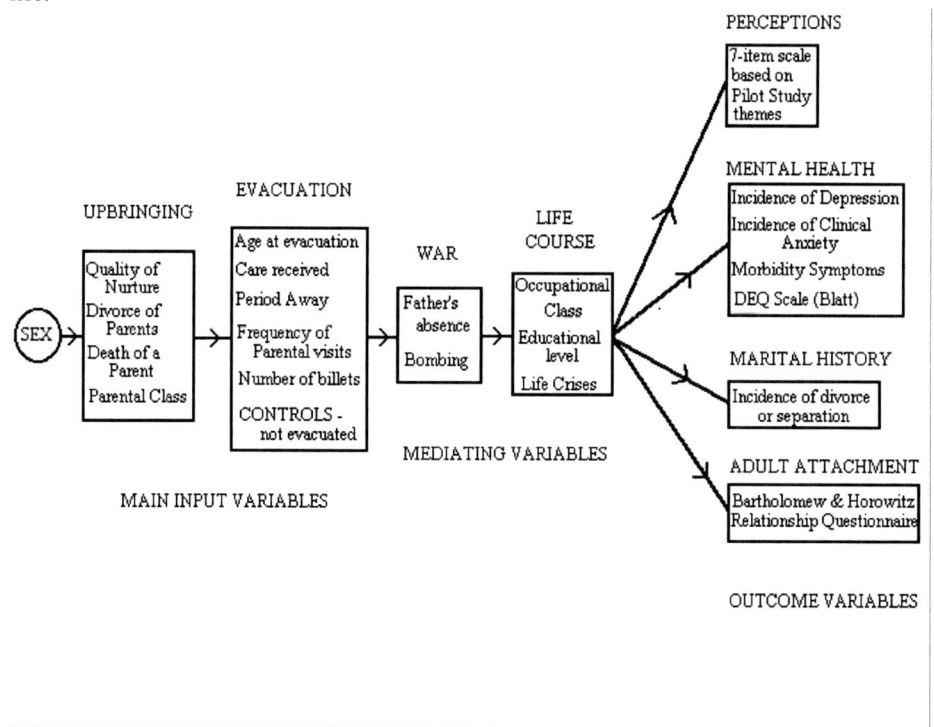

Figure 2.1 Respondent's pathway through life, with the main input and mediating variables and those outcome variables selected for the analysis.

This model includes those upbringing variables which have already featured in the discussion on the possible antecedents to affective disorders, divorce and adult attachment. The evacuation experience of respondents is covered by five variables based on the provisional conclusions of the pilot study, plus two war-related variables which are believed to be relevant to this developmental study. Life course variables have been limited to occupational class, educational level and certain life crises, and the outcome variables are those selected and discussed in the previous sections of this chapter. The way in which this model has been operationalised will be discussed in detail in the following chapter on the methodology of the investigation.

Chapter 3 Methodology

In this chapter we will describe the samples, procedures, measures and statistics used to operationalise this quantitative study of the long-term effects of evacuation on those outcomes selected and discussed in Chapter 2. Certain of the statistical tests employed, including concerns regarding data limitations and validation, will be discussed in further detail in the context of the following chapters to which they apply and which describe the results of each analysis for each of the selected outcome variables. Ethical agreement for the research was granted in August 1997 by the Department of Psychology Ethical Committee of Birkbeck College (Approval reference No. 9713) following a description of the proposed survey and questionnaire.

3.1 Samples and Procedures

It was decided to concentrate respondent recruitment in the county of Kent. This had certain advantages. Although close to London, the level of bombing in towns and villages in the county had been modest by comparison with London and since the study was concerned with evacuation, rather than the effects of enemy action on young people, this helped to reduce related confounding effects, particularly with regard to the recruitment of the non-evacuated, or control sample. From a practical point of view too it had the advantage that a large percentage of the children from the county's primary and secondary schools were evacuated from there during the war, mainly to the west country and Wales, partly because of its strategic importance and the fact that it lay under the path of German bombers targetting London. Possibly a disadvantage of concentrating on one such county was a certain loss of generalisabilty across the United Kingdom, particularly in relation to more urban areas which had large-scale evacuation schemes.

In order to provide sufficient power for the statistical analyses envisaged a projected sample size of some 1000 respondents was required, ideally split evenly between men and women. In addition a much lower non-evacuated control sample was needed for the initial comparisons. The evacuated sample should have a wide distribution in age at the start of evacuation from 5 to 15 years and this entailed recruiting respondents between the ages of 62 to 72 years of age when recruitment began in 1998. No form of direct advertising was employed or any payments made in recruiting respondents, i.e. no newspaper advertising, mail drops, unsolicited phone calls, or invitations via Kent Radio, for fear of skewing the distribution through overt 'marketing' pressure. Recruitment was effected through letters and short articles in all Kent regional and free issue newspapers and state school association magazines, also through short descriptions of the survey placed on county library notice boards and in newsletters of various organisations. No private or boarding schools were approached since these children were unlikely to have been fostered by families in the evacuation areas. In no case did the text refer explicitly to evacuation being the subject of the survey, rather it asked for volunteers from those whose home was in Kent during the war to complete a questionnaire concerned with their wartime experiences (see for example Appendix 2 - *'A survey of the lives of war children from Kent'*). As a result of this approach both recruitment of the evacuated and non-evacuated samples occurred at the same time and via the same procedures and so avoided a self-selected sample on evacuation. It was hoped that this recruitment scheme would not only provide the necessary respondent numbers but that their demographic distribution would be reasonably representative of the occupational class structure of the county population.

By this means 1467 volunteers replied to the invitation and were sent questionnaires marked with a reference number and the sex of the volunteer. If they wished to enjoy complete anonymity they were invited to cut off the reference number. Of the above number 1118, or 76%, returned the despatched questionnaires, of which 41, or 4%, were returned anonymously. With the acceptance criteria that only completed questionnaires should be employed, and also none from those evacuated with their mothers or from those who had attended boarding schools, this left 869 respondents, aged 62 to 74, to take part in the survey. Of these 487 were females and 293 were males who had been evacuated and 36 were females and 53 were males who had remained at home during the war. The percentage who returned the questionnaire, at 76%, was surprisingly high, particularly as it was 20 pages long (see Appendix 3 - A survey of the lives of war children from Kent). From accompanying letters and reports from the Evacuees Reunion Association it would appear that the survey occurred at a time when many past evacuees were wanting to revisit their childhood experiences of evacuation, some 50 years after the event. This was encouraged by a more open climate in relation to the true legacy of war, and possibly by their personal ability in affective terms in later age to face this important phase of their lives. This suggests that those who did respond to the invitation and who completed the questionnaire had a greater 'developmental' investment in their wartime experience than those who did not respond, maybe in both a positive and negative sense.

The distribution by occupational class of the sample is compared in Table 3.1(a) to that of the Kent county population from the census results of 1991 using the *Simplified List of Social Class based on Occupation*, as published by the Office of National Statistics. Table 3.1(a) shows that the distribution of the evacuated and non-evacuated samples are in reasonable agreement with each other and with that of the overall Kent population. However, the percentage level for the evacuated sample is rather less in Class 3 than in the other samples and somewhat higher in class 4.
Table 3.1(b) is a comparable table giving the educational level between the evacuated and non-evacuated control samples. Both samples are in reasonable agreement although the non-evacuated sample has a slightly higher percentage with a university degree.

Table 3.1(a) Occupational class distribution of the recruited sample compared to that of the population of Kent

Simplified list of Social Class based on Occupation	Kent population (1991 census) %	Evacuated sample (1998) N=780 %	Not evacuated sample (1998) N=89 %
Class 1	4.3	3.3	3.6
Class 2	28.5	25.4	27.7
Class 3	46.6	39.4	45.8
Class 4	14.8	26.5	20.5
Class 5	5.8	5.5	2.4
Total	100.0%	100.0%	100.0%

Table 3.1(b) Educational level distribution of the recruited sample

Educational level	Evacuated sample N=773 %	Not evacuated sample N=85 %
Secondary level only	70.8	70.6
Technical/Professional qualification (no degree)	19.6	16.5
University Degree	9.6	12.9
Total	100.0%	100.0%

3.1.1 Characteristics of the evacuation experience

The mean period of evacuation in years of the evacuated sample is shown below in Figure 3.1 as a function of the age when they were first evacuated.

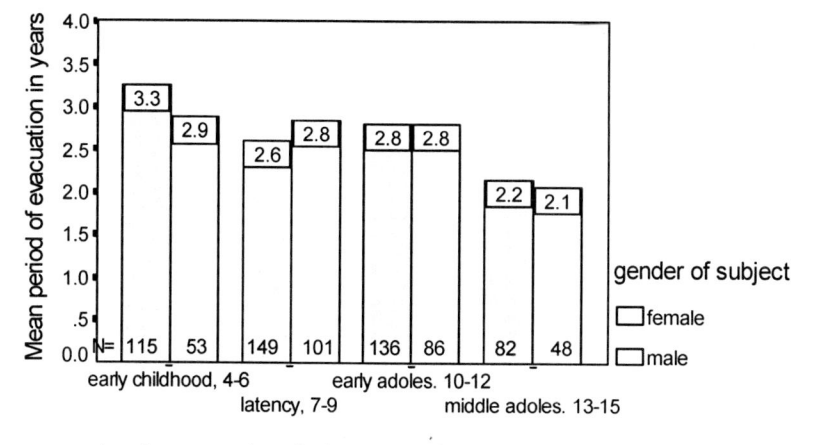

Figure 3.1 Mean period of evacuation in years as a function of sex and age at evacuation

It can be seen from this figure that there is a decrease in the evacuation period as a function of age which applies to both sexes in a similar manner, falling from about 3 years to 2 years from early childhood to middle adolescence. The numbers of male and female respondents in each age group is included in the figure at the base of each bar, where it can be seen that the numbers in each age group, for both sexes, are of similar magnitudes.

Figure 3.2 shows a plot of the mean number of visits made by a parent or parents during the total period of evacuation as a function of the age at the start of evacuation.

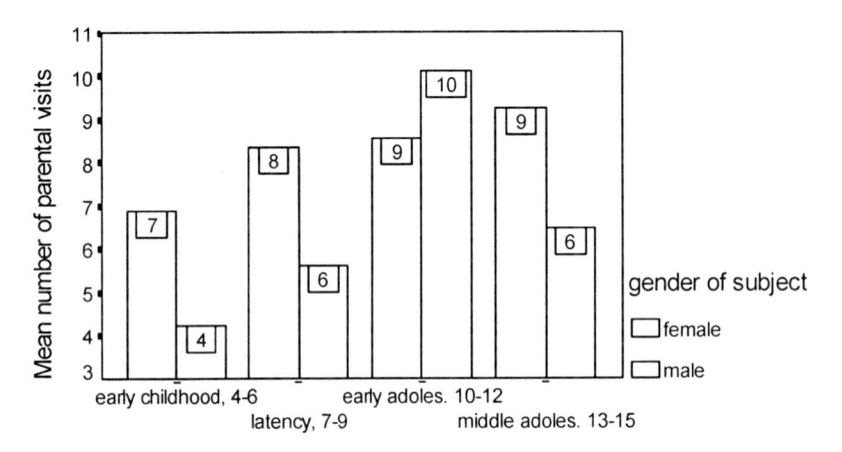

Figure 3.2 Mean number of visits made during the total evacuation period as a function of sex and the age when first evacuated.

Bearing in mind from Figure 3.1 that there is a reduction in the mean length of evacuation with age it can be seen from Figure 3.2 that the frequency of parental visits increases with age. This is particularly the case for male evacuees where the frequency increases from just over 1 visit per year in early childhood to over 3 visits per year in early adolescence.

Figure 3.3 gives a plot of the mean number of billets occupied as a function of the age at the start of evacuation for both sexes.

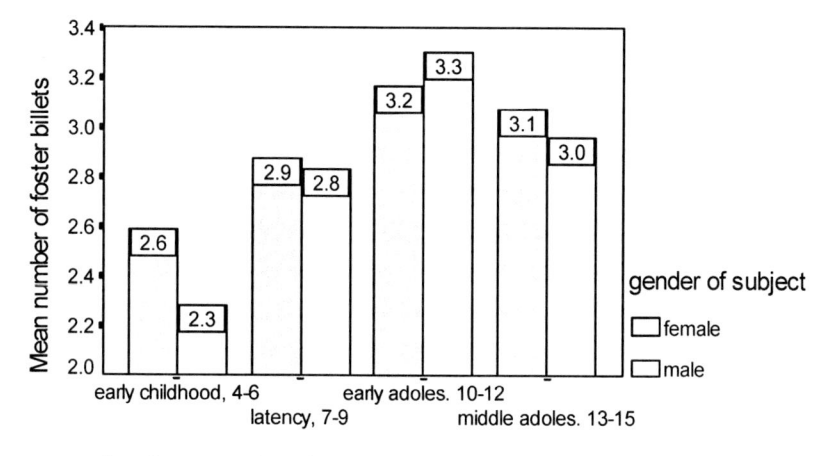

Figure 3.3 Mean number of foster billets as a function of age when first evacuated.

The variation in the number of billets occupied as function of age at evacuation is not great, but does peak in early adolescence for both sexes.

The relevance of these descriptive plots to both the univariate and multivariate results will be discussed later in the relevant chapters.

3.2 Measures

The diagram given at the end of the previous chapter, in Figure 2.1, illustrates respondents pathway through life and forms the model for the subsequent statistical analyses. It includes those input, mediating and outcome variables selected for inclusion in the study. Before discussing these variables in detail it is worth briefly looking at the layout of the questionnaire and to indicate which sections provided the appropriate data.

3.2.1 The Questionnaire

The layout of the questionnaire, given in Appendix 3 (*A survey of the lives of war children from Kent*), goes from Sections 1-17, effectively moving through the life cycle of a respondent. To a degree this chosen order was based on the pilot study interviews in which participants were asked first to recount their early family upbringing before describing their war experiences and adult and later lives.

At the start of the questionnaire they were asked to give their sex, date of birth and certain family details and this was followed by an invitation to give a brief description of their parents and their relationship with them in childhood and adolescence, including something on the form of their upbringing. They were also asked to include their family social situation and comment on any family problems or crises, including parental loss or divorce, and any financial or employment difficulties experienced by their parents during their childhood. This brief account, or short essay, formed the major part of Section 1 and was often continued by respondents on separate sheets included by them within the returned questionnaire. However, omission of this account by any respondent did not preclude acceptance of the questionnaire for the subsequent data analysis so long as the remainder of the questionnaire had been completed. This introductory section was followed in Section 2 by the Relationship Closeness Scale developed by Coffman et al. (1993) which required respondents to estimate the degree of closeness they had to their mothers and fathers at various stages of childhood and adulthood, using a series or scale which diagrammatically represented this closeness. These two sections provided data for the selected input variables under UPBRINGING in Figure 2.1.

Following these introductory sections, if they had been evacuated they were then asked details of their evacuation experiences in Section 3, or if not evacuated they were directed to Section 5. Section 3 on evacuation included a measure of the care received and details of any abuse experienced, and in Section 4 they were asked to mark a 7-point, 10-item scale based on themes which emerged from the pilot study on how they thought the evacuation experience might have contributed to their development as an adult. The answers given in Section 3 formed the basis for the variables included under EVACUATION in Figure 2.1 and those under Section 4 provided the data for the outcome variable on PERCEPTIONS.

All the subsequent sections in the questionnaire were answered by all respondents irrespective of whether or not they had been evacuated. Section 5 is concerned with respondents home life during the war, including any enemy action, and as in Section 1 asks for a brief account of family relationships and any crises, including problems of 'fitting-in' on return if the respondent had been evacuated. This section provided data for the variables entitled WAR in Figure 2.1. Section 6 asks about details of respondent's adult life since the war, including further education, employment and family and marital history (i.e. the LIFECOURSE mediating variables in Figure 2.1). Section 7 is the Bartholomew and Horowitz (1991) Relationship Questionnaire with four short paragraphs to be scored, each with a 7-point scale, which provided data for the outcome measure of ADULT ATTACHMENT. Following this Section 8 has 6 items related to respondents' belief of the degree of intimacy, involvement and sense of identity etc. enjoyed by them in their adult relationships with others, but which were not used in the present analysis. Section 9 is the 26 item F-scale developed by Adorno et al. (1950) for the measurement of authoritarianism but which was not analysed here, and Section 10 is the 66-item Depression Experiences Questionnaire (DEQ) developed by Blatt et al. (1976) and included here as a component of the MENTAL HEALTH data analysis. Section 11 asks three questions about the influence of marriage on their adult development. Section 12 lists 18 mental health disorders or symptoms and respondents are asked to tick any boxes which apply and provide brief details, including any relevant family or other crises which might have contributed to the condition, and these are incorporated in the MENTAL HEALTH analysis. Section 13 asks for brief details, with dates, of any major physical illnesses, treatments or operations. Finally Sections 14-17 are concerned with obtaining details of main interests, present relationships and important life events etc. which provided further background material but were not entered into the statistical analyses.

3.2.2 The chosen variables

Using Figure 2.1 as a guide we will describe how the data was obtained for each of the groups of input, mediating and outcome variables, moving from left to right in the diagram as through the course of a respondent's life.

3.2.2.1 Upbringing variables

As a result of an examination of the research cited in Chapter 2 with particular regard to the three outcome variables related to mental health, marital history and adult attachment it was decided to include four variables under the group title 'Upbringing'. These were Quality of nurture, Divorce of parents, Death of a parent and Parental class, all categorical variables.

The first of these, Quality of nurture, was a simple dichotic variable in which a control group was identified which consisted of those respondents with a 'good enough' upbringing in the sense employed by Winnicott (1965), i.e. those who had enjoyed reasonable care, affection and support from both parents and had experienced no significant abuse or serious family conflicts during their childhood. As a corollary to this the second, or 'comfortless' category consisted of those who had experienced a lack of care and affection and/or a harsh, very strict upbringing or serious parental conflict. Assessment was made by two raters, an experienced social worker who had specialised in working with families and children and the present author, and their assessment was based on the retrospective account of family life given in Section 1 of the questionnaire. 100 such accounts were randomly selected and were rated according to the above two definitions, 'good enough ' and 'comfortless'. The measure of inter-rater agreement was assessed by Cohen's kappa (Cohen, 1960), which after correcting for chance agreement, gave a value of $\kappa = .75$. i.e. an agreement of 75%. For the purposes of the subsequent analyses this level of agreement was taken to be acceptable. This dichotic measure was supplemented by the Relationship Closeness scale of Coffman et al (1993) which assesses by a series of diagrams the closeness of a respondent to either parent as a function of age. This main emphasis on a descriptive account of early upbringing was based on the findings of the pilot study which showed such participants in later life enjoyed the opportunity to think through their early family life and led to a certain richness in their interview accounts which a more structured approach would not so easily tap. It was believed this would also apply to the present study in that a formal instrument such as the Parental Bonding Instrument (Parker, 1979) would not elicit the relationship details and nuances which would be evident in a descriptive account. Support for this came from the number of respondents who took the opportunity to add an additional page to their descriptions and the fact that these accounts when summarised led to some 200 different abstracts, coded under Upbringing, being listed in the final data table.

However there still remain the perceived limitations of such historical, retrospective accounts. In the classic work by Harris and her colleagues over a period of 20 years, from 1977 to 1997, and referred to in Chapter 2, retrospective accounts from interview transcriptions were used by raters to assess the degree of neglect and abuse in childhood suffered by women and its impact on their adult mental health. As Bifulco & Moran (1998) say in their book *Wednesday's Child*, the Royal Holloway team were among the first to tackle such a long recall period and this approach was viewed initially with some scepticism by the scientific community. In an attempt to verify these accounts every effort was made in these Royal Holloway studies to examine the factual aspects of women's childhood experience and to use these to corroborate the more subjective descriptions given of their childhood upbringing, including the use of the Childhood Experience of Care and Abuse (CECA) instrument which the team developed for this purpose (Bifulco et al., 1994). In a study of 100 pairs of sisters designed, in part, to validate such retrospective accounts, Bifulco et al. (1997) were able to examine the corroboration existing between sister's accounts in terms of the quality of upbringing, including the incidence of neglect or abuse, and also to compare their findings with such data when using the CECA instrument. Although one would not expect perfect agreement, they did find that the correlation between the sisters' accounts was generally high and they also confirmed the performance of the CECA instrument, which had been employed in a number of their previous studies. Unfortunately the present survey by questionnaire does not lend itself to such an examination of validity; however the research by the Royal Holloway team does suggest that retrospective accounts of childhood upbringing may be more valid than was previously believed.

Returning to Figure 2.1, knowledge of the occurrence of either Divorce of parents or Death of a parent was obtained from Section 1 or Section 5 of the questionnaire depending on when the event might have occurred. Finally Parental Class was assessed by reference to father's occupation, using the guide *A Simplified list of Social Class based on Occupation* published by the Office of National Statistics (1998). For the purposes of the analysis Classes 2 and 3 were pooled as being 'middle class' and Classes 4 and 5 were pooled as being 'working class'. No parents of respondents were in Class 1, and this no doubt partly reflected the lack of any respondents who had attended private schools.

3.2.2.2 Evacuation variables

From the conclusions of the pilot study the hypothesis arose by induction that participants' perceptions of the long-term effects of their evacuation experience were largely a function of certain variables based on their evacuation experience. It was suggested that the main factors were: Age at the start of evacuation, the care received during evacuation, the total period away, the degree of parental contact maintained and the number of billets occupied. These conclusions were supported by the related research studies discussed in Section 2.2. and were further considered in Section 2.3.1. when discussing participants' perceptions of the evacuation experience on their development and lives. These selected factors which form the input variables for evacuation shown in Table 2.1 are also the major factors of the evacuation experience which are likely to be linked with the outcome variables of mental health, marital history and adult attachment from the discussions in Sections 2.3.2, 2.3.3 and 2.3.4. They are also the main contributors to the research questions posed at the end of each of these sections.

Since there was a possibility that some respondents might incorrectly recall their age at evacuation it was decided not to ask for this information directly in the questionnaire but rather to calculate it from their date of birth and the date of their first evacuation, using information from Sections 1 and 3. Corroboration for the date of evacuation was obtained from cross-checking with the returns of other respondents attending the same schools.

In Section 3 of the questionnaire respondents were asked to rate the care received during their evacuation, with five gradings available from 'very good to 'very poor'. There was also a 'mixed' box which could be marked, and an invitation to comment in detail on the quality of the care received. Since the majority of respondents had been placed in more than one billet this enabled them to describe their overall experience of the care they received in some detail. From an assessment of this description, in conjunction with the above scale markings, the input variable 'Care received' was rated by the present author under one of three possible categories: 'good', 'moderate/mixed' or 'poor'. In addition Section 3 also asked them to mark the appropriate boxes if they believed they had been physically, sexually or emotionally abused during the evacuation, or exploited as free labour. Again comments were invited.

Data for the last three variables of this group, Period away, Frequency of parental visits and Number of billets, were also obtained from answers to Section 3 of the questionnaire. Since some respondents were likely to have been evacuated twice, particularly so since Kent was under the path of the V1 attacks on London in 1944, there was space given for answers relative to both periods. For statistical purposes Period away was defined as the total, or aggregated, period away, and the same applied to the count of the Number of billets occupied during the separate periods of evacuation. Frequency of parental visits, i.e. visits per year, was calculated from a knowledge of the number of visits paid and the total period a respondent was away from home.

3.2.2.3 War-related variables

From the evidence in Chapter 2 and the conclusions of the pilot study the direct influence of the war for the purposes of this analysis was limited to two categorical variables: whether a father was at home or away for most of the five war years, and whether the family was affected by bombing.

Both of these variables were obtained from replies to Section 5 in the questionnaire. A father's temporary absence was invariably due to military service, and unless discharged for any reason usually meant he was away for most of the war. The influence of bombing was examined independently for respondents who had been present and for those absent from home during the enemy action. Bombing was further considered under three categories: no enemy action, bombs dropped within the local neighbourhood and, thirdly, bombing which directly affected the home causing serious damage or the loss of the home. Respondents were invited to give details, including information about the loss or serious injury of any family members.

3.2.2.4 Life-course variables

Life-course variables included in the statistical analysis were social class of respondents based on occupation, educational level achieved and the incidence of any severe life crises. For each variable the categories employed in the analyses are those listed below in Table 3.2.

Table 3.2 Categories of Occupational class, Educational level and Life-crises employed in the statistical analyses

---

1. Occupational class:

    Class 1 - Senior managers, senior administrators and senior public servants. Members of the legal, medical, scientific, engineering and other professions.

    Class 2 - General managers, administrators and public servants (with administrative and executive functions). Officers, inspectors, teachers, nurses, social workers etc. Designers, writers, artists, musicians etc. Farm, property, catering managers etc.

    Class 3 - Clerks, secretaries, IT operators, draughtpersons, photographers, instructors etc. Retail managers and owners. All skilled trades.

    Class 4 - Storekeepers, telephone operators, machine, construction and process plant operators and motor fitters. Prison and security guards, catering and retail staff etc. Farm workers, gardeners, horticultural trades. Care assistants. Maritime and fishing workers. Other trades.

    Class 5 - Labourers, dockers, messengers, couriers, porters, cleaners, car park attendants, railway staff, refuse collectors, road sweepers, etc.

2. Education level:

    - No vocational or higher education (Low)
    - Vocational or higher education (High)

3. Life crises:

    - None
    - One or more

The definition of social class based on occupation used for coding is that listed by the Office of National Statistics in their user guide 6.1 (1998), and the above table summarises the type of occupation used to define the five classes. Data was obtained from answers to Section 6.

Educational level is a simple Yes/No dichotomy between those who have, or have not, received either a college vocational training or, alternatively, any university degree. For the purposes of the analyses college vocational training does not include further education studies for City and Guilds and Ordinary National Certificates etc., but does include the more advanced studies for Higher National Diplomas etc. Information regarding training and any other further or higher education studies was also obtained from Section 6.

The final variable employed, Life crises, was also a Yes/No dichotomous variable where a positive answer meant that a respondent had experienced one or more of the events in adulthood listed in Table 3.3.

Table 3.3 Critical events in a respondent's life which qualify as a Life crisis in terms of the statistical analysis

---

1 - Death of a spouse
2 - Divorce or separation
3 - Life threatening illness of self or spouse
4 - Long-term disability of self or spouse
5 - Death of a son or daughter

Information for these was obtained from Section 6, concerned with details of respondents' adult life since the war, and from Sections 13 to 17 towards the end of the questionnaire, where respondents are asked to give details of any major family crises, illnesses, disabilities etc.

3.2.2.5 Outcome variable - Perceptions

For the purpose of providing guidance for this quantitative study a wide range of psychologically and physically based concepts were found from the pilot study which related to the main categories of evacuation, and these in turn could be associated with certain post-evacuation categories. (See Appendix 1 - Summary of the project report: *Wartime evacuation: a pilot study of some effects using grounded theory*). From this grounded theory analysis (Strauss & Corbin, 1990) there emerged the following main categories for the two periods:

Evacuation period -
- Evacuation organisation
- Physical well-being
- Emotional experience
- Parental contact
- Age when evacuated
- Length of evacuation period
- Number of billets
- Sexual experience
- Cultural experience
- Economic experience

Post-evacuation period -
- Fitting back
- Gains in development
- Emotional legacy
- Fears
- Security in marriage
- Need to keep in touch

As an example of the way these two groups of categories are assumed to be related we can look at two main effects, covered by the post-evacuation categories labelled 'Gains in development' and 'Emotional legacy'. In terms of Strauss and Corbin's guidance these two post-evacuation main effects are 'consequences' of individuals' perceived evacuation experience and the sum of this experience is mediated by the range of causal conditions or categories from the evacuation period, as listed above. The properties of these input categories from the evacuation period will have a wide range of dimensions and these are assumed to determine the post-evacuation outcome. For example we can list the derived input categories, or variables with their most important properties and dimensions and these are given in Table 3.4. These input variables, together with each individual's temperament and pre-evacuation history, are assumed to affect the perceived post-evacuation outcome of a participant's evacuation experience. This is an example of the inductively-based, 'theory-discovery', premise of Glaser and Strauss' (1967) original grounded theory construct.

Table 3.4 Evacuation input categories with their most important properties and dimensions

Category	Major property	Main dimension
Evacuation organisation	Control	Well monitored - Lax control
Physical well-being	Care	Well cared for - Poorly cared for
Emotional experience	Security	Secure - Rejected
Parental contact	Frequency	Frequent contact - Infrequent contact
Age when evacuated	Years	Older (15) - Younger (5)
Length of evacuation	Years	Long (4-5 years) - Short
Number of billets	Number	Large - small
Sexual experience	Abuse	Yes - No
Cultural experience	Contrast	High - Low
Economic experience	Exploitation	Severe - negligible

In this context it soon became clear when analysing the transcribed data that the outcome of a period of evacuation was perceived by interviewees in different ways, leading to certain believed gains and losses in terms of subsequent development and the ability to make secure relationships. In the pilot study there are 24 concept labels referring to a wide variety of positive outcomes under the category 'Gains in development' and 47 concept labels of negative outcomes under the category 'Emotional legacy' (Rusby,1995). Examples of these are listed in Appendix 1 of this study and include both developmental and relational characteristics perceived to be linked to the evacuation experience by participants. The most substantive of these are given below in Table 3.5 in the form of 7-point scales where it can be seen that the maximum and minimum of each scale is defined by 'in vivo' quotations from the interview transcriptions. These scales form the basis for the outcome variable marked PERCEPTIONS in the pathway diagram shown in Figure 2.1.

Table 3.5 Scales used in the analysis to measure seven components of the general perception of the influence of the evacuation experience on respondents' development and lives

Positive Perceptions	Strongly agree	Moderately agree	Slightly agree	No effect	Slightly agree	Moderately agree	Strongly agree	Negative Perceptions
	<-------------------------------				------------------------------->			
OVERALL - 'it made me'	3	2	1	0	-1	-2	-3	'it ruined my life'
CONFIDENCE - 'evacuation gave me confidence'	3	2	1	0	-1	-2	-3	'it made me nervy and insecure'
OUTLOOK - 'it broadened my horizons and interests'	3	2	1	0	-1	-2	-3	'it narrowed my outlook on life'
COMPANY - 'it helped me to come out of myself'	3	2	1	0	-1	-2	-3	'it has made me something of a solitary person'
FAMILY - 'it has made me let go of my children'	3	2	1	0	-1	-2	-3	'it has made me protective of my family'
ANGER WITH MOTHER - 'it drew me very close to my mother'	3	2	1	0	-1	-2	-3	'deep down it has made me very angry with my mother'
UNFINISHED BUSINESS - 'I did not feel a sudden loss on parting - there was no unfinished business'	3	2	1	0	-1	-2	-3	'it has left a dreadful urge... to put a name to the chapter'

For comparison and computational purposes the positive perceptions or attributes have all been placed on the left of the scales in the above table. In the questionnaire, reproduced in Appendix 3, the scales of OUTLOOK, FAMILY, ANGER WITH MOTHER and UNFINISHED BUSINESS have all been reversed to reduce any response bias.

As discussed in Section 2.3.1 these measures will provide an opportunity to test the hypothesis that a period of separation due to evacuation may be perceived as a long-term gain for development, or at the other extreme, an emotional legacy through life, depending on a range of input conditions or variables. The results of the analysis can also be compared with the results of similar analyses for the remaining outcome variables using the same input variables of evacuation to examine whether such subjective perceptions are reflected in standardised measures of their mental health, marital history and adult attachment style.

3.2.2.6 Outcome variables - Mental health

The second group of outcome variables shown in the pathway diagram in Figure 2.1 is concerned with the mental health of respondents. When discussing the relevant literature in Chapter 2 the hypothesis was proposed that the childhood experiences of evacuation may be associated with adult mental health in the form of affective disorders and a range of related measures have been selected to investigate this proposition. These include the incidence of depression and clinical anxiety, a score of the total number of morbidity symptoms experienced and two components of Blatt et al.'s (1976) Depression Experiences Questionnaire. Each of these will be discussed in turn.

The measures for the incidence of depression or clinical anxiety are both simple categorical variables obtained from responses to the questions included in Section 12 of the questionnaire. If respondents had experienced such a disorder they were asked to provide brief details and dates, including any relevant family or other crises which they believed may have contributed to the condition. From these comments it was clear that the disorders described were of the neurotic, i.e. reactive type. Mild forms of dysphoria or anxiety were not included in the analysis and respondents must have received a minimum of some form of primary care to be categorised as having such a disorder, that is at least level 2 in the index of severity quoted by Goldberg & Huxley (1992).

Symptoms of psychological morbidity were selected after discussions with Stephen Davies (1996), Head of Clinical Psychology Services for Older People at the Princess Alexandra Hospital. Sixteen such symptoms are listed in Section 12 of the questionnaire (see Appendix 3) and respondents were asked to tick the appropriate boxes if they had experienced any of them. Seven of these sixteen symptoms were finally selected for the analysis based on their association with the incidence of depression and these are listed in Table 3.6. These seven symptoms are believed to be primarily of the depressive type and in this study were selected because they all showed highly significant associations with the depressive category, with Kappa values lying between .18 and .36 (all $p < .001$).

Table 3.6 Seven morbidity symptoms selected for the mental health analysis

1. Sleep disruption
2. Severe or long-lasting headaches
3. Extreme fatigue
4. Severe irritability
5. Phobias or irrational fears
6. Extreme loneliness
7. Feelings of unreality

The final scale used to examine the possible connection between childhood experiences of evacuation and adult mental health was the Depressive Experiences Questionnaire (DEQ) developed by Blatt and his colleagues (Blatt et al., 1976). It was designed to assess the likelihood of two types of depressive experience and was based on a 66-item questionnaire using 7-point Likert scale items that were selected from the clinical literature and which were believed to represent a wide range of feelings and experiences frequently associated with depression or dysphoria but were not in themselves symptoms of these disorders. Items on the DEQ, which are found in Section 10 of this studies' questionnaire, assess characteristics such as:

(a) a distorted or depreciated sense of self and others
(b) dependency
(c) helplessness
(d) egocentricity
(e) fear of loss
(f) ambivalence
(g) difficulty dealing with anger
(i) self-blame
(j) loss of autonomy
and (k) distortions in family relations.

Blatt et al. (1976) conducted a factor analysis of the scores from university students presented with these items and defined three orthogonal factors which were labelled Factor 1- Dependency, Factor 2- Self-criticism and Factor 3- Efficacy. The first two factors are related to dysphoria and subsequent research has indicated that these two factors are stable over time with test-retest reliabilility coefficients of 0.80 for Dependency and 0.75 for Self-criticism over periods of 3 months and 12 months (Blatt & Zuroff, 1992). Factor 1, Dependency, involves items that are primarily externally directed; they refer to interpersonal relationships, i.e. feelings of abandonment, loneliness and helplessness, and a wish to be close to and dependent upon others. Items on this factor also reflect concerns about being rejected and hurting and offending people, and having difficulty expressing anger and aggression for fear of losing the other. Factor 2, Self-criticism, consists of items that are more internally directed and concern feeling guilty, empty, hopeless, unsatisfied and insecure, and are directed critically towards the self for failing to meet internal expectations and standards (Blatt & Zuroff, 1992). The Self-criticism factor correlates highly with traditional measures of depression such as the Beck and Zung depression scales (Beck et al, 1961; Zung, 1965). The Dependency factor has significant but rather lower correlations with these scales, but Blatt & Zuroff (1992) believe it may assess a dimension of depression often overlooked in the more usual methods of assessment, and which may relate to a form of near anaclitic depression due to deprivation, or separation, at a young age. In addition to these two dimensions of dysphoria or depression, the factor analysis of responses to the DEQ identified a third factor, Efficacy, which includes items indicating a sense of confidence about one's resources and capacities. These items contain themes of high standards and personal goals, a sense of responsibility, inner strength, and a sense of pride and satisfaction in one's achievements. This last factor was not used in this analysis relating to mental health.

A request was made to Dr Blatt in the Department of Psychiatry at Yale University to use the DEQ measure and he kindly forwarded a copy of the questionnaire plus the item statistics and factor score coefficients derived from the original factor analysis based on the scores of 500 female and 160 male participants. A table was also provided which showed that the alpha coefficients of congruence for the split-half factor analyses for the three factors were .958, .904, and .948 for Factors 1, 2 and 3 respectively. The original program for the reduction of the data to compute factor scores from the 66-item individual scores was written in Fortran 4 in a punched card format, but this was rewritten for use on a personal computer. This program allowed the factor scores to be evaluated from the individual respondents' scores for the 66 questionnaire items listed. As mentioned earlier only the factor scores for Factor 1, Dependency, and Factor 2, Self-criticism, were used in the subsequent statistical analysis to investigate the long-term effect of the evacuation experience on mental health.

3.2.2.7 Outcome variables - Marital history

In Chapter 2, Section 2.3.3, we introduced the evidence for an association between risk factors in childhood and the subsequent marital history of individuals. So that in the same way that certain aspects of the evacuation experience may place individuals at risk and so predispose them to poor mental health it is also hypothesised that there may be a similar connection with the incidence of divorce or separation.

In order to test for this a simple categorical measure was used based on the incidence of divorce or separation reported in answers to Section 6 of the questionnaire. To operationalise this different levels of marital status found have been translated into the simple coding given in Table 3.7.

Table 3.7 Coding as a function of marital status for the statistical analyses

Coded as	Marital status
1. MARRIED	[Married [Widowed [Widowed and remarried [Widowed, remarried and widowed
2. DIVORCED	[Divorced [Separated [Divorced and remarried [Divorced, remarried and widowed [Widowed, remarried and divorced [Divorced more than once
3. MULTIPLE DIVORCE	Divorced more than once (for unique tests or plots)
4. SINGLE	Never married

The simple form of coding given in Table 3.7 was adopted for both the univariate and multivariate analyses undertaken so that the incidence of divorce or separation could be derived and examined as a function of the input variables of evacuation and upbringing. The MULTIPLE DIVORCE category was not used as part of the main univariate analysis but only to examine specific associations or trends.

3.2.2.8 Outcome variables - Adult attachment

Following the discussion of the possible association between the evacuation experience of respondents and adult attachment, in Section 2.3.4 of Chapter 2, it was decided to employ the Bartholomew and Horowitz (1991) Relationship Questionnaire as the outcome variable in the analysis. This measure is introduced here in the context of attachment theory and its operational use in the analysis is described.

There has recently been considerable debate as to how adult attachment constructs can best be assessed (see Crowell and Treboux, 1995; Hazan and Shaver, 1994) and the need to delineate the content, focus and assumptions underlying the different measures so that they can be critically compared and the theory of adult attachment sensibly tested. Such measures can be obtained by interview, such as the Adult Attachment Interview (George, Kaplan and Main, 1984) and the Current Relationship Interview (Crowell, 1990), or by questionnaires or self-report rating scales, such as those developed by Hazan and Shaver (1987) and Bartholomew and Horowitz (1991). Generally it has been found that interview-based classifications are well related to each other but that their relationships to, and correlations with, self-report measures are not straightforward (Crowell and Treboux, 1995).

The apparent common theoretical ground of the measures has led to some confusion in the study of adult relationships and has obscured the fact that several of the measures appear to address rather different constructs (Crowell & Treboux, 1995). All are agreed, however, that attachment theory suggests that working models of attachment develop initially in childhood relationships with parents, and serve as prototypes for later, adult, relationships. Because of this concern about the variety of measures available it is important to examine the origin, and to give a full description, of the construct which lies at the heart of a chosen measure and to try and understand its relationship to other forms of attachment measures.

The Bartholomew and Horowitz (1991) model is a development of the adult attachment measure of Hazan & Shaver (1987), itself based on the theoretical and empirical work of Ainsworth and Main, described in Section 2.3.4. The forced-choice measure of Hazan & Shaver adopts a 'style- or 'type'-based approach used to identify the form of romantic relationship styles that parallel the three major attachment styles discussed earlier, i.e. Secure, Avoidant and Anxious/ambivalent. Bartholomew &

Horowitz however have argued on theoretical grounds that attachment styles are defined by two underlying dimensions of *self* and *other* proposed by Bowlby (1969) to describe prototypic forms of adult attachment (Bartholomew & Horowitz, 1991). In such a model an individual's abstract image of the self and other are both dichotomised as positive or negative, so four combinations are conceptualised. Figure 3.4 shows the four attachment patterns that are derived from a combination of these two dimensions:

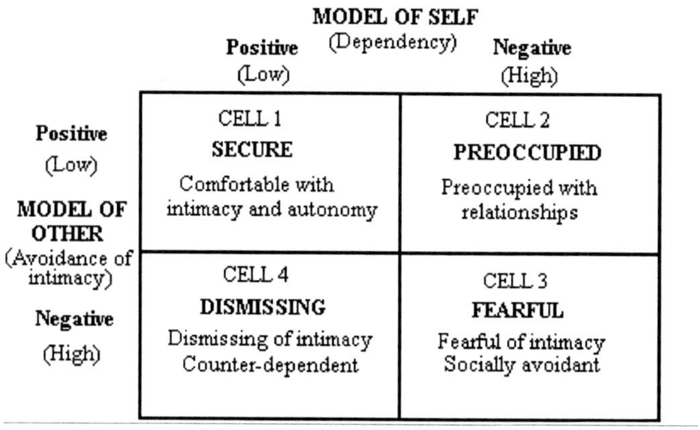

	MODEL OF SELF Positive (Low) (Dependency)	Negative (High)
Positive (Low) MODEL OF OTHER (Avoidance of intimacy)	CELL 1 **SECURE** Comfortable with intimacy and autonomy	CELL 2 **PREOCCUPIED** Preoccupied with relationships
Negative (High)	CELL 4 **DISMISSING** Dismissing of intimacy Counter-dependent	CELL 3 **FEARFUL** Fearful of intimacy Socially avoidant

Figure 3.4 Bartholomew and Horowitz model of Adult Attachment.

In Figure 3.4 Cell 1 indicates a sense of self-worthiness or lovability plus an expectation that other people are generally accepting and responsive, and is labelled **Secure** and corresponds to categories that other workers call securely attached (e.g. Hazan & Shaver, 1987; Main et al., 1985). Cell 2 indicates a sense of unworthiness (unlovability) of self combined with a positive evaluation of others, leading such a person to strive for self-acceptance by gaining the acceptance of valued others, and corresponds to Hazan and Shavers' ambivalent group and to Main's enmeshed or preoccupied with attachment pattern. Here it is labelled **Preoccupied**. Cell 3 indicates a sense of unworthiness (unlovability) of self combined with an expectation that others will be negatively disposed to oneself (untrustworthy and rejecting). By avoiding close involvement with others, this style enables people to protect themselves against anticipated rejection by others. Bartholomew and Horowitz believe it may correspond in part to the avoidant style described by Hazan and Shaver (1987), and they have labelled it **Fearful-avoidant**. Finally Cell 4 indicates a sense of self-worthiness combined with a negative disposition towards other people. Such people would protect themselves against emotional pain and disappointment by avoiding close relationships and maintaining a sense of independence and invulnerability. Bartholomew and Horowitz believe this style corresponds conceptually to the detached or dismissing attitude described by Main, but with no equivalent in the Hazar & Shaver model, so they have labelled it **Dismissive-avoidant**. They also show that the dimensions in Figure 3.4 can be considered in terms of *dependency* on the horizontal axis and the *avoidance of intimacy* on the vertical axis (see labels in brackets in Figure 3.3). Dependency can vary from being low, where a positive self-regard is established internally and does not require external validation, to high where a positive self-regard can only be maintained by others' continuing acceptance. Avoidance of intimacy reflects the degree to which people avoid close contact with others as result of their expectations of aversive consequences or rejection. The dismissing and fearful styles are alike in that both reflect the avoidance of intimacy; they differ, however, in the individuals' need for others' acceptance to maintain a positive self-regard. Similarly the preoccupied and fearful groups are alike in that both exhibit a strong dependency on others to maintain a positive self-regard, but they differ in their readiness to become involved in close relationships. Whereas the preoccupied cell implies a reaching out to others in an attempt to fulfil dependency needs, the fearful cell implies an avoidance of closeness to minimise eventual disappointment or rejection. Therefore, cells in adjoining quadrants of Figure 3.3 are believed, by Bartholomew and Horowitz, to be more similar conceptually than those in opposite quadrants.

This construct of adult attachment has been operationalised through the development of their Relationship Questionnaire which consists of four statements describing the four attachment styles, and each respondent is asked to rate the degree to which they resemble the four styles on a 7-point scale. In this way it differs from the simple categorical depiction required by Hazan & Shaver. These statements are found in Section 7 of the questionnaire (Appendix 1) and are reproduced below in Table 3.8 in terms of their relationship to the cells shown in Figure 3.3.

Table 3.8 Statements formulated by Bartholomew & Horowitz for use in their Relationship Questionnaire

---

CELL 1 - SECURE

'It is easy for me to become emotionally close to others. I am comfortable depending on others and having others depend on me. I don't worry about being alone or having others not accept me'.

CELL 2 - PREOCCUPIED

'I want to be completely emotionally intimate with others, but I often find that others are reluctant to get as close as I would like. I am uncomfortable being without close relationships, but I sometimes worry that others don't value me as much as I value them'.

CELL 3 - FEARFUL

'I am uncomfortable getting close to others. I want emotionally close relationships, but I find it difficult to trust others completely, or to depend on them. I worry that I will be hurt if I allow myself to become too close to others'.

CELL 4 - DISMISSING

'I am comfortable without close emotional relationships. It is very important for me to feel independent and self-sufficient, and I prefer not to depend on others, or have others depend on me'.

Bartholomew and Horowitz (1991) have carried out a series of studies to describe and help validate their self-report measure by comparing the results with those from semi-structured interviews. Seventy seven students were asked about their friendships, romantic relationships and feelings about close relationships, and the transcripts of these were independently rated and compared to the students' own assessment of their relationships using the self-report Relationship Questionnaire. They found that the internal structures of the interview ratings and the self-report ratings of the four attachment styles were consistent and this was tested both by correlation procedures and by factor analysis. They showed that a 2-dimensional structure spatially reproduced the hypothesised relationships among the four styles, and that this was supported by both sets of ratings. From this analysis, Bartholomew and Horowitz concluded their results helped to confirm Bowlby's model of the self and other in adult relationships.

As a further aspect of their investigation of the validity of their instrument they also asked the raters to assess the students on 15 separate dimensions which they believed related to the four attachment styles, and used these as correlates to effectively describe each style (Bartholomew & Horowitz, 1991). They found that the *secure* group obtained the highest ratings on coherence of their interviews and the degree of intimacy of their friendships. They also received the highest ratings on warmth, balance of control in friendships, and level of involvement in romantic relationships. The *dismissing* group scored the highest on self-confidence and lowest on emotional expressiveness and warmth. They also scored lower than the *secure* and *preoccupied* groups on all scales reflecting closeness in personal relationships: That is self-disclosure, intimacy, level of romantic involvements, capacity to rely on others, and use of others as a secure base. They were also more in control than their social partners in both friendships and romantic relationships. The profile shown by the *preoccupied* group was opposite to that of the *dismissing* group in almost every respect. They scored the highest on elaboration, inappropriate self-disclosure, emotional expressiveness, reliance on others, use of others as a secure base and in care-giving. They were also rated high on level of romantic involvement and low on coherence and balance of control in friendships. Finally, the *fearful* group was rated significantly lower than the *secure* and *preoccupied* groups on self-disclosure, intimacy, level of romantic involvement, reliance on others and use of others as a secure base when upset. They were also rated as lowest in self-confidence and balance of control in both friendships and romantic relationships.

Bartholomew and Horowitz warn, however, that many subjects were rated as showing elements of two, three and occasionally all four of the attachment styles, so that a great deal of individual variability was lost when the four continuous ratings from the Relationship Questionnaire were collapsed into a simple 4-category classification. Nonetheless they say that their conclusions were very similar whether a correlational analysis was used, involving four continuous ratings, or a between-groups comparison of the four groups was made. Crowell and Treboux (1995) quote a test-retest stability figure for young adults over an 8 month period for the Relationship Questionnaire giving only moderate reliability levels of 56-63% over the period. However since Bartholomew and

Horowitz recruited first year students for their study we may expect rather higher levels of stability for adults in the 60-70 age range recruited for this present study.

When evaluating adult attachment measures of this kind, concerned with adult relationships, it is important to investigate how they might correspond with respondents' mental representations of their parents, which is the focus of the Adult Attachment Interview and object relations theory. Levy and Blatt (1993), using a sample of 196 undergraduates, found a correspondence between young adults' attachment styles and the structure of these individuals' mental representations of their parents. This was assessed through the single-item checklist and Likert scale measures of the Bartholomew and Horowitz 4-category Relationship Questionnaire and compared with object representations assessed from written descriptions of their parents (Blatt et al., 1992). The parental descriptions were scored for both structural and qualitative dimensions as well as for the degree of self/other differentiation on a 10-point scale. The findings indicated that the parental representations of securely attached young adults were differentiated and organised at a higher conceptual level than those who were insecurely attached. Insecurely attached respondents also described their parents as more malevolent and punitive. Blatt et al. (1992) say that their findings, and those by Levine et al. (1991), provide support for the hypothesis that working models of attachment and object representations are overlapping, if not identical, modes of conceptualising the internalised cognitive-affective schemata that form the bedrock of the intrapsychic world, and that in turn shape interpersonal relationships.

In summary, as Crowell and Treboux (1995) warn, care is clearly needed when assessing adult attachment. Many different measures have been developed, and they differ in their areas of focus and emphasis and may not be equally well validated. Unfortunately the shared terminology implies considerable overlap of meaning which is often not supported by research. These caveats will be borne in mind when we use the Relationship Questionnaire in Chapter 7 to provide a simple categorical measure of the incidence of adult attachment style.

3.3 Statistical procedures

This section introduces the statistical tests used which are common to the subsequent four chapters relating to respondents' perceptions, mental health, marital history and adult attachment (see Figure 3.2). The majority of results are based on univariate tests, but certain multivariate analyses were used and these are also described. All univarate tests and certain of the multivariate tests were made using the SPSS software program (Norušis, 1993) and the Confirmatory Factor Analysis (CFA) and Structural Equation Modelling (SEM) computations were carried out on the EQS program developed by Bentler (1988; 1995).

3.3.1 Univariate statistics

From the earlier description of the chosen input, mediating and output variables it is clear that some are categorical in form and some are continuous and so amenable to parametric analysis. As an example, of the five outcome variables which have been chosen as measures of a respondent's mental health two are categorical in form, i.e. Incidence of Depression and Incidence of Clinical Anxiety, and three are parametric, i.e. DEQ Factor 1 (Dependency), DEQ Factor 2 (Self-criticism) and the Morbidity symptom aggregate score. This distinction applies to the outcome variables in all four chapters. Due to the large number of univariate tests carried out, of either form, there is a probability that some of the results in the first level of significance will be due to chance.

In the univariate analyses the categorical data, which are always mutually exclusive, were examined by Pearson's chi-square tests designed to test the independence of two variables, i.e. whether or not the null hypothesis can be rejected (see Howell, 1992). The contingency tables involved vary in the number of cells depending on the number of levels or categories in the outcome variable. In every case expected frequencies are computed and examined using the criterion of Tabachnick and Fidell (1989), to ensure that they were greater than 1 and that no more than 20% were less than 5. The univariate tables are annotated accordingly by the label 'cell too small' if the expected frequencies are below these limits.

The univariate parametric data was analysed by one-way ANOVA computations to test for significant differences between factor levels. In each case the data was first screened by using box plots to identify outliers, and both the distribution of the data and its variance were also examined. Any outliers found were referred back to the particular respondent's questionnaire return, and a decision taken on whether to include or exclude the data. If any data distributions were found to be severely skewed from normality then the reader is alerted in the text. Likewise if differences in variance between factor levels or groups were found to exceed 4:1 by Levene's criterion (Levene, 1960) the reader is alerted. However, as Glass & Stanley (1970) and Box (1954) point out the analysis of variance is a robust procedure and the assumptions of normality and homogeneity of variance can be violated with relatively minor affects on Type 1 errors. What is agreed by statisticians, though, is that heterogeneity of variance and unequal sample sizes do not 'mix' (Scheffé, 1959; Box, 1954); so that the probability of a Type 1 error increases considerably if fewer individuals are sampled from the population with larger variances, and conversely there is a reduction in the probability if the reverse applies. From Scheffé's analysis it can be seen that so long as the ratio of the maximum to minimum sample sizes does not exceed 5:1, when the differences in variance do not exceed 30%, then any change in Type 1 error is likely to be small. In addition it is important to maintain adequate sample sizes, N, in the different factor levels to provide statistical power in order to limit Type 2 errors. From the analysis in Howell (1992) power is a function of the statistic δ given in this case by:

$$\delta^2 = d^2.N \ ; \quad \text{so that} \quad N = (\delta/d)^2$$

where d = effect size required in terms of the standardised difference between two mean levels. The value of δ may be found from the table given by Howell for a range of significance levels and power values. Assuming a two-tailed significance level of $\alpha = .05$ and a power value of .80 then δ = 2.80. Using this value in the above equation for N we get:

For a small effect size (Cohen, 1988), d = .20 and so N = 196
And for a medium effect size, d = .50 and so N = 31

These minimum sample sizes need to be borne in mind when considering the reported one-way ANOVA results.

Because of the importance of differences, and magnitudes, in sample sizes, the numbers of respondents in each level or group are given alongside the column headings in each table of the univariate results. Sample sizes are also included at the base of the first plotted figure in each section of the results. The reader is alerted in the text if either the differences, or magnitudes, of samples are likely to affect the results of either the chi-square or one-way ANOVA results.

3.3.2 Multivariate statistics

Unlike the univariate analyses in this study which followed a common, systematic pattern through each of the following four chapters, certain of the multivariate tests were not routinely made. Tests for interaction, however, were routinely made by loglinear or 2-way ANOVA tests and are reported in the appropriate sections of results. Other multivariate tests were carried out on an ad hoc basis according to theoretical considerations and conclusions drawn from the univariate analyses. This applied to multiple or logistic regression to predict outcome variables and SEM for confirmatory factor analyses and to build causal path models to test structural hypotheses. All, except SEM, were implemented on the SPSS program using the standard procedures. SEM, on the other hand, is not such a common analysis and it is worth examining why it was used in this study.

Several aspects of SEM set it apart from the older generation of multivariate procedures (see Fornell, 1982, also Mueller, 1996). First, it takes a confirmatory rather than an exploratory approach to data analysis and, secondly, by demanding that the pattern of intervariable relation be specified a priori, SEM lends itself to the analysis of data for inferential purposes (Byrne, 1994). By contrast most other multivariate procedures are essentially descriptive in nature so that hypothesis testing may be more difficult. Other advantages of a practical or analytic nature are listed below in Table 3.9.

Table 3.9 Structural and analytical advantages of SEM over multiple regression analysis

1. It allows for the estimation of direct, indirect and total structural effects and so for the inclusion of multiple mediating and outcome variables.

2. It permits the inclusion of latent, unobserved, factors in an analysis for the estimation of effects between variables or constructs that cannot be directly measured or observed.

3. It allows the use of more generalised estimation methods than ordinary least squares (OLS) used in multiple regression, such as maximum likelihood (ML) and generalised least squares (GLS) methods that depend on less restrictive assumptions (Mueller, 1996).

4. It provides explicit estimates of measurement error.

5. It includes and estimates covariances, or correlations, between variables.

6. It permits the inclusion of both continuous and categorical variables in the same analysis (EQS only), so long as the categorical data can be assumed to have an underlying numerical base (Bentler, 1995).

All of these attributes listed in Table 3.9 were of advantage in the present study. The particular SEM program employed was EQS, developed by Bentler over a period of some years (Bentler, 1980, 1988, 1995). It is one of a few programs available in this context designed to use matrix algebra to examine the validity of a given model structure. Its particular advantage lies in its relative ease of use and, in its later form, the fact that it can accommodate both continuous and categorical data in a single analysis. In the present analyses this is an invaluable characteristic since both types of data are of importance. It is used in this study to investigate and confirm model hypotheses of certain structural patterns or pathways which link input and mediating variables to an outcome variable or variables. It is also used to carry out a confirmatory factor analysis (CFA) where the loading of scale items on an inferred latent factor is estimated and compared. Like other such programs the plausibility of the postulated relationship among variables is tested statistically in a simultaneous analysis of the entire structure in which an iterative process is employed to minimise the difference between the covariance matrix of the observed and modelled data. A measure of this data fit among the variables is given by 'goodness of fit' indices. A structural model which includes both types of variable is analysed by the arbitrary least squares estimator (AGLS) which permits non-normal distributions, after the categorical data has been converted to polytomous coefficients (Lee, Poon & Bentler, 1994). Further details of the EQS program and its procedures are given in the relevant sections in the following chapters which relate to particular analyses and their results.

3.4 Layout of results chapters and summary of key hypotheses

The following four chapters give the results of the statistical analyses for each of the outcome variables shown in Figure 2.1. As far as is practical the layout of these chapters follows a common format. The univariate tables of results for the main input variables of evacuation and upbringing are first listed, each in separate main sections, followed by those for the mediating variables concerned with war and the life-course of respondents. Each of these main sections includes a brief summary of the findings followed by a discussion of these results. In the case of Chapter 5 on mental health these univariate analyses and results are followed by a structural equation modelling (SEM) analysis with a summary and discussion. Each chapter ends with a general conclusions section discussing the overall results and how these may relate to the theoretical and empirical evidence given in the relevant sections of Chapter 2, including the hypotheses which emerged. Table 3.10 gives a summary of these hypotheses, particularly as they relate to the evacuation experience:

Table 3.10. Summary of the hypotheses given in Chapter 2 relating to the evacuation experience

Key hypotheses	Outcome Measures	Variables[1]	Analyses and Results
Re Perceptions:			
Evacuation experience is perceived, at one extreme, as a positive gain for development and at the other as an emotional legacy through life	7-item Perceptions scale (Table 3.5)	All evacuation variables (Section 3.2.2.2)	Chapter 4
Re Mental health:			
Long-term effects of the mental health of respondents is associated with the age at evacuation, the care received and significant life events	Categorical measures of depression and clinical anxiety. Blatt's DEQ scale. Aggregate 7-item scale of morbidity symptoms (Table 3.6)	Age at start of evacuation. Care received during evacuation. (Section 3.2.2.2) Life crises (Table 3.3)	Chapter 5
Re Marital history:			
Divorce is associated with age at evacuation, care received and the degree to which parental attachment is maintained	Categorical measure divorce/separation. Also multiple divorce (Table 3.7)	Age at start of evacuation. Care received during evacuation. Frequency of parental visits (Section 3.2.2.2)	Chapter 6
Re Adult Attachment:			
Adult attachment is associated with age at evacuation, care received, the period away and the degree to which parental connection is maintained	Bartholomew & Horowitz Relationship Questionnaire (Section 3.2.2.8)	Age at start of evacuation. Care received during evacuation. Period away. Frequency of parental visits (Section 3.2.2.2)	Chapter 7

1. In Table 3.10 upbringing is not included as a variable to be considered since the emphasis here is on the variables related to the evacuation experience. However the evidence from theoretical and empirical studies given in Chapter 2 relating to the chosen outcome variables suggest that upbringing is likely to be of major significance.

The final chapter, Chapter 8, considers possible relationships between the outcome variables in terms of the long-term effects found, and discusses the general conclusions of the study, including the degree to which the range of perceptions of respondents are reflected in their performance in the chosen outcome measures.

Chapter 4. The evacuation experience and respondents' perceptions of how this influenced their development and life.

4.1 Introduction

A general description of the Government's evacuation plan was given in the introductory chapter, and a description of the sample recruited in Kent for this study was included in Chapter 2 and in Section 3.1 of Chapter 3. The prime purpose of this chapter is to examine whether this sample's perceptions of the influence of the evacuation experience on their development and adult lives can be explained in terms of their individual experience of evacuation. The conclusions of the pilot study were that such perceptions varied very widely, ranging from the experience being 'life enhancing' to those who believed it had left an 'emotional legacy' (see Section 2.3.1). The hypothesis was put forward at the end of Section 2.3.1, and summarised in Table 3.12, that these perceptions are associated with an individual's evacuation experience and can be represented by the variables given in Section 3.2.2.2, that is Age at evacuation, Care received, Total period away, Frequency of parental visits and the Number of billets occupied. To test this hypothesis a 7-item scale was derived, based on *in vivo* extracts from the pilot study, to assess respondents perceptions of the influence of their experience on their development and adult lives and this is given in Table 3.5. Univariate analyses will be used in this chapter to test for any such associations and the results discussed both generally and in terms of the above hypothesis.

4.2 Respondents' perceptions of the evacuation experience on their development and adult lives.

4.2.1 Analysis

Missing scores were treated listwise in the one-way ANOVA computations made, with 465 females and 280 males entered in the analysis. Examination of the data showed that the distributions were near-normal in form. Less than half the computations made satisfied the Levene test for homogeneity of variance in the ANOVA computations. These limitations, plus the variation in the number of respondents in each category of the input variables, are likely to mean that the initial level of significance may be unreliable ($p<.05$, two-tailed) but they should not effect the higher levels of significance. Standard deviations lay in the range from 1.5 to 2.0, and this distribution width should be borne in mind when interpreting the mean scores and trends displayed in Table 4.1 below and those plotted in the figures which follow.

4.2.2 Results

The mean scores for the seven measures of perception of the effects of respondents' evacuation experience are given below in Table 4.1 with the results of the one-way ANOVA F-value computations and significance levels.

Table 4.1 (a) and (b). Respondents' perception of the effect of their evacuation experience on their development and adult lives as a function of the evacuation experience variables

(a) Re: Age at evacuation, Care received and Period away.

	EVACUATION EXPERIENCE		
	Age at evacuation 4-6 7-9 10-12 13-15	Care received Poor Mod Good	Period away (years) .1-.9 1-1.9 2-6.9
$N_F =$	114 148 136 81	89 159 234	115 92 276
$N_M =$	53 101 86 48	36 83 172	57 65 169

PERCEPTIONS		F		F		F
OVERALL						
Female	0.2^a 0.5^{ab} 0.9^{bc} 1.1^c	6.0***	-0.5^a 0.5^b 1.2^c	42.7***	0.6 0.6 0.6	0.0
Male	0.5^a 1.1^b 1.3^b 1.6^b	4.6**	-0.2^a 0.8^b 1.5^c	26.3***	0.6^a 1.1^{ab} 1.3^b	4.8**
CONFIDENCE						
Female	-0.7^a 0.2^b 0.5^b 1.3^c	19.1***	-1.3^a 0.0^b 1.1^c	55.4***	0.4 0.4 0.2	0.8
Male	0.4^a 0.7^a 1.2^a 1.8^b	6.0***	-1.0^a 0.7^b 1.5^c	36.0***	0.5 1.2 1.0	2.2
OUTLOOK						
Female	0.9^a 1.1^a 1.6^b 1.6^b	6.9***	0.2^a 1.2^b 1.7^c	36.8***	1.2 1.2 1.4	0.8
Male	1.2^a 1.6^{ab} 1.8^{ab} 2.0^b	2.8*	0.7^a 1.3^a 2.0^b	14.2***	1.2^a 1.7^{ab} 1.8^b	3.3*
COMPANY						
Female	-0.7^a 0.1^b 0.1^b 0.8^c	14.1***	-1.2^a 0.2^b 0.7^c	43.1***	0.2 0.1 -0.1	1.2
Male	0.0^a 0.3^a 0.7^{ab} 1.1^b	3.6*	-0.9^a 0.3^b 1.0^c	16.8***	0.3 0.7 0.6	1.1
FAMILY						
Female	-0.9^a -0.3^b -0.5^{ab} 0.0^b	4.2**	-1.4^a -0.4^b 0.1^b	14.7***	-0.5 -0.4 -0.4	0.1
Male	-0.4 -0.6 -0.1 0.0	1.7	-1.2^a -0.4^b 0.1^b	6.1**	-0.1 -0.2 -0.5	1.3
ANGER						
Female	0.0^a 0.1^a 0.4^a 1.0^b	6.2***	0.0 0.3 0.4	1.9	0.7^a 0.4^{ab} 0.1^b	4.6*
Male	0.6 0.6 0.9 0.6	1.1	0.7 0.6 0.7	0.1	0.6 0.6 0.7	0.1
UNFINISHED						
Female	-0.2^a 0.0^a 0.5^b 0.7^b	4.8**	-0.6^a 0.3^b 0.5^b	10.4***	0.3 0.3 0.1	0.8
Male	-0.1^a 0.6^b 0.4^{ab} 1.1^b	4.0**	-0.1 0.7 0.5	2.2	0.5 0.6 0.5	0.2

Mean scores are listed and the results of one-way ANOVA tests. Significance key: * $p<.05$, ** $p<.01$ and *** $p<.001$; all two-tailed tests. Significant differences labelled by Newman-Kreuls' post-hoc tests; mean scores marked by different superscripts are significantly different at $p<.05$.

(b) Re: Frequency of parental visits per year and Number of billets.

EVACUATION EXPERIENCE

	Frequency of parental visits/year						Number of billets			
	0	1	2	3-7	>8	F	1	2-4	5-15	F
N_F =	69	92	79	178	56		131	260	91	
N_M =	43	74	49	102	16		78	157	56	

PERCEPTIONS

OVERALL
Female	0.6	0.6	0.4	0.8	0.6	1.3	0.6	0.6	0.7	0.1
Male	0.8^a	0.8^a	1.4^b	1.3^b	1.0^{ab}	2.7*	0.9	1.2	1.2	1.6

CONFIDENCE
Female	0.1^{ab}	-0.2^a	0.1^{ab}	0.7^b	0.5^{ab}	3.5**	0.2	0.3	0.2	0.5
Male	0.5^a	0.5^a	1.0^{ab}	1.4^b	1.5^b	4.1**	0.6	1.1	1.1	2.9

OUTLOOK
Female	1.3	1.2	1.2	1.5	1.2	1.0	1.2	1.2	1.5	1.3
Male	1.5	1.4	1.7	2.0	1.6	1.9	1.4^a	1.6^{ab}	2.0^b	3.4*

COMPANY
Female	0.2^a	-0.6^b	-0.1^{ab}	0.3^a	0.0^{ab}	4.4**	0.0	0.0	-0.2	0.7
Male	0.3	0.3	0.6	0.7	0.5	1.0	0.3	0.6	0.6	1.1

FAMILY
Female	-0.8	-0.7	-0.4	-0.2	-0.1	2.2	-0.5	-0.5	-0.3	0.3
Male	-1.0	-0.2	-0.4	-0.1	-0.6	2.1	-0.2	-0.4	-0.3	0.6

ANGER
Female	-0.2^a	0.1^a	0.1^a	0.7^b	0.5^{ab}	4.3**	0.3	0.4	0.2	0.6
Male	0.1^a	0.8^{ab}	0.5^{ab}	0.9^b	1.3^b	2.9**	0.6	0.7	0.8	0.3

UNFINISHED
Female	-0.6^a	0.3^b	0.1^b	0.5^b	0.2^b	4.3**	0.2	0.2	0.2	0.0
Male	0.3	0.5	0.5	0.7	-0.4	1.4	0.2	0.6	0.5	1.4

Mean scores are listed and the results of one-way ANOVA tests. Significance key: * p<.05, ** p<.01 and *** p<.001; all two-tailed tests. Significant differences labelled by Newman-Kreuls' post-hoc tests; mean scores marked by different superscripts are significantly different at p<.05.

From an examination of Table 4.1 it is clear that most of the seven Perceptions of the effect of respondents' evacuation experience are significantly dependent on two of the evacuation experience variables: Age at evacuation and Care received, and this applies to both sexes. They are seen to be less dependent on Period away, Frequency of parental visits and Number of billets. This dependency is illustrated in Figures 4.1 and 4.2 given below, where the seven Perceptions of the evacuation have been plotted as a function of Age at evacuation and Care received for both sexes. All plotted lines above the origin indicate a positive perception or believed outcome of the evacuation experience, while those below refer to a negative perception. These positive and negative perceptions or attributes are synonymous with the end quotations given in the scales from the questionnaire and reproduced earlier in Table 3.5.

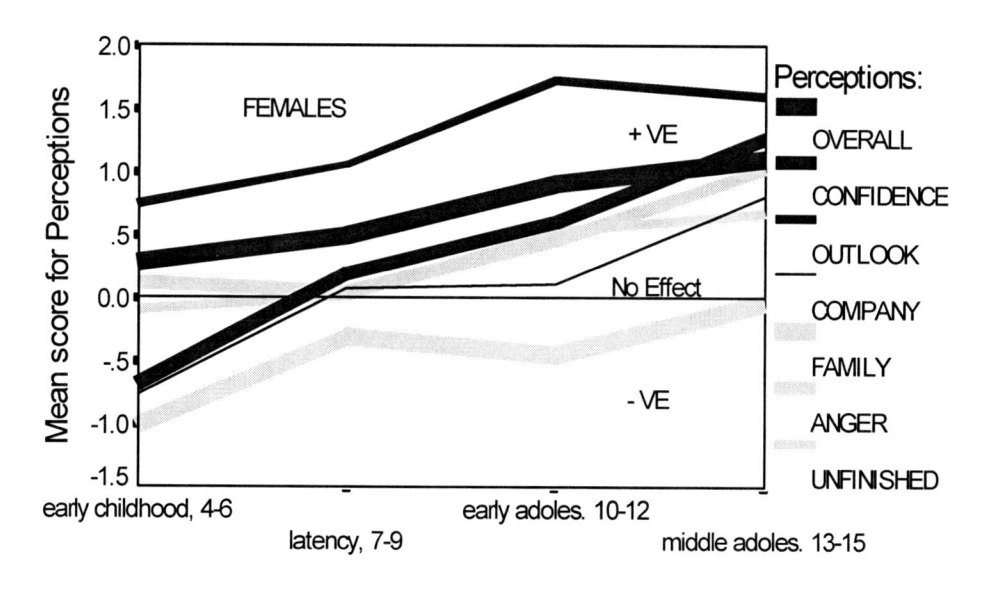

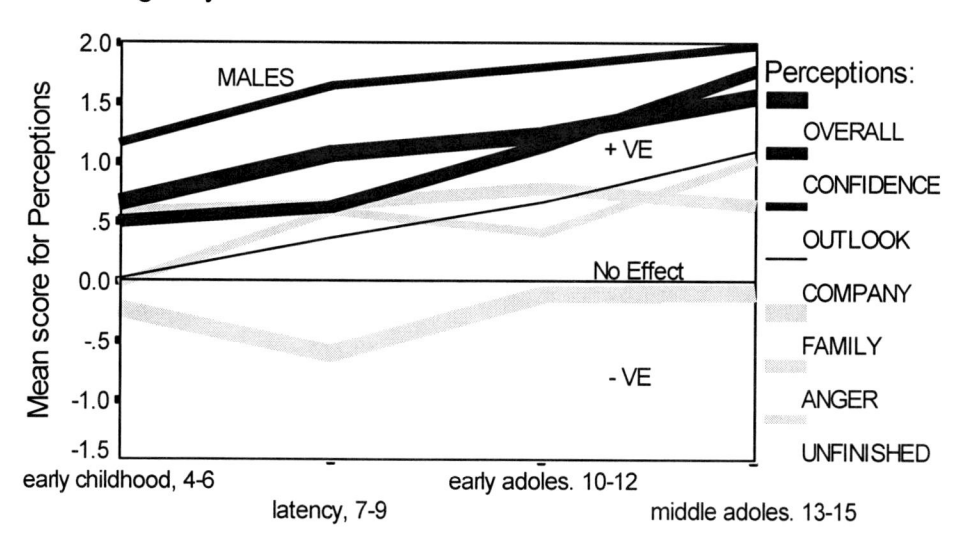

Figure 4.1 Mean scores for respondents' Perceptions of the effect that the evacuation experience had on their development and lives, as a function of their Age when first evacuated and their gender.

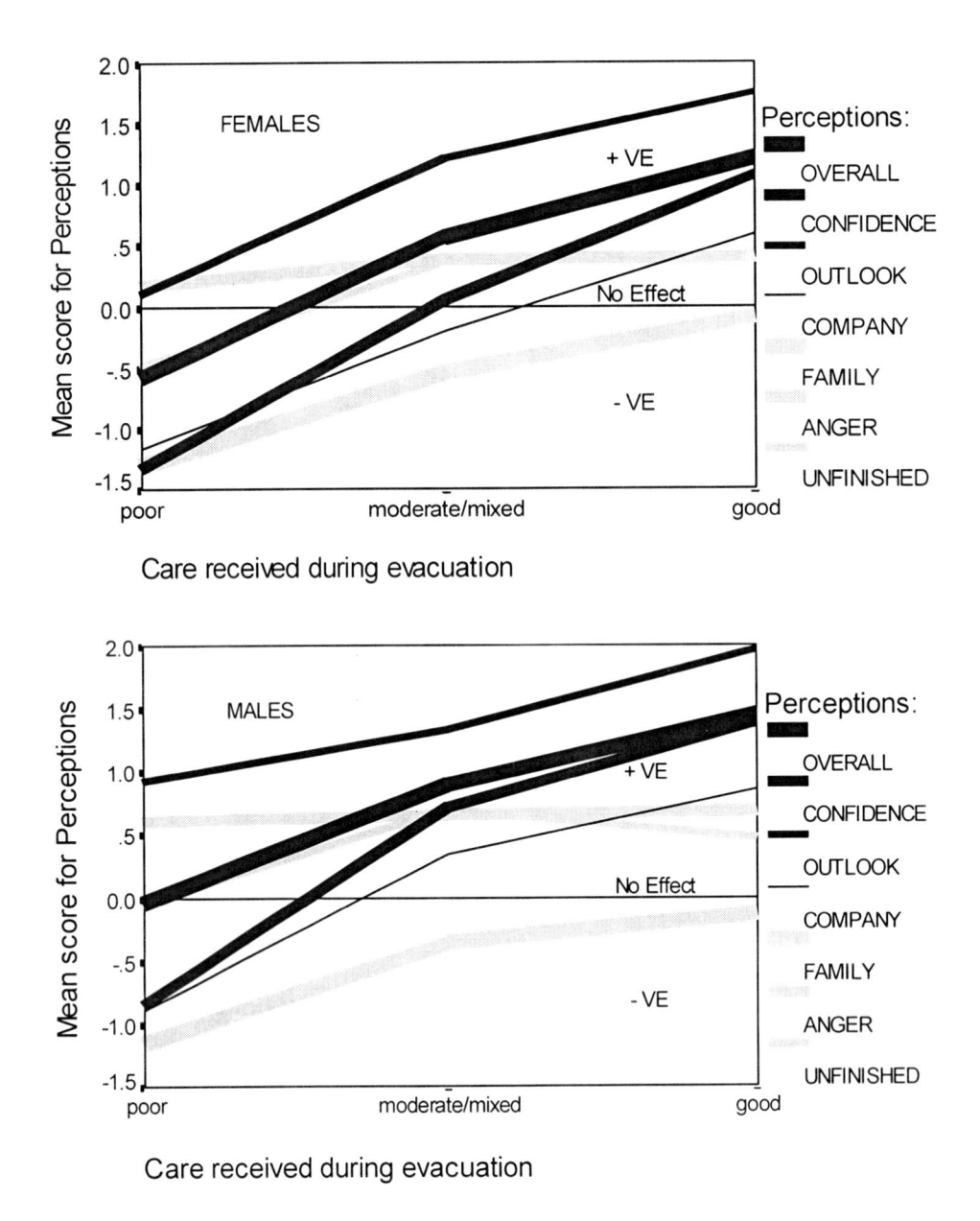

Figure 4.2 Mean score for respondents' Perceptions of the effect that the evacuation experience had on their development and adult lives, as a function of the Care received during evacuation and gender.

The most striking aspect of the plots displayed in Figures 4.1 and 4.2 are the rising trends which the majority of the Perception variables show as either Age at evacuation increases, or as Care received improves, and which applies to both sexes. Females evacuated between 4-6 years of age have a negative image of the effects of their experience, particularly attributing a lack of confidence (CONFIDENCE in Figure 4.1) and a certain 'solitariness' in adulthood (COMPANY) to their evacuation. Male respondents adopt a more positive attitude in this respect. However, these perceptions change if respondents were evacuated in adolescence, and both sexes believe they have gained in confidence and developed in social ability through their experience. Other Perceptions show similar trends as a function of Age when first evacuated, with particularly high positive levels of OUTLOOK where respondents attribute a 'broadening of horizons and interests' to the evacuation experience. If we look at Figure 4.2 a similar pattern of rising scores is exhibited as a function of Care received during evacuation. Both sexes attribute the same lack of confidence and social isolation to their evacuation experience if care was poor, rising to highly significant positive levels if care received was good. It can be seen from Table 4.1(a) just how high the F-values are for both sexes for the first four Perceptions, that is for OVERALL, CONFIDENCE, OUTLOOK and COMPANY, as a function of Care received. Interestingly, ANGER with mother (in Figure 4.2) is the only perception which does not show this trend, the plot remaining flat on the positive side of the 'no effect' origin, suggesting that for most respondents they believed their relationship to their mother was made closer by the experience. The response to FAMILY (in Figure 4.2) was similar for both sexes, rising significantly from a low starting value when care was poor to near the origin when it was good. Since the plot remains in the negative part of the frame it means that respondents believe evacuation made them protective of their own families in adulthood. Female respondents were more likely than males to be concerned with any unfinished business as a result of their childhood experience (UNFINISH - in Figure 4.2), but only if care had been poor, with a wish to 'revisit' that period of their lives and to confront its emotional associations (see Pilot study themes - Appendix 1).

From Table 4.1 it can be seen that by comparison with the very significant effects of Age at evacuation and Care received the remaining Evacuation Experience variables have had very much less effect on the seven listed Perceptions. A long Period away (2-6.9 years) is associated by male respondents with a positive OVERALL outcome, i.e. 'it made me', and again in OUTLOOK with a 'broadening of horizons and interests'. Females show a tendency to be angry with their mother (ANGER) if they were evacuated for a long period, but males do not show this significant effect. According to both sexes CONFIDENCE is a function of the frequency of Parental visits, with perceived levels in adulthood rising significantly if parental contact during evacuation was maintained at a minimum of about 3 visits a year. Frequency of parental visits was also associated with respondents' attitude to their mothers in later life (ANGER), so that regular parental contact has helped to maintain a continuing close relationship. The Number of billets had surprisingly little effect on respondents Perceptions of their evacuation experience; the only significant effect was for males where an increase in interests and a broadening of horizons (OUTLOOK) was associated with an increase in the Number of billets.

Finally, it is important to bear in mind that notwithstanding the very high levels of significance found for most of the seven Perceptions as a function of Age at evacuation and Care received the width of the distributions of scores for each level or category of these input variables remains high. Because of this the scores of many respondents will be far removed from the means, due to individual circumstances, and these wide distributions will, generally, include both positive and negative effects. An example of this is given in Figures 4.3 and 4.4 for the mean score of CONFIDENCE plotted as a function of Age at evacuation and Care received during evacuation. The plots include limiting bars defining one standard deviation either side of each mean value for the various input levels or categories. It can be seen how these wide distributions cover a range of responses in each category.

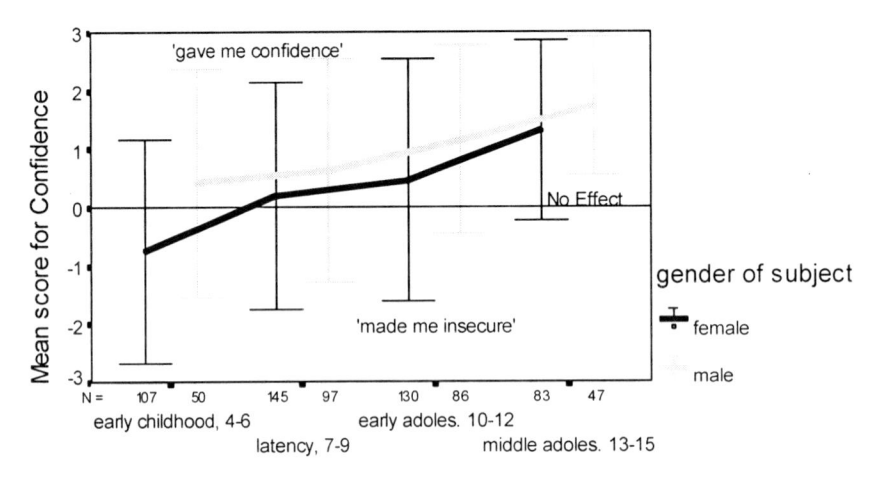

Figure 4.3 Mean score for CONFIDENCE as a function of Age in years when first evacuated.

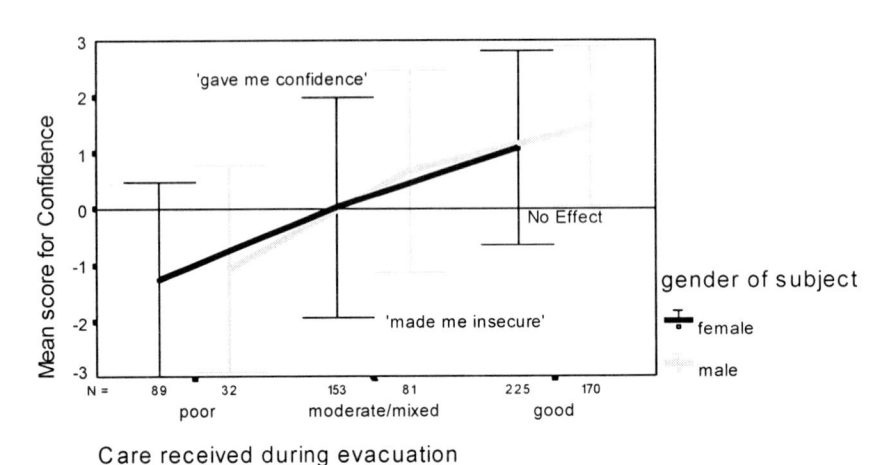

Figure 4.4 Mean score for CONFIDENCE as a function of Care received during evacuation.

4.3 Conclusions

The results of this analysis of respondents' perceptions of the long-term effect that childhood evacuation had on their development and adult lives shows clearly that these perceptions were modulated by the age at which evacuation took place and the care they received. Evacuation at a young age, or with poor care, tended to induce a more negative attribution compared to that given by those who were evacuated at an older age, or who were fortunate to receive good care. This was found to apply to both sexes and respondents believed that the experience had affected their adult lives in an overall sense as well as in their levels of development in terms of self-confidence, social ability and in widening their horizons and interests. To a lesser extent they also believed it had affected the way they have related to their own children in terms of protectiveness. These conclusions are in agreement with those found from the grounded theory analysis used in the pilot study (see Appendix 1).

When examining the plots for the mean scores of men and women's Perceptions, given in Figures 4.1 and 4.2 as a function of Age when first evacuated and Care received, it is striking to see their similarity in form and gradient. This does suggest that, in broad terms, there is a continuum from negative to positive beliefs about the effect of evacuation, dependent on respondents' individual circumstances, and which underlies these particular perceptions. If this is correct then the underlying concept of these perceptions of evacuation ranges from a developmentally 'inhibiting' experience to a developmentally 'enhancing' one. In order to test this hypothesis a confirmatory factor analysis (CFA) was carried out using the EQS program (Bentler, 1988). From this analysis it was found that of the seven Perception titles listed in Table 3.5 all but the seventh, UNFINISHED, contributed significantly to a common latent outcome factor. The loadings from this latent factor to the six perception variables were broadly similar for the two sexes, demonstrating high loadings for OVERALL, CONFIDENCE, OUTLOOK and COMPANY, and lesser values for FAMILY and ANGER. In each case CONFIDENCE receives the highest loading, and this is supported by a Coefficient of Determination of 0.751 and 0.762 for females and males respectively, indicating that 75% and 76% of the variance of the latent factor is explained by this item. Again this is in agreement with the provisional findings of the pilot study, and taken together with the loadings on OVERALL, OUTLOOK and COMPANY confirms the original hypothesis given in Table 3.10 that the latent factor represents a 'development' factor based on respondents' perception of their experience. This factor tracks the perceived effects of the Evacuation Experience on their development and adult lives over a wide and continuous spectrum from a negative, 'inhibiting' attribution through to a positive, 'enhancing' one.

We have seen in Table 4.1 how these Perceptions of evacuation are affected by the chosen Evacuation Experience variables, and it will be possible to compare these results in subsequent chapters with measures relating to mental health, marital history and adult attachment. In general, respondents who were evacuated at a young age, or who received poor care while away, believed the experience inhibited their development, whilst those who were evacuated, say, in adolescence or who received good care, believed it was a liberating and enhancing one. If these perceptions are correct then we may expect the same evacuation input variables to affect the outcome variables we will be examining in the following chapters.

Chapter 5. Mental health

5.1 Introduction

Although little was found in the literature review in Chapter 2 which directly related to an association between mental disorders in adulthood and childhood separation nevertheless clear evidence was found that childhood experience of inadequate child care, or maternal loss or family conflict may predispose young people to affective disorders in later life (Brown and Harris, 1978; Roy, 1978; Parker, 1983; Bifulco et al., 1987; Birtchnell, 1988; Harris, 1988; Tweed et al., 1989; O'Connor et al., 1999). Furthermore, one of the output categories which emerged from the pilot study was named *emotional legacy* and this was found to include a variety of themes which relate to mental health (see Section 2.3.1 of Chapter 2). Many of these themes, or characteristics, are also mentioned in the Finnish studies of the long-term effects of wartime evacuation (Serenius, 1995: Lagnebro, 1994, 2002). So that in the context of this chapter this evidence suggests that just as inadequate child care, or maternal loss or family conflict may predispose to depressive or anxiety disorders in later life so may extended periods of childhood separation, particularly if the separation occurred in early childhood and was followed by a lack of care or any close attachment to a caring adult. It is this hypothesis which will be examined in this chapter, including the mediating effects of life-course variables.

As described in Section 3.2.2.6 of Chapter 3, concerning the Methodology employed in this study, the outcome variables selected for this analysis of the mental health of respondents included categorical measures of the incidence of depression and clinical anxiety, two factors from the DEQ scale (Blatt et al., 1976) and a mean score of the total number of morbidity symptoms experienced. In the following sections of this chapter these measures are used as outcome variables in univariate statistical tests to assess the long term effects of evacuation, upbringing and certain mediating variables on mental health in adulthood. Figure 5.1, based on Figure 2.1 in Chapter 2, shows the relevant path through life which is being investigated in this chapter. Following the univariate analyses a SEM analysis will be carried out to confirm the univariate results and to delineate the structural paths which may lead to Depression, either directly or indirectly via the mediating variables.

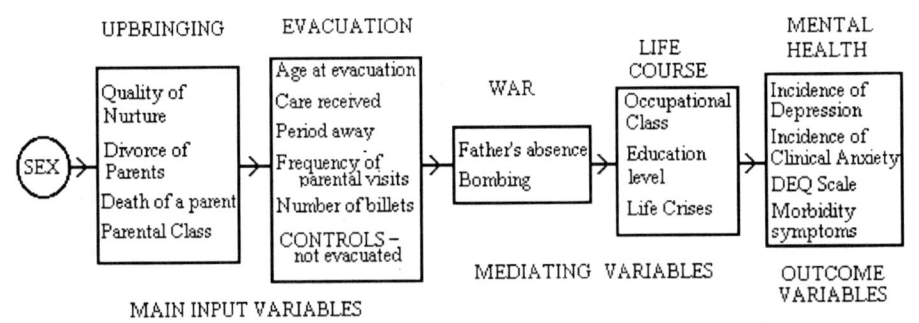

Figure 5.1. Respondents' pathway through life, with the input, mediating variables and mental health outcome variables selected for analysis in this chapter.

5.2 Long term effects of evacuation on mental heath.

The first input variables to be considered in the following analysis are those associated with evacuation, shown in Figure 5.1 above, with those subjects who were not evacuated acting as controls.

5.2.1 Analysis

The following five outcome, or dependent variables were employed in this analysis of mental health:

1. Incidence of Depression
2. Incidence of Clinical Anxiety
3. Mean score for Factor 1 - Dependency (DEQ scale)
4. Mean score for Factor 2 - Self-criticism (DEQ scale)
5. Mean score for Morbidity symptoms.

These have been discussed in Section 3.2.2.6 in Chapter 3. The first two are categorical variables, but subjects were asked to provide a brief resume of case information, including any family crises etc. which may have been relevant (see Appendix 3). The next two are scores from the factor analysis of the DEQ 66-item scale using only the factor coefficients obtained from Blatt et al.'s (1976) work with 500 university women. Blatt has provided the present author with both this set of coefficients and also those from the 150 men tested at the same time, but because of the importance of making a gender comparison a single gender set was used in the computation, as used in the study of gender and depression by Chevron et al. (1978). The final variable given is the result of aggregating the number of morbidity symptoms a subject has experienced from the following list:

1. Sleep disruption
2. Severe or long-lasting headaches
3. Extreme fatigue
4. Severe irritability
5. Phobias or irrational fears
6. Extreme loneliness
7. Feelings of unreality

One-way ANOVAs show that the above measure of Morbidity symptoms, and Self-criticism and Dependency from the DEQ scale, are all effective indicators of the Incidence of Depression ($F(1, 851)$ of 271.6, 96.2 and 29.1 respectively, all at $p<.001$). They are also indicators of the Incidence of Anxiety, at slightly reduced F-values ($F(1,853)$ of 142.3, 35.4 and 22.5 respectively, all at $p<.001$).

Missing cases were treated listwise in the computations, with 518 females and 343 males entered into the analysis, of which 52 and 34 respectively were not evacuated (controls). Pearson's chi-square tests were made separarately for each gender for each of the five evacuation input variables given in Figure 5.1 for Incidence of Depression and Clinical Anxiety. One-way ANOVA tests were made in a similar way for the three dependent variables involving mean scores: Dependency, Self-criticism and Morbidity symptoms.

In the case of the categorical data, i.e. for the Incidence of Depression and Clinical Anxiety, the expected cell frequencies were examined, using the criterion of Tabachnik and Fidell (1989), to ensure that they were greater than 1 and that no more than 20% were less than 5. None were found to lie outside these limits. For the three dependent variables involving scores, i.e. Dependency, Self-criticism and the number of Morbidity symptoms, boxplots were used to check the distribution of cell scores and to detect the presence and number of outliers. It was found that the first two dependent variables, Dependency and Self-criticism, were normally distributed, and since the outliers did not represent more than 2% of the total numbers of cases in each cell they were left in the computations. The homogeneity of variance between these cells was found to be high, according to Levene's criterion (Levene, 1960). Although there was considerable variation in the number of cases between some cells, because of this homogeneity of variance in the scores it was assumed, from the analysis included in Glass and Stanley (1970), that this would have little effect on changing the alpha probability for Type 1 errors (see Section 3.3.1 in Chapter 3 on Methodology). The final dependent variable, for the number of Morbidity symptoms, was not as well conditioned, and the boxplots showed that in cells where the mean score was low the distribution was affected by the resulting floor effect. Because of this, although trends in mean scores will be unaffected, the initial levels of significance from ANOVA tests, where $p<.05$, are likely to be unreliable. Higher levels of significance, at $p<.01$ and $.001$, are likely to be unaffected.

5.2.2. Results

The first section of these univariate results is concerned with examining possible associations between the overall incidence of evacuation and of gender with the selected mental health outcome variables. This will be followed by sections where the Evacuation Experience variables, and those variables related to upbringing, war and the life-course, are examined in a similar way.

5.2.2.1 Overall effect of the Incidence of evacuation and Gender as a function of the outcome variables of Mental health

The Incidence of Depression and Clinical Anxiety, and the mean scores for Dependency, Self-criticism and Morbidity symptoms, are given in Table 5.1 as a function of the split between evacuees and controls in the first column and the overall sample in the second column, both as a function of gender. The third column gives the results of loglinear and 2-way ANOVA analyses to test for any interaction between the evacuated / non-evacuated conditions and gender for each of the mental health variables. An examination of the first column, which gives the split between those who were, or were not evacuated, shows that 40% and 41% respectively of females and 27% and 23% of males have suffered depression. The equivalent figures for clinical anxiety are 12% for females of either sample and 9% and 10% of males for those evacuated and not evacuated respectively.

Table 5.1. Outcome variables for mental health as a function of gender on the occurrence of evacuation and the overall sample

	Evacuated			Overall by Gender		Evacuated x Gender
$N_F =$	484	34		518		
$N_M =$	291	52		343		
			χ^2		χ^2	
Incidence of Depression						
Female	40%	41%	0.0	40%	16.7***	Not significant
Male	27%	23%	0.3	26%		
Incidence of Clinical Anxiety						
Female	12%	12%	0.0	12%	1.4	Not significant
Male	9%	10%	0.0	9%		
Mean score Factor 1 Dependency						
Female	-0.3	-0.3	0.1	-0.3	51.2***	0.0 (NS)
Male	-0.7	-0.7	0.1	-0.7		
Mean score Factor 2 Self-criticism						
Female	-0.2	-0.3	0.0	-0.2	5.6*	0.0 (NS)
Male	-0.4	-0.4	0.1	-0.4		
Mean score Morbidity Symptoms						
Female	1.7	1.8	0.1	1.8	49.5%***	0.0 (NS)
Male	0.9	1.0	0.2	1.0		

Chi-square tests have been carried out for categorical data and one-way ANOVA tests for interval scores. Significance key: * p<.05, ** p<.01, and *** p<.001; all two-tailed. Tests for the interaction Evacuated x Gender were made by loglinear analysis and 2-way ANOVA tests.

From the first column in Table 5.1 it can be seen that there is no effect of the occurrence or non-occurrence of evacuation on any of the five mental health variables for either sex. For the total sample, i.e. including those evacuated and not evacuated, given in the second column there are significant effects of gender on the Incidence of Depression, Dependency, Self-criticism and Morbidity, but not on clinical anxiety. In column three the interaction Evacuated x Gender is tested and found to be not significant for any of the five mental health variables, where the categorical variables Incidence of Depression and Clinical anxiety were tested by loglinear analysis and the remaining three by two-way ANOVA.

It is somewhat surprising, and certainly interesting, that there is no effect of the occurrence of evacuation on the mental health of respondents. This will be examined in detail in the following sections when the Evacuation Experience is deconstructed into its selected component variables. It is also interesting that, notwithstanding the major effects of gender found, the interaction test shows that these are not a function of the occurrence or non-occurrence of evacuation.

Results indicating the main effect of gender dominate the results in Table 5.1. Looking first at the Incidence of Depression percentages given in the second column of Table 5.1 these show that there is a highly significant difference between women and men ($\chi^2(1) = 16.7$, $p < .001$), where 40% of females and 26% of males have reported some form of depression. Bearing in mind that in this community sample this is largely the incidence in primary care and not psychiatric admission this large gender difference is not unexpected, and has been reported previously by a number of workers (see Goldberg and Huxley, 1992). Goldberg and Huxley have reviewed the rates for common mental health disorders in the community and at different levels of clinical and psychiatric care and report female to male sex ratios of about 2.2:1 in the community, dropping to about 1.2:1 for psychiatric in-patients. In the community and in primary care 90% of these disorders are accounted for by depressive and anxiety states. However Table 5.1 also shows that there is no effect of gender on the Incidence of Clinical Anxiety, but this result is questionable because of the lower statistical power, i.e. the low incidence levels involved.

The remaining three mental health variables show significant effects of gender, and these are particularly strong in the case of Dependency ($F(1,853) = 51.2$, $p<.001$) and Morbidity $(1,806) = 49.5$, $p<.001$). By selection (see Chapter 3) we know that the number of morbidity symptoms is an indicator of depression for both sexes, and it would appear from the gender difference that the DEQ Factor 1 measure, Dependency, is similarly, an indicator of depression for both sexes. However, the reality appears to be rather more complicated. If the upper and lower quartiles in the distributions of

Dependency and Self-criticism are selected then the percentage of respondents who have suffered depression are given below in Table 5.2 for three different logical conditions related to these quartiles:

Table 5.2 Incidence of Depression as a function of three conditions based on the upper (>75%) and lower (< 25%) quartiles of each distribution

	Dependency Distribution (quartiles)	Self-criticism distribution (quartiles)	Incidence of Depression Female (N_F) Male (N_M)	
Group 1.	> 75% AND	> 75%	58% (144) 38% (87)	$p < .01$
Group 2.	< 25% AND	> 75%	43% (112) 39% (85)	N/S
Group 3.	> 75% AND	< 25%	44% (112) 18% (87)	$p < .05$

If we compare the depression percentages in Group 2 they show that a high level of Self-criticism alone is a good indicator of the incidence of depression for both sexes with no significant difference between the percentages, however when the upper quartile for Dependency is included (Group 1) the incidence rises for Females but not for males, and the difference between the sexes is now significant. This contrast in the relevance of Dependency between the sexes is confirmed by the results in Group 3 where high levels of Dependency alone maintain female incidences of depression, comparable to those in Group 2, but that the percentage for male respondents drops to 18%, leading to a significant difference between the sexes. So not only are females more prone to high mean levels of Dependency than males (see Table 5.1), they are also more vulnerable to these levels. This gender difference in such a personality trait, as defined by Factor 1 of the DEQ scale, could be innate and may be mediated by nurture received in infancy or early childhood. As a guide to this personality characteristic ten of the items from the DEQ scale that load most heavily on the Factor 1 axis, all of which have factor coefficients $> +0.6$ are given below:

1. 'Without support from others who are close to me, I would be helpless.'
2. 'I would feel like I'd be losing an important part of myself if I lost a very close friend.'
3. 'I often think about the danger of losing someone who is close to me.'
4. 'I am very sensitive to others for signs of rejection.'

5. 'I constantly try, and very often go out of my way, to please or help people I am close to.'
6. 'I find it very difficult to say 'No' to the requests of friends.'
7. 'I worry a lot about offending or hurting someone who is close to me.'
8. 'If someone I cared about became angry with me, I would feel threatened that he (or she) might leave me.'
9. 'After a fight with a friend, I must make amends as soon as possible.'
10. 'After an argument, I feel very lonely.'

The dominant theme throughout these items is a fear of rejection, and in terms of Fairbairn's Object-Relations Theory of the personality they seem to express 'infantile' rather than 'mature' dependency (Fairbairn, 1952), so it is perhaps not surprising that a high 'Dependency' score can be a predictor of depression. Birtchnell (1984, 1988) has written extensively on the concept of dependency and its relation to depression. He sees an overtly dependent person 'as an adult behaving as a child', and that such dependence can be understood as a failure to separate successfully from the principal parent figure and thus a failure to establish a secure personal identity in adulthood. In Birtchnell's view Bowlby's (1973) 'anxious attachment' is the affectional component of such dependency and should be coupled with Laing's (1965) ontological approach which is concerned with the nature of being or identity. Such concepts and theories were mentioned earlier in Chapter 2 when adult attachment was selected as an outcome variable and will be discussed further in Chapter 7 in relation to attachment.

5.2.2.2 Evacuation Experience variables and Gender as a function of the mental health outcome variables

In the previous section the *overall* effect of evacuation was examined and was, surprisingly, found to be not significant in terms of the mental health output variables. In this section the evacuation experience will now be deconstructed into the five factors or variables given in Section 3.2.2.2 and tested for possible associations with the same mental health variables. The univariate and bivariate results for the outcome variables of mental health as a function of these selected Evacuation Experience variables and of Gender are listed in Table 5.3 (a) and (b) below. These results will be examined first for each mental health variable in turn and then for each of the evacuation variables. Loglinear and 2-way ANOVA tests were made to determine if there were any significant interactions between Gender x Evacuation Experience with any of the Mental health variables. The only significant interactions found were for Gender x Age at evacuation with both Depression and Clinical Anxiety, these results will be discussed under the relevant subsections.

Table 5.3 (a) Outcome variables for Mental Health as a function of gender and the three Evacuation Experience variables, Age at evacuation, Care received and Period away

	EVACUATION EXPERIENCE		
	Age at evacuation 4-6 7-9 10-12 13-15	Care received Poor Mod Good	Period away (years) .1-.9 1-1.9 2-6.9
$N_F =$	114 148 136 81	89 159 234	115 92 276
$N_M =$	53 101 86 48	36 83 172	57 65 169

MENTAL HEALTH

	χ^2	χ^2	χ^2
Incidence of Depression			
Female	50%a 35%b 38%ab 37%ab 6.7*	48% 37% 38% 3.5	37% 38% 42% 1.0
Male	36%a 35%a 19%b 15%b 12.0**	47%a 23%b 24%b 8.8*	32% 25% 26% 0.9
	(Figure 5.2)	(Figure 5.3)	
Incidence of Clinical Anxiety			
Female	13%ab 9%a 18%b 6%a 7.9*	17% 14% 9% 5.3	10% 10% 13% 1.3
Male	19%a 8%bc 4%c 13%ab 9.8*	19%a 11%a 6%b 6.4*	5% 11% 10% 1.4
	(Figure 5.4)	(Figure 5.5)	

	F	F	F
Mean score Factor 1 Dependency			
Female	-0.3 -0.4 -0.4 -0.5 0.9	-0.2 -0.4 -0.4 1.4	-0.4 -0.4 -0.3 0.2
Male	-0.7 -0.7 -0.8 -0.8 0.6	-0.3a -0.8b -0.8b 6.0**	-0.7 -0.7 -0.8 0.3
		(Figure 5.6)	
Mean score Factor 2 Self-criticism			
Female	-0.0a -0.4b -0.1a -0.5b 6.0***	-0.1a -0.1a -0.4b 6.4**	-0.4a -0.3ab -0.1b 4.0*
Male	-0.0a -0.3b -0.5b -0.7b 4.6**	-0.1 -0.3 -0.5 2.3	-0.5ab -0.6a -0.3b 4.1*
	(Figure 5.8)	(Figure 5.9)	(Figure 5.10)
Mean score Morbidity Symptoms			
Female	2.1a 1.7ab 2.0a 1.3b 3.7*	2.3a 2.0a 1.5b 8.3***	1.5 1.8 2.0 1.9
Male	1.3 1.0 1.0 0.7 2.1	1.7a 1.0b 0.8b 7.3***	1.1 0.8 1.0 1.0
		(Figure 5.11)	

Chi-square tests have been carried out for categorical data and one-way ANOVA tests for interval scores. Significance key: * $p<.05$, ** $p<.01$ and *** $p<.001$; all two-tailed. Significance in the chi-square tests was followed by bivariate tests and in the ANOVA analysis by Newman-Kreuls' post-hoc tests. Percentage values and mean scores for each

Table 5.3 (b) Outcome variables of Mental Health as a function of gender and the two Evacuation Experience variables, Frequency of parental visits and Number of billets

EVACUATION EXPERIENCE

	Frequency of parental visits/year						Number of billets			
	0	1	2	3-7	>8		1	2-4	5-15	
$N_F =$	69	92	79	178	56		131	260	91	
$N_M =$	43	74	49	102	16		78	157	56	

MENTAL HEALTH

						χ^2				χ^2
Incidence of Depression										
Female	51%	43%	39%	33%	39%	7.3	35%	39%	49%	4.8
Male	35%^{ab}	39%^{b}	18%^{ac}	18%^{c}	25%^{abc}	13.5**	31%	27%	20%	2.1
Incidence of Clinical Anxiety										
Female	20%	9%	13%	11%	11%	5.9	12%	11%	14%	0.7
Male	12%	14%	8%	7%	6%	2.7	5%	12%	9%	2.6
						F				F
Mean score Factor 1 Dependency										
Female	-0.3	-0.3	-0.3	-0.4	-0.4	1.0	-0.2	-0.4	-0.4	2.7
Male	-0.8	-0.8	-0.7	-0.8	-0.9	0.1	-0.6^a	-0.8^b	-1.0^b	4.6*
								(Figure 5.7)		
Mean score Factor 2 Self-criticism										
Female	-0.2	-0.1	-0.3	-0.3	-0.3	0.9	-0.3	-0.3	-0.1	1.2
Male	-0.2	-0.2	-0.5	-0.6	-0.2	2.6	-0.5	-0.4	-0.2	1.8
Mean score Morbidity Symptoms										
Female	2.2	2.0	1.6	1.7	1.5	2.3	1.7	1.8	2.0	0.7
Male	1.2^{ab}	1.3^a	0.8^{ab}	0.8^b	0.6^{ab}	3.3*	1.1	0.9	0.9	0.9

Chi-square tests have been carried out for categorical data and one-way ANOVA tests for interval scores. Significance key: * $p<.05$, ** $p<.01$ and *** $p<.001$; all two-tailed. Significance in the chi-square tests was followed by bivariate tests and in the ANOVA analysis by Newman-Kreuls' post-hoc tests. Percentage values and mean scores for each gender marked by different superscripts are significantly different at $p<.05$.

5.2.2.2.1 Incidence of Depression

In Table 5.3 the evacuation experience is broken down into the five input variables selected in Chapter 2 from considerations of previous developmental studies, including the pilot study. The first column gives the Incidence of Depression as a function of age in years when first evacuated, for each gender. These percentage incidences have been plotted in Figure 5.2, as well as reference lines for each gender indicating the incidence levels for those not evacuated. Numbers of respondents in each age category are also included at the top of each bar.

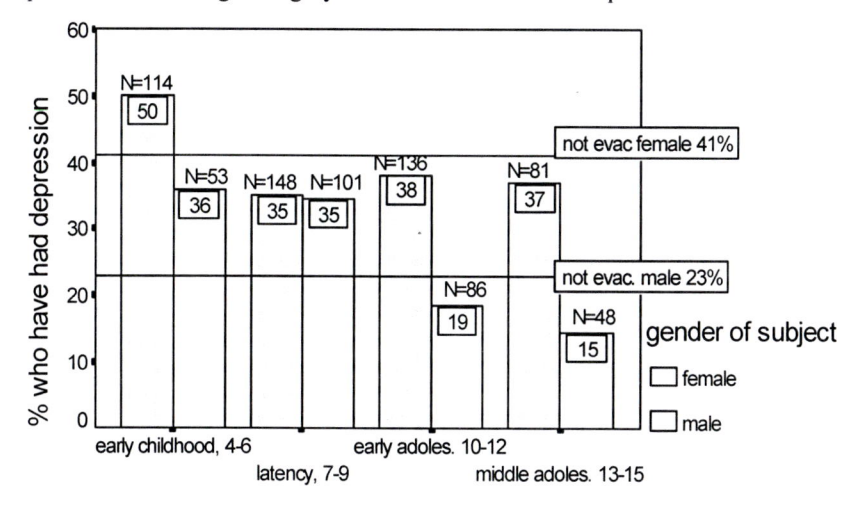

Figure 5.2. Incidence of Depression as a function of Age when first evacuated.

Females who have been evacuated in early adulthood, at 4-6 years, suffer a very high mean rate of depression in adulthood, 50%, and this drops and remains steady for the other age ranges of childhood evacuation, between 35-38%, comparable to the incidence for non-evacuated controls, at 41%. On average, men do not appear to have been so affected by their experience in early childhood with an adult depression incidence of 36%, which then drops significantly after latency to 15-19% if evacuation first occurred in adolescence ($\chi^2(3) = 12.0$, $p<.01$). It is interesting to see that these levels are lower than the incidence for controls, at 23% for males, which suggests that the evacuation experience may have provided male respondents with some 'protection' against adult depression, although the difference does not reach significance ($\chi^2(2) = 1.2$, $p=.29$). As mentioned earlier a loglinear test shows that there is a significant difference between the sexes in terms of the association between depressive incidence and age at evacuation ($p=.04$).

The second column in Table 5.3 (a) gives the incidence rates of depression as a function of the Care received during evacuation and is plotted in Figure 5.3:

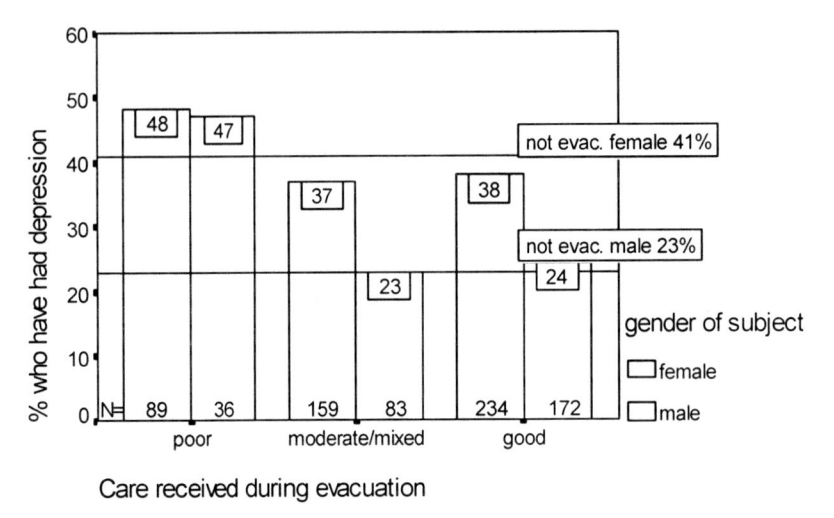

Figure 5.3. Incidence of Depression as a function of Care received during evacuation.

These results tend to mirror the general trends seen in Figure 5.2 for the two sexes. There is no significant difference in the female values, but the level is higher if care received during evacuation was poor, at 48%, compared to 37-38% for moderate or good care. Male values are significantly different as a function of care received ($\chi^2(2) = 8.8$, p<.05), and this effect is clearly seen in the figure where depression levels drop from 47% to 23-24% with improved care. The former figure is comparable to that for females when care was poor, and the latter figures are comparable to the non-evacuated figure for males of 23%.

The third column in Table 5.3 (a) lists incidence rates as a function of the length of the total evacuation period in years. Although the gender difference is maintained there is, rather surprisingly, no significant difference with Period away for either sex.

In Table 5.3 (b) the first column lists the depressive rates as a function of the number of parental visits made per year, and indicates that there are trends in the expected direction for both sexes but no significant difference in the rates for females, but that there is for males ($\chi^2(4) = 13.5$, p<.01) where the incidence of depression drops significantly if parental visits occurred at least twice per year.

The second column in Table 5.3 (b) gives the depressive rates as a function of the number of billets and no significant differences were found for either sex.

Summarising, the main evacuation variables which affect the Incidence of Depression in adulthood are Age at evacuation and Care received. It is suggested that the combined mediation of these two variables, plus the distribution of subjects in the cells, is the main reason for the overall lack of a significant effect of evacuation shown in column one in Table 5.1. The large difference in the occurrence of depression between the sexes, and the possible protection afforded to male subjects by evacuation in adolescence, will be discussed in Section 5.2.4.

5.2.2.2.2 Incidence of Clinical Anxiety

In Table 5.3 (a) both sexes reach significance for the Incidence of Clinical Anxiety as a function of Age at evacuation (Females $\chi^2(1) = 7.9$, p<.05; Males $\chi^2(1)=9.8$, p<.05), and these results have been plotted in Figure 5.4.

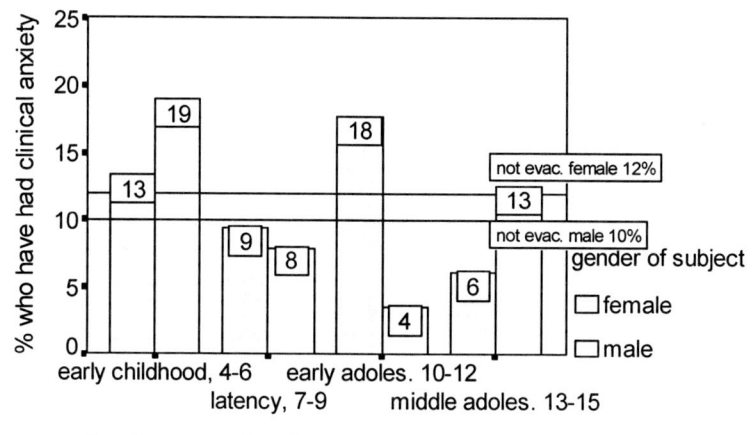

Figure 5.4. Incidence of Clinical Anxiety as a function of Age when first evacuated.

Because the incidence of clinical anxiety among respondents is noticeably less than that for depression it is likely that these results for clinical anxiety are more prone to variability between the data sets for the four age periods than those for depression. Nevertheless the Incidence of Clinical Anxiety is shown to be rather higher if evacuation took place in early childhood, particularly for males. Females, however, show a second marked increase in anxiety if evacuation occurred in early adolescence where the value of 18% is found to be significantly different from both the 9% and 6% values recorded in latency and middle adolescence. This is an interesting result and suggests that the separation of female subjects from their parents near puberty has significantly affected their later psychological development. The importance of effective parent-child relationships in early adolescence as a precursor for the later achievement of a mature identity has been emphasised by Erikson (1968) and his co-workers (see Marcia, 1980). Paikoff & Brooks-Gunn (1991) have reviewed more recent work which confirms the importance of parent-child relationships during puberty, a time of relational change, including conflict, at the start of the individuation process. It is likely that this could have been a critical time for females who were evacuated, particularly at the menarche if care was poor and unsupportive, and this will be discussed further in Section 5.2.4. For males anxiety levels drop to 4% in early adolescence, but rise significantly to 13% in middle adolescence. This may be due to the later onset of puberty in males (see Paikoff and Brooks-Gunn, 1991), but it is nevertheless difficult to see why the level is so low in early adolescence. These differences between the sexes for the Incidence of Clinical Anxiety as a function of the Age at evacuation are found to be significant in a test for interaction by loglinear analysis (p=.004).

In column two of Table 5.3 (a), plotted in Figure 5.5, both sexes show a marked reduction in anxiety levels as Care received improves, reducing from 17% to 9% for females and 19% to 6% for males ($\chi^2(2) = 6.4$, p<.05), dropping below the control values for both sexes.

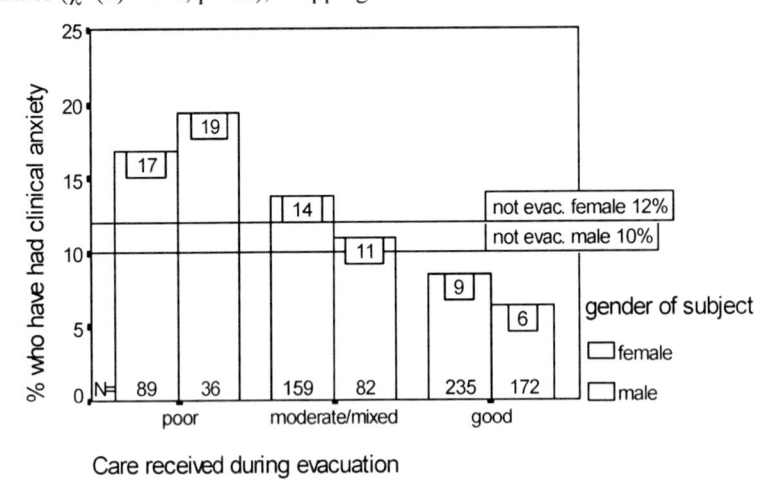

Figure 5.5. Incidence of Clinical Anxiety as a function of Care received during evacuation.

None of the results listed for the Incidence of Clinical Anxiety as a function of the last three evacuation input variables in Table 5.3 (a) and (b) reached significance for either sex. However, the trend in the values for Period away and for Frequency of parental visits is in the expected direction for both sexes, suggesting a lack of power in the analysis because of the limited incidence of clinical anxiety reported.

5.2.2.2.3 Mean score for Factor 1 - Dependency

In the first column of Table 5.3 (a), for Age at evacuation, the highly significant difference between the sexes in Dependency is maintained ($F(3, 755) = 42.4$, p<.001), but the mean scores as a function of Age are not significantly different for either sex, and show only a slight trend to lower Dependency with increasing Age at evacuation.

The next column in Table 5.3 (a), for Care received, does show a trend towards lower Dependency with improved care, particularly for males where the scores are significantly different ($F(2, 286) = 6.0$, p<.01). These are plotted in Figure 5.6 which also shows the divergence between the two functions as care improves, starting from a common high level when care is poor. The non-evacuated levels emphasize this difference between the sexes.

Figure 5.6. Mean score for Dependency as a function of Care received during evacuation.

The mean scores in the next two columns, Period away in Table 5.3 (a) and Frequency of parental visits in Table 5.3 (b), show no clear trends and no significant differences. The results in the final column, for the Number of billets experienced during evacuation, plotted in Figure 5.7, shows little change for females but a significant downward trend for male respondents as the number of billets increases ($F(2, 286) = 4.6$, $p<.05$), below that of the non-evacuated level.

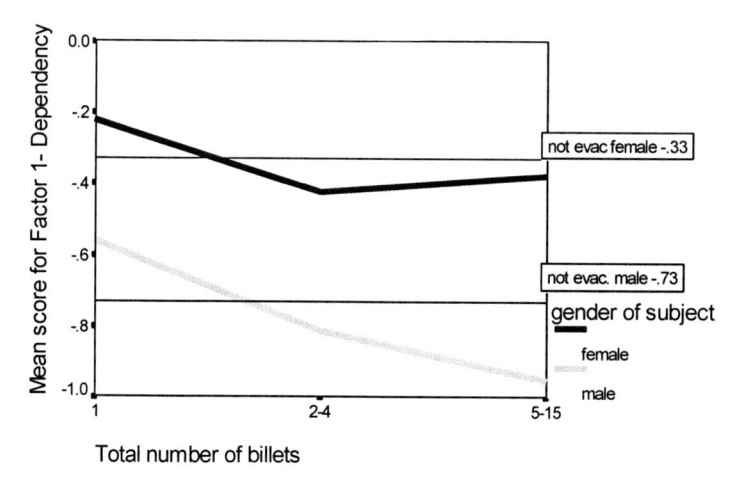

Figure 5.7 Mean score for Dependency as a function of the Number of billets occupied by respondents.

The most striking characteristic of all these results for Dependency are the very large differences in mean scores maintained between the sexes across all five evacuation input variables, and the relatively small changes seen in the female scores across the outcome factor levels. The two significant results found are both for male respondents, as a function of Care received and Number of billets experienced

5.2.2.2.4. Mean score for Factor 2 - Self-criticism

In column one of Table 5.3 (a) both sexes show significant levels for Self-criticism as a function of Age at evacuation (Female $F(3, 473) = 6.0$, $p<.001$; Male $F(3, 282) = 4.6$, $p<.01$) and these mean scores have been plotted in Figure 5.8.

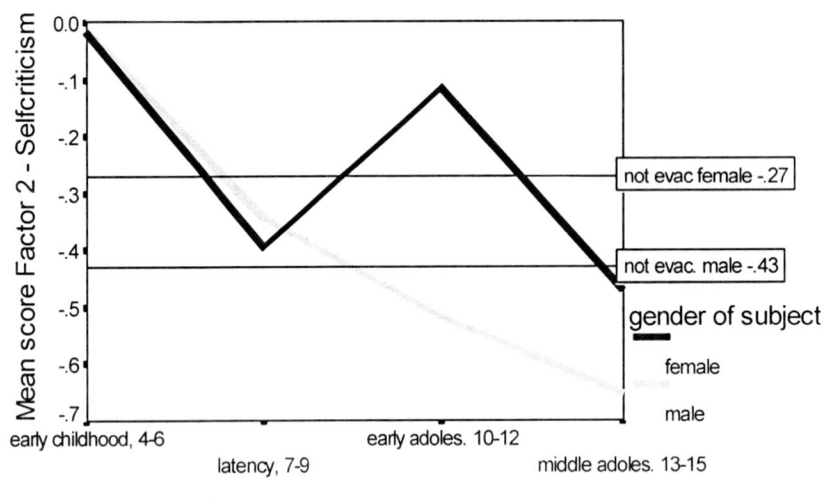

Figure 5.8 Mean score for Self-criticism as a function of Age when first evacuated.

These graphs in Figure 5.8 have interesting features. The first is the high and equal level of Self-criticism of adults of both sexes if evacuation took place in early childhood, followed by a steep reduction to a low level if evacuation first occurred in middle adolescence, below the control values of -.27 and -.43 for female and male subjects respectively. However the plot for female subjects shows, in addition, a significant rise in early adolescence above both the levels at latency and middle adolescence (see superscript marking of significance in Table 5.3 (a)). A similar, anomalous, result in early adolescence was observed in Figure 5.4 for females, where the Incidence of Clinical anxiety is plotted as a function of Age at evacuation; this rise was also significantly higher than the levels at latency and middle adolescence. Since Self-criticism, Factor 2 on the DEQ, is a predictor of an anxious as well of a depressive state, it is suggested that these two anomalous features are associated. This will be discussed further in Section 5.2.4.

The plots for both sexes in Figure 5.9, for the mean score of Self-criticism as a function of Care received during evacuation, have slopes in the expected direction, that is as care improves Self-criticism drops. However only the variation in female values is significant ($F(2, 477) = 6.4$, $p<.01$), although the male values lie close to significance.

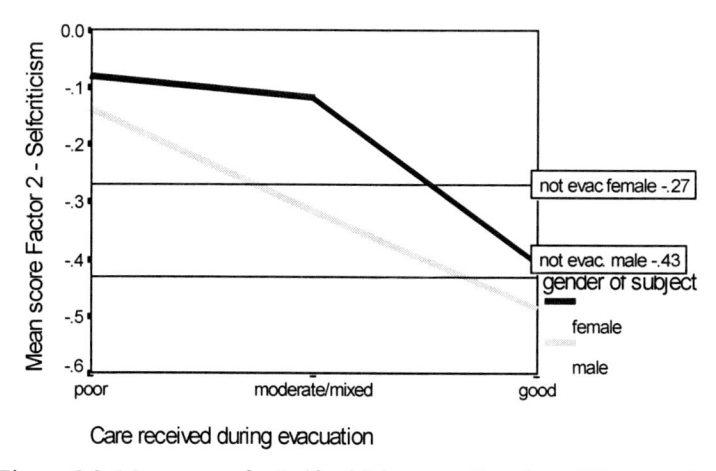

Figure 5.9 Mean score for Self-criticism as a function of Care received during evacuation.

The values given in column three of Table 5.3 (a) for Self-criticism as a function of Period away are plotted in Figure 5.10. Mean scores for both sexes are significant and show trends in the expected direction, increasing in Self-criticism as the evacuation period increases in years, but where the drop in self-criticism for males at a period of 1-1.9 years is not significant.

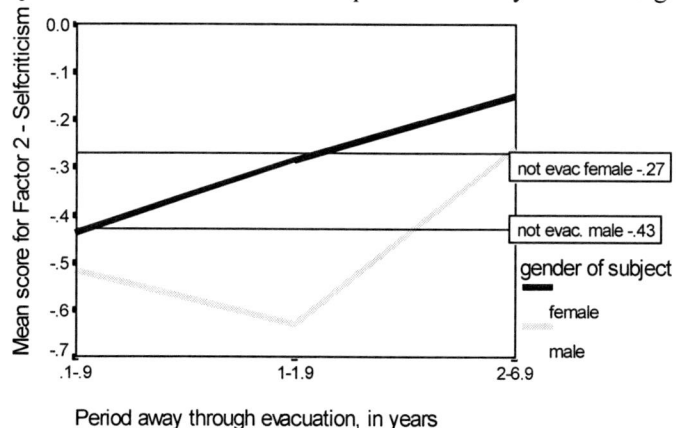

Figure 5.10. Mean score for Self-criticism as a function of length of evacuation period in years.

Neither of the last two sets of mean scores given in Table 5.3 (b) for Self-criticism as a function of Frequency of parental visits or Number of billets are significant.

Apart from the anomalously high value of Self-criticism for those females evacuated in early adolescence or puberty, the other features of particular interest in these results for Self-criticism is the sharp decline in mean scores with increasing Age at evacuation and with improving Care received during evacuation. This is similar to the decline seen in the Incidence of Depression as a function of the same input variables. This relationship will be examined and discussed in Section 5.2.4.

5.2.2.2.5. Mean score of Morbidity symptoms

The mean scores for Age at evacuation in column one of Table 5.3 (a) show a trend in the expected direction, i.e. reducing number of symptoms with increasing Age at evacuation, but only the results for females are significant ($F(3, 448) = 3.7$, $p<.05$). The score for females evacuated in early adolescence is higher than that at latency or in middle adolescence, and is comparable to that for early childhood; a similar anomaly to that seen for Clinical anxiety and Self-criticism.

The results for both sexes in column two of Table 5.3 (a) for Care received are highly significant (Female $F(2, 452) = 8.3$, $p<.001$; Male $F(2, 266) = 7.3$, $p<.001$) and are plotted in Figure 5.11 which shows the trend for the number of symptoms to decrease as care improves, and where the effect of gender remains highly significant ($p<.001$).

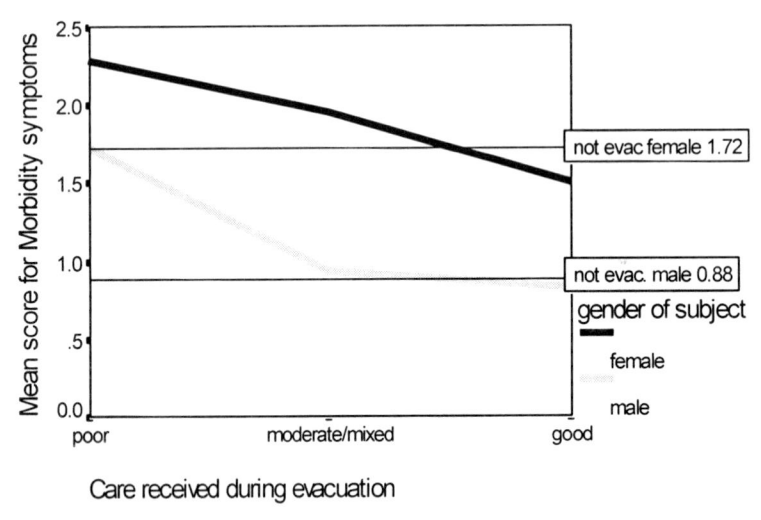

Figure 5.11. Mean score for Morbidity symptoms as a function of Care received during evacuation.

In column three of Table 5.3 (a) there is no significant effect for Period away for either sex, and only a slight trend of increasing morbidity symptoms with increasing years away, but for female respondents only. In the first column of Table 5.3 (b) there is a marked trend for a decrease in the number of morbidity symptoms as the Frequency of parental visits increases. Both sexes show this effect, which levels off when visits are made at least twice per year, but only the results for males are significant ($F(4, 258) = 3.3$, $p<.05$). The last column, for the effect of the number of billets, is not significant.

Again, the most striking characteristic in these results for the number of morbidity symptoms is the great difference between the sexes, across all input variables, similar in magnitude to those seen for Depression and Dependency. Also the highly significant effect of Care received, and to a lesser extent Age at evacuation. Trends are consistent with the other dependent variables in the sense that good care and older age at evacuation are protective against poor outcomes in terms of the number of morbidity symptoms experienced.

Thus far each mental health outcome variable has been examined in turn as a function of the chosen evacuation variables. In the following sub-sections the relationships between each evacuation input variable and the outcome variables will now be examined, i.e. by columns rather than rows in Table 5.3 (a) and (b).

5.2.2.2.6. Age at evacuation

If we compare the results given in column one of Table 5.3 (a), where the input variable is Age at evacuation, then certain inferences can be drawn, all of which have been mentioned in previous subsections of this chapter:

1. Those, of both sexes, evacuated in early childhood (4-6 years) are more likely to suffer depression and anxiety than those evacuated in adolescence (see Figures 5.2 and 5.4).

2. Males evacuated in adolescence appear to be at a lower risk of depression than those not evacuated, whereas females evacuated in adolescence do not benefit from this 'protection' (see Figure 5.2).

3. Females evacuated in early adolescence have a significantly higher probabilty of suffering from clinical anxiety than those evacuated in latency or middle adolescence, and this anomalous peak is also found in the values for Self-criticism (Figures 5.4 and 5.8).

4. Dependency scores do not significantly change with Age at evacuation for either sex, but gender is highly significant.

5. Self-criticism scores are very high, and equal, for both sexes evacuated in early childhood, and fall sharply with increasing Age at evacuation, apart from the anomaly mentioned in paragraph 3 above (see Figure 5.8).

When considering these results, and others in this chapter, all given as a function of Age at evacuation, i.e. at the start of evacuation, it should be borne in mind that subjects were then away from home for an average of 2-3 years. Figure 3.1 in Chapter 3 gives the mean period of evacuation for both sexes as a function of Age at evacuation. It is highest in early childhood, at some 3 years duration, and lowest in middle adolescence at 2 years duration.

5.2.2.2.7. Care received during evacuation

An examination of column two in Table 5.3 (a) for Care received, shows that the results for all five outcome variables contain significant values, and that the trend in these values indicates improving mental health as the Care received during evacuation improved. The difference between the sexes is again apparent for the Incidence of Depression (see Figure 5.3). As discussed earlier, this incidence approaches 50% for both sexes evacuated who reported receiving poor care, but falls to about half this value for males, 23-24% (equal to the control value), as care during evacuation improved, but remains at 37-38% for females. This is in contrast to the trend plotted in Figure 5.5 for the Incidence of Clinical Anxiety where the difference between the sexes is not significant, and there is a steady decline in the adult incidence for both sexes as the quality of care improved in evacuation.

Taking the results for Dependency and Self-criticism together (see Figures 5.6 and 5.9) they show rather different trends. Female Dependency values remain nearly constant with changing Care received, whereas male values drop significantly with improved care. Self-criticism values drop sharply for both sexes as Care received improves from 'poor' to 'good'. The characteristics of these two plots, taken in conjunction with the trends for the two sexes seen in Figure 5.3 for Incidence of Depression, support the supposition given earlier that it is the female respondents' trait of continuing Dependency in adult life, plus their vulnerability to this factor in terms of mental health, which may override any possible development advantages they may have gained from a 'good' evacuation experience.

Although not listed in Table 5.3, but relevant to this discussion on care received, respondents were also asked to indicate if they had suffered any emotional, sexual, or physical abuse, or believed they were exploited during evacuation. Some 42% of females and 29% of males believed they were emotionally abused during evacuation in early childhood, and this level reduced with age at evacuation for both sexes, but remained high for females (see Figure 5.12 below). Also 8% of females and 3% of males reported being sexually abused during evacuation, and this was most common for female evacuees in early childhood and early adolescence (10% for each age group). Physical abuse was most common in early childhood at an incidence of about 20% for both sexes, falling to neglible values in adolescence. Overall about 14% reported being exploited as free labour and this figure was highest for females in early adolescence (21%). Of these types of abuse the most damaging in terms of mental health was emotional or physical abuse; some 50% of those females and 45% of males who reported either or both forms of such abuse suffered from depression in later life. In terms of the incidence of clinical anxiety in adulthood females were most affected by emotional abuse, where rates for clinical anxiety increased from 9 to 20% if such abuse was reported. Males were more affected by physical abuse, which led to clinical anxiety rates increasing from 8 to 25%.

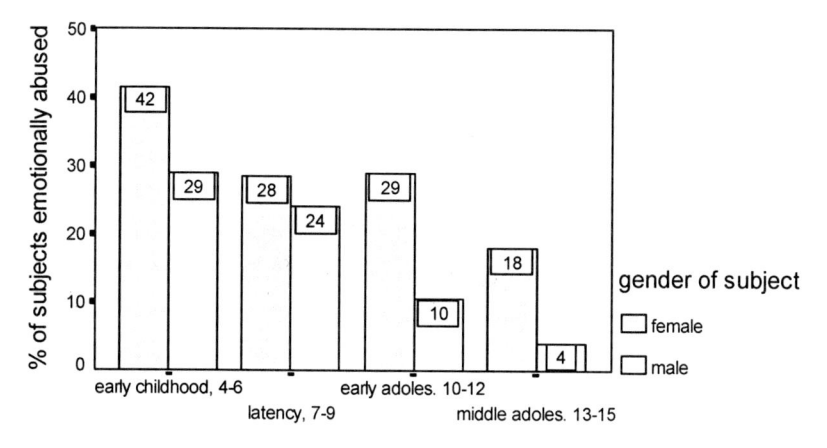

Figure 5.12 Percentage of respondents emotionally abused as a function of age at the start of evacuation

5.2.2.2.8 Period away, Frequency of parental visits and Number of billets

There is little to comment on in summarising the results for the five outcome variables as a function of either Period away, Frequency of parental visits or Number of billets which has not been covered earlier. Most of these results show trends in the expected direction but any likely significance may have been limited by a lack of power in the samples. As discussed in Section 5.2.2.2.4 on Self-criticism both sexes show a significant association with Period away and Figure 5.13 is a plot of these variables as a function of Age at evacuation for the female sample only.

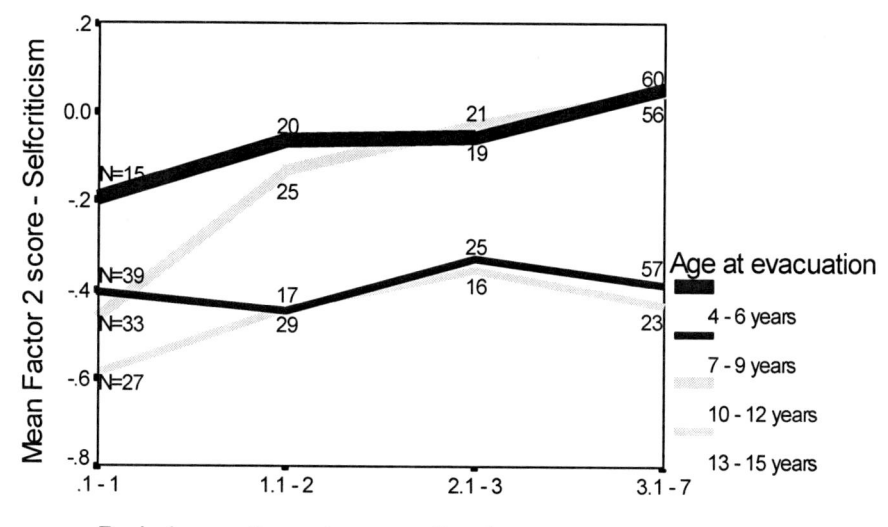

Figure 5.13 Mean Self-criticism score of female respondents as a function of the Period away for each of the Age at evacuation groups

Figure 5.13 shows that for evacuation periods in excess of one year the mean Self-criticism scores for the female sample are split into two groups. Those evacuated at 4-6 and 10-12 years are in the high Self-criticism group and those evacuated at 7-9 and 13-15 years are in a lower group. These differences in Self-criticism as a function of Age at evacuation are significant and were seen in Figure 5.8 and discussed in Section 5.2.2.2.4, but the interesting thing about this further plot is that it shows how the characteristics of the Age at evacuation curves vary with the length of the evacuation period. Not only are they in two separated paired groups but the anomalous 10-12 age sample only rises to a comparable mean level of Self-criticism to that of the youngest sample after a period of one year's separation. This finding has a bearing on the discussion in Section 5.2.4 on the possible origin of this high level of Self-criticism, linked to Clinical Anxiety.

This section will conclude with a short summary of the main findings on the effect of the evacuation experience on respondents' adult mental health, and this will be followed by a discussion of these results.

5.2.3. Summary

The main results for the long-term effects of evacuation are summarised below in Table 5.4, and these will be used as the basis for a discussion in the next section.

Table 5.4. Summary of the main results for the long-term effects of evacuation on mental health

1. For each mental health variable there was no significant difference in the overall results between those who had been evacuated and those who had not been evacuated. In view of the significant effects of the mediating Evacuation Experience variables this is primarily due to the integration of positive (protective) and negative (risk-inducing) aspects of each respondent's evacuation experience. (Tables 5.1 and 5.3).

2. Females are significantly more likely to suffer depression and have high scores on Dependency and the number of Morbidity symptoms than males. In terms of the onset of depression females also appear to be more vulnerable to the personality characteristic defined by that Dependency, i.e. Factor 1 of the DEQ scale. (Tables 5.1 and 5.2, and Section 5.2.2.1).

3. High levels of Self-criticism predict adult depression in both sexes, but high levels of Dependency are primarily related to depression in females only. (Section 5.2.2.1).

4. Evacuation in early childhood, at 4-6 years, predicts an increased probability of depression or clinical anxiety in adult life for both sexes, compared to those evacuated at a later age or those not evacuated. The exception to this is for females evacuated in early adolescence, 10-12 years, who have a significantly higher probability of suffering clinical anxiety in later life. (Figures 5.2 and 5.4. and Section 5.2.2.2.2).

5. Males evacuated in adolescence have a significantly reduced likelihood of depression in adulthood compared to those not evacuated. Females do not enjoy the same 'protection'. (Figure 5.2).

6. Both sexes are more prone to depression and clinical anxiety in adult life if the care received during evacuation was poor, or they reported being emotionally or physically abused, i.e. the circumstances are 'risk inducing'. If the care received was good then the incidence of depression and clinical anxiety is reduced and for clinical anxiety it lies below the incidence value for those not evacuated, i.e. the circumstances are 'protective'. (Figures 5.3 and 5.5. and Section 5.2.2.2.7).

7. There is no significant change in Dependency with Age at evacuation for either sex, but there is a highly significant effect of gender with females scoring higher than males. (Tables 5.1 and 5.2).

8. Dependency is high for both sexes when Care received was poor, and drops significantly with improved care, but for males only. (Figure 5.6).

9. Dependency reduces significantly in adulthood for males if they experienced multiple billets, i.e. greater than 2-4 moves, during evacuation. There was no significant change for females. (Figure 5.7).

10. There is a significant reduction in Self-criticism with Age at evacuation for both sexes, apart from an anomalously high, and significantly different, high value for females in early adolescence. It is suggested that this anomaly is associated with the peak in the Incidence of Clinical Anxiety mentioned in paragraph 4 above. (Figures 5.4 and 5.8).

11. Self-criticism scores are high for both sexes when Care received was poor and reduce with improving care. When Care received was good these scores are lower than the non-evacuated values, i.e. the circumstances are 'protective'. (Figure 5.9).

12. Self-criticism scores increase significantly with the length of the evacuation period for both sexes. (Figure 5.10).

13. The number of Morbidity symptoms reduces significantly for both sexes when the Care received during evacuation improved. (Figure 5.11).

14. The number of Morbidity symptoms, and the Incidence of Depression and of Clinical anxiety, increase in adulthood for both sexes if the Frequency of parental visits during evacuation was less than about two per year. (Table 5.3).

5.2.4. Discussion

From the research referred to in the introduction to this chapter, and previously discussed in Chapter 2, it was expected that there would be some long-term effects of evacuation on mental health. These suppositions were supported by the findings of the pilot study and the hypothesis emerged that these would primarily be associated with the age at the start of evacuation and the care received during evacuation (see Table 3.12: Summary of the hypotheses relating to the evacuation experience).

In fact what was found was that, overall, there was no effect of evacuation on subjects when tested against controls who had not been evacuated, and that this was the case for both sexes and all five mental health variables examined (Table 5.1). However, it was also found that within this overall assessment there were significant differences in the values for all mental health measures dependent on the Evacuation Experience variables, primarily on the Age at evacuation and the Care received (Table 5.3). This apparent contradiction can be explained by the belief that the evacuation experience can have both a positive, i.e. protective, and negative, i.e. risk-inducing, effect on adult mental health, depending on the individual circumstances involved. This interpretation is in line with the perceptions of respondents regarding the long-term effects of their evacuation experience which was confirmed in Chapter 4.

Another initial finding of the analysis, which has a bearing on the effect of evacuation, was the highly significant gender difference found for the Incidence of Depression, the mean scores of Dependency and the mean scores for Morbidity symptoms (Table 5.1). This result is in agreement with the literature on the subject of gender differences in depressive states and on the number of morbidity symptoms suffered (Goldberg and Huxley, 1992). However it is particularly interesting to find that not only are females higher on Dependency as defined by Factor 1 of the DEQ scale, but that this factor is a more effective predictor of depression for females, than it is for males (analysed in Section 5.2.2.1).

As mentioned in the introduction to this chapter Blatt and Zuroff (1992) have made a clear distinction between two types of depression: (1) a dependent type characterised by feelings of helplessness and weakness, by fears of being abandoned and by wishes to be cared for, loved and protected; and (2) a self-critical or guilty type characterised by intense feelings of inferiority, guilt and worthlessness and by a sense that one must struggle to compensate for failing to live up to expectations and standards. Bowlby (1980), from a rather different theoretical position, makes a similar split when he contrasted anxiously attached and compulsively self-reliant individuals and their vulnerability to depression. However, Blatt and his colleagues do not appear to have made any comparative gender studies for adults of the relationship between their DEQ factors and the incidence of depression, since their research with adults has involved female college students only. Their recent work at Yale has been concerned with adolescents and the use of the more recently derived DEQ-A scale to examine social functioning at this stage of development (Henirch et al., 2001). The only studies found which compare the DEQ factors for adults as a function of gender, either directly or indirectly, are by Chevron et al. (1978) and Langer (2001). The former authors obtained a significant, difference in Dependency (Factor 1) between the sexes when they compared 87 female and 41 male university students, with mean Dependency scores of -.14 and -.70 for females and males respectively. This difference can be compared with the scores found in this study for non-evacuated respondents, i.e. -.33 and -.73 respectively. However Chevron et al. did not specifically comment on this large gender difference but rather concentrated on the congruence evident between the sex roles for females and males and that between the dimensions of Blatt's Dependency (Factor 1) and Self-criticism (Factor 2) scales respectively. Langer also recruited undergraduates, 150 female and 72 male students, in a study employing the DEQ scale, the Mutual Psychological Development Questionnaire (MPDQ) and the Beck Depression Inventory (BDI). She found from structural path analysis that for females both dependency and self-criticism had a positive, direct, effect on the level of self-reported depression using the BDI, whereas for male students only self-criticism was significant.

Whatever the biological or cultural contributions to this gender difference, it is likely to have an effect on the mental health of respondents who have experienced separation from parents as a result of evacuation in their youth. It is clear from the results given in this chapter that males tend to respond more positively to the experience, particularly if they were evacuated in adolescence. This 'protection' is not so apparent in the mental health outcome results for females in this age group (see

Summary, Table 5.4, paragraphs 3, 4 and 5). It would appear that females, with their higher 'investment' in all the characteristics of dependency, are not only more vulnerable to family and relationship factors in adulthood, but are not so able in adolescence to benefit, in terms of increased confidence and self-reliance, from a good evacuation experience.

Looking more closely at the anomalously high Incidence of Clinical Anxiety and Self-criticism scores for females evacuated in early adolescence (Table 5.4, paragraphs 4 and 10), there were 24 out of 136 female respondents evacuated in early adolescence (10-12 years) who have suffered from clinical anxiety in their adult life, i.e. 18%. They are characterised by having high Dependency, high Self-criticism and high Morbidity Symptom mean scores, i.e. -0.1, 0.1 and 3.0 respectively. In addition 19 out of the 24 have also reported Depression. The most common symptoms listed by the 24 respondents were Sleep disorder (19), Phobias (13), Fatigue (12), Headaches (9), Avoidance behaviour (9) and Feelings of unreality (8). Most respondents reported that they received good *physical* care during evacuation but the main theme in their accounts given in the questionnaire was the feeling of isolation, of being treated as an outcast with no mother or family to go to for reassurance and love. In this context it is pertinent to see from Figure 5.13 that it is only after one year's separation from a parent that the anomalous rise in Self-criticism occurs when the average age of a female respondent would be 13. The lack of inclusion and emotional care is illustrated by the quotations given in Table 5.5 below when asked to comment in the questionnaire on the care received.

Table 5.5 Comments made on the quality of care received by those female respondents who were evacuated at 10-12 years of age and suffered clinical anxiety in adulthood.

Case Number

97 '....there was a lack of emotional support - made to feel different in many ways, especially when I needed mother's help. Never hugged, couldn't run to anyone for reassurance. Yearned for love, warmth and recognition.'

143 '....it was a an unfamiliar religious background. Made to eat separately. Felt isolated - mother love and familial love were not considered necessary.'

248 '.... kept downstairs with servants - shared bedroom upstairs with Hungarian maid. Impersonal life - Miss S cuddled her dogs but not us.'

324 '.... foster parents spoke unkindly about parents - such as looking old - very hurtful. Also I remember remarks about knicker linings re menstruation - very distressing. I was emotionally affected.'

492 '.... billeted with elderly widow. Not sympathetic to little girls. Expected to work hard and say little. Exploited on small farm.'

514 '.... taken in by elderly couple with grown-up daughter who made her dislike of us plain. Periods started when 11 and stopped when evacuated.'

The importance of a close and effective parent-child relationship in puberty for the later achievement of a secure identity was briefly discussed earlier in Section 5.2.2.2.2. In adulthood, the immediate, precipitating events given by these 24 respondents which led to the onset of clinical anxiety varied widely, but included a sense of isolation, rejection, death, cruelty or loss reflected in the following life events:

> Death of parents
> Death of relatives
> Marriage breakdown
> Parental antagonism towards, and rejection of, the respondent
> Post-operational and post-natal effect
> Witnessing an internment
> Any threatening behaviour by others
> Witnessing cruelty to children or animals
> Being involved in a car accident.

Returning to the summary of the results given in Table 5.4 it is clear that the quality of care received during evacuation, in both physical and emotional terms, is of equal importance with the age at which evacuation took place. When the care received was poor both sexes have incidence levels for depression and clinical anxiety well above those who were not evacuated, and conversely, when such care is good these levels lie below the control levels (Table 5.4, paragraph 6). Some of this 'gain' may be due to evacuees being removed from the worst effects of bombing and the associated exigencies of war, although none of the 86 respondents who remained at home reported any family losses or serious injuries, or serious trauma.

By comparison with Age at evacuation and Care received the effects due to the other mediating variables, i.e. the length of the evacuation period, the frequency of parental visits and the number of billets occupied, were of secondary importance, although the trends seen were in the expected direction. Self-criticism was the only outcome variable to be significantly affected by the length of the evacuation period, increasing significantly for both sexes if the evacuation period exceeded 2 years. The incidence of depression and clinical anxiety, and the number of morbidity symptoms, rose if parental visits were less than about two per year (Table 5.4, paragraphs 12 and 14). The only significant effect of the number of billets related to male respondents, and showed a drop in Dependency with increasing numbers of billets occupied.

Taken together these results suggest that so long as the age at evacuation was greater than 6 years, the care received was moderate or good and parental visits were made a few times per year, then, on average, there were no significant effects on mental health in adulthood. If evacuation occurred when a respondent was younger than 6, with poor care received and with infrequent parental contact, then the long-term, negative, effects on adult mental health were significant for both sexes. Adolescent male evacuees generally enjoyed a more robust mental health and were more likely to gain from a good evacuation experience; such an experience seems to have led to the development of increased self-confidence and self-reliance, and often to widened horizons (see Rusby, 1995). The level of adult depression for this group was significantly lower than that for respondents who remained at home.

It must be remembered, however, that these results refer to mean trends, and an examination of the individual scores, and accompanying brief accounts, show great individual variability, which, unfortunately, this quantitative analysis cannot address. In the end, one is left with an impression of the resilience of some young people when confronted by such a crisis of family separation and the loss of immediate parental care. Perhaps this is exemplified by the fact that, overall, no significant difference was found in adult mental health between those who were, and those who were not, evacuated.

5.3 Long term effects of upbringing on mental health.

This section is concerned with the long term effects that the quality of parenting and the family situation and any crises may have had on the adult mental health of respondents. Apart from Evacuation, Upbringing is the other input group variable shown in the 'pathway through life' block diagram in Figure 5.1, which includes a number of related factors which are described below. As discussed in Chapter 2 it is important to establish if there are any direct long-term effects of upbringing on adult mental health for this present population sample, and to test if the quality of such upbringing has a moderating influence on the evacuation results considered in Section 5.2. Any moderating influence will be discussed in the next main section, Section 5.4. In Section 2.3.2 of Chapter 2 the research linking childhood adverse experiences in the family with subsequent psychological well-being was examined and a number of workers have linked inadequate child care, or parental loss or divorce, or family conflict in childhood to poor adult mental health.

5.3.1 Analysis.

The choice of input variables for this analysis are shown in Figure 5.1 and their selection and the measures employed were discussed in Chapter 3 (see Section 3.2.2.1) after considering the theoretical background in Chapter 2. They are the Quality of Nurture, defined as being Good enough or Comfortless, Divorce of parents, Death of a parent and Parental class. For the purposes of this present analysis these are treated as being dichotomous, i.e. presence or absence of effect. They will be tested against the same outcome variables for mental health as before.

Missing cases were treated listwise in the computations, with 368 females and 250 males available, of which 310 females and 222 males were in the Good enough category of nurturance, used as controls. This is a reduction in the number of cases from those available for analysis in Section 5.2.1 since 98 female and 59 male respondents did not wish to give a description of their family upbringing. Respondent numbers are given at the top of each column of the univariate results in

Table 5.6, where the same 'Good enough' control sample was used to test each of the three input variables, i.e. Nurture, Divorce of parents and Death of a parent. It can be seen that the ratio of respondent numbers between the two levels in each of the above three input variables is high, ranging from 310/72 = 4.3 to the worst case of 222/12 = 18.5. This is acceptable for the chi-square analysis for the outcome categorical variables Incidence of Depression and Incidence of Clinical Anxiety, since the expected frequency criterion of Tabachnick & Fidell (1996) given in Section 3.3.1 was applied as a check and Table 5.6 has been annotated 'cells too small' where this applies. In the case of the three outcome variables tested by ANOVA analyses, mean scores of Dependency, Self-criticism and Morbidity symptoms, it does mean that, according to Scheffe's (1959) analysis discussed in Section 3.3.1, the lowest level of significance may be unreliable, even though the homogeneity of variance was found to be acceptable.

As before Pearson's chi-square tests were made separately for each gender for each input variable as a function of the Incidence of Depression and Clinical Anxiety. In a similar way one-way ANOVA tests for each gender were made for those tests involving the three outcome mental health variables with mean scores: Dependency, Self-criticism and Morbidity symptoms. The same qualification that was mentioned in Section 5.2.1 applies to the reliability of the lowest significance level for Morbidity symptoms due to floor effects.

5.3.2. Results

The results of this univariate and bivariate analysis are given below in Table 5.6, in a similar format to Table 5.3 for evacuation, using the same mental health outcome variables. Interaction tests by Loglinear and 2-way ANOVA statistics gave only one significant effect, for Death of a parent x Gender as a function of the Incidence of Depression. We will examine the results given in Table 5.6 by input variable, starting with the first column on the effect of Nurture.

Table 5.6 Outcome variables for mental health as a function of gender and childhood upbringing

	Nurture Good enough Comfortless	Divorce of parents No Yes	Death of parent No Yes	Parental Class Middle Working
$N_F =$	310 55	310 28	310 72	146 361
$N_M =$	222 28	222 12	222 36	85 253

MENTAL HEALTH

	χ^2	χ^2	χ^2	χ^2

Incidence of Depression
Female	36% 58% 9.5**	36% 46% 1.2	36% 39% 0.2	36% 41% 1.1
Male	20% 43% 7.2**	20% 50% 5.9*	20% 44% 10.0**	20% 28% 2.3
	(Figure 5.14)	(Figure 5.18)	(Figure 5.20)	

Incidence of Clinical Anxiety
Female	10% 25% 9.1**	cells too small	10% 8% 0.3	12% 12% 0.0
Male	7% 21% 6.2*		7% 8% 0.0	6% 11% 1.8
	(Figure 5.15)			

Mean score Factor 1 Dependency
	F	F	F	F
Female	-0.4 -0.3 1.0	-0.4 -0.4 0.1	-0.4 -0.3 0.1	-0.4 -0.4 0.2
Male	-0.7 -0.9 2.6	-0.7 -0.7 0.0	-0.7 -0.8 1.1	-0.7 -0.8 0.8

Mean score Factor 2 Self-criticism
Female	-0.4 0.3 24.1***	-0.4 0.0 3.9*	-0.4 -0.2 1.4	-0.3 -0.2 0.3
Male	-0.6 0.1 13.4***	-0.6 0.2 7.1**	-0.6 -0.3 2.4	-0.5 -0.4 1.6
	(Figure 5.16)			

Mean score Morbidity symptoms
Female	1.6 2.9 23.4***	1.6 2.2 3.6	1.6 1.8 1.4	1.6 1.9 3.3
Male	0.8 1.2 3.2	0.8 2.2 12.7***	0.8 1.2 2.3	0.9 0.9 0.1
	(Figure 5.17)	(Figure 5.19)		

Chi-square tests have been carried out for categorical data and one-way ANOVA tests for interval scores. Significance key: * p<.05, ** p<.01 and *** p<.001; all two-tailed.

5.3.2.1. Nurture

Column one in Table 5.6 gives the results for 'good enough' and 'comfortless' Nurture in childhood. The Incidence of Depression increases significantly for both sexes with poor nurturance ($\chi^2(1) = 9.5$, p<.01 for females, and $\chi^2(1) = 7.2$, p<.01 for males), and these results are plotted Figure 5.14, which shows large percentage increases in depression for both sexes as Nurture deteriorates. By loglinear analysis, in line with the results given in Table 5.1, the gender difference is highly significant (p<.001), and in addition there is a highly significant main effect of Nurture (p<.001) but no significant interaction was found between Depression x Nurture x Gender.

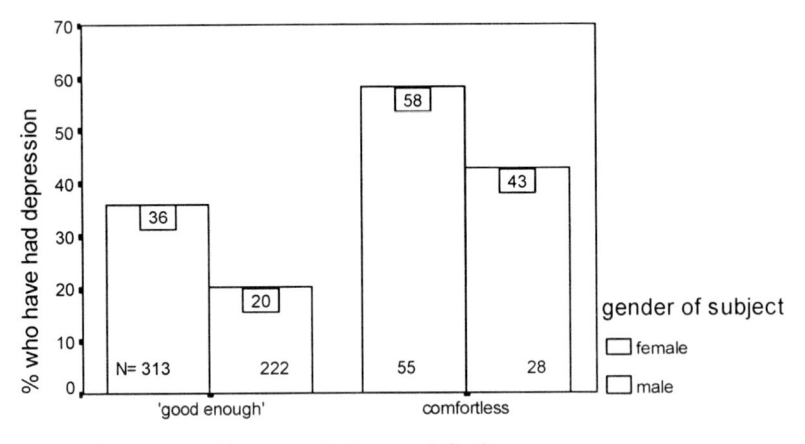

Figure 5.14 Incidence of Depression as a function of nurture received in upbringing.

Results for the Incidence of Clinical Anxiety given in Table 5.6 are also significant ($\chi^2(1) = 9.1$, $p<.01$ for females, and $\chi^2(1) = 6.2$, $p<.05$ for males) and are plotted in Figure 5.15, and show a high percentage increase in Clinical Anxiety with Comfortless nurture. By loglinear analysis it was found that the significant difference in the gender response to depression seen in Figure 5.14 was not maintained, but there is a highly significant main effect of Nurture and, again, no 3-way interaction.

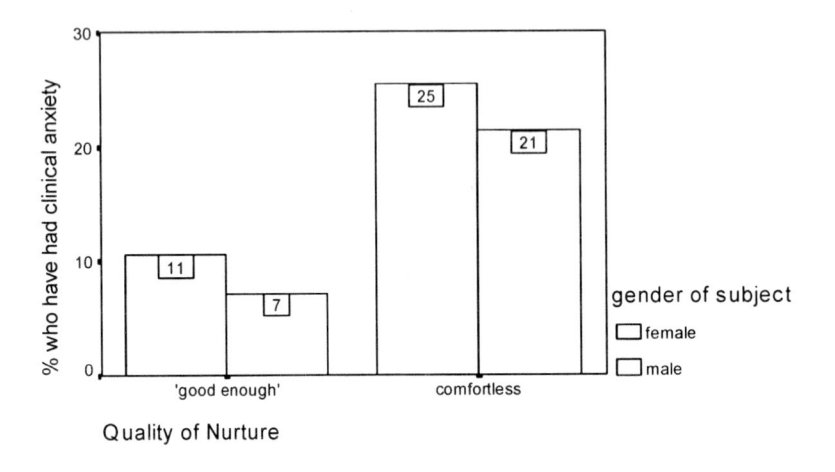

Figure 5.15 Incidence of Clinical Anxiety as a function of nurture received in upbringing.

For Dependency, in Table 5.6, although neither of the results for either sex are significant there is a suggestion of an interaction between gender and nurture, since the female value slightly increased while the male value decreased with comfortless nurture. From a 2-way ANOVA analysis the interaction effect was found to lie close to significance ($F(1, 610) = 3.5$, $p = .06$), suggesting that male subjects respond differently, on average, to females when nurturance is poor in childhood by moving to a rather less dependent state, and this effect is reflected in adulthood.

As in the evacuation analysis, Self-criticism would appear to be the prime indicator of poor mental health for both sexes, and is highly significant in these results ($F(1,361) = 24.1$, $p<.001$ for females, and $F(1, 248) = 13.4$, $p<.001$ for males), but with no main gender effect and no interaction of Gender x Nurture as analysed by 2-way ANOVA. These results are illustrated in Figure 5.16, showing the steep and parallel increase in Self-criticism with loss of nurture, with no indication of any interaction.

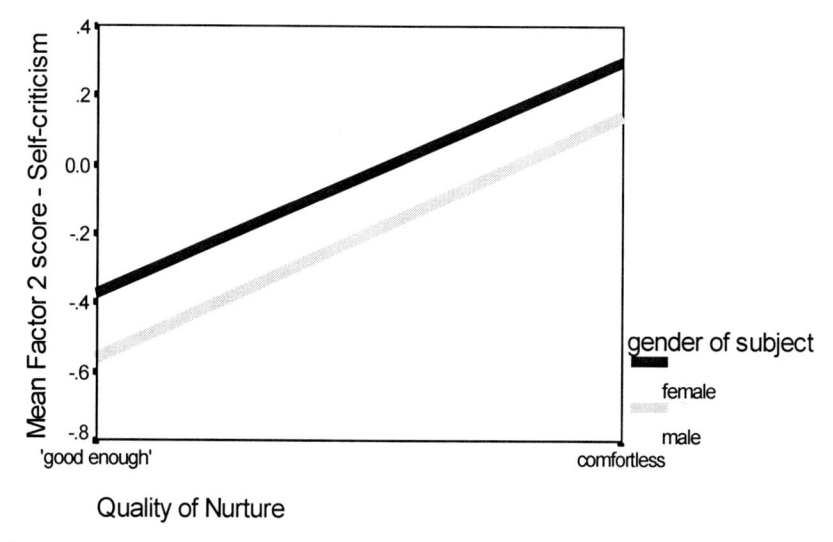

Figure 5.16 Mean score for Self-criticism as a function of nurture received in upbringing.

The effect of Comfortless Nurture on the number of Morbidity symptoms is shown in Figure 5.17. The results are highly significant for females but only approach significance for males ($F(1, 339) = 23.4$, $p<.001$ for females, and $F(1, 235) = 3.2$, $p=.07$ for males), giving a significant interaction level between Gender and Nurture ($F(1, 572) = 4.8$, $p<.05$) as analysed by 2-way ANOVA. In terms of the effect on each gender this is a rather different result from that found for Care received during evacuation seen in Table 5.3, and plotted in Figure 5.11, where values for both sexes were highly significant. However it should be borne in mind, as mentioned in Chapter 3, that there are floor effects for this Morbidity symptom variable which will affect its reliability in an analysis.

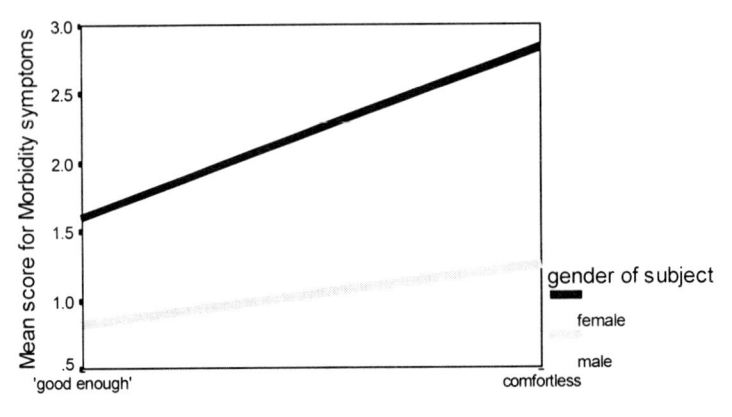

Figure 5.17 Mean score for Morbidity symptoms as function of nurture received in upbringing.

5.3.2.2. Divorce or Separation of parents

In column two of Table 5.6 the effect of divorce or separation of parents in childhood has significantly affected the Incidence of Depression in adulthood for males ($\chi^2(1) = 5.9$, $p<.05$), so that incidence rates have increased by a factor of 2.5, from 20 to 50%. Females appear to be less affected by marriage breakdown, with incidence rates remaining high but only increasing from 36 to 46%, below the level of significance. These results have been plotted in Figure 5.18. Loglinear analysis of the interaction between Depression x Gender x Divorce only approaches significance ($p=.09$) but confirms the highly significant effect of gender on the Incidence of Depression ($p<.001$).

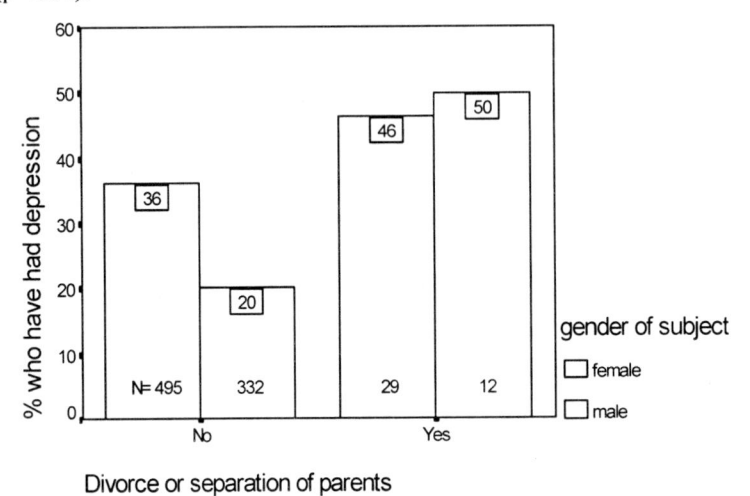

Figure 5.18 Incidence of Depression as a function of the divorce or separation of parents in childhood.

For the effect of parental divorce on the Incidence of Clinical Anxiety the expected frequencies in certain of the cells for each sex in the 2 x 2 contingency tables were <5, therefore, according to the criterion of Tabachnik and Fidell (1989) adopted in Chapter 3 no chi-square test was carried out.

In Table 5.6 there was no effect of parental divorce on Dependency for either sex, although the main effect of gender remains highly significant ($F(1) = 7.6$, $p<.001$). The effect of divorce or separation on Self-criticism in Table 5.6 was greater for male subjects, but results for both sexes are significant (for females $F(1) = 3.9$, $p<.05$ and for males $F(1) = 7.1$, $p<.01$). A 2-way ANOVA analysis showed there was no effect of gender and no interaction.

The result for the mean score for morbidity symptoms in Table 5.6 was highly significant for male respondents ($F(1, 217) = 12.7$, $p<.001$)) but not for females and these results are plotted in Figure 5.19.

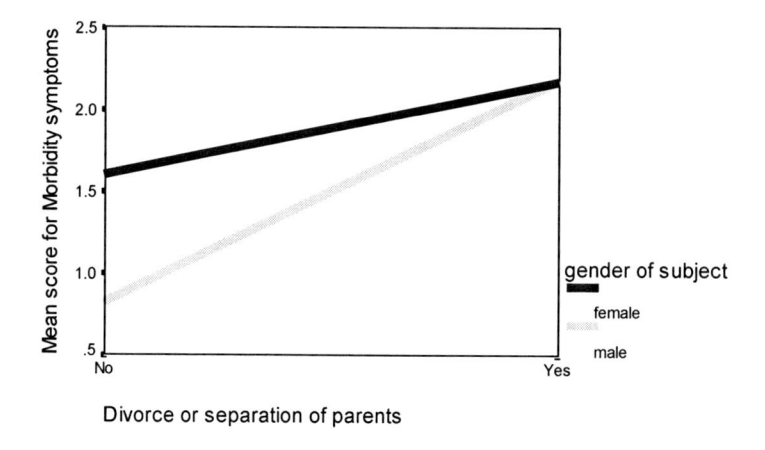

Figure 5.19 Mean score for Morbidity symptoms as a function of the divorce or separation of parents in childhood.

A two-way ANOVA of Gender x Divorce gave an interaction level of $p =.13$, only approaching significance. This differentiation between the sexes as a result of parental divorce is similar in form to that seen for the Incidence of Depression and Self-criticism and will be commented on later in this section. It is interesting to contrast the inversion in the significance of gender between the effect of parental divorce and comfortless nurture on the number of morbidity symptoms. This is seen by a comparison between Figures 5.17 and 5.19.

5.3.2.3. Death of a parent

With death of a parent in childhood the Incidence of Depression more than doubles for male respondents, increasing very significantly from 20 to 44% in adulthood ($\chi^2(1) = 10.0$, $p<.01$).

Female respondents' levels are little changed by comparison, at 36-39%. This differential effect between the sexes is illustrated in Figure 5.20, and is almost identical to that seen in Figure 5.18 as a function of parental divorce. Loglinear analysis confirms the highly significant effect of Gender on the Incidence of Depression (p<.001) and shows that the interaction Depression x Gender x Death of a parent is significant (p<.05).

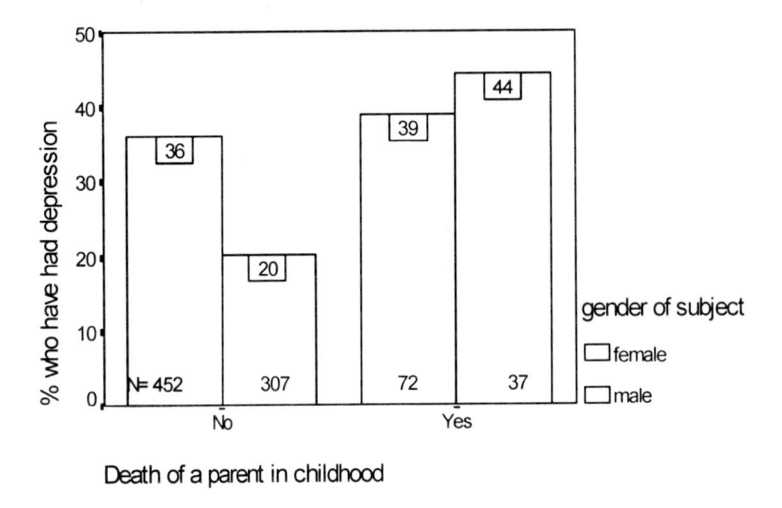

Figure 5.20 Incidence of Depression as a function of Death of a parent in childhood.

The results in Table 5.6 also show that Death of a parent is not associated with clinical anxiety in adulthood for either sex, nor does it affect the Dependency ratings of respondents. There is, however, an increase in the mean score for Self-criticism and Morbidity symptoms with death of a parent, particularly for males, but these changes do not reach significance.

5.3.2.4. Parental Class

As described in Chapter 3 on Methodology, Section 3.2.2.1, respondents were divided into those that came from a middle and working class backgrounds, defined by parental occupation. None were found who came from Class 1. Of the total number of respondents 147 females and 86 males had middle class parents (Classes 2 and 3) and 363 females and 253 males had working class backgrounds (Classes 3 and 4).

From an examination of Table 5.6 it can be seen that, overall, there is very little effect of parental class on the mental health of respondents in adulthood. None of the results reach significance and the only discernible trends are for males. The Incidence of Depression for males increases from 20% for middle class to 28% for working class, both values below the incidence for females at 36 to 41%. Again it is only males that show a change in the Incidence of Clinical Anxiety, from 6% for middle class to 11% for working class, just below 12% for females. There is no trend for

Dependency, just the usual gender difference (p<.001), and no effects for Self-criticism or Morbidity symptoms.

5.3.3 Summary

The main conclusions from these results are summarised below, and will be discussed in the following section.

Table 5.7 Summary of the main results for the long-term effects of upbringing in childhood on adult mental health

---

1. Gender differences, where females score more highly than men, remain highly significant for the Incidence of Depression, and the mean scores of Dependency and Morbidity symptoms (all p<.001).

2. There are significant increases in the Incidence of Depression and Clinical anxiety for both sexes in adulthood as a function of a deteriorating quality of nurture in childhood. (Figures 5.14 and 5.15).

3. Factor 2 of the DEQ scale, Self-criticism, a strong indicator of a vulnerability to depression and clinical anxiety in adulthood, is associated with poor nurture in childhood. Factor 1, Dependency, is not associated in this way. (Table 5.6 and Figure 5.16).

4. Divorce of parents is associated with an increased likelihood of adult depression, particularly for male respondents, and this gender difference is also reflected in the mean scores of Self-criticism and Morbidity symptoms. (Figures 5.18 and 5.19).

5. Death of a parent has a significant effect on the Incidence of Depression for males in adulthood only. The Incidence of Clinical anxiety is not affected. (Table 5.6 and Figure 5.20).

6. The effect of Parental class is minimal. Only male respondents show a small related change: An increase in the Incidence of Depression and Clinical anxiety if males come from a working class, rather than a middle class background. (Table 5.6).

5.3.4. Discussion

Bearing in mind the limitations of a retrospective account of a respondent's upbringing (discussed in Chapter 3, Section 3.2.2.1), the results for the effect of Nurture on adult mental health do, nevertheless, have a certain internal consistency. There are large increases in the incidence of adult depression and clinical anxiety for respondents of both sexes who reported a childhood background lacking in affection, or who suffered parental conflict or a harsh upbringing, compared to those reporting a more loving and secure family background. And these significant differences in mental health are strongly supported, for both sexes, by the scores for Self-criticism, Factor 2 of the DEQ scale, where the rise in values are large and highly significant between the two categories of Nurture, 'Good enough' and Comfortless (see Table 5.6). It is worth looking at the items in this 66-item scale which load most heavily on to Factor 2 of the DEQ factor analysis, both to see what makes it such an effective indicator of poor mental health and to understand the way such respondents, from a nurtureless upbringing, view themselves in adulthood. The eight items that load most strongly on to Factor 2, Self-criticism, of the DEQ scale are given below in Table 5.8.

Table 5.8 The 8 items of the DEQ scale which load most strongly onto Factor 2, Self-criticism, of the DEQ scale, from the items listed in Section 10 of the questionnaire in Appendix 3

Item No.

11. Many times I feel helpless.
13. There is a considerable difference between how I am now and how I would like to be.
16. There are times when I feel empty inside.
17. I tend not to be satisfied with what I have.
35. I never feel secure in a close relationship.
43. I often feel guilty.
36. The way I feel about myself frequently varies: There are times I feel good about myself and other times when I feel like a total failure.
56. In my relationships with others I am very concerned with what they can give to me.

These items have a common theme: a lack of self-worth or self-esteem. In Frosh's terms, and that of the title of his book, there is an *Identity crisis* (Frosh, 1991), and he quotes Guntrip (1973) on the concerns of such people seeking 'for a secure core of self' and unable to form healthy, and mature relations with others. This is also the concern of Object Relations Theory, reflected in the need for mature, rather than infantile, dependence (Fairbairn, 1952).

Whereas the effect of poor nurture influences both sexes in nearly equal measure, that of divorce and parental death do not. In Table 5.6 it can be seen that it is male subjects who are more affected by divorce and parental death, and this is particularly clearly demonstrated by the significant values for χ^2 given for males for the Incidence of Depression as a function of both Divorce of parents and Death of a parent. The same differential effect between the sexes is also seen in the mean scores for Self-criticism and Morbidity symptoms as a function of Divorce. It is suggested that this difference in response is due to the fact that, for the children of the family, both divorce and parental death result in a greater probability of paternal loss: In this sample no respondent reported living with father following divorce or separation and in the case of parental death 71% were paternal deaths. If we look specifically at the Incidence of Depression as a function of death of a *father* then there is a highly significant effect for male respondents, where the incidence rises from 23% to 60%, and there is no comparable effect for female respondents (for males, $\chi^2(1) = 16.3$, $p<.001$ and for females, $\chi^2(1) = 0.0$, $p = 0.9$). This is a very strong indicator of gender diversity in development through loss of a father, and it is supported by a loglinear analysis of the three categorical variables involved, Depression x Gender x Death of a Father, which results in a significant 3-way interaction where $p<.01$. There is also evidence that this male response to loss by divorce and by death leads to different levels for both Self-criticism and Morbidity symptoms. Divorce of parents leads to a highly significant effect on both these mental health variables, but Death of a parent does not (see Table 5.6). This suggests that the developmental response of males to these two types of loss may be different, but both 'losses' are associated with later depression. This difference is highlighted by an examination of the number and type of morbidity symptoms experienced by males who lost fathers by (1) divorce or separation and (2) by death, *and* who suffered depression. There were 6 respondents in the first category (divorce) with a mean score of 4.0 Morbidity symptoms; there were 15 respondents in the second category (death) with a mean Morbidity symptom score of 1.9. Three of those 6 respondents whose parents were divorced marked the symptom list box 'Feelings of unreality' (see Section 12 in Appendix 3), none of the 15 who lost their fathers by death did so. This evidence, plus that from the brief case notes provided by respondents in response to their marking of the symptom list suggests that the long-term effect on male mental health associated with parental divorce may be more severe than that associated with loss of a father by death. This difference may have a 'developmental' basis, and/or, following the work of Harris (1988), it may be related to any neglect or conflict associated with parental divorce or separation, or possibly loss of family support. The vulnerability of male respondents to loss of a father in childhood should be contrasted with the vulnerability of females to loss of a mother, found by Brown and Harris (1978) in their studies of young mothers' vulnerability to depression. In this present work it was not possible to make this comparison since there were insufficient cases of loss of a mother for a meaningful analysis to be made.

Clearly a lot more work needs to be done on the differential effect on the two sexes of these two 'upbringing' variables, divorce and parental death, both in regard to general development and the subsequent adult mental health of the two sexes. Most workers in this field have concentrated on females subjects, and few comparisons have been made between the sexes in developmental quantitative research.

Finally, a word on the effect of parental death and nurture on the Incidence of Clinical Anxiety. Death of a parent has no effect on the Incidence of Clinical Anxiety, but the quality of Nurture has a very marked effect (see Table 5.6). This difference, plus the very large proportional increases in Clinical Anxiety for both sexes between the two Nurture categories, lends support to the idea that a predisposition to clinical anxiety may be formed in early childhood due to a lack of maternal bonding or attachment (see Bowlby, 1969; Tizard and Hodges, 1978; Rutter 1980; and Main et al., 1985).

5.4 Long term effect of the quality of nurture in upbringing and care received during evacuation on adult mental health

In Sections 5.2 and 5.3 we have seen how the care received during evacuation, and the quality of nurture received in upbringing, have each affected the mental health of respondents in adulthood. In this section the two variables have been separated to determine if the quality of upbringing has moderated the way care received during evacuation affects mental health in adulthood. For example it might be that good nurture in the early childhood years may have had a protective effect for those respondents who had a poor evacuation experience, or, conversely, it may be that a good experience in evacuation went some way to ameliorating the negative effects of a poor upbringing. Such considerations follow on from the theoretical discussion of possible antecedents to poor mental health given in Section 2.3.2 of Chapter 2.

5.4.1. Analysis

The analysis is based solely on the quality of nurture received by the respondent in the home environment and the quality of care during evacuation. The relevant categorical input variables are those used and described in the earlier sections: i.e. 'good enough' or 'comfortless' Nurture and poor, moderate or good Care received during evacuation.

The mental health outcome variables employed are the same as those used in Sections 5.2 and 5.3, except that the Incidence of Clinical Anxiety has been omitted due to the small expected frequencies predicted in the 'comfortless' category. As before, all cases were treated listwise in the computations, with a total of 337 females and 208 males available. Loglinear analysis was used to examine any interaction between Nurture, Care received and the Incidence of Depression. Pearson chi-square tests were made separately for each gender and Nurture category as a function of Care received for the outcome variable Incidence of Depression. Interactions between Nurture and Care received were examined by factorial ANOVA computations for the three outcome variables Dependency, Self-criticism and Morbidity symptoms, and these were followed by one-way ANOVA tests for each gender and nurture category as a function of Care received.

5.4.2 Results

The results of the interaction tests will be reported under their respective outcome variables in the subsections which follow. The chi-square and one-way ANOVA results are given below in Table 5.9 using a similar format to Tables 5.3 and 5.6. These results will be examined by looking at the effect of Nurture and Care received on each of the mental health outcome variables in turn. As before the sexes have been treated separately.

Table 5.9 Outcome variables for mental health as a function of gender, the quality of childhood upbringing and the care received during evacuation

		Nurture	Care received poor	moderate	good	
MENTAL HEALTH						
Incidence of Depression						χ^2
	Female	'good enough'	38%	34%	36%	0.2
		'comfortless'	53%	67%	53%	0.9
	Male	'good enough'	36%	20%	19%	3.2
		'comfortless'	\multicolumn{3}{c}{cells too small}		
			\multicolumn{3}{c}{(Figure 5.21)}		
Mean score Factor 1 - Dependency						F
	Female	'good enough'	-0.2	-0.4	-0.4	0.5
		'comfortless'	-0.1	-0.4	-0.3	0.6
	Male	'good enough'	-0.4[a]	-0.7[b]	-0.8[b]	3.2*
		'comfortless'	-0.5	-0.9	-1.2	0.8
			\multicolumn{3}{c}{(Figure 5.22)}		
Mean score Factor 2 - Self-criticism						
	Female	'good enough'	-0.3	-0.3	-0.4	0.5
		'comfortless'	0.3	0.5	0.0	0.6
	Male	'good enough'	-0.6	-0.4	-0.6	0.7
		'comfortless'	0.9	0.4	0.0	2.1
			\multicolumn{3}{c}{(Figure 5.23)}		
Mean score Morbidity symptoms						
	Female	'good enough'	2.0	1.7	1.5	2.5
		'comfortless'	3.0	3.5	1.8	2.2
	Male	'good enough'	1.4	0.9	0.8	2.9
		'comfortless'	2.8[a]	1.7[a]	0.7[b]	5.8*
			\multicolumn{3}{c}{(Figure 5.24)}		

Chi-square tests have been carried out for categorical data and one-way ANOVA tests for interval scores. Significance key: * p<.05, ** p<.01 and *** p<.001; all two-tailed. Significance in the ANOVA analysis was followed by Newman-Kreuls' post-hoc tests. Mean scores marked by different superscripts are significantly different at p<.05.

5.4.2.1 Incidence of Depression

Interactions between Incidence of Depression, Nurture and Care received were examined by hierarchical loglinear analysis in which the sexes were pooled due to the low expected frequencies for males in some cells. No significance was found for the 3-way interaction Depression x Nurture x Care received, but 2-way interactions were significant for both Depression x Nurture and Nurture x Care received. The likelihood ratio chi-square change when these were deleted was 15.3 (p<.001) and 10.7 (p<.01) respectively. The first interaction reflects and confirms the bivariate results for both sexes given in Table 5.6, i.e. that the quality of Nurture in childhood significantly affects the Incidence of Depression in adulthood, and the second result shows that Nurture and Care received are not independent. From an examination of the observed and expected frequencies the effect is due to a tendency for those from a 'comfortless' family background to report poor Care received during evacuation. This could be due to retrospective bias by the respondents involved (N=20), or difficulties experienced by foster parents in caring for those from unsupportive or neglectful families, or possibly an affect of the lack of an informed and sensitive billeting selection procedure (see Chapter 1). If it is predominantly due to personal bias then it will have some skewing effect on the results given in Table 5.9.

From Table 5.9 it can be seen that there is no significant effect on the Incidence of Depression for Care received for females for either level of Nurture. The lack of any trend is illustrated in Figure 5.21 where the Incidence of Depression appears largely unaffected by Care received (cf Table 5.3 (a)). What is apparent, though, is the highly significant difference in Incidence of Depression between the two levels of Nurture, which has already been reported in Section 5.3.2.1 (see Table 5.6). No equivalent results for male respondents are given since certain of the expected cell are below the acceptable criterion.

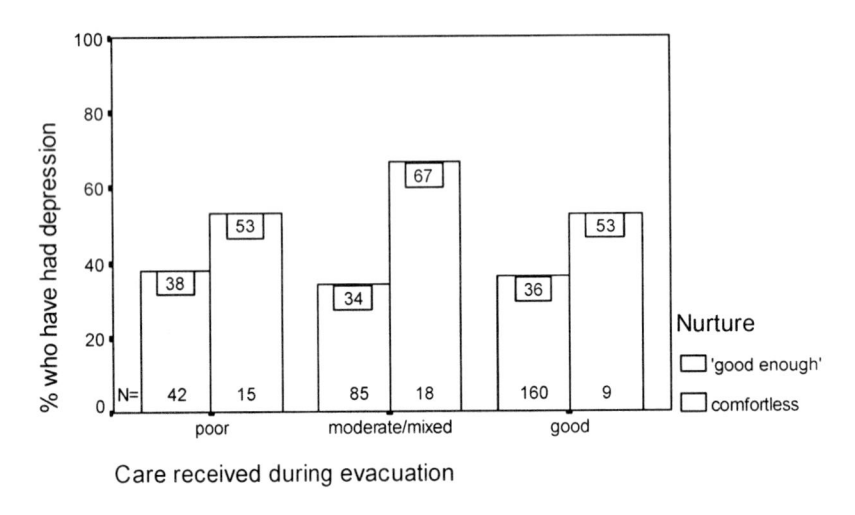

Figure 5.21 Incidence of Depression for female respondents as a function of Nurture received during upbringing and Care received in evacuation.

From these plotted results for the Incidence of Depression for females it can be seen that the quality of Nurture directly adds or subtracts from the way that the Care received during evacuation affects the Incidence of Depression in adulthood.

5.4.2.2 Mean score for Factor 1 - Dependency

Interactions for Nurture, Care received and Gender were tested by factorial ANOVA as a function of Dependency and no interactions of either a 3-way or 2-way nature were found to be significant. As determined in previous sections involving Dependency, gender was highly significant ($F(1,540) = 14.4$, $p<.001$).

From Table 5.9 it can be seen that only the 'good enough' Nurture category for males shows a significant difference across Care received for mean scores of Dependency. These results have been plotted in Figure 5.22 for the two sexes. Figure 5.22(a) for female respondents clearly illustrates the lack of any effect of either Care received or Nurture on the mean score of Dependency, and reflects the results given in Tables 5.3 and 5.6 respectively for the same variables. The results plotted in Figure 5.22(b) show reduced levels of Dependency for males and a trend to lower values as Care received improves. This trend is significant for the 'good enough' Nurture category ($F(2,206) = 3.2$, $p<.05$) but fails to reach significance for the 'comfortless' category due to the small cell frequencies. It is interesting to note that this trend is in the opposite sense from that due to Nurture, i.e. where males become more Dependent as Nurture improves. The very low value for Dependency, i.e. -1.2, when Care received was good for the 'comfortless' category should be compared with the non-evacuated, control, value of -.73 given in Figure 5.6.

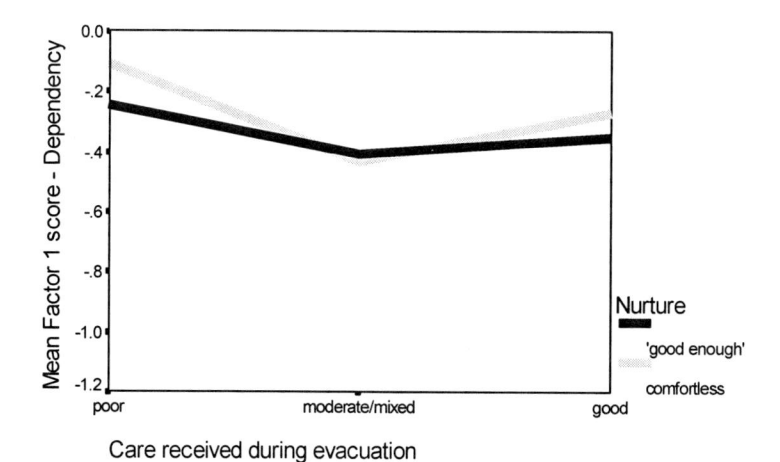

(a) For Female respondents

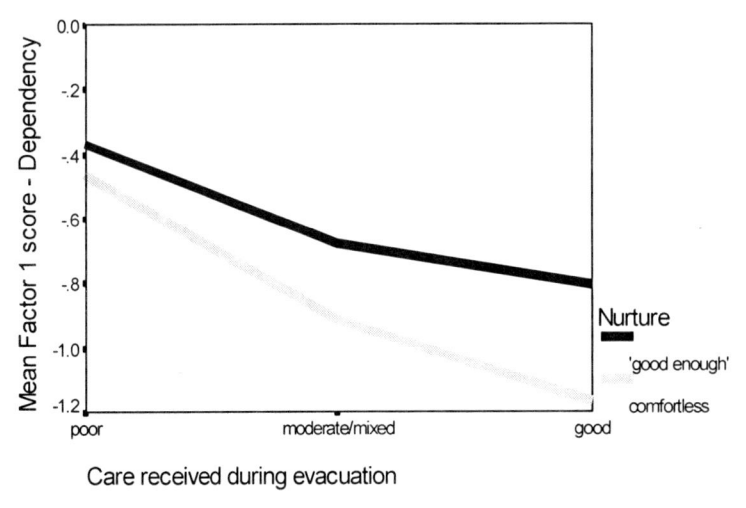

[Figure: Mean Factor 1 score - Dependency plotted against Care received during evacuation (poor, moderate/mixed, good), with Nurture categories 'good enough' and comfortless]

(b) For Male respondents

Figure 5.22 Mean score for Dependency as a function of Nurture received during upbringing and Care received in evacuation, plotted separately by gender.

5.4.2.3 Mean score for Factor 2 - Self-criticism

Interactions for Nurture x Care received x Gender were tested by factorial ANOVA as a function of Self-criticism and no interactions were found to be significant. There was no main effect of gender.

From Table 5.9 it can be seen that none of the univariate results are significant; these have been plotted in Figure 5.23 for the two sexes. Figure 5.23(a) illustrates the lack of any marked trend in Self-criticism for Care received during evacuation for females and the highly significant difference for the two Nurture categories ($F(1,310) = 15.8$, $p<.001$). Examination of Table 5.3 in Section 5.2.2 does, however, show a significant effect of Care received for females, and this difference between the results given in the two tables is due to the inclusion of 122 respondents in Table 5.3 who did not wish to provide a description of their family upbringing; the corollary being that there is a correlation between poor Care received and comfortless Nurture. This will be examined later in the chapter when structural path analysis is employed. Figure 5.23(b) illustrates the equivalent results for male respondents, again showing a highly significant effect of Nurture ($F(1,206) = 20.2$, $p<.001$) but no significant effect of Care received. There is, however, a marked trend for Self-criticism to reduce as Care received in evacuation improved for those who reported a 'comfortless' Upbringing, but cell numbers are low.

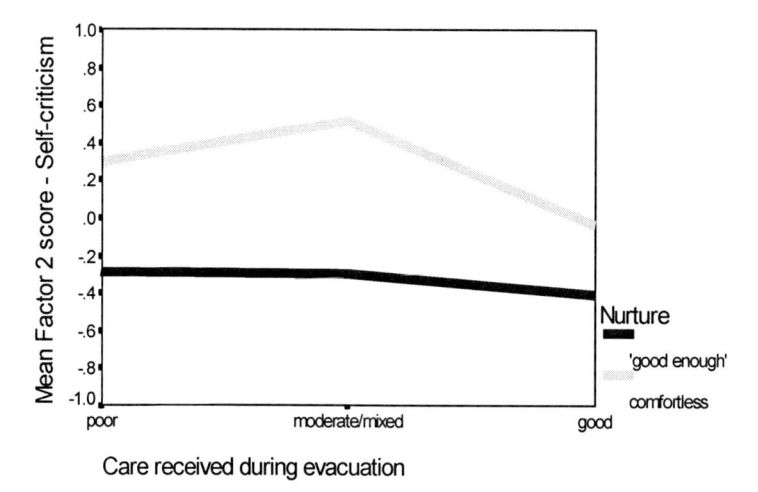

(a) For Female respondents

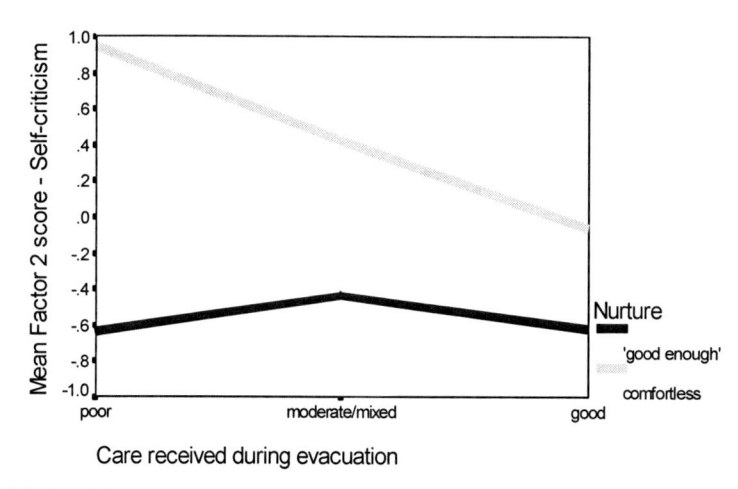

(b) For Male respondents

Figure 5.23 Mean score for Self-criticism as a function of Nurture received during upbringing and Care received in evacuation, plotted separately by gender.

5.4.2.4 Mean score for Morbidity symptoms

Interactions for Nurture x Care received x Gender were tested by factorial ANOVA as a function of Morbidity symptoms. There was no 3-way interaction but a 2-way interaction was found for Nurture x Care received (F(2,507) = 3.5, p<.05). Examination of the results shows that this interaction was in the sense that good compared with poor Care received during evacuation led to a smaller difference in the number of morbidity symptoms between the two Nurture categories, i.e. to a beneficial effect. From Table 5.9 it can be seen that only the univariate results for males in the 'comfortless' Nurture category are significant (F(2,24) = 5.8, p<.05). The univariate results from

Table 5.9 have been plotted in Figure 5.24 for the two sexes. Figure 5.24(a) illustrates the significant difference between the two Nurture categories for females (F(1,313) = 13.9, p<.001) and Figure 5.24(b) the main effect of Care received for males (F(2,313) = 4.6, p<.05), with a trend to lower numbers of Morbidity symptoms as Care received in evacuation improves. The effect of the 2-way interaction between Nurture x Care received, mentioned above, can be seen in both Figures 5.24(a) for females and (b) for males, where the beneficial effect of good Care received has reduced the difference in mean scores for Morbidity symptoms to near zero between the two Nurture categories for both sexes. This suggests that good Care received in evacuation can help to ameliorate the negative influence of comfortless Nurture.

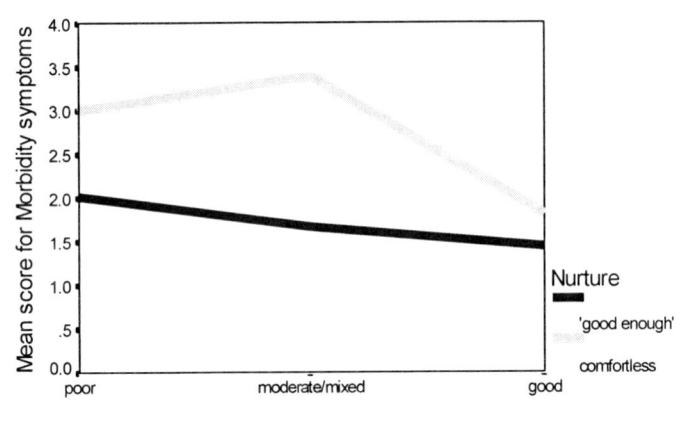

(a) For Female respondents

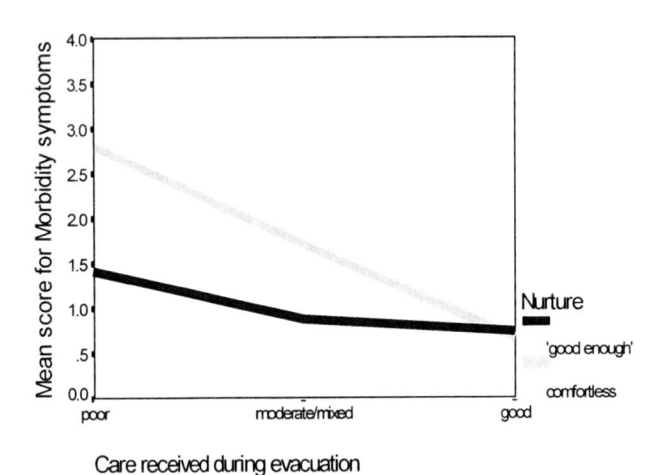

(b) For Male respondents

Figure 5.24 Mean score for Morbidity symptoms as a function of Nurture received during upbringing and Care received in evacuation, plotted separately by gender.

5.4.3. Summary

The main conclusions from these results are summarised below and will be discussed in the following section.

Table 5.10 Summary of the results for the effect of quality of upbringing and care received in evacuation on adult mental health.

---

1. Quality of upbringing is a stronger predictor of adult mental health than that of care received during evacuation for both sexes. The effect is additive, so that 'good enough' Nurture appears to underwrite emotional security during evacuation, whereas comfortless nurture has a negative effect.

2. A significant interaction was found for Nurture x Care received for the mean score for Morbidity symptoms, where good Care received reduced the differential in the number of Morbidity symptoms between the two levels of Nurture (Figures 5.24(a) and (b)). The same, interactive, trend was seen in the results for male respondents for the mean score of Self-criticism (Figure 5.23(b)).

3. Males are more affected by 'comfortless' Upbringing followed by poor Care received in evacuation, demonstrated by the high level of Self-criticism scores (Figures 5.23(b)). If Nurture was 'good enough' they were less affected by varying levels of Care received during evacuation.

4. For the outcome variable Dependency there is no effect of Nurture or Care received for females, and no clear trends (Figure 5.22(a)). Mean scores for males are significantly less than for females, as expected, and show a significant reduction in Dependency as Care received improves in evacuation (Figure 5.22(b)).

5.4.4 Discussion

The object of separating out the input variables of Nurture and Care received was to investigate if there were any interactions between them which would affect the adult mental health of respondents. It might be expected, for instance, that a 'good enough' upbringing in the family, prior to evacuation, would help to moderate the long term effects of poor care received during evacuation or that good care during evacuation might make up to some extent for comfortless nurture. The only significant interaction in this sense was found for the mean score of Morbidity symptoms and which applied to both sexes, although the trend was in this direction for male respondents for the mean score of Self-criticism. This interaction showed that good Care received during evacuation did help to ammeliorate the long-term effects of comfortless Nurture, particularly as it applied to the onset of certain morbidity symptoms in adulthood. Overall, though, the most noticeable feature in these results is the large main effect of Nurture, which clearly has a greater influence on adult mental health than the quality of Care received during evacuation. The only exception to this is the Dependency result for females which is of considerable interest and will now be considered.

It is surprising that the level of Dependency for females, so much higher than that for males, is largely unaffected by both the quality of upbringing and the care received in evacuation (see Figure 5.22(a)). In fact if Tables 5.3 and 5.6 are examined there is no significant effect of Dependency for females for any of the nine input variables considered in these tables:

For evacuation	Age at evacuation
- Table 5.2	Care received
	Period away
	Frequency of parental visits
	Number of billets
For Upbringing	Nurture
- Table 5.6	Divorce of parents
	Death of parents
	Parental class

In general Dependency is lower for those females experiencing a good home or evacuation experience, but the effect is surprisingly small and is less than the equivalent trend for males. These results not only underline the difference in levels of Dependency between the sexes but also the almost invariant nature of mean Dependency in female respondents when experiencing a very wide range of family and evacuation variables. This suggests that the high level of dependency in females, as measured in adults by Factor 1 of the DEQ scale, may be largely innate and that the variables measured play a limited role in moderating it. If correct, this has a direct bearing on the relatively high incidence of depression suffered by females in adulthood since it has already been shown that a high level of Dependency (Factor 1), even without a high level of Self-criticism (Factor 2), is a reliable indicator of depression in females, but not for males (see Table 5.2). So that such women, starting life with a high level of Dependency may be predisposed to depression by precipitating events in later life. The invariant form of these results, which suggest that the high levels of dependency experienced by females could be primarily due to nature, with any influence of nurture possibly limited to the first few months of life, provide support for the supposition of Blatt and Zuroff (1992) that Factor 1, Dependency, in the DEQ scale is a predictor for an anaclitic form of depression, with its origin in early childhood. This subject will be discussed again later in this chapter after testing a structural path model for Depression which includes the contributions of both Dependency and Self-criticism as a function of gender.

5.5 Long term effect of bombing and of father's absence due to the war.

In the path diagram shown in Figure 5.1, in the box entitled WAR, there are two variables listed which relate directly to the exigencies of hostilities, and which may have affected the adult mental health of respondents, one due to aerial bombing of a respondent's neighbourhood or home and the other due to the effect of a father's temporary absence from home because of war service. Death of a father due to enemy action has been already subsumed within the variable Death of a parent included in Section 5.3 on the effects of Upbringing, where only 5 such cases occurred. Although every attempt was made to recruit respondents who were evacuated from areas of Kent, rather than south London, so that their families' experience of bombing was minimised, inevitably the sample contained many whose families had been bombed.

5.5.1 Analysis

The analysis is based on the following categories, where the effect of bombing is tested for both a respondent being present in, and absent from, the family home:

    1. Bombing - Respondent present or absent
- No bombing
- Town or neighbourhood bombed
- Family home bombed

    2. Absence of father
- At home
- Absent on war service

As before, all cases were treated listwise in the computations, with a total of 503 female and 329 male respondents available. Pearson chi-square tests were made separately for each gender as a function of the above categories for the outcome variables Incidence of Depression and Incidence of Clinical Anxiety. One-way ANOVA tests were made for the three outcome variables Dependency, Self-criticism and Morbidity symptoms.

5.5.2 Results

The results of the bivariate chi-square and one-way ANOVA tests are given below in Table 5.11 in a similar format to that used in previous tables. Tests by Loglinear and 2-way ANOVA statistics gave no significant interactions between Gender x War variables for any of the mental health outcome variables.

Table 5.11 Outcome variables for mental health as a function of gender, the absence of a father due to war service and of bombing

		WAR						
		Father			Bombing			
		At home	Absent		None	Nearby	Home bombed	
$N_F =$		365	96		147	254	102	
$N_M =$		244	71		91	193	55	

MENTAL HEALTH

				χ^2	Respondent				χ^2
Incidence of Depression									
	Female	38%	37%	0.0	Present	37%	44%	41%	2.6
					Absent	37%	38%	36%	0.2
	Male	22%	26%	0.5	Present	20%	32%	24%	3.0
					Absent	19%a	24%a	45%b	6.9*
						(Figure 5.25)			
Incidence of Clinical Anxiety									
	Female	13%	10%	0.6	Present	11%	17%	11%	1.6
					Absent	11%a	8%a	23%b	8.6*
	Male	8%	8%	0.0	Present	7%	8%	17%	3.1
					Absent	7%a	8%a	25%b	8.5*
						(Figure 5.26)			
Mean score Factor 1 Dependency				F					F
	Female	-0.3	-0.4	0.2	Present	-0.3	-0.3	-0.5	1.2
					Absent	-0.3	-0.4	-0.3	0.5
	Male	-0.7	-0.9	2.2	Present	-0.8	-0.7	-0.7	0.5
					Absent	-0.8	-0.8	-0.5	1.5
Mean score Factor 2 Self-criticism									
	Female	-0.3	-0.3	0.0	Present	-0.2	-0.3	-0.1	0.7
					Absent	-0.2	-0.3	-0.2	0.1
	Male	-0.5	-0.3	1.8	Present	-0.5	-0.3	-0.2	1.5
					Absent	-0.5	-0.4	-0.1	2.4
Mean score Morbidity Symptoms									
	Female	1.8	1.6	0.7	Present	1.6	2.1	1.9	2.2
					Absent	1.6	1.7	1.9	0.7
	Male	0.9	1.0	1.0	Present	0.7	1.0	1.1	1.0
					Absent	0.7	1.0	1.3	2.6

Chi-square tests have been carried out for categorical data and one-way ANOVA tests for interval scores. Significance key: * $p<.05$, ** $p<.01$ and *** $p<.001$; all two-tailed. Significance in the chi-square tests was followed by bivariate tests, so that percentage values marked by different superscripts are significantly different at $p<.05$.

These test results will be examined by looking first at the effect of father's temporary absence on each of the five mental health outcome variables and this will be followed by a similar examination of the long term effect of enemy bombing, dependent on whether the respondent was at home or evacuated at the time of the attacks.

5.5.2.1 Absence of Father

Examination of the percentage values and mean scores for the five mental health outcome variables given in Table 5.11 show that there are no significant effects due to the temporary absence of a father for the major part of the war. For male respondents only there was a trend for the mean scores of Dependency to decrease and for those of Self-criticism to increase with absence of a father.

5.5.2.2 Effect of Bombing

Examination of Table 5.11 shows that there are three significant test results and that in each case they apply to respondents who were *absent*, i.e. evacuated, rather than being present during the bombing of their homes or home neighbourhoods. The first listed is for the Incidence of Depression for males ($\chi^2(2) = 6.9$, $p<.05$), and the other two are for the Incidence of Clinical Anxiety for both female and male respondents ($\chi^2(2) = 8.6$, $p<.05$ and $\chi^2(2) = 8.5$, $p<.05$ respectively). These three significant test results are illustrated in Figures 5.25 and 5.26.

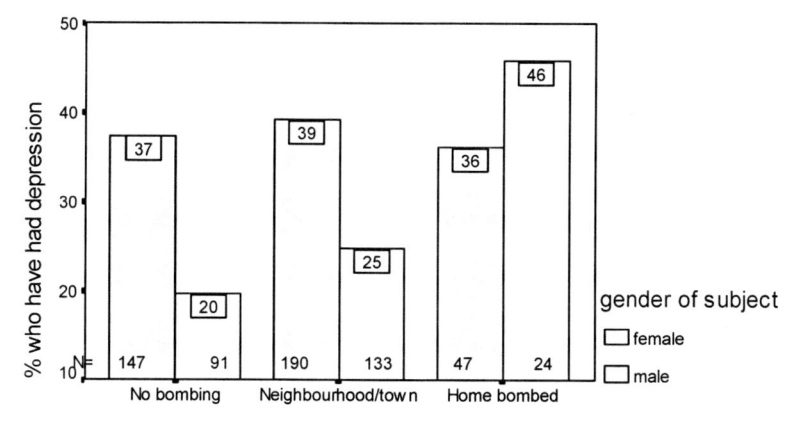

Figure 5.25 Incidence of Depression as a function of the Bombing of home or neighbourhood while the respondent was away from home.

Figure 5.26 Incidence of Clinical Anxiety as a function of the Bombing of home or neighbourhood while the respondent was away from home.

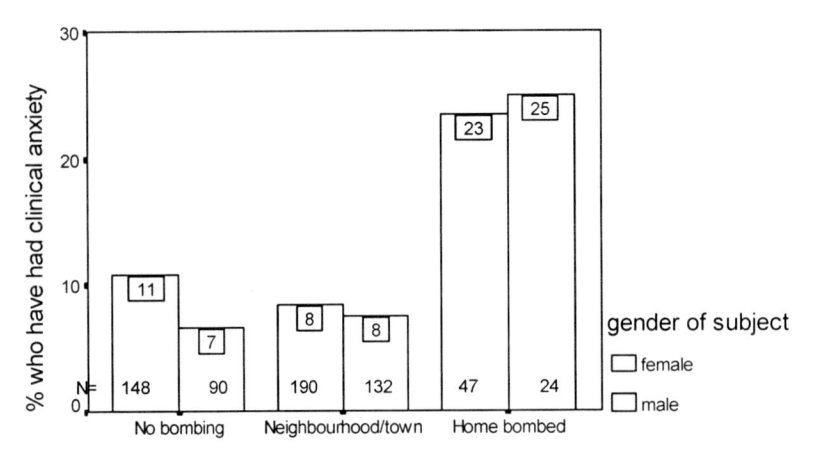

Figure 5.25 shows the high and unvarying level of depression for females, in contrast to an increase in the incidence of depression for males, starting from a lower level, as the danger to their home and family had increased. By contrast Figure 5.26 shows a different gender pattern for the onset of clinical anxiety. Both sexes respond in a similar way, with a sharp rise in the incidence of clinical anxiety associated with the bombing of family homes in their absence.

5.5.3 Summary

The conclusions from these results are summarised below and will be discussed in the following section.

Table 5.12 Summary of the results for the long term effect of fathers' absence due to the war and of bombing

1. There were no significant effects on the measured mental health variables due to the absence of fathers on war service, although there was a male-only trend for the mean scores of Dependency to decrease and for those of Self-criticism to increase with the absence of a father.

2. There were three significant effects of bombing on the measured mental health variables, all three of which were associated with the *absence*, rather than the *presence*, of the respondent in the home at the time of the aerial attacks. The incidence of adult depression increased significantly, for males only, as the danger to the family had increased, and both sexes displayed an increase in the incidence of clinical anxiety in adulthood associated with these events.

5.5.4 Discussion

Looking first at the results for Fathers' presence/absence during the war, there are no significant effects to report for the five mental health variables examined. However there are trends for male respondents to show less Dependency and an increase in Self-criticism if their fathers were away on war service (see Table 5.11). In view of the association between both death of a parent (71% were fathers) and parental divorce on the adult mental health of male respondents discussed in Section 5.3.4 it is not too surprising to find the above trends although in the case of temporary absence the trends were slight. A test was made to determine if there was a 2-way interaction between Fathers' presence/absence and Age at evacuation as a function of the mean score for Self-criticism (Factor 2). The result was not significant ($F(3,260) = 1.7$, $p = 0.16$).

As mentioned earlier, examination of the effects of bombing on mental health, when respondents were either present or absent from home, realised three significant results, all of which related to those who were away from home, i.e. evacuated, at the time. The first showed that there was an association between the bombing of the family home and Incidence of Depression in later life for male respondents. There was no comparable effect for females, and their levels reflected earlier results in this chapter which indicate the high and near-invariant nature of the incidence of female depression generally. The second and third significant results indicated an association between the bombing of the family home and the onset of Clinical anxiety in adulthood for both female and male respondents. There were a total of 17 respondents who reported suffering from such clinical anxiety and 12 of these also reported some form of depression in adulthood. The most common symptoms reported were:

> Sleep disruption
> Severe or long-lasting headaches
> Extreme fatigue
> Severe irritability
> Phobias or irrational fears
> Fear of sickness, injury or death
> Avoidance behaviour
> Feelings of unreality

An examination of their replies suggested these symptoms were usually recurrent throughout adult life, being activated by a wide variety of events including physical health worries and family and marital crises. Initially it may appear surprising that, relatively speaking, bombing of the home environment had a greater effect on the adult mental health of those respondents who were absent from home during the attacks rather than on those who shared the immediate fear and danger with their families. From the comments made by respondents in the questionnaire it does appear that the combined effect of the two components of insecurity, that of being evacuated and that of being absent when the family was in danger has reinforced those feelings of insecurity and loneliness, and fear of loss, and so contributed to poor mental health in adult life.

In conclusion we can say that in statistical and psychological terms being evacuated from home during the enemy bombing campaign had a greater effect than being present with the family during such action. Stephen Davies, a clinical psychologist at the Princess Alexandra Hospital in Harlow, who has treated many affected by the events of World War 2, says that from his caseload he finds that evacuation per se is a greater predictor of poor mental health in adulthood than a personal experience of the blitz (Davies, 1996, 1997).

5.6 Effect of occupational class, educational level and life crises on the mental health of respondents.

Following on through the path diagram shown in Figure 5.1 we are concerned in this section with three life-course variables which may have a direct, or mediating effect on a respondent's mental health in adulthood. These are occupational class, educational level and certain individual or family crises. Each of the five mental health outcome variables used in earlier sections will be evaluated as a function of these three life-course variables.

5.6.1 Analysis

The analysis is based on the categories for the three chosen life-course variables which have been given in Tables 3.2 and 3.3 in Chapter 3. The definition of Occupational Class is that listed by the Office of National Statistics in their *User Guide 6.1, A Simplified list of Social Class based on Occupation (1996)*. Educational level is a dichotomy between those who have or have not, received either a college vocational training or a university degree. Life crisis covers the following events in adulthood,

> Death of a spouse
> Divorce or separation
> Life-threatening illness of self or spouse
> Long-term disability of self or spouse
> Death of a son or daughter.

As before all cases were treated listwise in the computations, with a total of 511 female and 340 male respondents available. Pearson chi-square tests were made separately for each gender as a function of the above categories for the outcome variables Incidence of Depression and Incidence of Clinical Anxiety. One-way ANOVA tests were made for the three outcome variables mean score of Dependency, Self-criticism and Morbidity symptoms.

5.6.2 Results

The results of the bi-variate and univariate tests are given below in Table 5.13 in a similar format to that used in previous tables. Tests by Loglinear and 2-way ANOVA statistics gave significant interactions for Gender x Life Crises as a function of the Incidence of Depression and also for Gender x Occupational class as a function of the Incidence of Depression and of Morbidity symptoms. These interaction results are considered in the relevant sections which follow.

Table 5.13 Outcome variables for mental health as a function of gender, occupational class, education level and life crises

	\multicolumn{6}{c}{LIFE COURSE}					
	\multicolumn{6}{c}{Occupational Class}	\multicolumn{2}{c}{Education Level}		\multicolumn{2}{c}{Life Crises}	
	1	2	3	4	5		Low	High		No	Yes
$N_F =$	6	84	204	181	33		292	110		249	262
$N_M =$	22	134	135	38	10		172	75		228	112

MENTAL HEALTH

Incidence of Depression						χ^2			χ^2			χ^2
Female	33%	36%	44%	39%	33%	2.4	43%	35%	2.4	31%	48%	15.6***
Male	5%a	17%a	34%b	37%b	50%b	20.5***	28%	19%	2.4	17%	45%	30.6***
			(Figure 5.27)								(Figure 5.29)	
Incidence of Clinical Anxiety												
Female	-	11%	14%	9%	9%	3.8	12%	12%	0.0	9%	14%	3.2
Male	4%	8%	10%	13%	10%	1.6	9%	9%	0.0	7%	14%	4.7*
Mean score Factor 1 Dependency						F			F			F
Female	-0.8	-0.4	-0.4	-0.4	-0.2	1.1	-0.3	-0.4	0.9	-0.3	-0.4	0.4
Male	-0.8	-0.8	-0.8	-0.6	-0.7	0.6	-0.7	-0.9	5.6*	-0.8	-0.7	1.4
Mean score Factor 2 Self-criticism												
Female	-0.6	-0.3	-0.2	-0.3	-0.3	0.4	-0.2	-0.2	0.0	-0.4	-0.1	11.4***
Male	-0.6	-0.5	-0.4	-0.2	-0.2	0.8	-0.4	-0.3	1.1	-0.5	-0.2	7.6**
											(Figure 5.30)	
Mean score Morbidity Symptoms												
Female	1.0	1.6	1.8	1.8	1.7	0.9	1.8	1.6	1.6	1.5	2.1	21.3***
Male	0.5a	0.8a	0.9a	1.3a	2.3b	4.4**	1.0	0.9	1.0	0.8	1.3	13.5***
			(Figure 5.28)								(Figure 5.31)	

Chi-square tests have been carried out for this categorical data. Significance key: * p<.05, ** p<.01 and *** p<.001; all two-tailed. Significance in the chi-square tests was followed by bivariate tests: Percentage values and mean scores for each gender marked by different superscripts are significantly different at p<.05.

The effect of each life-course variable on the five mental health outcome variables will now be examined in turn.

5.6.2.1 Occupational Class.

Looking first at the association between Occupational Class and the Incidence of Depression it is clear that the trends in this incidence as a function of class for females and males are different. Whereas incidences are high and fairly constant across class for females, those for males start at a low value of 5% in Class 1 and increase fairly linearly to a high value of 50% in Class 5. This difference in gender characteristics is illustrated in Figure 5.27.

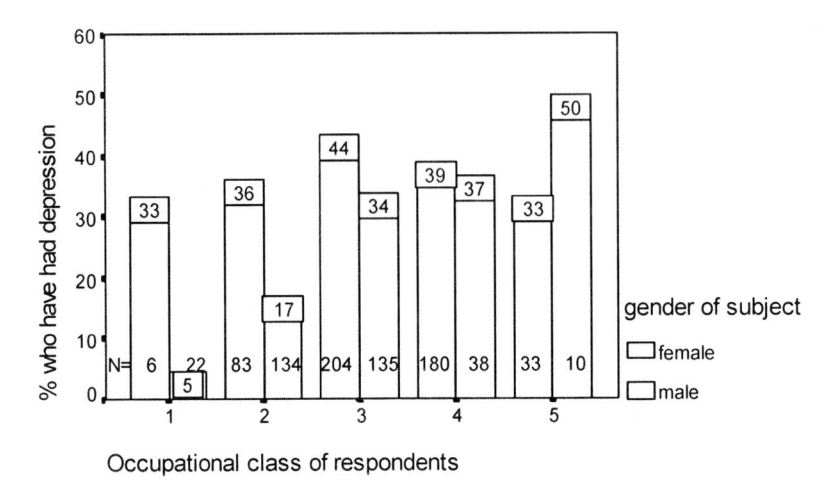

Figure 5.27 Incidence of Depression as a function of the Occupational Class of respondents.

Not surprisingly, the chi-square test values are very different for the two sexes, with no significant difference across class for females ($\chi^2(4) = 2.4$, $p = 0.65$) and a highly significant difference for males ($\chi^2(4) = 20.5$, $p<.001$). Although the cell frequencies in Class 1 and Class 5 are low (see Figure 5.27 for N values) neither gender has more than 20% of expected cell frequencies less than 5, an accepted criterion for contingency tables greater than 2 x 2 in cell numbers (see Chapter 3 - Methodology). For the loglinear analysis Class1 and 2 were pooled because of low female numbers in Class 1 (n=6). The 3-way interaction Gender x Occupational Class x Depression was found to be significant (p=.045).

Incidence levels for Clinical Anxiety with Class are much lower than those for Depression for both sexes, and neither shows any level of significance or clear trends. The mean scores for Dependency and Self-criticism as a function of Class do not show any significant differences for either gender.

Mean scores for the number of Morbidity symptoms as a function of Occupational Class reflect the results for Depression, in that is there is no significant effect for females ($F(4,472) = 0.93$, $p = 0.44$) but there is a significant effect for males ($F(4,313) = 4.4$, $p<.01$). These different gender responses to Occupational class are shown in Figure 5.28, where the high level for males in Class 5 reflects the high Incidence of Depression in the same class in Figure 5.27. The 3-way interaction

Gender x Morbidity symptoms x Occupational Class was found to be significant (F(3,794) = 3.2, p<.05).

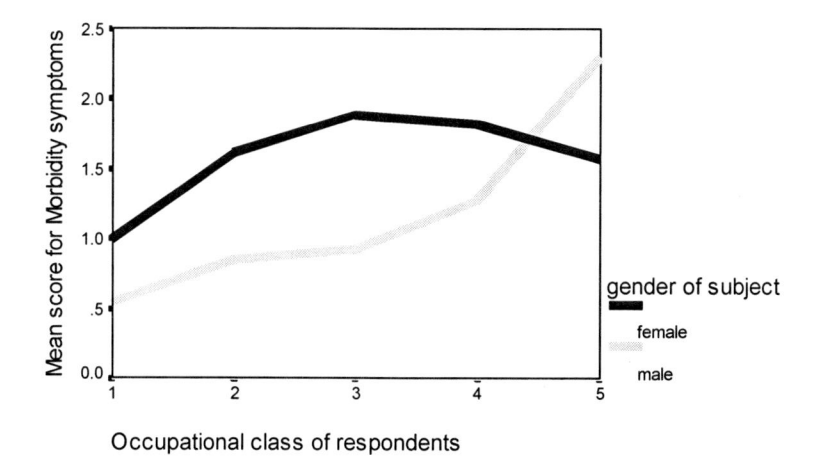

Figure 5.28 Mean score for Morbidity symptoms as a function of the Occupational Class of respondents.

5.6.2.2 Educational level

Both sexes showed a reduction in the Incidence of Depression with a higher level of Education, but neither result quite reached significance. There was no change in the Incidence of Clinical Anxiety with Education level for either sex. There was little effect of Dependency or Self-criticism on Educational level, although a drop in Dependency for males with a higher level of Education was found to be significant (F(1,243) = 5.6, p <.05). There was no significant effect for the mean score for Morbidity symptoms for either sex.

5.6.2.3 Life Crises

Life Crises, as defined in Section 5.6.1, had a very significant effect on the Incidence of Depression for both sexes ($\chi^2(1)$ = 15.6, p<.001 and $\chi^2(1)$ = 30.6, p<.001 for females and males respectively). The rise in incidence was particularly marked for male respondents and the value of the corresponding Pearson chi-square coefficient of 30.6 is noticeably high. This difference in response between the sexes was found to be significant by loglinear analysis (p=.04). These results are illustrated in Figure 5.29.

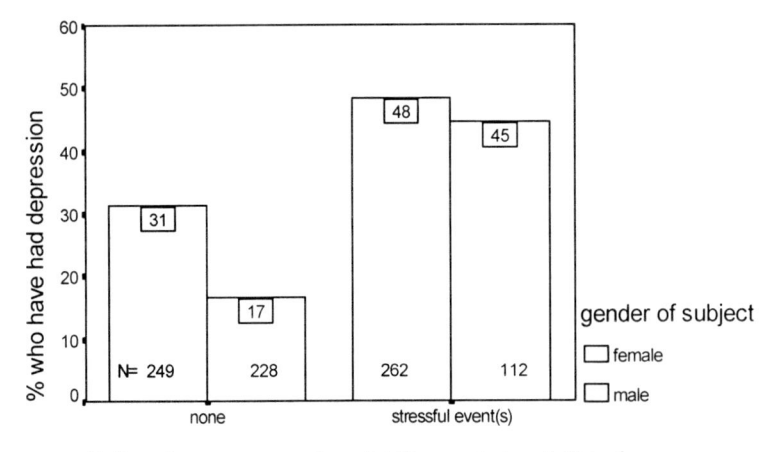

Figure 5.29 Incidence of Depression as a function of a respondent suffering one or more stressful life events in adulthood.

Clinical Anxiety also increased with the occurrence of Life Crises in adulthood; the difference for females lay close to significance, while that for males was significant ($\chi^2(1) = 3.2$, $p = 0.07$ and $\chi^2(1)$ 4.7, $p<.05$, for females and males respectively). There was no interaction between the sexes.

There was no effect due to Dependency, but there were highly significant increases in both the mean scores for Self-criticism and those for the number of Morbidity symptoms for both sexes with the occurrence of Life Crises. These trends, which show no interaction, are illustrated in Figures 5.30 and 5.31 respectively.

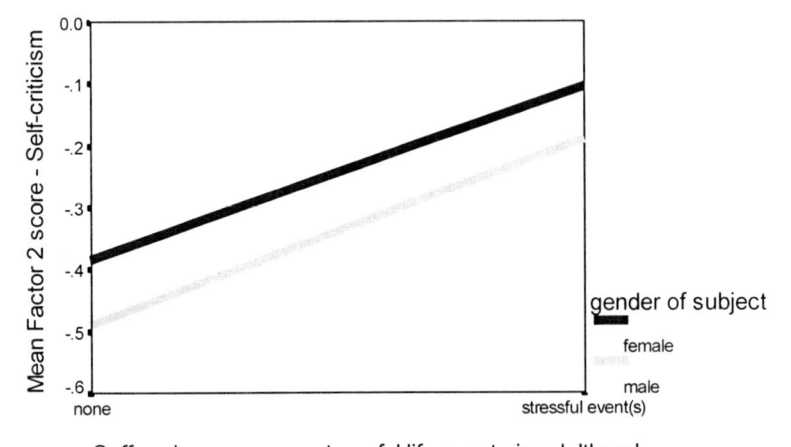

Figure 5.30 Mean score for Self-criticism as a function of a respondent suffering one or more stressful life events in adulthood.

Figure 5.31 Mean score for Morbidity symptoms as a function of a respondent suffering one or more stressful life events.

5.6.3 Summary

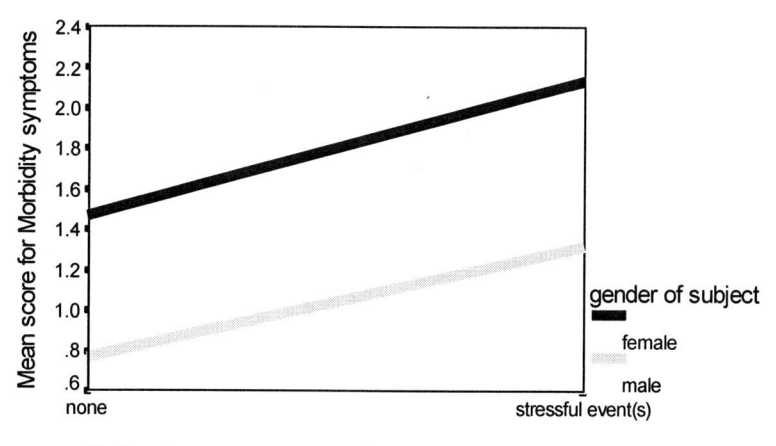

The conclusions from these results are summarised below and will be discussed in the following section.

Table 5.14 Summary of the results for the effect of occupational class, educational level and life crises on the mental health of respondents

---

1. There was found to be a marked difference in the effect of Occupational Class on the Incidence of Depression for the two sexes. The incidence was high (~38%) and with little variation with class for females, whereas incidence levels increased, with significance, from 5% to 50% from Class 1 to Class 5 for males (Figure 5.27). Mean scores for Morbidity symptoms reflected these results for Depression in that there was no significant effect for females but a significant increase from 0.5 to 2.3 in the mean number of symptoms across the Classes for males (see Figure 5.28). There were no significant effects for either the Incidence of Clinical Anxiety or the mean scores of Dependency (Factor 1) or Self-criticism (Factor 2).

2. There was no effect of educational level for the Incidence of Depression or Clinical Anxiety or the mean scores for Self-criticism or Morbidity symptoms. However, Dependency for males reduced significantly with a higher level of Education.

3. The occurrence of any Life Crises had a very significant effect on the Incidence of Depression for both sexes (see Figure 5.29), and the Incidence of Clinical Anxiety also increased, although only that for males reached significance. Dependency was not affected, but both the mean scores for Self-criticism and Morbidity symptoms increased very significantly for both sexes, mirroring the effect on the Incidence of Depression (see Figures 5.30 and 5.31).

5.6.4 Discussion

The results for the effects of Occupational Class on the Incidence of Depression for the two sexes are particularly interesting. The two incidence characteristics across class are very different (see Figure 5.27). Females show high values with modest variation with class (33-44%), whereas males exhibit a low incidence in Classes 1 and 2 (5-17%) rising very significantly to much higher levels in Classes 4 and 5 (37-50%). This difference in the two characteristics is mirrored by the mean scores for the number of Morbidity symptoms as a function of Class.

It is widely accepted that female levels of minor morbidity and depression are significantly higher than for males, particularly for those seen in primary care, and this has been found throughout the results given in this Chapter (see Goldberg and Huxley, 1992). However recent work has suggested the higher incidence of minor morbidity found for females may be largely explained by taking into account occupational grade or class. In an examination of minor morbidity among full-time employees of a British university Emslie et al. (1999) found that, using hierarchical multiple regression analysis, the significant effect of gender on morbidity was eroded when account was taken of occupational grade and working conditions. However, in view of the imbalance in recruitment of the two sexes to the three grades being examined, academic/technical/clerical, the present author believes it would have been better to have analysed the two sexes separately and then to have compared the results. This would have discriminated more clearly between the effects of gender and grade on minor morbidity in the Emslie et al. study. The results given in Figures 5.27 and 5.28 show that for this present sample there is an effect of gender *and* that the characteristics for the effect of class on Depression or Morbidity is very different for the two sexes.

Moving on to the effect of Education level it was found that although there was a reduction in the Incidence of Depression with a higher level this reduction did not reach significance and generally Education level does not appear to be such a clear mediator of mental health as Occupational class for this sample. In fact only Dependency for males shows any significant change with Educational level, all other outcome variables, i.e. Clinical Anxiety, Self-criticism and Morbidity symptoms, do not vary for either sex. This suggests that education is a mediator towards Occupational class, but that personal attributes are equally important.

The occurrence of one or more Life Crises, as defined in Section 5.6.1, does have a very strong effect on the Incidence of Depression and on the mean scores for Self-criticism and Morbidity symptoms for both sexes. The rise in the Incidence of Depression for male respondents is particularly steep, from 17 to 45%, showing that they are equally vulnerable with females to such stressful events in adulthood. The Incidence of Clinical Anxiety does increase for both sexes with the occurrence of Life Crises, but the effect is not so strong as that for the Incidence of Depression. Dependency is not affected, tending to reinforce the concept that this factor is primarily a function of early life. These results reflect the work of Brown and Harris (1978) and other researchers, that loss of a close relationship by death or separation, or the life-threatening illness of someone close has an effect on the mental health of individuals. It is also known that social support is important in mitigating the effects in such cases, but this was not assessed in this present work (see Goldberg and Huxley, 1992; Billings et al., 1983).

5.7 Testing the validity of a model structure linking the major input variables of evacuation and upbringing to the Incidence of Depression.

The computational analysis described in this section is an attempt to integrate the major univariate and bivariate effects on the Incidence of Depression, found in the earlier sections of this chapter, into a structural model. Rather than using a multiple or logistic regression analysis it was decided to employ a Structural Equation Modelling (SEM) approach in which an hypothesised, 2-dimensional, path model can be tested and, hopefully, confirmed. SEM is unique in this respect in that it allows for the inclusion of mediating variables and multiple paths and hence for the estimation of direct, indirect and total structural effects through the model, and also for the estimation of residual error variances. Covariances or correlations between independent variables, including those between residual errors, can also be included. It can also use more generalised estimates which depend on less restrictive assumptions regarding data distribution than the ordinary least squares (OLS) estimates normally available in regression analyses. In Bentler's (1995) version the inclusion of categorical variables is allowed so long as they have a numerical basis. SEM's particular merits and characteristics are described in Section 3.3.2 of Chapter 3 on Methodology which introduces the multivariate statistics employed in the study.

5.7.1 Analysis

The selection of measured variables for the SEM analysis was based on those input and life-course variables which had shown a significant association with Self-criticism, Dependency or the Incidence of Depression from the univariate and bivariate results, and which were deemed to have an underlying numerical base defining the measure. The hypothesised model structure is illustrated in Figure 5.32.

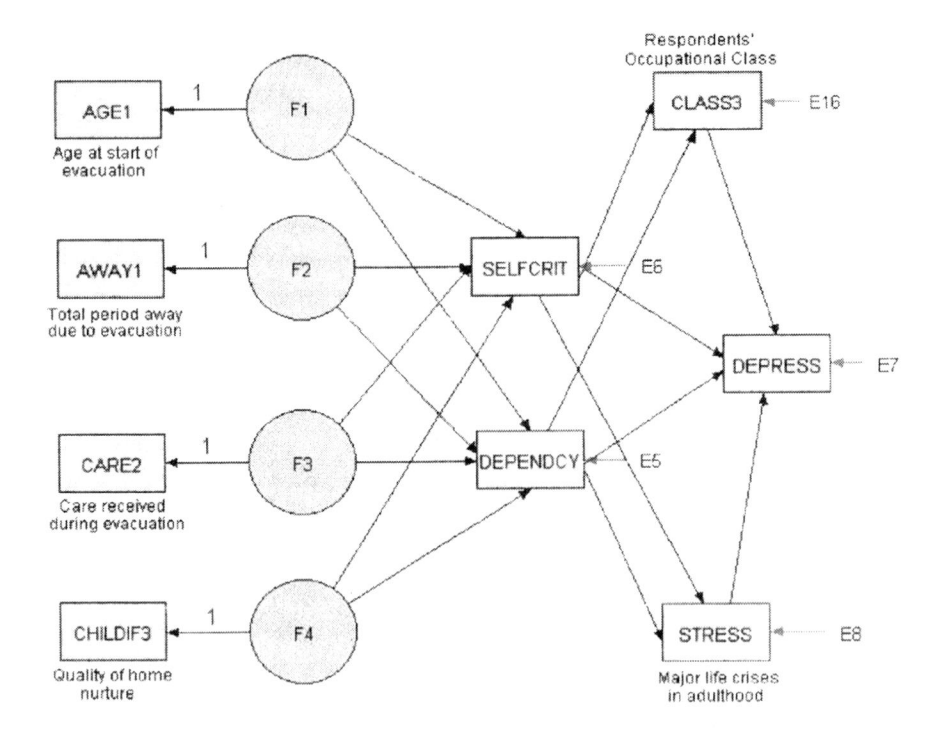

Figure 5.32 Hypothesised path structure to Depression based on the univariate and bivariate results.

It is assumed that the three evacuation-related variables and one upbringing variable on the left of the figure operate through the two measured variables Dependency and Self-criticism of Blatt's DEQ scale. In turn these two variables are assumed to affect the incidence of Depression either directly, or through the mediation of a respondents' Occupational Class or the incidence of Life Crises in adulthood. These input and mediating variables selected for use in this model, and which have been found to have had a major effect on the incidence of depression for one or both sexes, are listed below in Table 5.15. In this table reference is given to the chapter sections in which the relevant univariate results were reported, also the variables' titles or codes used in the analyses and the numerical type of data involved. All variables have been described earlier in Section 3.2.2 of Chapter 3 on Methodology.

Table 5.15. Measured variables selected for use in the SEM analysis

	Chapter Section	Variable Code	Type of data (levels)	Categories
MEASURED VARIABLES				
Age at start of evacuation	5.2	AGE1	Interval	-------------------
Total period away	5.2	AWAY1	Categorical (3)	.1-.9 1-1.9 2-6.9 years
Care received	5.2	CARE2	Categorical (3)	Poor / Mod. / Good
Quality of home nurture	5.3	CHILDIF3	Categorical (2)	Good / Comfortless
Occupational Class	5.6	CLASS3	Assumed Interval*	(Occ. Classes 1 to 5)
Major life crises in adulthood	5.6	STRESS	Categorical (2)	None / One or more life crises
Factor 1, Dependency		DEPENDCY	Interval	-------------------
Factor 2, Self-criticism		SELFCRIT	Interval	-------------------
CRITERION VARIABLE				
Incidence of Depression		DEPRESS	Categorical (2)	None / Suffered depression

*In order to limit the computer memory allocation needed to compute the required polyserial and polychoric coefficients for the categorical variables, it was decided to enter CLASS3 data as interval data rather than categorical (with 5 levels).

From the original univariate and bivariate results it is clear that the two gender samples represented separate populations with significant differences so it was necessary to keep the two data sets separate in the subsequent structural analyses.

In Bentler's notation any variable with at least one path arrow pointing towards it becomes a dependent variable and all others are independent variables, including the residual errors of the dependent variables, labelled 'E' in Figure 5.32. Because any model that includes categorical variables is not permitted to have measured variables as independent variables, any such variables need to be converted to dependent variables and this is accomplished by adding a dummy latent factor to represent each of these variables (Bentler, 1995); hence the latent factors labelled F1-F4 in Figure 5.32, which are independent variables with unity loadings on their respective measured variables. All other measured variables in this model are dependent variables by the 'path arrow' definition.

EQS can only handle complete data sets which have no missing values, so it was necessary to carefully screen the data sets for both sexes and see if any missing values could be recovered from an examination of the relevant questionnaire returns. When this was not possible the particular cases were erased from the set. Some 20 cases were lost in this way. In 12 cases the DEQ scale had not been completed, so rather than lose these cases the mean value of each factor, dependent on the gender, was computed and inserted. After this examination 483 female and 290 male cases remained in the complete data sets for the structural analysis, and only respondents who had been evacuated were included in these totals. With 16 structural coefficients and 5 error variances in the model there are 21 parameters to be estimated, giving ratios of 23:1 and 14:1 between sample sizes and the number of parameters for females and males respectively. Bentler (1993) recommends a minimum of 5:1, and preferably 10:1 or 20:1 for this ratio, if statistical significance tests are to be trusted. With 21 parameters to be estimated and a total of 45 pieces of information in the samples' variance/covariance matrices the models are 'over identified', a necessary criterion for the solution of the simultaneous equations involved, and each has 45-21=24 degrees of freedom.

5.7.2 Results

Evaluation of the model in Figure 5.32 indicated that it was a poor fit to the observed data for both female and male data sets. The goodness of fit index used, as recommended by both Bentler (1995) and Byrne (1994), was the Comparative Fit Index (CFI), which compensates for sample size. It is defined as:

$$CFI = [(\chi_0^2 - df_0) - (\chi_k^2 - df_k)] / (\chi_0^2 - df_0)$$

where χ_0^2 = the chi-square value for the null, or observed model
χ_k^2 = the chi-square value for the hypothesised model
df_0 = degrees of freedom for the null model
df_k = degrees of freedom for the hypothesised model

The CFI has a value lying between 0 and 1, and any value in excess of 0.9 is deemed to indicate an acceptable degree of fit (Bentler, 1992). In the case of both female and male models based on Figure 5.32 the value of the CFI was close to 0.6 and the distribution range of the standardised residuals was unacceptably wide. However, EQS incorporates the Wald test for indicating those free parameters in a model that could be fixed to zero for parsimony without significantly eroding the overall fit (i.e. redundant paths). It also includes the Lagrange Multiplier (LM) test which indicates whether certain fixed parameters such as missing paths or covariances set to zero in the model could, with advantage, be made free parameters and estimated on a future run. The program provides a parameter change statistic that indicates the chi-square value that would be expected if a particular fixed parameter were to be freely estimated. Care has to be taken in using this post hoc test and the rule is that parameters should only be set free, or covariances included, if these modifications are strictly in line with, and contribute to, the theoretical rationale of the model (Mueller, 1996; Kaplan, 1990).

After removing those paths which did not contribute to the overall fit, through the use of the Wald test, and by incorporating paths and covariances which might usefully be freed from zero through the LM test, and which were in accordance with the underlying theoretical hypothesis, modified structural path models for each sex were then computed. The effect of these changes, particularly through freeing certain paths and by allowing the latent factors representing the measured input variables to covary, led to a large change in the CFI index for both sexes, which increased from 0.6 to 0.978 for females and 0.6 to 0.989 for males. These levels of fit between the covariance matrices were achieved after 6 and 8 iterations respectively, with 95% and 100% of the standardised residuals for each model lying in the range -0.1 to +0.1. The resulting two structural path models with their respective standardised structural, or regression, coefficients are given below in Figures 5.33 and 5.34.

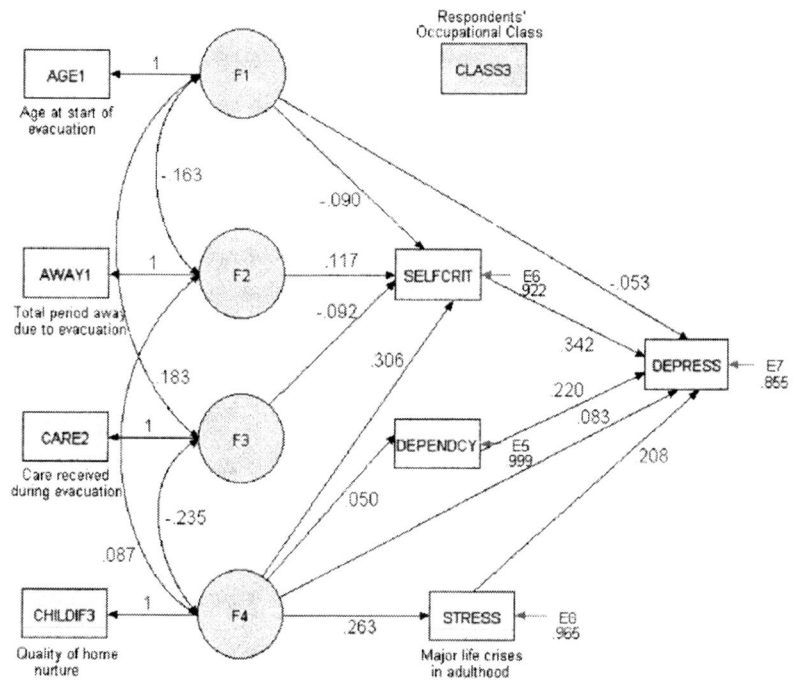

CFI = 0.978

Coefficient of Determination
R^2

DEPRESS = .270
DEPENDCY = .003
SELFCRIT = .150
STRESS = .069

Effect on DEPRESS
Direct   Indirect   Total

AGE1   = -.053 + -.031 = -.084
AWAY1   =   0 + .040 = .040
CARE2   =   0 + -.032 = -.032
CHILDIF3 = .083 + .171 = .254

Figure 5.33 Final structural path model to Depression for females who were evacuated. Standardised coefficients displayed.

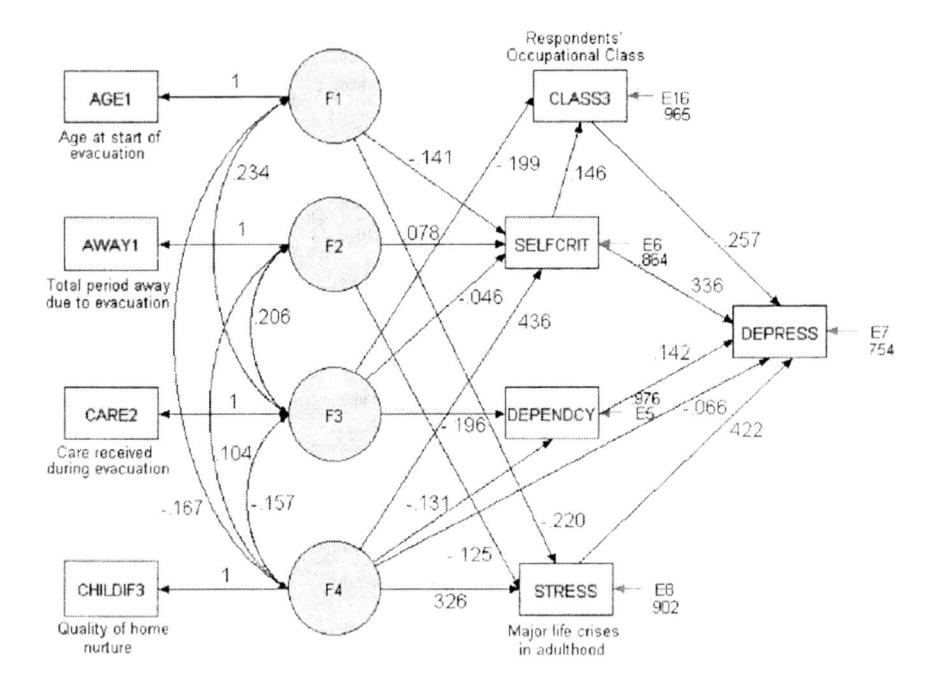

[Figure: Structural path model diagram with latent factors F1–F4 connected to observed variables AGE1, AWAY1, CARE2, CHILDIF3 and outcomes CLASS3, SELFCRIT, DEPENDCY, STRESS, DEPRESS with various standardised path coefficients.]

CFI = 0.989

Coefficient of Determination
R^2

DEPRESS   = .431
DEPENDCY = .047
SELFCRIT = .254
STRESS   = .186
CLASS3   = .069

Effect on DEPRESS
Direct Indirect Total

AGE1   = 0 + -.146 = -.146
AWAY1   = 0 + -.024 = -.024
CARE2   = 0 + -.096 = -.096
CHILDIF3 = -.066 + .282 = .216

Figure 5.34 Final structural path model to Depression for males who were evacuated. Standardised coefficients displayed.

Before discussing these two models in detail the reader is reminded that, unlike the previously reported univariate and bivariate results, the structural coefficients given do not carry any information on the magnitude of either occurences or of means. The SEM analysis employed here does not include the intercept in the regression equations involved so that the standardised coefficients reported in Figures 5.33 or 5.34 are a measure of the association between any predictor, or any mediating variable and the criterion variable connected with them by a particular path. In the same way that a simultaneous multiple regression analysis only gives information on the unique variance contribution of a predictor variable so in this SEM simultaneous equation analysis no information is given on the shared variance contributed by more than one predictor (Tabachnick and Fidell, 1996). These standardised structural coefficients, given next to each path arrow in the figures, can be shown to be equivalent to the simple estimate of the Pearson product-moment correlation coefficient between any two measured variables.

The Coefficient of Determination, R^2, which is a measure of the overall variance of a dependent variable explained by the model, can be calculated from the value of the standardised coefficient, θ_E, printed immediately below each residual error term E in the diagrams and is given by the equation:
$$R^2 = 1 - \theta_E^2$$

These calculated values of R^2 for each of the dependent variables are listed below the path diagrams in Figures 5.33 and 5.34. In addition the Direct, Indirect and Total Effect on the incidence of Depression (DEPRESS) is also listed in this way, for each of the four input variables from childhood. This is a measure of the association or correlation between each of them with DEPRESS via direct and indirect (mediated) paths. A negative sign simply identifies an inverse relationship, i.e. in both figures increasing AGE1 and improving CARE2 reduce the likelihood of depression (DEPRESS).

5.7.2.1 Female structural path model to Depression

The final path model for females shown in Figure 5.33 is noticeably less complex than that for males in Figure 5.34. Given the univariate and bivariate results reported in the previous sections of this chapter this is not surprising; all along it has been evident that females are less affected, in terms of reported mental health, by evacuation and other childhood variables than males. Again, the earlier bivariate results for the effect of Occupational Class in adulthood on Depression are not significant for females, whereas they are highly significant for males (p<.001), and this difference is confirmed by the SEM analysis modelled in the two diagrams; that for females respondents has no significant paths associated with CLASS3 but the model for males does.

In the process of refining the original hypothesised path structure given in Figure 5.32 a number of the paths originally postulated have been removed due to a lack of significance demonstrated by the Wald test so that all the remaining paths, including the covariances, are significant by the appropriate t-test. Most noticeably, apart from the path 'isolation' of CLASS3, there are no paths linking F1, F2 or F3 to Dependency, and no significant mediating paths from SELFCRIT or DEPENDCY to DEPRESS via STRESS. Paths previously fixed to zero, and which from the LM test could, with advantage, be set free are:
1. covariances between F1 and F2, F1 and F3, F2 and F4, and F3 and F4
2. a direct path from AGE1 to DEPRESS
3. a direct path from CHILDIF3 to DEPRESS and
4. a mediating path from CHILDIF3 to DEPRESS via STRESS.

In general terms the final structural model for females given in Figure 5.33 confirms the hypothesis illustrated by the path structure of Figure 5.32. This supports the idea that Blatt's two factors, SELFCRIT and DEPENDCY, are mediators between childhood experiences and the onset of a possible state of depression in adulthood. However, there is one important caveat to this in that with a Coefficient of Determination for DEPENDCY of .003 only a very small part of the variance of DEPENDCY is explained by the existing model, and what there is emanates from CHILDIF3, the quality of nurture received. But from the path linking DEPENDCY to DEPRESS the magnitude of the loading is high, with a standardised coefficient of .220, so the question is where does this effect come from? In Section 5.2.2.1 and Table 5.2 we have shown that whereas Self-criticism scores are a good indicator of Depression for both sexes those for Dependency are a more effective predictor for females than they are for males. So not only are females more prone to high mean levels of Dependency, they are also more vulnerable to these levels. It is suggested in Sections 5.2.2.1 and the discussion in Section 5.2.4 that high Dependency scores may relate more to 'infantile' rather than 'mature' dependency in Fairbairn's terms (Fairbairn, 1952) so it is possible that the missing Dependency variance arises from a naturally higher level of dependency in females, possibly mediated by the experience of early infancy. Related to this is the fact that in this structural model for females CLASS3, respondents' Occupational Class, plays no part and so cannot explain the higher levels of depression suffered by females compared with males (see the discussion on this in Section 5.6.4).

Looking at the model in greater detail we will examine below the standardised covariances and standardised coefficients, starting on the left of the figure and working 'with the path flow' to the right and towards DEPRESS. Standardised covariances are identical to Pearson correlation coefficients. While evaluating the model it should be borne in mind from Section 3.2.2 in Chapter 3 that whereas CARE2, the care received during evacuation, has three categorical levels increasing from 'poor' to 'good', CHILDIF3, the quality of home nurture, has two such levels but they are specified in the reverse sense and go from 'good enough' to 'comfortless' (see also Table 5.15).

Not surprisingly there is a negative correlation between age at the start of evacuation, AGE1, and the total period away due to evacuation, AWAY1, of -.163, and this is in agreement with the plot in Figure 3.1. There is a positive correlation between AGE1 and CARE2, the care received during evacuation, of +.183. This could be due to a number of possibilities:

    1. The greater need of young children for love and care,

    2. The retrospective perceptions of 'care received' changing with the age at which evacuation occurred for respondents,

    3. Poor monitoring of care received by parents who evacuated their children at a young age,

4. The ability of older children to cope better with aspects of poor care.

AWAY1 and CHILDIF3, the quality of home nurture, are positively correlated at a lower level of +.087, suggesting that there is a trend for those evacuated for long periods to come from home environments providing poor nurture. Finally there is a relatively strong negative correlation between CARE2 and CHILDIF3 of -.235, which could be due to:

1. Poor monitoring of the care being received by their children during evacuation by those parents living in a disturbed and comfortless household,

2. A bias in the perception of respondents of the care received during evacuation due to a comfortless upbringing,

3. Response of the foster parents to a child from a disturbed background.

Moving across the model to the loading on SELFCRIT we find that it is affected equally by the three evacuation variables AGE1, AWAY1 and CARE2, but that CHILDIF3 provides a much higher loading of +.306, about equal to the combined loading of the three evacuation related variables. This confirms the relative levels of significance of these variables as a function of self-criticism listed in Table 5.3 and 5.6 of the univariate results. As discussed earlier only CHILDIF3 loads on DEPENDCY at a very modest level of +.050, no other loadings are significant.

Moving further across towards the effects on DEPRESS we find that the largest coefficient is that from SELFCRIT at +.342, followed by levels of +.220 from DEPENDCY and a level of +.208 from STRESS which acts as a mediating variable for CHILDIF3. In addition there are more modest loadings from AGE1 and CHILDIF3 direct to DEPRESS, in the expected sense. The figures given under Effect on DEPRESS in Figure 5.33 for the four input childhood variables show that if both direct and indirect paths are summed then CHILDIF3, with four paths which link to DEPRESS, provides by far the highest loading at +.254. AGE1 is next with both a direct and a mediated path, through SELFCRIT, giving a total effect of -.084. AWAY1 and CARE2 have more modest effects at +.040 and -.032 respectively, both mediated by SELFCRIT. Since the observed, or null, correlation between CHILDIF3 and DEPRESS is +.265 (from the EQS computer output) that from the model of +.254 explains 96% of the correlation between these two measured variables. The remaining 4% is associated with the correlations between CHILDIF3 and the evacuation variables.

As mentioned previously, the very low Coefficient of Determination for the dependent variable (in Bentler's terms) of DEPENDCY of .003 may be compared with that of SELFCRIT at .150. The value of DEPRESS at .270 shows that the model explains about 1/4 of the variance of this measured dependent variable, which is encouraging. A large part of this explained variance emanates indirectly from the quality of home nurture through Self-criticism and through Life crises, with the remainder from an, as yet, undefined source mediated by Dependency.

5.7.2.2 Male structural path model to Depression

The same measured variables were employed for the path model for males, shown in Figure 5.34, and, as mentioned at the start of the previous subsection, the model is noticeably more complex than that for females. This agrees with the univariate and bivariate results where it was found that the majority of childhood variables, including those of evacuation as well as certain mediating variables in adulthood, had a greater significance for males. In this male model CLASS3, respondents' Occupational Class, becomes a significant mediating variable and both AGE1 and AWAY1 load on to STRESS, representing major life crises in adulthood.

The same Wald and Lagrange test criteria were used to arrive at this final path model with a CFI of 0.989 for male respondents, and like that for females it broadly confirms the basic hypothesis illustrated in Figure 5.32 that the DEQ factors SELFCRIT and DEPENDCY act as predictors of depression in adulthood based on certain childhood experiences. Before looking at the path model in detail it is worth pointing out two important differences between the results for the two sexes. The first is the high value for the coefficient of determination for DEPRESS at .431, showing that 43% of the variance of DEPRESS has been accounted for by the male model, a considerably higher figure than that for females at 27%. The second is the finding that, unlike the small positive female loading between CHILDIF3 and DEPENDCY in Figure 5.32 of .050 there is a more significant negative loading of -.131 for male respondents. This confirms the trend in the univariate results shown in Table 5.6 of Section 5.3.2 that, unlike females, male respondents show a *reduction* in dependency as home nurture deteriorates in childhood. Poor care during evacuation, on the other hand, has the opposite effect with dependency increasing significantly as care deteriorates. This is shown by the loading of -.196 between CARE2, or F3, and DEPENDCY, bearing in mind that there is reverse relationship between the category levels of CARE2 and CHILDIF3. This anomalous effect does not influence SELFCRIT, which, as the Lagrange test has demonstrated, has zero correlation with DEPENDCY, as one would expect from the original derivation of the two factors which are orthogonal components of an exploratory factor analysis (Blatt and Zuroff, 1992). In fact CHILDIF3 has a very high positive loading on SELFCRIT of .436 which is in agreement with the highly significant univariate results given in Table 5.6 of Section 5.3.2. As a result we can say that the model suggests that a deterioration in home nurture for males can lead to an independence in relationships and to a high level of self-criticism or low self esteem, i.e. feelings of unworthiness, inferiority, failure and guilt (Blatt and Zuroff, 1992).

When we come to look at the model in greater detail we can see that, compared to the hypothesised model, the paths dropped through the Wald test for significance are those from:

1. SELFCRIT and DEPENDCY to STRESS
2. AGE1 and AWAY1 to DEPENDCY and
3. DEPENDCY to CLASS3.

In addition the Lagrange test has freed the following paths which were previously fixed in the hypothesised model:

1. Covariances between F1 and F3, F1 and F4, F2 and F3, F2 and F4, and F3 and F4
2. A path from CARE2 to CLASS3
3. Paths from AGE1 and AWAY1 to STRESS and
4. A direct path from CHILDIF3 to DEPRESS.

As before, starting from the left of the figure, we will look at the model in greater detail, examining the standardised covariances and structural path coefficients.

A comparison between Figures 5.34 and 5.33 shows that the standardised covariances or correlations between the childhood variables have similarities and some differences. Compared with female respondents:

1. There is no significant correlation between AGE1 and AWAY1 for males
2. There is an additional correlation between AGE1 and CHILDIF3 for males, of -.167
3. There is an additional correlation between AWAY1 and CARE2 for males, of +.206.

Regarding the first difference an examination of the mean total periods away due to evacuation as a function of age show that there was little difference in the mean evacuation period of male children who were first evacuated between the ages of 5 and 13 years, averaging about 2.8 years. However, female children at the youngest ages from 5 to 7 years were, on average, evacuated for 3.3 years, and this declined with age at the start of evacuation. The second difference listed above suggests that male children were more likely to be evacuated at a young age if effective nurture was lacking at home. This correlation was not significant for females. The third difference, a significant positive correlation between AWAY1 and CARE2 of +.206, which is not found in the female sample is of particular interest and suggests that either:

1. Male children were more inclined to be moved to new and better billets by parents if evacuation was found to be poor, or
2. Male children were more effective at drawing their parents' attention to poor care.

Related to this, an examination of the distribution of the samples for the two sexes show that more male respondents reported good care, 60%, as against 48% for females, and that for poor care the difference was 12% versus 19% respectively. This may well be influenced by the different criteria and the different perceptions of the two sexes.

Continuing across the male model path diagram in Figure 5.34, and looking at the way these childhood variables load on to the four mediating variables we find that the main differences from the female path structure and loadings in Figure 5.33 are:

1. All childhood variables load on to SELFCRIT, in the same sense as in Figure 5.33, with CHILDIF3 providing the largest effect at a loading of .436. The coefficient for determination is higher for SELFCRIT at .250 indicating that a significant part of the variance of SELFCRIT is explained by this male model.

2. CARE2 and CHILDIF3 are the two childhood variables that load on to DEPENDCY for males; where poor care received during evacuation increases dependency but comfortless upbringing has the opposite effect. By comparison for females there is no significant path between CARE2 and DEPENDCY in Figure 5.33 and the small loading of .050 between CHILDIF3 and DEPENDCY is in the opposite sense so that a 'comfortless' upbringing tends to increase dependency.

3. AGE1, AWAY1 and CHILDIF3 all load on to STRESS, as a mediating variable to DEPRESS. By comparison only CHILDIF3 does so for females. AGE1 loads in the expected sense, that is those male respondents evacuated at a younger age are more likely to suffer depression through major life crises in adulthood. AWAY1 loads in the contra-intuitive sense; that depression is less likely to be mediated by life crises for those evacuated for longer periods. This may be related to the improved care received by those respondents who ere away for longer periods (see discussion of positive correlation between AWAY1 and CARE2 above). CHILDIF3 loads on to STRESS in the expected sense and is the major predictor of DEPRESS via STRESS.

CLASS3 mediates two paths to DEPRESS, one directly from CARE2 and one via SELFCRIT. So that poor care received during evacuation is associated with a low occupational class in adulthood leading to a greater likelihood of depression. A high level of self-criticism has the same effect. This important influence of Occupational Class for males confirms the previous highly significant bivariate results reported in Table 5.13 of Section 5.6.2.

Finally, all four mediating variables load on to DEPRESS with positive coefficients. There is one, direct, counter-intuitive loading of -.066 from CHILDIF3, which in the multivariate analysis only just reaches significance on a t-test ($t = 2.36$, critical value $t_c = 1.96$). This may be associated with the negative loading through DEPENDCY discussed earlier. From the values for the Coefficient of Determination we find that the structural path model for male respondents explains 43% of the variance of DEPRESS, compared to 27% for females, and that SELFCRIT is the most important mediating variable for depression. Looking at the Total Effect figures also given in Figure 5.34 we can see that AGE1 and CHILDIF3 have the highest association or correlation with DEPRESS. The figure for AGE1 of -.146 being noticeably higher than that for females at -.084, and this confirms the difference in the bivariate results given in Table 5.3 of Section 5.2.2.2.

5.7.3 Summary

The conclusions from the examination of the structural path models for evacuated female and male respondents are summarised below and will be discussed in the following section.

Table 5.16 Summary of an examination of the structural path models to depression for evacuated female and male respondents

---

1. In general terms the final structural path models for the two sexes confirm the original hypothesised model, i.e. that Dependency and Self-criticism, Factors 1 and 2 of the Blatt DEQ scale, act as mediators between childhood experience, including evacuation, and the Incidence of Depression in adulthood. Comparative Fit Indices (CFI) of .978 and .989 for the final female and male models are an indication of the good fit obtained between the covariance matrices for these models and the observed, or null models, for each sex.

2. The structural path model for males is noticeably more complex than that for females and this diversity of loading tends to agree with the univariate and bivariate results reported in earlier sections which show that male respondents are more affected by childhood experiences than females. Furthermore 43% of the variance of the measured variable Incidence of Depression is accounted for by the male structural model, but only 27% of the female variance is explained by the female model.

3. All three evacuation-related variables load on to Self-criticism, i.e. Age at start of evacuation, Period away and Care received, for both sexes, but the largest effect is due to Age at start of evacuation for male respondents. In addition the quality of Nurture loads heavily on to Self-criticism and this applies to both sexes. Only Nurture loads on to Dependency for females, where comfortless Nurture is associated with an increase in Dependency, but this fails to explain the high loading between Dependency and the Incidence of Depression. Less than 1% of the variance of Dependency is accounted for in this way. For males both Care received during evacuation and the Quality of home nurture load on to Dependency, but in opposite senses: Dependency decreases with

improved Care received during evacuation but increases with improved home nurture. This anomalous finding is in agreement with the univariate results (see Tables 5.3 and 5.6).

4. No input or mediating variables load on to Occupational Class for females and there is no significant path from Occupational Class to Depression. But for male respondents good Care received and low levels of Self-criticism are associated with higher Occupational Class and this is associated with a reduced Incidence of Depression. This difference between the sexes in the relevance of Occupational Class to Depression is in agreement with the univariate and bivariate results (see Table 5.13).

5. For males Age at evacuation, Period away and the quality of home Nurture all load on to major Life Crises in adulthood, as a mediating variable to the Incidence of Depression. Only the quality of Nurture does so for females. All such loadings are in the expected direction except for Period away for males which loads in a contra-intuitive sense, i.e. longer values of Period away are associated, through major Life Crises, with a reduction in the Incidence of Depression. Quality of Nurture has the largest effect for both sexes, in that good nurture protects respondents from the possibility of depression as a result of a major life crisis in adulthood, i.e. loss or severe illness of a spouse or near relative, or divorce or separation.

6. The largest total effect on the Incidence of Depression from the four childhood variables, by both direct and indirect paths, is due to the quality of Nurture for both sexes.

5.7.4 Discussion

Within the limitations of a structural path analysis based on a limited number of input variables the models derived for female and male respondents confirm the hypothesis that the two factors Dependency and Self-criticism act as mediating variables between childhood experience and the possible onset of depression in adulthood. In addition the models confirm, and in a 2-dimensional structural format, help to explain the significant associations and trends found in the univariate and bivariate results. In the models the three evacuation related variables, Age at start of evacuation, Total period away and Care received, contributed significantly to the total effect, or loading on the Incidence of Depression, with Age at evacuation being the most important evacuation variable for both sexes. However, the largest total effect on the Incidence of Depression was due to the Quality of home nurture experienced.

Comparison of the structural models for each sex confirmed earlier impressions that male respondents were more affected by childhood events, including evacuation, than females. This was seen from both the relative complexity and loadings of the paths in the male model compared to the female, and the fact that some 43% of the variance of the Incidence of Depression was explained by the male model, as compared with only 27% for females. Again both mediating variables included in the SEM analysis from adulthood, respondents' Occupational Class and the occurrence of Life Crises, were active components in the male model, but only the latter played a significant role for female respondents. The lack of any significant associations in paths to or from Occupational Class for females is of considerable interest, and is contrary to the conclusion of Emslie et al. (1999) who found that occupational grade, rather than gender, explained the major proportion of malaise symptoms observed in their work with bank employees. Concerns over their analysis, in which the scores for the two sexes were not examined separately, have been briefly discussed earlier in Section 5.6.4.

From the original pilot study (Rusby, 1995) for this research it was concluded that evacuation for male respondents could have a beneficial effect, exemplified by the following concepts or themes which arose from an inductive analysis of the tape transcriptions by grounded theory and are listed under the category title 'Gains in development' in the project report (see Rusby, 1995, also Appendix 3):

Confidence   Widened horizons
Independence   Love of countryside
Self-reliance   Love of books
Achieving   Music
Positive gain

These gains in self confidence, and possibly also those concerned with widened horizons and interests, are contingent on the age at which evacuation took place, and this is illustrated by Figure 5.2 in Section 5.2.2.2.1 which shows that if evacuation took place when male respondents were in early or middle adolescence they were less likely to suffer some form of depressive disorder in adulthood compared with those evacuated at a younger age or *who were not evacuated* (controls). This did not apply to female respondents. If the structural path diagram for males in Figure 5.34 is examined, then there are indications of the way some male respondents may have benefited from evacuation in their adult life. With the above age proviso in mind, it would appear that a longer Period away correlates with improved Care received ($\rho = +.206$) and that this in turn leads to low Self-criticism, i.e. higher self-esteem and confidence, and a higher Occupational Class in adulthood (standardised effect coefficients of -.046 and -.199 respectively). In addition a longer Period away leads to some protection from the mediating effect of Life Crises in adulthood on the Incidence of Depression (standardised coefficient = -.125). Not surprisingly, Age at evacuation has an even greater effect in this respect (standardised coefficient = -.220). Related to this tendency is the negative path loading between Care received during evacuation and Dependency (standardised coefficient = -.196) in Figure 5.34, which is also shown by the univariate scores displayed in Figure 5.6; females do not exhibit this association. This demonstrates that good care received during evacuation is associated with reduced dependency, i.e. increased male self-reliance and independence. Most respondents were evacuated to homes in the West Country or in South Wales, and experienced the relative freedom of living in small communities or the countryside, a rather different environment from their more urban and possibly sheltered life at home. So in this sense it is understandable that horizons were broadened and often a love of the countryside was engendered. However the above list of themes from the pilot study, and the analysis of those related perceptions from respondents examined in Chapter 4, do also suggest that separation from the home environment for these male adolescents led to a gain in independence and self-reliance in their adult life. This conclusion, plus the observed reduction in Dependency (always very much lower than the female mean levels anyway, see Table 5.1), might imply a lack of mature adult dependence in Fairbairn's terms (Fairbairn, 1952), possibly leading to a certain emotional detachment and coldness and a need for control and achievement in adulthood. This supposition will be examined in Chapter 7 when we consider Adult Attachment.

Finally we are left with the contribution of Dependency to the Incidence of Depression, particularly for females where the loading is highly significant at +.220 yet less than 1% of the variance of Dependency is explained by the model (Coefficient of Determination = .003). The importance of Dependency as a predictor of depression for females was discussed earlier in Section 5.2.2.1, where it was shown in Table 5.2 that if the individuals who were in both the top quartile of Dependency *and* the lowest quartile of Self-criticism were selected then the Incidence of Depression was >44%. The only path in the model linked to Dependency for females arises from the Quality of home nurture, and for this the loading is only just significant (standardised coefficient = +.050, t = 3.73, t_{crit} = 1.96). So, in a somewhat negative sense, the structural model does not contradict the suggestion that both the higher levels of Dependency in female respondents, and the mediating effect it has on the Incidence of Depression, may arise from an innate characteristic of gender, possibly mediated by the nurture received in early infancy.

5.8 General conclusions regarding mental health

In this final section of the chapter we will comment on the most significant results and draw together the main conclusions from the univariate, bivariate and SEM analyses related to mental health.

Possibly the most surprising finding was that for each mental health dependent variable there was no significant difference in the overall results between those who had, and had not, been evacuated, and that this applied to both sexes. In view of the significant effects which were found when the evacuation experience was examined in detail, particularly in terms of Age at start of evacuation, Care received and Period away, this overall lack of significance was evidently due to the integration of positive (protective) and negative (risk-inducing) effects arising from each respondent's evacuation experience. The belief that evacuation can have both a positive and negative outcome in developmental terms was expressed by those taking part in the pilot study which preceded this research (Rusby, 1995), and these perceptions were confirmed in this study in terms of the Evacuation Experience variables Age at evacuation and Care received through the analysis given in Chapter 4.

A second, equally clear-cut finding was that there was a highly significant gender effect relating to the Incidence of Depression and the mean scores of Dependency and Morbidity symptoms, and that this applied to both evacuated and non-evacuated samples. Female respondents were 1.6 times more likely to report some depressive experience in adulthood than males, and their scores of Dependency and Morbidity symptoms were also much higher. The Incidence of Clinical anxiety and of mean scores of Self-criticism did not exhibit this gender difference. Many workers have found this same gender imbalance in reported cases for depressive illness and these have been effectively summarised by Goldberg & Huxley (1992). Examination of descriptions of respondents' depressive experiences from the questionnaires suggest that the majority of those affected fall into level 4 of the Goldberg & Huxley model, as psychiatric out-patients, and these authors give a female to male ratio of 1.4:1 for all types of mental disorder at this level. Epidemiological data collected from around the world by Weissman & Olfson (1995) demonstrates that this difference does not appear to be culturally dependent. The difference in mean scores of Dependency between the sexes is particularly interesting and evidence has been given in Section 5.2.2.1 that females are more vulnerable, in depressive terms, to high levels of Dependency, and this is confirmed by both the univariate and SEM analyses. These higher levels, and female respondents' vulnerability to them, go some way to explaining the higher incidence of depression found. However, neither the univariate or SEM analyses demonstrate how this high level of Dependency arises. In this study Dependency for females is not significantly affected by Nurture, Age at evacuation, Care received, Period away, Frequency of parental visits, Number of billets, Divorce of parents, Death of a parent, Parental class or Occupational class, which tends to point to a significant innate component. Examination of the items in the DEQ (see Section 5.2.2.1) which load highly on to this factor (Factor 1) suggest that, in terms of Fairbairns' (1952) object-relations theory, the more extreme levels represent 'infantile' rather than 'mature' dependence. No evidence was found from either the univariate or SEM analyses for the suggestion by Emslie et al. (1999) that the significant difference in depressive or morbidity experiences between the sexes can be explained by membership of occupational class. This difference between the sexes, and the suggestion of a significant innate or biological component for women in terms of Dependency, is supported by the work of Reiss et al. (1995) who found from twin studies that the genetic and environmental variance components of separation anxiety were different between the sexes. Females were found to be biologically more affected with an innate variance component of 31-74% whereas men had a near neglible innate variance component of 0-19%.

If we examine the chosen mental health variables as a function of Age at the start of evacuation, Care received and Period away then certain associations emerge. Both Age at the start of evacuation and Care received significantly effect the Incidence of Depression, Clinical Anxiety, Self-criticism and Morbidity symptoms for both sexes in the expected sense, i.e. increasing Age at evacuation and improving Care are associated with a reduction in these outcome measures, while increase in Period away is associated with an increase in Self-criticism. When these results are compared with controls (non-evacuated respondents) then some interesting trends are found. In particular, male respondents evacuated after early adolescence (10-12 years) benefit in a reduced Incidence of Depression, so long as Care received was adequate, whereas females are not affected to the same extent, their levels remaining more constant with Age at the start of evacuation. If we look at the Incidence of Clinical Anxiety as a function of Age at evacuation we find it is more varied for both sexes, and part of this is no doubt due to the smaller case numbers involved, particularly of male respondents. However those evacuated in early childhood (4-6 years) show incidence levels higher than controls, but these drop in latency (7-9 years) below controls and then, for females, rise again in early adolescence and for males in middle adolescence, both above control levels. From these descriptions of the variation of depression and clinical anxiety as a function of evacuation age it can be understood how it is possible for mental health, in the limited way it is considered here, to be independent of the occurrence or non-occurrence of evacuation. The above rise in the Incidence of Clinical Anxiety for females evacuated in early adolescence is mirrored by a sharp and highly significant rise in Self-criticism. Both these results, and possibly the rise for males relating to evacuation one or two years later, may be associated with separation from parents occurring soon after puberty. This suggestion has been discussed in Section 5.2.2.2.2 for the female sample in relation to the work of Erikson (1968), Marcia (1980) and Paikoff & Brooks-Gunn (1991), where the importance of a close and effective parent-child relationship following menarche for the later achievement of a secure identity was emphasised. In Section 5.2.4 quotations are given relating to the quality of the care received during evacuation by this female sample and these are followed by a list of those events in adulthood that those same 24 respondents gave for precipitating their clinical anxiety in adulthood. The former relate to feelings of isolation with no mother or family to go to for reassurance and love. The latter, in adulthood, reflect these same feelings of isolation, rejection and loss. By contrast, the 6 male respondents who reported clinical anxiety and who were evacuated at middle adolescence associated their anxiety more with work stress and concerns over their health.

Good Care received during evacuation provided some protection against poor mental health in adulthood for both sexes, though this was more pronounced for male respondents. It is interesting to note that good Care received is associated with reduced Dependency for males, and this is confirmed by the SEM results, while good nurture at home is associated with a small increase in Dependency. Discussions in Section 5.7.4, based on the SEM results and themes from the pilot study, suggest that evacuation has led to a measure of independence and self-reliance for males which is supported both by this reduction in Dependency and a similar reduction in Self-criticism, i.e. an increase in self-esteem. The SEM analysis shows that one of the outcomes of good care for males in evacuation during adolescence has been to load positively on to the mediating variable Occupational Class in adulthood so that the Incidence of Depression is reduced. However, it is possible that this increase in independence and self-reliance has been achieved at the expense of a loss in primary attachment. This will be examined in Chapter 7 when we consider Adult Attachment.

There is no doubt that the input variable which has the greatest influence on adult mental health for the respondents of both sexes is the quality of home Nurture enjoyed. This significantly effects the Incidence of Depression, Clinical Anxiety and Self-criticism in the univariate and bivariate results and provides the highest loadings towards the Incidence of Depression in the SEM structural path analyses, not directly, but through the mediating variables of Self-criticism and the incidence of major life crises in adulthood. This applies equally to both sexes, and is clearly shown by the Total Effect on Depression listed in the SEM diagrams, where Quality of home nurture has a value of .254 for females and .216 for males, both considerably greater than the equivalent evacuation input variables.

In terms of other variables which relate to upbringing Divorce of parents is associated with an increased Incidence of Depression, particularly for males in adulthood, and this gender difference is also reflected in the mean scores of Self-criticism and of Morbidity symptoms. Death of a parent, where in 71% cases the losses were of fathers, had a significant effect on the Incidence of Depression for males, but not for females. Taken together these results suggest that a large part of the greater effect on male respondents is because both divorce, and also in this case death, led effectively to loss of a father. As discussed in Section 5.3.4 this provides a strong indicator of gender diversity in development through loss of a father and evidence is given for the suggestion that developmental response of males to these two types of loss may be different. This evidence, particularly from an examination of the morbidity symptoms involved, suggests that the long-term effect on mental health associated with parental divorce may be more severe than that due to loss of a father by death. But since most research has involved young females it is difficult to make meaningful comparisons with results from the literature. There is evidence that part of the increased risk of affective disorders, and particularly depression, in later life may be due to the attendant loss of care, or neglect, which may ensue after divorce or loss of a parent rather than the event itself (Birtchnell, 1988; Parker, 1983; Harris, 1988).

If we look at the combined effects of home nurture and the care received during evacuation on adult mental health then the former is a stronger predictor. The effects are additive in terms of a model of 'protection' and 'risk', so that 'good enough' Nurture provided some emotional security during evacuation whereas comfortless Nurture placed respondents at risk. The only interaction determined, which was common to both sexes, involved the mean score for Morbidity symptoms, where good Care received had the effect of reducing the difference in the number of Morbidity symptoms between the two levels of Nurture. Again the high levels of Dependency are in evidence for females, largely unaffected by both the quality of Nurture and the Care received during evacuation, and this is confirmed by the SEM structural model.

Regarding the more direct effects of the war, no evidence was found for a significant effect of fathers' absence due to the war, but there were trends for a reduction in Dependency and an increase in Self-criticism for males only. In view of the effect of divorce and death of a parent on male respondents these trends are not surprising. Of more import was the effect of bombing, where significant increases in the Incidence of Clinical Anxiety occurred for both sexes if their home was bombed in their *absence*. This also applied to the Incidence of Depression, but for male respondents only. No significant effects were found if respondents were at home during the bombing. These results provide some insight into the effect of direct wartime action on the emotional life of children, emphasizing the importance of close family contact during such a time of great danger and potential loss. Absence appears to have internalised the separation anxiety associated with possible parental loss so that it can surface in later life when life course events occur that can be associated with such feelings of personal loss and rejection.

Examination of the life course variables Occupational Class, Education Level and Life Crises as a function of mental health showed up differences in gender. There was a marked difference in the effect of Occupational Class on the Incidence of Depression. The incidence was high with no significant variation with class for females, whereas incidence values increased, with a high level of significance, from 5% to 50% from Class 1 to Class 5 for male respondents; this was also reflected in the mean number of Morbidity symptoms. This difference between the sexes was confirmed by the SEM structural models, with no significant paths present in the female model which related to Occupational Class. As a result no part of the variance of the Incidence of Depression for females can, in this study, be attributed to Occupational Class, contrary to the conclusion of Elmslie et al. (1999). The SEM model for male respondents showed a highly significant path from Care received during evacuation to Occupational Class, indicating that good care is associated with a higher Occupational Class in adulthood leading to a lower probability of Depression. Education Level had surprisingly little effect on mental health, although there were trends in the expected direction for the Incidence of Depression. This suggests that it is not educational level per se that affects mental health, but rather whether it permits entry into a higher occupational class.

The occurrence of Life Crises had a highly significant effect for both sexes on the Incidence of Depression, Self-criticism and the number of Morbidity symptoms; the Incidence of Clinical Anxiety also increased, although only that for males reached significance. These results are in general agreement with those of Brown & Harris (1978) and Brown, Harris & Hepworth (1995), albeit for a rather younger female sample, who found that the type of life events most likely to provoke depression or anxiety were those involving close relationships. In both SEM models Life crises was an important mediating variable between Nurture and the Incidence of Depression, and for males only there were also input paths from both Age at evacuation and Period Away. For Age at evacuation this was in the expected direction, i.e. evacuation at a young age led to a vulnerability to Depression via Life Crises, but the loading for Period Away was counter-intuitive, i.e. for male respondents increased length of time away gave some protection from the effect of life crises in adulthood. The direction of this effect was also found in the bivariate results, but there it was not significant. The SEM male model also gives a clue as to how such an effect can arise: there is a significant level of positive correlation between Care received during evacuation and Period Away, so that separation from home under good care can develop a sense of self-reliance and independence, with the proviso that evacuation did not take place in early childhood. This is in agreement with comments on the positive aspect of evacuation made by male respondents in the questionnaires, and was also apparent from the grounded theory analysis in the pilot study (Rusby, 1995).

Summing up it is clear that there are long-term effects of evacuation in childhood, and that these can be risk-inducing or protective depending on the experience of the individual. If respondents were evacuated at a young age, between 4-6 years, or the care received was poor, then they were likely to be predisposed to poor mental health in adulthood. If they were evacuated at a later age, with good care, then the prognosis was more favourable, and they could even fare better than those who were not evacuated. This particularly applied to male respondents evacuated after early adolescence who were less likely to suffer depression in later life than those who were not evacuated, so long as the care received was moderate or good, and their parents visited at regular intervals, at least twice per year. In general the sexes were found to differ in their response to evacuation. Male respondents were more affected by the chosen input variables, but females were found to have had a higher overall incidence of depression, clinical anxiety and morbidity symptoms. Self-criticism was found to be the major mediating variable to depression for both sexes, but females had higher levels of Dependency and they were more vulnerable to these levels. It was suggested that this vulnerability largely accounted for the difference in the incidence of depression between the sexes. The origin of these high Dependency levels was not explained by the univariate, bivariate or SEM results and the suggestion is made that they may be primarily innate, possibly mediated by the nurture received in infancy or early childhood. There was evidence that evacuation for females at the time of the menarche could lead to a later vulnerability to clinical anxiety and a high level of Self-criticism; unfortunately few respondents enjoyed a sufficiently close relationship with their foster mothers to provide the necessary emotional support and practical guidance at this critical time in their development. In terms of upbringing the quality of home nurture had the largest effect in predisposing both sexes to the incidence of adult depression and clinical anxiety, and male respondents were particularly affected by parental divorce and loss of a parent in childhood, which in the majority of cases was a father. Both the occupational class of respondents in adulthood and the advent of life crises were shown by the SEM analysis to be important mediating variables towards depression. The first variable was only significant for male respondents where a high occupational class was associated with good care during evacuation and a low incidence of depression, and vice versa. The second, the occurrence of life crises in adulthood, was a major factor between the quality of home nurture and the onset of later depression for both sexes.

the overall effect of evacuation and then with the details of the Evacuation Experience: That is Age at evacuation, Care received, Period away, Frequency of parental visits and Number of billets, all as a function of gender. The analysis section which follows describes the dependent, or outcome, variables related to marital history selected for the bivariate statistical tests. Towards the end of the chapter a multiple regression analysis will be undertaken involving those input variables found to have had a significant association with the incidence of divorce.

6.2.1 Analysis

For the statistical tests in this chapter marital history was simply defined by placing respondents into three categories: 1. Married, 2. Divorced and 3. Single. The married category included those who had been widowed, and those who remarried as a result of the death of a spouse, but with no divorce or separation history involved. The Divorced category also covered those who had separated, and those who had experienced multiple divorces or separations. The Single category covered those who did not marry, and by default included any respondents who cohabited. Results were analysed in the same univariate way as in Section 5.2.1 of Chapter 5. Missing cases were treated listwise in the computations, with 518 females and 342 male respondents available, of which 52 and 34 respectively were not evacuated (controls). Pearson chi-square tests were made separately for each gender for the above three marital history variables chosen for analysis. Data were accepted for statistical analysis if they fell within the criteria for categorical tests given in Chapter 3 on the methodology employed. For the table of results which follows the numbers in each category were converted into percentages of each sample.

6.2.2 Results

As in the previous chapter the first results to be considered are those concerned with the overall sample and also the effect of considering evacuees and control samples separately, both as a function of gender. These are listed in Table 6.1 for the three marital history categories considered in this analysis. These results are followed by those in Table 6.2 for the five Evacuation Experience variables of Age at evacuation, Care received, Period away, Frequency of parental visits and Number of billets. In the following subsections each of these variables will be considered separately. It should be remembered that the three marital history percentage values listed relate to the proportion of the total sample within a given category, so that the three percentage values always total 100%.

6.2.2.1 Overall effect of the incidence of evacuation and gender on the outcome variables of marital health

The Incidence of Married, Divorced and Single respondents are given in Table 6.1 as a function of the overall sample in the first column and the split between evacuees and controls in the second respondents increased length of time away gave some protection from the effect of life crises in adulthood. The direction of this effect was also found in the bivariate results, but there it was not significant. The SEM male model also gives a clue as to how such an effect can arise: there is a significant level of positive correlation between Care received during evacuation and Period Away, so that separation from home under good care can develop a sense of self-reliance and independence, with the proviso that evacuation did not take place in early childhood. This is in agreement with comments on the positive aspect of evacuation made by male respondents in the questionnaires, and was also apparent from the grounded theory analysis in the pilot study (Rusby, 1995).

Summing up it is clear that there are long-term effects of evacuation in childhood, and that these can be risk-inducing or protective depending on the experience of the individual. If respondents were evacuated at a young age, between 4-6 years, or the care received was poor, then they were likely to be predisposed to poor mental health in adulthood. If they were evacuated at a later age, with good care, then the prognosis was more favourable, and they could even fare better than those who were not evacuated. This particularly applied to male respondents evacuated after early adolescence who were less likely to suffer depression in later life than those who were not evacuated, so long as the care received was moderate or good, and their parents visited at regular intervals, at least twice per year. In general the sexes were found to differ in their response to evacuation. Male respondents were more affected by the chosen input variables, but females were found to have had a higher overall incidence of depression, clinical anxiety and morbidity symptoms. Self-criticism was found to be the major mediating variable to depression for both sexes, but females had higher levels of Dependency and they were more vulnerable to these levels. It was suggested that this vulnerability largely accounted for the difference in the incidence of depression between the sexes. The origin of these high Dependency levels was not explained by the univariate, bivariate or SEM results and the suggestion is made that they may be primarily innate, possibly mediated by the nurture received in infancy or early childhood. There was evidence that evacuation for females at the time of the menarche could lead to a later vulnerability to clinical anxiety and a high level of Self-criticism; unfortunately few respondents enjoyed a sufficiently close relationship with their foster mothers to provide the necessary emotional support and practical guidance at this critical time in their development. In terms of upbringing the quality of home nurture had the largest effect in predisposing both sexes to the incidence of adult depression and clinical anxiety, and male respondents were particularly affected by parental divorce and loss of a parent in childhood, which in the majority of cases was a father. Both the occupational class of respondents in adulthood and the advent of life crises were shown by the SEM analysis to be important mediating variables towards depression. The first variable was only significant for male respondents where a high occupational class was associated with good care during evacuation and a low incidence of depression, and vice versa. The second, the occurrence of life crises in adulthood, was a major factor between the quality of home nurture and the onset of later depression for both sexes.

The simple hypothesis relating to mental health given at the end of Section 2.3.2 and summarised in Table 3.10 was affirmed by these results: that the prime long-term associations of the evacuation experience with mental health will be due to the age at which evacuation took place and the care received, and that such associations will be mediated by significant life events. Furthermore these results also confirmed the perceptions of respondents that the evacuation experience can rightly be perceived, at one extreme, as a positive gain for development and at the other as an emotional legacy.

Chapter 6. Marital history

6.1 Introduction

In Chapter 5 we have found that there is an association between exposure to risk factors in childhood and the mental health experienced by respondents in adulthood. For some time evidence for this association has been growing and the background research was discussed in Chapter 2, but in addition there is evidence for a similar connection between such risk factors and the subsequent marital history of individuals, which was also discussed in Chapter 2. This is particularly the case for the generational association between parental divorce or separation and the likelihood that any offspring will also experience divorce in adulthood (Amato, 1996; Bumpass et al., 1991; Pope & Mueller, 1976). O'Connor et al.(1999) have examined this connection by obtaining predictive and outcome data from over 8000 mothers with an average age of 28 years. They found by regression analysis that these respondents were significantly more likely to suffer divorce if their own parents had divorced, but also if there had been parental marital conflict or if home care had been poor. Evidence such as this would suggest that the insecurity engendered by the evacuation experience could lead to insecurity in marriage. This is supported by interviews conducted by Lagnebro (1994) with those who had been evacuated from Finland to Sweden in the Second World War where she found evidence for high divorce rates. Serenius (1995) also comments on the prevalence of divorce and separation among those who had been evacuated to Sweden during the war.

This chapter on the marital history of respondents follows the same format used in the preceding chapter, and Figure 6.1, based on Figure 2.1 in Chapter 2, shows the path through life which is being investigated.

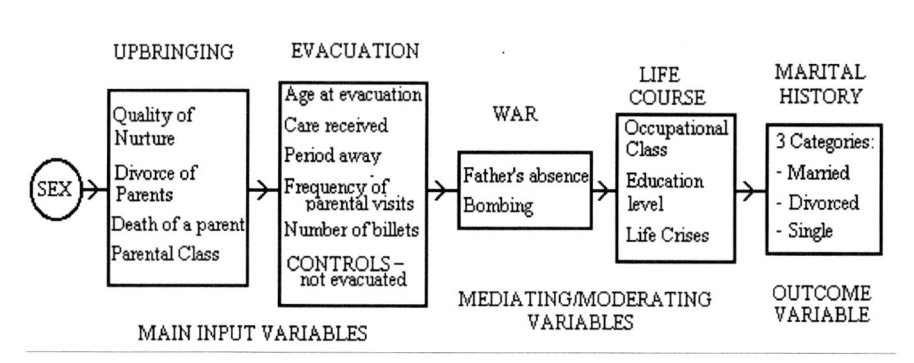

Figure 6.1 Respondent's pathway through life, with the main input and mediating variables and the Marital history outcome variables to be considered in this chapter.

6.2 Long-term effects of evacuation on marital history

Following the same approach as in the previous chapter the initial analysis is first concerned with the overall effect of evacuation and then with the details of the Evacuation Experience: That is Age at evacuation, Care received, Period away, Frequency of parental visits and Number of billets, all as a function of gender. The analysis section which follows describes the dependent, or outcome, variables related to marital history selected for the bivariate statistical tests. Towards the end of the chapter a multiple regression analysis will be undertaken involving those input variables found to have had a significant association with the incidence of divorce.

6.2.1 Analysis

For the statistical tests in this chapter marital history was simply defined by placing respondents into three categories: 1. Married, 2. Divorced and 3. Single. The married category included those who had been widowed, and those who remarried as a result of the death of a spouse, but with no divorce or separation history involved. The Divorced category also covered those who had separated, and those who had experienced multiple divorces or separations. The Single category covered those who did not marry, and by default included any respondents who cohabited. Results were analysed in the same univariate way as in Section 5.2.1 of Chapter 5. Missing cases were treated listwise in the computations, with 518 females and 342 male respondents available, of which 52 and 34 respectively were not evacuated (controls). Pearson chi-square tests were made separately for each gender for the above three marital history variables chosen for analysis. Data were accepted for statistical analysis if they fell within the criteria for categorical tests given in Chapter 3 on the methodology employed. For the table of results which follows the numbers in each category were converted into percentages of each sample.

6.2.2 Results

As in the previous chapter the first results to be considered are those concerned with the overall sample and also the effect of considering evacuees and control samples separately, both as a function of gender. These are listed in Table 6.1 for the three marital history categories considered in this analysis. These results are followed by those in Table 6.2 for the five Evacuation Experience variables of Age at evacuation, Care received, Period away, Frequency of parental visits and Number of billets. In the following subsections each of these variables will be considered separately. It should be remembered that the three marital history percentage values listed relate to the proportion of the total sample within a given category, so that the three percentage values always total 100%.

6.2.2.1 Overall effect of the incidence of evacuation and gender on the outcome variables of marital health

The Incidence of Married, Divorced and Single respondents are given in Table 6.1 as a function of the overall sample in the first column and the split between evacuees and controls in the second column, both as a function of gender. The third column gives the results of loglinear tests for any interaction between the evacuated / non-evacuated conditions and gender for each of the marital history variables. From the second column it can be seen that there is no difference in the percentage incidence of married females between those who were evacuated and those not evacuated at 74%, whereas there is a small difference for males of 81% and 84% respectively. Divorced levels for females are similar between the two samples at 20% and 21% while those for males are lower at 15% and 14%. Males are less likely to be single at 3% and 2% respectively compared to 6% for both female samples.

Table 6.1 Outcome variables for marital history as a function of gender on the overall sample and on the occurrence of evacuation

		Overall by Gender		Evacuated Yes	Evacuated No		Evacuated x Gender
$N_F =$		518		466	52		
$N_M =$		342		308	34		
MARITAL HISTORY			χ^2			χ^2	
Married							
	Female	74%	7.7**	74%	74%	0.0	Not significant
	Male	82%		81%	84%	0.2	
Divorced							
	Female	20%	3.5	20%	21%	0.0	Not significant
	Male	15%		15%	14%	0.1	
Single							
	Female	6%	4.2*	6%	6%	0.0	cells too small
	Male	3%		3%	2%	0.3	

Chi-square tests have been carried out for this categorical data. Significance key: * p<.05, ** p<.01 and *** p<.001; all two-tailed.

Looking at the Overall effect of gender in the first column of Table 6.1 there are two significant differences between the sexes. Females are less likely to have had a stable married relationship and are also more likely to have remained single, although in the latter case the percentages involved are low.

Results listed in the second column of Table 6.1 show no effects for the experience of evacuation taken as a simple dichotomy between those who were and those who were not evacuated. This is surprising but may reflect the similar result for mental health in Table 5.1 where there was also no effect of evacuation taken across the whole sample. No interaction was found for either Evacuated x Gender x Married or for Evacuated x Gender x Divorced tested by loglinear analysis.

6.2.2.2 Outcome variables of Marital history as a function of the Evacuation Experience variables and of Gender

The bivariate results for the outcome variables of Marital History as a function of the selected Evacuation Experience variables and of Gender will now be examined and discussed and these are listed in Table 6.2 (a) and (b) below. Loglinear tests were also made to determine if there were any significant interactions between Gender x Evacuation Experience with any of the Marital history variables. Significant interactions were found for Gender x Age at evacuation with both the outcome variables Married and Divorced and for Gender x Care received with Divorced. These interactions will be discussed under the relevant subsections.

Table 6.2 (a). Outcome variables for Marital history as a function of gender and the three Evacuation Experience variables, Age at evacuation, Care received and Period away

	EVACUATION EXPERIENCE		
	Age at evacuation 4-6 7-9 10-12 13-15	Care received Poor Mod Good	Period away (years) .1-.9 1-1.9 2-6.9
$N_F =$	114 148 136 81	89 159 234	115 92 276
$N_M =$	53 101 86 48	36 83 172	57 65 169

MARITAL HISTORY		χ^2		χ^2		χ^2
Married						
Female	62%^{a} 79%^{b} 77%^{b} 75%^{b}	10.4*	65%^{a} 71%^{ab} 78%^{b}	6.3*	71% 83% 72%	4.8
Male	68%^{a} 78%^{ab} 84%^{b} 98%^{c}	16.0**	86% 78% 82%	1.1	81% 85% 80%	0.6
Divorced						
Female	35%^{a} 17%^{b} 16%^{b} 13%^{b}	19.6***	33%^{a} 20%^{b} 15%^{bc}	12.7**	22% 11% 22%	5.9
Male	30%^{a} 17%^{ab} 13%^{b} 0%^{c} (Figure 6.2)	18.5***	8% 20% 14%	3.3	16% 16% 15%	0.1
Single						
Female	4% 5% 8% 12%	6.9	2% 8% 7%	3.5	8% 7% 6%	0.5
Male	cells too small		cells too small		cells too small	

Chi-square tests have been carried out for this categorical data. Significance key: * p<.05, ** p<.01 and *** p<.001; all two-tailed. Significance on the chi-square tests was followed by bivariate tests; percentage values for each gender marked by different superscripts are significantly different at p<.05.

Table 6.2 (b) Outcome variables for marital history as a function of gender and the Evacuation Experience variables, Frequency of parental visits and Number of billets

EVACUATION EXPERIENCE

	Frequency of parental visits/year					Number of billets		
	0	1	2	3-7	>8	1	2-4	5-15
$N_F =$	69	92	79	178	56	131	260	91
$N_M =$	43	74	49	102	16	78	157	56

MARITAL HISTORY

						χ^2				χ^2
Married										
Female	66%	70%	69%	78%	78%	5.9	77%	73%	71%	1.4
Male	80%	82%	82%	85%	69%	2.8	81%	81%	82%	0.0
Divorced										
Female	31%^{a}	24%^{ab}	24%^{ab}	14%^{b}	15%^{b}	11.8*	17%	21%	20%	0.8
Male	20%	11%	16%	13%	25%	3.7	14%	16%	14%	0.2
Single										
Female	3%	5%	8%	8%	7%	2.2	5%	6%	9%	1.3
Male		cells too small						cells too small		

Chi-square tests have been carried out for this categorical data. Significance key: * p<.05, ** p<.01 and *** p<.001; all two-tailed. Significance on the chi-square tests was followed by bivariate tests; percentage values for each gender marked by different superscripts are significantly different at p<.05.

6.2.2.2.1 Age at evacuation

It is clear from the results listed under Age at evacuation in Table 6.2 (a) that the marital history of respondents is significantly affected by the age at which they were first evacuated. Both sexes show the same general trend, with married percentages increasing with Age at evacuation and Divorced percentages decreasing. Married incidence rises from 62% to 75% for females, and from 68% to 98% for males, with corresponding reductions in the divorce rate from 35% to 13% for females and 30% to 0% for males over the age range. This trend is illustrated for the divorce rates in Figure 6.2, which also shows the levels of divorce for females and male respondents who were not evacuated.

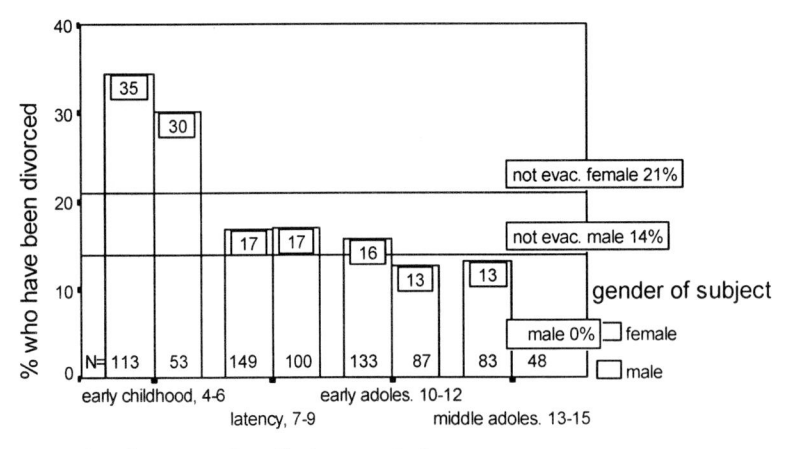

[Chart: % who have been divorced vs Age in years when first evacuated, showing bars with values 35, 30, 17, 17, 16, 13, 13, 0 for female/male across age groups (early childhood 4-6, latency 7-9, early adoles. 10-12, middle adoles. 13-15); N values: 113, 53, 149, 100, 133, 87, 83, 48. Control rates: not evac. female 21%, not evac. male 14%.]

Figure 6.2 Incidence of respondents who have been divorced as a function of their age when first evacuated.

These control rates, at 21% for females and 14% for males, are higher than the equivalent evacuated rates of 13% and 0% respectively for those evacuated in middle adolescence. However only the difference for male respondents reaches statistical significance (Female: $\chi^2(1) = 1.0$, $p = .32$; Male: $\chi^2(1) = 7.1$, $p<.01$). Finally, in Table 6.2 (a) there has been an increase in the number of single female respondents with Age at evacuation which lies close to significance ($\chi^2(3) = 6.9$, $p = .08$). Although this trend is small it is contra-intuitive and may relate to the increase in clinical anxiety and self-criticism found in those evacuated in early adolescence which was discussed in Chapter 5.

6.2.2.2.2 Care received

Looking at the second column in Table 6.2 (a) it is clear that females have been significantly affected by the quality of the Care received during evacuation in terms of their marital history, whereas males have not. Female married rates rise from 65% when Care received is poor to 78% when good ($p<.05$), whereas males show no significant change across the three levels. Divorce rates drop significantly from 33% to 15% for females ($p<.01$), but male differences do not reach significance. Percentages for the single category for females are low and do not reach significance.

6.2.2.2.3 Period away

No results under Period away reached significance, however in Table 6.2(a) an intermediate period away, from 1 year but less than 2 years, nearly reaches significance associated with a lower level of divorce for females at 11% compared with 22% if the period away was shorter or longer ($\chi^2(2) = 5.9$, $p = .06$).

6.2.2.2.4 Frequency of parental visits

Female respondents show a significant drop in divorce rates, from 31% to 15% in Table 6.2 (b), if the Frequency of parental visits increases from zero to greater than 8 visits per year. The equivalent male results are not significant. This again suggests that sustained parental contact was of particular importance to female respondents during evacuation.

6.2.2.2.5 Number of billets

As we found in the last chapter when considering the mental health of respondents there are no significant effects for the Number of billets occupied during evacuation, and no trends.

6.2.3 Summary

The main results for the long-term effects of evacuation on the marital history of respondents are summarised below in Table 6.3 and these will be discussed in the section which follows.

Table 6.3 Summary of the main results for the long-term effects of evacuation on the marital history of respondents

---

1. The age at which evacuation first took place has been found to be significantly associated with the marital history of both sexes. Divorce rates for both sexes fall significantly with increasing age at evacuation (Figure 6.2).

2. The care received during evacuation has been found to be significantly associated with the marital history of female respondents, but male results have not been affected.

3. Female respondents show a significant drop in divorce rates with increasing frequency of parental visits made per year. Male results were not significant.

6.2.4 Discussion

Clearly the age at which respondents were evacuated has been found to have had a highly significant effect on their divorce rates and this applies equally to the sexes. This steady reduction in rates, from 30-35% if evacuated at ages between 4 to 6 years to 0-13% if evacuated between 13-15 years, is reflected in the improvement of mental health found as a function of age at evacuation (see Table 5.3 (a) in Chapter 5). In the case of the male respondents their divorce rates if evacuated in middle adolescence, at age 13-15 years, fall significantly below those who were not evacuated and this suggests a positive outcome of the evacuation experience. Respondents of both sexes who were evacuated in early childhood, between 4-6 years of age, also experienced a much higher rate of multiple divorces than those evacuated at later ages. These rates have been plotted in Figure 6.3 for both sexes, and the differences between those in the youngest category and those in the pooled, three older age ranges are highly significant (Females $\chi^2(1) = 17.1$, $p<.001$; Males $\chi^2(1) = 13.4$, $p<.001$).

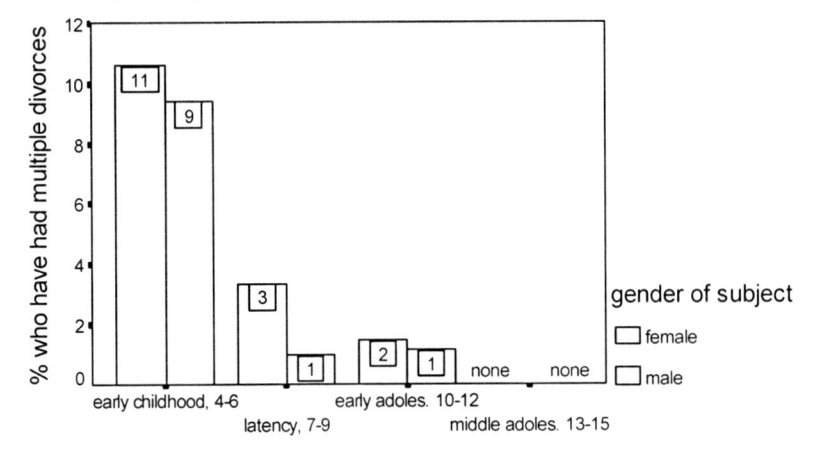

Figure 6.3 Percentage of respondents who have experienced multiple divorces, as a function of age when first evacuated.

Finally regarding the effect of age at evacuation, there is an interesting trend where the incidence of single female respondents increases from 4% to 12% over the age range, but does not quite reach significance. This may be associated with an increase in clinical anxiety and self-criticism found in Chapter 5; anecdotal evidence (Gunn, 1995; Serenius 1995) describes a tendency for women evacuated in later childhood to remain single.

By contrast the quality of the Care received during evacuation has significantly affected the divorce rates of only the female respondents and this may be associated with the high degree of Fearful insecurity shown by females who received poor care. This is discussed in the following chapter on adult attachment where such Fearful insecurity was found to be more highly associated with Divorce rates than the other insecure attachment styles. Of the other three evacuation input variables, Period away, Frequency of parental visits and Number of billets, only Frequency of parental visits had any significant effect, for females only, which led to a reduction in divorce rates with increasing frequency of parental visits. Again it will be shown that this result is associated with a significant reduction in the Fearful category of attachment over the visiting frequency range.

6.3 Long-term effect of upbringing on marital history

Following the same layout as that used in Chapter 5 on mental health we will consider here the effect of the four upbringing variables on the marital history of respondents.

6.3.1 Analysis

The input variables related to upbringing are those used in Chapter 5 on mental health and relate to the quality of nurture, divorce of parents, death of a parent and parental occupational class. The outcome variables employed for marital history are the same as those used in the last section of this present chapter. Results were analysed in the same way as before with a maximum of 508 females and 339 males in the analysis concerned with parental class, but reducing to a minimum of 339 females and 234 males when considering associations with parental divorce.

6.3.2 Results

Bivariate results for the effect of upbringing on the marital history of respondents are given below in Table 6.4. Certain of the cells involved had expected counts below the acceptable limits for chi-square tests given in Chapter 3. No interactions were found using these same limiting criteria for loglinear tests.

Table 6.4 Outcome variables for marital history as a function of gender and four input variables of childhood upbringing

	Nurture			Divorce of parents			Death of parents			Parental Class		
	Good enough	Comfortless		No	Yes		No	Yes		Middle	Working	
$N_F =$	310	55		311	28		310	72		147	361	

MARITAL HISTORY

			χ^2			χ^2			χ^2			χ^2
Married												
Female	79%	67%	4.0*	79%	54%	9.4**	79%	72%	1.6	73%	74%	0.0
Male	83%	68%	3.7	cell too small			83%	78%	0.6	80%	82%	0.2
Divorced												
Female	14%	28%	6.7**	14%	46%	19.8***	14%	24%	4.2*	20%	19%	0.0
Male	13%	32%	7.0**	cell too small			13%	19%	1.1	15%	15%	1.0
		(Figure 6.4)										
Single												
Female	7%	6%	0.2	cell too small			7%	4%	0.4	7%	6%	0.0
Male	cell too small			cell too small			cell too small			5%	3%	0.7

Chi-square tests have been carried out for this categorical data. Significance key: * $p<.05$, ** $p<.01$ and *** $p<.001$; all two-tailed.

The effects associated with each of the above four Upbringing variables will be examined in turn in the following sections.

6.3.2.1 Nurture

The quality of home nurture has a significant association with the marital history of respondents. Divorce rates have been plotted in Figure 6.4 and illustrate how similarly the sexes have been affected by the quality of Nurture as defined in this study, where divorce rates have doubled in value between the two Nurture categories (females $\chi^2(1) = 6.7$, p<.01; males $\chi^2(1) = 7.0$, p<.01). This is very much in line with the conclusions drawn from recent work by O'Connor et al. (1999) and Bifulco and Moran (1998) where the links between divorce and the quality of childhood nurture have been made clear and were discussed in Section 2.3.3 of Chapter 2.

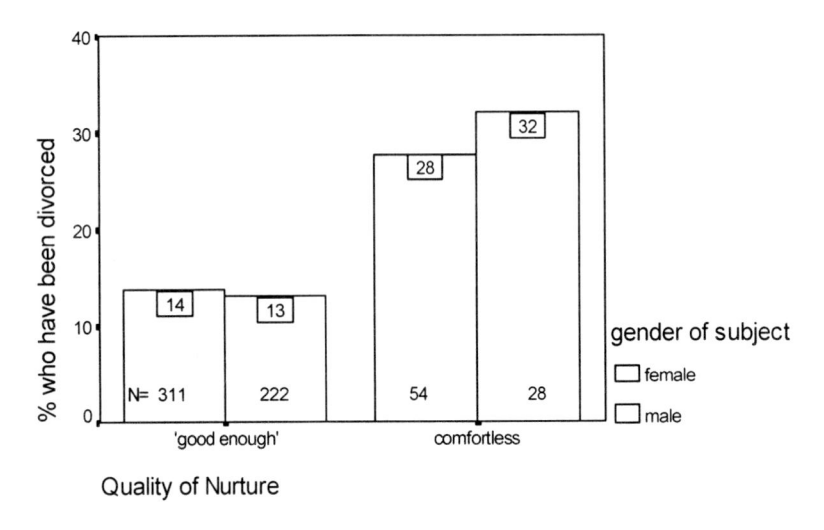

Figure 6.4 Divorce rate of respondents as a function of the quality of nurture received at home.

6.3.2.2 Divorce of parents

Looking at the second column in Table 6.4 we can see that female respondents' incidence of divorce is clearly associated with the divorce of their parents, rising from 14% to 46% ($\chi^2(1) = 19.8$, p<.001). This is also in agreement with the conclusions of recent workers discussed in Section 2.3.3 of Chapter 2. For males one of the expected cell counts is below the acceptable limit of chi-square tests, in both the married and divorced categories, and the counts for both sexes are below the limit in the single category.

6.3.2.3 Death of parents

The only significant result is for females which showed an increase in divorce rate with Death of a parent ($\chi^2(1) = 4.2$, p<.05), but with a less significant association compared to the above result for Divorce of parents, in agreement with the findings of Diekmann & Engelhardt (1999) (see Section 2.3.3). The marital history of male respondents was not associated with loss of a parent which is surprising since 75% of those who died were fathers, and this loss has been shown to have had a very significant effect on the incidence of Depression (see Table 5.6 in Chapter 5). There was no association with loss of a parent for those in the single category.

6.3.2.4 Parental class

There were no effects or trends in the marital history of respondents associated with the occupational class of parents in Table 6.4. This independence was also found for the outcome variables of mental health listed in Table 5.6.

6.3.3 Summary

The results for the long-term effects of upbringing on the marital history of respondents are summarised below in Table 6.5, and these will be discussed in the section which follows.

Table 6.5 Summary of the results for the long-term effects of upbringing on the marital history of respondents

---

1. The divorce rate of both sexes was found to be significantly associated with the quality of nurture provided during respondents' upbringing, with poor nurture associated with a higher divorce rate.

2. Divorce or separation of parents was significantly associated with female respondents rates of divorce, which increased from 14% to 46%.

3. Loss of a parent, through natural causes or by war action, was significantly associated with the rate of divorce of female respondents.

6.3.4 Discussion

Following the work of Bowlby (1988), Rutter (1994), O'Connor et al (1999) and others it is not surprising to find that when respondents recalled comfortless nurture in their home upbringing, as defined in this study, it is associated with the capacity to maintain close and secure relationships in adult life, as evidenced by high levels of marital instability. The increase in divorce rates found for this effect of upbringing was similar for both sexes. By comparison it does appear that the divorce of parents may have had a significant effect only on female respondents. It would have been valuable to have had more reliable evidence of this possible difference, particularly as there is limited reference in the literature to the effect of parental divorce on male offspring. Loss of a parent during childhood, of which 75% were fathers, had a significant effect on female respondents, but a similar trend for males did not reach significance. This is surprising because such a loss had the opposite association with mental health, where it was male respondents which showed a steep increase in depression as a result of parental death. Finally, it is interesting to note that the incidence of divorce is not associated with parental class and that this applies to both the sexes.

Although the background research studies discussed in Section 2.3.2 in Chapter 2 have limited direct relevance to the main interest of this present work, i.e. the effects of temporary childhood separation on marital history, they do underline the difficulty of isolating the mechanisms at work in the intergenerational effect of divorce and relating these to the diversity of family history (Pope & Mueller, 1976; Teachmann, 2002). The results given in this section have confirmed the simple intergenerational effect of divorce for females and in addition have demonstrated an association between the quality of home nurture received and the incidence of divorce which was found to apply to both sexes. The results also give tentative support to the current thinking that parental divorce and parental death have different implications for later psychological adjustment (Dickmann & Engerlhardt, 1999; Teachman, 2002).

6.4 Long-term effect of the quality of home nurture and care received during evacuation on the marital history of respondents

Following the same analysis given in Section 5.4 of the previous chapter on mental health we will determine if the quality of home nurture has moderated the way care received during evacuation affected the marital history of respondents.

6.4.1 Analysis

The input variables of Nurture and Care received are the same as those employed together in Sections 5.4 in Chapter 5 on mental health. The outcome variables are those used in the previous sections for marital history, except that the expected cell sizes for single respondents were below the acceptable limit and so percentage values for this category have not been included in the analysis.

As before all cases were treated listwise in the computations, with a total of 337 female and 208 male respondents available. Pearson chi-square tests were made separately for each gender and Nurture category as a function of Care received for each of the outcome variables, Married and Divorced.

6.4.2 Results

The results listing the percentages in the Married and Divorced marital history categories are presented below in Table 6.6 as a function of Care received for the two levels of Nurture. Those cells with expected counts below the acceptable limit for analysis were not listed. For females there were no interactions found by loglinear analysis between Nurture x Care x Marital History; male results were not tested due to the small cell counts.

Table 6.6 Outcome variables for marital history of respondents as a function of Gender, the Quality of nurture and the Care received during evacuation

		Nurture	Care received poor	moderate	good	
MARITAL HISTORY						χ^2
Married						
	Female	'good enough'	74%	81%	79%	1.0
		comfortless	60%	56%	63%	0.4
	Male	'good enough'	83%	76%	84%	1.9
		comfortless	cells too small			
Divorced						
	Female	'good enough'	26%	12%	13%	6.1*
		comfortless	35%	37%	33%	0.1
			(Figure 6.5)			
	Male	'good enough'	cells too small			
		comfortless	cells too small			

Expected cell counts for the single category were too small for statistical analysis. Chi-square tests have been carried out on the above data. Significance key: * p<.05, ** p<.01 and *** p<.001, all two-tailed.

From Table 6.6 we can see that the only significant result for the Marital history categories as a function of the Care received during evacuation was for the incidence of divorce amongst those female respondents who had received a 'good enough' Nurture. In all other cases for which incidence levels are given the Married or Divorced incidence is not associated with the quality of Care received during evacuation for either level of Nurture. In Figure 6.5 the percentage of those female respondents who have been Divorced has been plotted as a function of Care received for the two levels of Nurture.

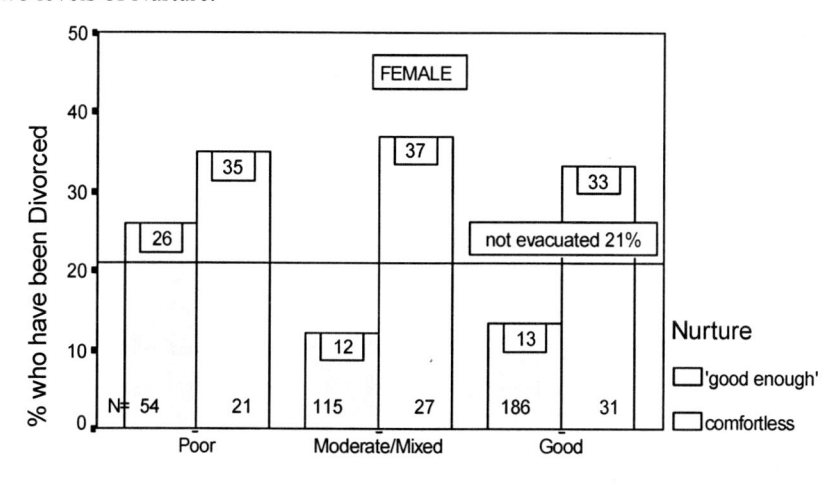

Figure 6.5 Percentage of female respondents who have been divorced as a function of the care received during evacuation for the two levels in the quality of home nurture.

The plot in Figure 6.5 illustrates the significant difference in the way the two Nurture levels have influenced divorce rates of female respondents across the three levels of Care received. Comfortless Nurture is associated with high and near-unvarying rates of divorce at about 35% irrespective of the three levels of care received; while 'good enough' nurture has led to a relatively high incidence of divorce of 26% when Care received was poor followed by low levels of 12-13% when Care received was moderate or good. So any mediating influence on the level of divorce from the quality of Care received during evacuation is only in evidence when home nurture has been 'good enough'. Loglinear analysis on the female sample confirms the effect of Nurture x Divorced ($p<.001$), as listed in Table 6.4, but that there is no equivalent effect of Care received and no interaction between Divorced x Nurture x Care received. The reason that there is an apparent discrepancy between the bivariate result listed in Table 6.6 for the significant difference found in the Divorced incidence for females as a function of Care received for the 'good enough' category and the fact that the loglinear analysis gives no equivalent effect of Care received is because in the loglinear analysis both levels of Nurture have been pooled.

6.4.3 Discussion

From the results for the incidence of divorce for female respondents given in Table 6.6, and the plot in Figure 6.5, it is clear that a secure, caring home background has provided some degree of isolation from the mediating effects of the quality of care received during evacuation. By contrast if home nurture is 'comfortless' then the mean incidence of divorce is nearly doubled and is invariant over the different care levels. In terms of risk and protection there is some similarity here with the results given in Section 5.4 of Chapter 5 when the long-term effects of Upbringing and Care received were examined in terms of mental health.

6.5 Long-term effects of fathers' absence due to war service and of bombing on the marital history of respondents

In this section we will examine whether the absence of a father due to war service, or the aerial bombing of a respondent's home neighbourhood or home may have affected their marital history.

6.5.1 Analysis

Following the procedures used in Section 5.5.1 of Chapter 5, the analysis is based directly on the presence or absence of a father due to war service and on three levels related to bombing:

- no bombing
- town or neighbourhood bombed
- family home bombed (no loss of life or serious injury)

for both the situations when the respondent was present or absent from home.

As before all cases were treated listwise in the computations, with a total of 461 female and 315 male respondents available. Pearson chi-square tests were made separately for each gender as a function of the above categories for the incidence of married, divorced and single respondents, as previously defined in Section 6.2.1.

6.5.2 Results

Results for the effects of the absence of a father on war service and of bombing on the three categories relating to the marital history of respondents are given below in Table 6.7. There were no interactions found for either Gender x Father (at home / absent) or Gender x Bombing with any of the Marital History categories.

Table 6.7 Outcome variables for the marital history of respondents as a function of gender, bombing and the absence of a father due to war service

			Father			WAR		Bombing		
			At home	Absent			None	Nearby	Home bombed	
	$N_F =$		365	96			147	254	102	
	$N_M =$		244	71			91	193	55	
MARITAL HISTORY					χ^2	Respondent				χ^2
Married										
	Female		77%	68%	3.5	Present	72%	74%	66%	1.0
						Absent	73%	78%	69%	2.4
	Male		81%	82%	0.0	Present	87%	82%	83%	0.8
						Absent	87%	80%	72%	3.5
Divorced										
	Female		17%	23%	1.8	Present	23%	15%	28%	2.9
						Absent	23%	15%	22%	3.4
	Male		16%	14%	0.1	Present	9%	15%	14%	1.5
						Absent	9%	18%	24%	5.2
Single										
	Female		6%	9%	1.4	Present	cells too small			
						Absent	5%	6%	8%	0.9
	Male		cell too small			Present	cells too small			
						Absent	cells too small			

Chi-square tests have been carried out on the above data; no results were found to be significantly different at $p<.05$ (two-tail tests).

Examination of the first columns in Table 6.7 show that there are no significant differences in the

Marital history of either sex as a function of Fathers' absence or presence at home during the war years. However, female respondents do show a trend to lower Married rates if a father was absent, falling from 77% to 68%; this reduction is compensated by increases in the Divorced and Single rates.

The results under the variable for Bombing show that there are no significant effects on the marital history of respondents as a function of the degree of aerial attack. There is, however, a trend for male respondents who were *absent* to exhibit an increase in Divorced rates, rising from 9% to 24%, between those whose homes or neighbourhoods were not affected and those whose homes were bombed.

6.5.3 Discussion

It can be seen that there is a trend for the Married rates of female respondents to have been more affected by a father's absence than those for males. By comparison there was no change in the Married rates for males, which at 82% when father was absent, was significantly higher than the equivalent rate of 68% for females ($\chi^2 = 4.1$, $p<.05$).

Under the variable, Bombing, no differences reached significance but there was a trend to increased Divorced rates with bombing severity, particularly for males if they were absent at the time of the action. This trend may be associated with the significant increases in both the incidence of Depression and Clinical Anxiety listed in Table 5.11 of Chapter 5 under the same conditions.

6.6 Relationship between occupational class and education level on the marital history of respondents

In this section, following the same procedure used in the previous two chapters, we will examine the relationship between Occupational Class and Education level on the marital history of respondents. Since the third mediating variable, Life Crises, used in the previous two chapters includes the effect of divorce, it has been omitted from the analysis.

6.6.1 Analysis

Both Occupational Class and Education level were defined in the previous chapter and were used here in the same form for this analysis (see Section 5.6.1). As before all cases were treated listwise in the computations with a total of 508 female and 339 male respondents available. Pearson chi-square bivariate tests were made separately for each gender as a function of the three marital history categories.

6.6.2 Results

The results of the bivariate analysis are given below in Table 6.8 using the same layout as in previous tables. Loglinear tests showed a significant level of interaction for Gender x Educational level with the Single category.

Table 6.8 Outcome variables for the marital history of respondents as a function of gender, Occupational Class and Education level

		LIFE COURSE						
		Occupational Class				Education level		
		1/2	3	4/5		Low	High	
$N_F =$		90	203	215		295	110	
$N_M =$		156	135	48		171	75	

MARITAL HISTORY					χ^2			χ^2
Married								
	Female	67%	74%	77%	3.4	73%	68%	1.0
	Male	80%	86%	75%	3.3	82%	81%	0.0
Divorced								
	Female	19%	17%	22%	2.1	24%	16%	3.0
	Male	17%	13%	17%	1.1	15%	15%	0.0
Single								
	Female	14%[a]	9%[a]	1%[b]	22.2***	2%	15%	24.6***
	Male		cells too small			3%	4%	0.2

Chi-square tests have been carried out on the above data. Significance key: * p<.05, ** p<.01 and *** p<.001; all two-tailed. Significance on the chi-square tests was followed by bivariate tests; percentage values marked by different superscripts are significantly different at p<.05.

Under Occupational Class the only significant result is for the female single category which falls from a high value of 14% in Occupational Class 1/2 down to 1% in Occupational Class 4/5 (p<.001). This is associated with a rising Married trend from 67% to 77% between the same class groups. Male expected cell counts were too small to be included in this analysis.

For Education level a similar situation prevails, where female respondents show a highly significant rise from 2% to 15% in the single status if they have received a higher education (p<.001). There is also a trend to a lower incidence in divorce associated with this rise in the unmarried rates. Male respondents showed no similar trends and incidences in all three categories appeared to be unaffected by the level of educational attainment achieved. This difference between the sexes was found to be significant using Loglinear analysis (p=.049).

6.6.3 Conclusions

The significant rise in female percentages found within the single category for both those in the higher occupational classes and those with a higher education are not unexpected given the generation from which the sample was drawn. In sociological terms it would appear that females with a good education, and so good career prospects, no longer felt the same compulsion to marry early or at all, whilst male respondents remained unaffected by such issues. These results are in agreement with contemporary studies of the decisions made by professional women in terms of marriage and the family (Carp, 1991; Roskies & Carrier, 1994).

6.7 Predicting divorce through multiple regression models

Within the previous sections of this chapter we have found that in terms of bivariate analyses certain input variables related to the evacuation experience and upbringing were significantly associated with the occurence of divorce in the marital history of respondents. However the life course mediating variables concerned with occupational class and educational level were not found to be significantly associated. Because of this it was possible to carry out a simple multiple linear regression analyses, rather than a structural path analysis, to determine if these same variables, under multivariate conditions, continued to predict adult divorce. This form of analysis will also allow comparison with the results of both O'Connor et al (1999) and Amato (1996) described in Section 2.3.3 of Chapter 2.

6.7.1 Analysis

Those variables from the bivariate tests significantly associated with adult divorce were selected for inclusion in the analyses. They were found to be in the Evacuation Experience and Upbringing groups:

> Evacuation Experience:
> - Age when first evacuated
> - Care received during evacuation.
>
> Upbringing:
> - Parental divorce
> - Quality of nurture

Only female respondents were included, some 424 cases, since the number of males whose parents had divorced or separated was low (N=12). Of the selected variables only the data in Age at evacuation was continuous, the other three contained discrete (categorical) data which was converted into continuous data by the polyserial and polychoric procedures in the EQS program (see Bentler, 1995). The EQS programme was also used to run the regression analyses, where the effect of Parental divorce alone was first tested in Model 1; this was followed by adding the second Upbringing variable, Quality of nurture, in Model 2; and finally the two Evacuation variables were included in Model 3.

6.7.2 Results

Table 6.9 below lists the results of the multiple regression analyses for the three models. The figures given are standardised regression coefficients, i.e. semipartial correlation coefficients (Howell, 1992), and are a measure of the magnitude of the unique contribution provided by each component in predicting the incidence of adult divorce. Those figures in brackets give the percentage of the total variance of adult divorce explained by the variables included in each model.

Table 6.9 Multiple linear regression analyses predicting the history of divorce for female respondents

	Model 1	Model 2	Model 3
(Variance explained:	14%	33%	44%)
Upbringing:			
Parental divorce	+ .38	+ .40	+.41
Quality of Nurture		+ .41	+.44
Evacuation experience:			
Age when first evacuated			- .23
Care received during evacuation			- .17

All these results are significant, and the algebraic signs are in the expected direction, i.e. the incidence of adult divorce increases with parental divorce and poor quality of nurture, and it decreases with increasing age at evacuation and improving care received. In terms of these multivariate analyses the largest contributions are made by each of the two upbringing variables, with the two evacuation variables together providing a third, major, component.

It had been expected that the regression coefficient for parental divorce would have reduced in magnitude when the other variables were entered into the analysis, but this has not occurred. Parental divorce remains a unique predictor of adult divorce both when the quality of nurture is included and when the two evacuation experience variables are also incorporated. What has changed is the overall percentage of variance explained, which has increased from 14% for Parental divorce entered alone to 44% when all four variables are included. This last figure is a high value and is an indication that the quality of care and family security provided in childhood can explain nearly half the variance in the occurrence of adult divorce for these respondents.

6.7.3 Discussion

The main reason for carrying out a regression analysis was to provide a comparison with the work of both O'Connor et al. (1999) and Amato (1996). As described in Chapter 2 O'Connor et al. found from a retrospective study of some 8000 women that the accepted generational association between parental divorce and the occurrence of offspring divorce was mediated by the quality of family relations in childhood as well as the age of leaving home and the educational attainment achieved. Using logistic regression analysis they found that the odds ratio linking parental divorce to divorce in adulthood reduced from 1.75 to 1.25 when such family and life course variables were included. Amato conducted a prospective study over a period of 12 years with a mixed gender sample of over 1000 respondents in the United States. He found that, like O'Connor et al, parental divorce was associated with an increased risk of offspring divorce. This effect was mediated by age at marriage, cohabitation and socioeconomic attainment. However he also found that interpersonal behaviour problems mediated the largest share of the association. He believes that these findings suggest that parental divorce elevates the risk of offspring divorce by increasing the likelihood that offspring exhibit behaviours that interfere with the maintenance of mutually rewarding intimate relationships.

Both these studies, with their different approaches, have found that although the occurrence of parental divorce is directly associated with offspring divorce there are also important family and relationship components which contribute to this prediction. In this present study, with its emphasis on the long-term effects of evacuation, we have also found that although the occurrence of parental divorce is a major element in the prediction of divorce in adulthood, nevertheless both the quality of home nurture experienced and respondents' evacuation experience are also important contributors. Taken together these three components explain nearly half of the variance in the measured occurrence of divorce in the marital history of the female respondents (Table 6.9).

6.8 General conclusions regarding marital history

Although we have found that there was no overall effect on the marital history of those respondents who were, or were not, evacuated, nevertheless when the evacuation experience is examined in detail significant differences were found. This is analogous to the form of the results for mental health in Chapter 5 and once again demonstrates the wide range of experience covered by the concept of evacuation which is also reflected in the perceptions of the respondents discussed in Chapter 4.

Examination of the bivariate results showed that the main input variables which affect the marital history of respondents are:

Upbringing:
> Quality of home nurture - both sexes
> Divorce of parents - females only

Evacuation:
> Age at evacuation - both sexes
> Care received during evacuation - predominantly females.
> Frequency of parental visits - females only

For both sexes the occurrence of divorce in adulthood was found to be inversely associated with the age when first evacuated. The strength of this association was further demonstrated by examining the numbers of both sexes who had experienced *multiple* divorces as a function of age at evacuation. Percentages for females and males fell from 11% and 9% if evacuated between 4-6 years of age, to 0% for both sexes if evacuated between 13-15 years of age. In terms of Rutter and Smith's (1995) 'dose-response' test of causality, quoted by Bifulco and Moran (1998) in *Wednesday's Child*, this would seem to point to a cause and an effect. It also supports the evidence of both Serenius (1995) and Lagnebro (1994) given in Chapter 1 in which they recall the effect on the lives of those evacuated from Finland at a very young age. The other evacuation variable of importance was Care received, which was associated with female rates of divorce only. In terms of upbringing the divorce rates of both sexes were associated with the quality of nurture experienced in childhood, and females were also affected by parental divorce, the male sample being too small to test.

In a comparison with the results of both O'Connor et al.(1999) and of Amato (1996) multiple regression analyses found that the above four input variables were also major predictors of the occurrence of divorce for female respondents when considered together in a multivariate model. The contribution of the parental divorce component did not reduce when the other three elements were added, and together the four variables explained nearly half the variance in the divorce rate. Both O'Connor et al. and Amato had found a reduction in the effect of parental divorce when family and life course variables were entered, but are in agreement with the association found here between childhood family conditions and the occurrence of divorce in adulthood.

On the positive side it has been found that a secure and caring home background provided a degree of protection for female respondents from poor care received during evacuation; unfortunately male cell numbers were too small to make a comparison. And for male respondents evacuation in middle adolescence, at 13-15 years, is associated with a sharp reduction in the occurrence of divorce compared with those not evacuated, in fact of the 48 male respondents evacuated in middle adolescence none reported that they had experienced divorce. This may be compared with the similar protection against Depression gained under the same evacuation condition discussed in Chapter 5.

It is clear that a number of the results reported in this chapter point towards a difference between the sexes regarding the influence of the variables on divorce rate. O'Connor et al.(1999) suggest that their results for a female sample are likely to also apply to males, but the above results suggest otherwise and certainly much more work needs to be done on the comparison between the sexes in this respect. Nearly all studies examined used female samples only, and where both sexes were included they were not analysed separately.

Finally, in general terms the simple hypothesis given in Table 3.10 of Chapter 3 that the incidence of divorce for respondents will be associated with the evacuation experience through the age at evacuation, the care received and the degree to which parental attachment is maintained i.e. the frequency of parental visits per year, was affirmed, particularly for female respondents.

Chapter 7. Adult Attachment

7.1 Introduction

In this chapter we will consider the possible effects of the evacuation experience on adult attachment style. The effects of home upbringing, the war and particular life course variables will also be examined, following the same layout as that used in Chapter 5 on mental health.

As discussed in Section 2.3.4 of Chapter 2 recent work has shown that attachment styles from infancy and early childhood maintain a degree of continuity and consistency into later childhood and adolescence, following the early studies of Bowlby (1960, 1969 and 1980) and Ainsworth (1967), and based on the research by Main and Cassidy (1988), Grossman and Grossman (1991), Kobak and Hazan (1991) and others. This has led to the hypothesis that adult attachment patterns are developmental successors of those found in early childhood through the emergence of internal working models and the expectations these bring to the formation of adult interpersonal relationships (Shaver and Hazan, 1993; Rothbard and Shaver, 1991; Feeney and Noller, 1990). However Bowlby (1982) suggested that change in adult life is possible and Rothbard and Shaver (1994) have also concluded that '...attachment styles are not fixed in stone, and seem not to be as stable as genetically-based personality traits; nonetheless they are consistent enough and in some cases dysfunctional enough to warrant both researchers' and clinicians' attention' (p. 65). They also ask the question as to what proportion of the variance in adult attachment can be accounted for by experiences occurring subsequent to the relationship between young children and their primary caregivers? We shall try to throw some retrospective light on that question through respondents' experience of evacuation, which occurred during a formative period in their lives and which for some was internalised as a period of rejection by their parents. It may also be possible to suggest the degree to which a secure early childhood has enabled respondents to come to terms with, and accept, any past feelings of rejection or separation.

The analysis and results sections of this chapter report how the Bartholomew & Horowitz Relationship Questionnaire, described in Section 3.2.2.8 of Chapter 3 on Methodology, has been used to delineate the adult attachment styles of respondents as outcome variables in statistical tests to assess the long- term effects of:

        1. Evacuation
        2. Upbringing
   and 3. certain mediating variables.

The layout of the chapter and the results of the statistical tests are presented in a similar format to Chapter 5 on mental health. Figure 7.1, based on Figure 2.1 in Chapter 2, shows the relevant path through life which is being investigated:

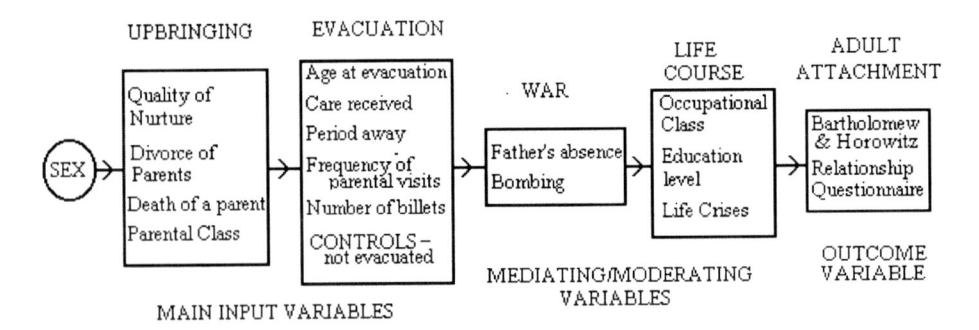

```
UPBRINGING        EVACUATION                         LIFE          ADULT
                                                    COURSE       ATTACHMENT
┌─────────────┐   ┌──────────────────┐              ┌──────────┐  ┌──────────────┐
│Quality of   │   │Age at evacuation │    WAR       │Occupational│  │Bartholomew   │
│Nurture      │   │Care received     │              │Class      │  │& Horowitz    │
│Divorce of   │→  │Period away       │→ ┌─────────┐→│Education  │→ │Relationship  │
│Parents      │   │Frequency of      │  │Father's │  │level      │  │Questionnaire │
│Death of a parent│  parental visits │  │absence  │  │Life Crises│  │              │
│Parental Class│  │Number of billets │  │Bombing  │  └──────────┘  └──────────────┘
└─────────────┘   │CONTROLS –        │  └─────────┘
                  │not evacuated     │                              OUTCOME
                  └──────────────────┘   MEDIATING/MODERATING       VARIABLE
    MAIN INPUT VARIABLES                       VARIABLES
```
(SEX)

Figure 7.1. Respondents' pathway through life, with the main input and mediating variables and the Adult Attachment outcome variable to be considered in this chapter.

7.2 Long-term effects of evacuation on adult attachment

Following the same layout as that used in Chapter 5 on mental health the first input variables to be considered are those associated with evacuation, that is the Overall occurrence/non-occurrence of evacuation followed by the Evacuation Experience variables: Age at evacuation, Care received, Period away, Frequency of parental visits and Number of billets.

7.2.1 Analysis

As discussed in the previous section the measure used in this chapter to assess adult attachment is the Relationship Questionnaire of Bartholomew and Horowitz (1991). The measure consists of four short statements describing the four attachment styles: Secure, Preoccupied, Fearful and Dismissing. Each respondent is asked to rate the degree to which they resemble the four styles on a 7-point scale. These paragraphs can be found in Table 3.8 in Chapter 3 on Methodology. Results for the long-term effects of evacuation were analysed in the same way as in Section 5.2 of Chapter 5. Missing cases were treated listwise in the computations, with 492 female and 320 male respondents available, of which 34 and 52 respectively were not evacuated (controls). Pearson chi-square tests were made separately for each gender for the four attachment categories. Data was accepted for statistical analysis if it fell within the criteria for categorical tests given in Chapter 2 on Methodology.

7.2.2 Results

The first results to be considered, following the layout of Chapter 5, are those concerned with the overall sample, and also the effect of considering evacuees and controls separately, both as a function of gender. These are listed in Table 7.1 for the four adult attachment categories. In terms of secure adult attachment it can be seen from the second column in Table 7.1 that the female percentages rise from 38% to 44% if not evacuated whereas the equivalent male percentages show a considerably larger difference increasing from 39 to 64%. Examination of the three insecure categories shows how these differences between the two sexes and the two conditions have been distributed.

Table 7.1 Outcome variables for adult attachment as a function of gender on the overall sample and the occurrence of evacuation

		Overall by Gender		Evacuated Yes	No		Evacuated x Gender
	$N_F =$	492		440	34		
	$N_M =$	320		286	52		
			χ^2			χ^2	
ATTACHMENT STYLE							
Secure							
	Female	39%	1.1	38%	44%	0.5	Not significant
	Male	42%		39%	64%	11.2***	
Dismissing							
	Female	37%	1.0	38%	35%	0.1	Not significant
	Male	41%		43%	28%	4.1*	
Proccupied							
	Female	8%	1.5	7%	9%	0.1	Not significant
	Male	5%		6%	2%	1.3	
Fearful							
	Female	16%	4.0*	17%	12%	0.5	Not significant
	Male	11%		12%	6%	1.6	

Chi-square tests have been carried out on this categorical data. Significance key: * $p<.05$, ** $p<.01$ and *** $p<.001$; all two-tailed.

7.2.2.1 Overall effect of gender

Looking first at the Overall effect of gender in the first column of Table 7.1 it is clear that only the Fearful attachment category shows a significant difference between the sexes, with a higher percentage of females in that category. While considering these Overall results as a function of gender it is helpful to have in mind the relationships between the four attachment styles and certain of the outcome variables employed in Chapter 5 on mental health as a function of gender. These relationships will now be briefly examined in the following sub-section before continuing with the examination of the results in
Table 7.1, followed by those relating to the details of the evacuation experience.

7.2.2.1.1. On the relationship between adult attachment styles and Depression, Morbidity and DEQ Dependency as a function of gender

If we look at Figure 7.2, where the incidence of depression has been plotted as a function of attachment style, it is clear for both sexes that those in the Preoccupied and Fearful categories are more prone to depression (Female $\chi^2(3) = 35.8$, p<.001; Male $\chi^2(3) = 26.4$, p<.001). It is also relevant to see that the Dismissing, insecure, style, like the Secure category affords a defence against depression.

Figure 7.2 Incidence of Depression as a function of Attachment style.

Also if we look at Figure 7.3, for the mean number of Morbidity symptoms, the same tendencies are found, with the Preoccupied and Fearful categories showing levels about twice those of the Secure and Dismissing categories. Both graph characteristics for each gender in Figure 7.3 are very similar in form with females showing a higher mean number of symptoms (Attachment: Female $F(3,458) = 23.9$, p<.001; Male $F(3,295) = 16.0$, p<.001. Gender: $F(1,753) = 33.1$, p<.001).

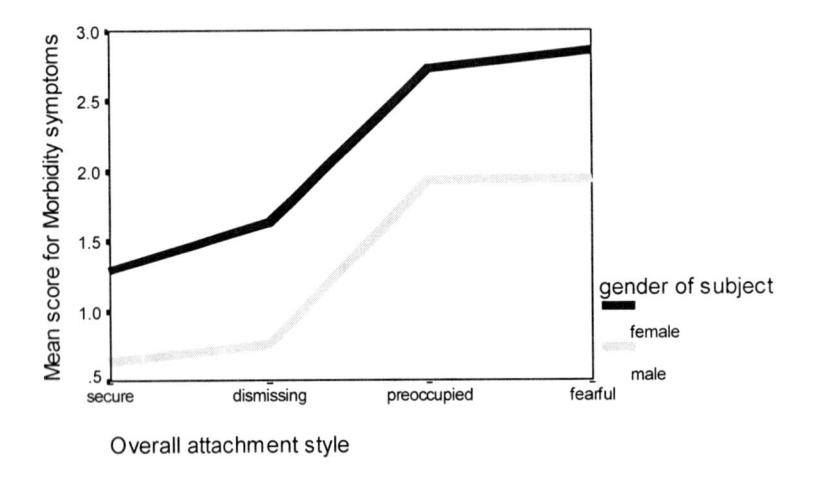

Figure 7.3 Mean score for Morbidity symptoms as a function of Attachment style

Lastly if we also look at the incidence of those who were high in DEQ Dependency (i.e. >0) (see discussion in Section 5.2.2.1 in Chapter 5) it can be seen that in Figure 7.4 those respondents, particularly females, in the Preoccupied and Fearful categories show the highest incidence. The lowest incidence is shown by those in the Dismissive category. Such results support the Bartholomew and Horowitz's model in Figure 3.4 in Chapter 3, where both the Preoccupied and Fearful categories in Cells 2 and 3 are premised to be high on *dependence* and the Secure and Dismissive in cells 1 and 4 to be low (Female: $\chi^2(3) = 37.9$, p<.001; Male: $\chi^2(3) = 16.0$, p<.001).

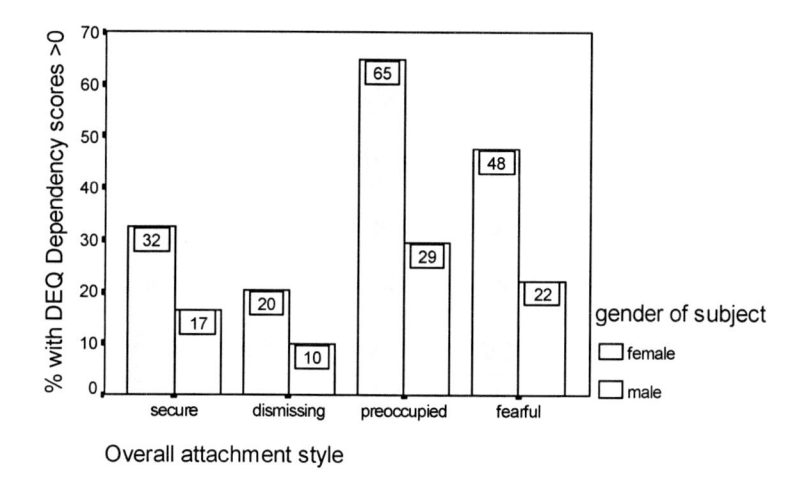

Figure 7.4 Incidence of high DEQ Dependency scores (>0) as a function of Attachment style

All these results, and the correlation existing between Fearful and DEQ Self-criticism (r = 0.43, p<.001), the variable which has been shown to be the prime indicator of depression (see structural path model to Depression, Figure 5.32), emphasize the close relationship between these attachment styles, as defined by Bartholomew and Horowitz (1991), and the mental health of respondents. These relationships should be borne in mind when we come to examine in some detail the effects of the evacuation experience variables on respondents' Adult Attachment in this chapter.

7.2.2.2 Overall effect of evacuation

The results given under the second column title in Table 7.1, between those who were and were not evacuated, show that, overall, male respondents suffered a significant reduction in the percentage in the Secure category on evacuation, from a markedly high level of 64% to 39%, which was largely compensated by a significant increase in the percentages in the Dismissing category. There is also a trend for both sexes to migrate to the Fearful category on evacuation. Figure 7.5(a) and (b) provides a cumulative plot of these percentage counts for both sexes and it can be seen that there is a greater movement between the male samples than there is for the equivalent female samples (Female: $\chi^2(3) = 0.9$, n/s; Male: $\chi^2(3) = 11.5$, p<.01).

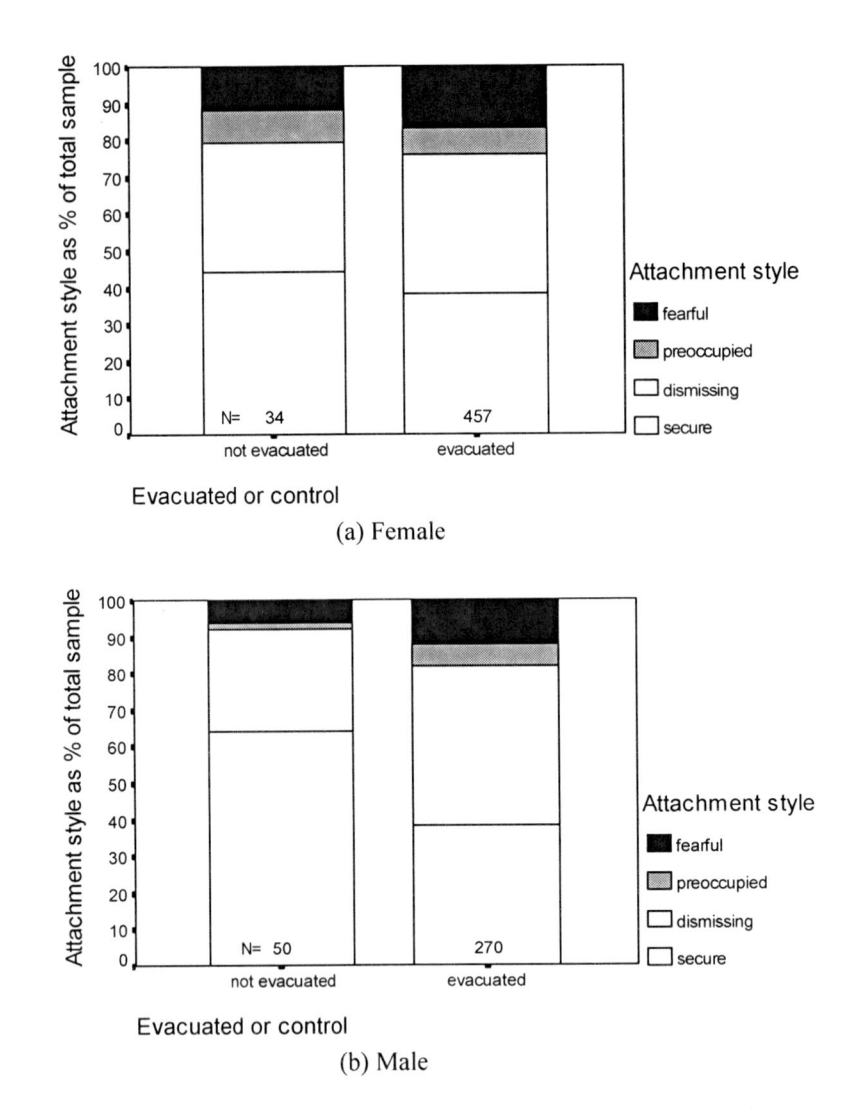

Figure 7.5 Attachment style as a percentage of respondents evacuated or not evacuated.

It should be remembered that here we are considering an overall, or pooled, sample of those who were evacuated without regard to their personal experiences. In the following sections, as in Chapter 5, this overall sample will be broken down and examined as a function of the Evacuation Experience variables listed earlier.

7.2.2.3 Outcome variables of Adult Attachment as a function of the Evacuation Experience variables and of Gender

In the next subsections we will examine the association between respondents' adult attachment style and their experience of evacuation using the selected Evacuation Experience variables. These bivariate results are listed in Table 7.2 (a) and (b). Loglinear analysis indicated significant interactions between Gender x Age at evacuation x Secure and also Gender x Care received x

Preoccupied, these results will be discussed in the relevant subsections.

Table 7.2 (a) Outcome variables for adult attachment as a function of gender and of Age at evacuation, Care received and Period away

EVACUATION EXPERIENCE

	Age at evacuation 4-6 7-9 10-12 13-15	Care received Poor Mod Good	Period away (years) .1-.9 1-1.9 2-6.9
$N_F =$	106 139 127 80	81 156 218	111 89 256
$N_M =$	47 95 78 47	31 76 163	55 60 155

ADULT ATTACHMENT STYLES

		χ^2		χ^2		χ^2
Secure						
Female	27%a 46%b 35%ab 44%b	10.6*	30%a 34%a 45%b	7.8*	44% 35% 37%	2.2
Male	38% 32% 37% 53%.	6.3	32% 38% 40%	0.6	33% 48% 37%	3.4
	(Figure 7.6)		(Figure 7.11)			
Dismissing						
Female	33% 34% 43% 44%	4.4	31% 42% 38%	2.7	40% 39% 36%	0.6
Male	30% 49% 49% 36%.	6.9	35% 39% 47%	2.0	45% 38% 45%	0.8
	(Figure 7.7)					
Preoccupied						
Female	11% 6% 7% 4%	4.2	5% 6% 9%	1.9	6% 9% 8%	0.3
Male	11% 4% 6% 4%	2.6	13% 8% 4%	4.7	cells too small	
Fearful						
Female	28%a 14%b 16%b 9%b	14.8**	35%a 18%b 8%c	30.5***	10% 6% 19%	4.9
Male	21% 15% 8% 6%	7.1	19% 14% 10%	2.7	9% 12% 14%	0.8
	(Figure 7.8)		(Figure 7.12)			

Chi-square tests have been carried out for this categorical data. Significance key: * p<.05, ** p<.01 and *** p<.001; all two-tailed. Significance was followed by bivariate tests; percentage values for each gender marked by different superscripts are significantly different at p<.05.

Table 7.2 (b) Re: Frequency of parental visits and Number of billets

EVACUATION EXPERIENCE

	Frequency of parental visit/year	Number of billets
	0 1 2 3-7 >8	1 2-4 5-15
$N_F =$	66 83 73 170 55	122 247 86
$N_M =$	39 67 47 93 17	77 145 48

ADULT ATTACHMENT STYLE

		χ^2		χ^2
Secure				
Female	39% 33% 37% 41% 42%	2.1	43% 37% 35%	1.5
Male	33% 25% 45% 47% 41%	9.1	31% 43% 35%	3.4
	(Figure 7.13)			
Dismissing				
Female	29% 36% 41% 40% 40%	3.2	34% 38% 41%	0.9
Male	26% 49% 43% 39% 47%	1.9	44% 42% 46%	0.2
Preoccupied				
Female	9% 8% 8% 5% 11%	2.5	8% 8% 6%	0.5
Male	8% 9% 2% 5% 6%	2.5	10% 3% 6%	4.4
Fearful				
Female	23%[a] 23%[a] 14%[b] 14%[b] 7%[b]	9.4*	15% 17% 19%	0.6
Male	15% 16% 11% 9% 6%	3.4	14% 11% 13%	0.5
	(Figure 7.14)			

Chi-square tests have been carried out for this categorical data. Significance key: * p<.05, ** p<.01 and *** p<.001; all two-tailed. Significance was followed by bivariate tests; percentage values for each gender marked by different superscripts are significantly different at p<.05.

7.2.2.3.1 Age at evacuation

Although only the results for female respondents under Age at evacuation show any significant differences, nevertheless most of these results for both sexes were found to lie close to significance in terms of their χ^2 value for attachment categories. The lower values of χ^2 for male respondents having similar percentage trends to females is mainly due to the reduced power in the statistical analysis since there are 267 males to 452 females in the evacuated sample.

Looking first at the Secure results, which have been plotted in Figure 7.6, it can be seen that those females evacuated in early childhood had the lowest incidence of Secure respondents at 27%, rising to 46% if evacuated in latency, falling to 35% in early adolescence and rising again to 44% in middle adolescence, equal to the control, or non-evacuated value. The fall in early adolescence may well reflect the results in Chapter 5 on mental health where a significant increase in Clinical anxiety and Self-criticism was found in this age group (see Table 5.3) and which was discussed in Sections 5.2.2.2.2 and 5.2.4. The incidence for male respondents is at a minimum for those evacuated in latency at 32% and rises to 53% in middle adolescence. It is of interest to see that this last value does not reach the level of 64% for those not evacuated. Also the mean incidence level for those evacuated in early childhood, latency and early adolescence is 35%, only about half the value of those who remained at home, a highly significant difference ($\chi^2(1) = 14.2$, p<.001). These differences between the sexes are significant by Loglinear analysis (p=.047).

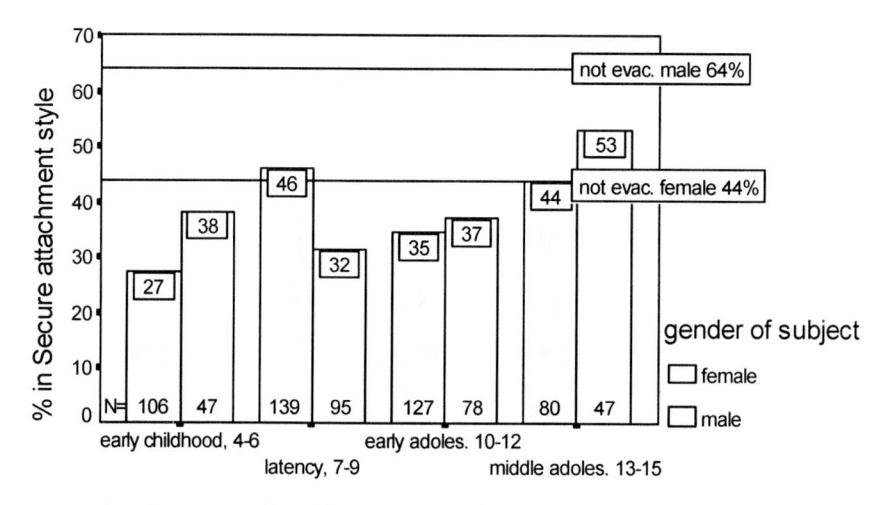

Figure 7.6 Incidence of Secure adult attachment category as a function of Age when first evacuated.

Although the difference in the Dismissing values for Age at evacuation do not reach significance, those for male respondents do lie close to significance ($\chi^2(3) = 7.1$, p = .07) and both sets of values have been plotted in Figure 7.7 to show the trends. Male respondents show slightly greater changes with age and it would appear that the high levels in the Dismissing category for those males evacuated in latency and early adolescence at 49% are related to the corresponding reduction in the Secure attachment style at these ages and seen in Figure 7.6. This level of 49% is significantly higher than that for non-evacuated controls at 28% ($\chi^2(1) = 7.0$, p<.01).

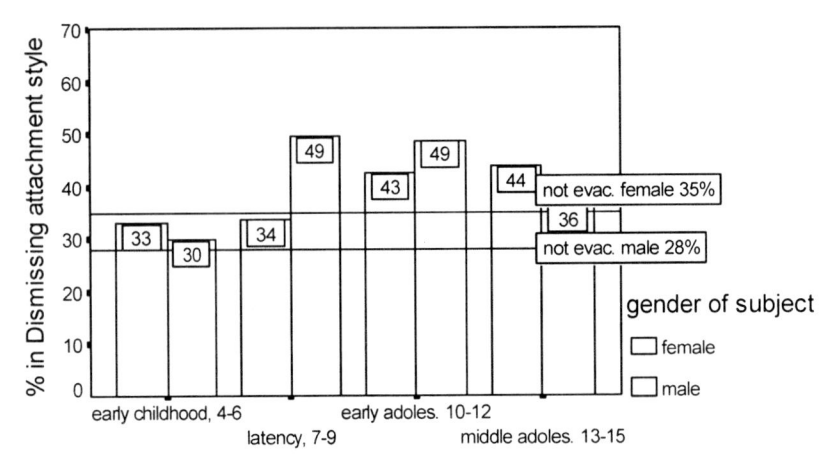

[Bar chart: % in Dismissing attachment style vs Age in years when first evacuated. Values shown: 33, 30 (early childhood, 4-6); 34 (latency, 7-9); 49, 43 (early adoles. 10-12); 49, 44 (middle adoles. 13-15); not evac. female 35%; 36; not evac. male 28%. Legend: gender of subject — female, male.]

Figure 7.7 Incidence of Dismissing adult attachment category as a function of age when first evacuated.

Both sexes exhibit a decrease in the incidence of the Preoccupied category with increasing Age at evacuation, although the respondent numbers are small and the values do not reach significance.

Results for the Fearful category are clear cut, both sexes show a relatively high incidence level if evacuated in early childhood, falling to low values in middle adolescence which lie close to the control levels. These results have been plotted in Figure 7.8. Although the trends for both sexes are comparable, only the differences for female respondents are significant ($\chi^2(3) = 14.8$, $p<.01$); however those for males lie close to significance
($\chi^2(3) = 7.1$, $p = .07$). As mentioned in Section 7.2.2.1.1 the Fearful rating scores have a high correlation with Self-criticism ($r =.43$) which in turn is a major indicator of Depression in the structural path diagrams shown in Figures 5.33 and 5.34.

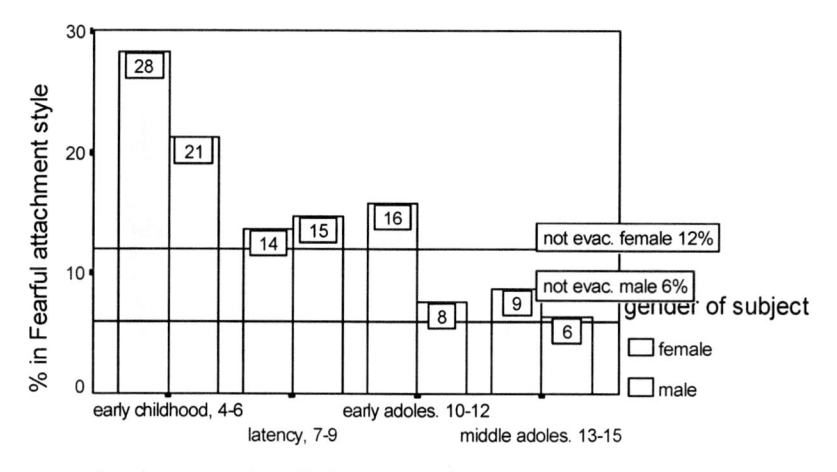

Figure 7.8 Incidence of Fearful adult attachment category as a function of age when first evacuated.

In Figure 7.9 (a) and (b) the percentage incidences for the four adult attachment styles, as a proportion of the total samples, have been plotted as a function of Age at evacuation for each sex. These help to illustrate the proportional changes which have occurred in the attachment categories with Age at evacuation, and which were discussed above.

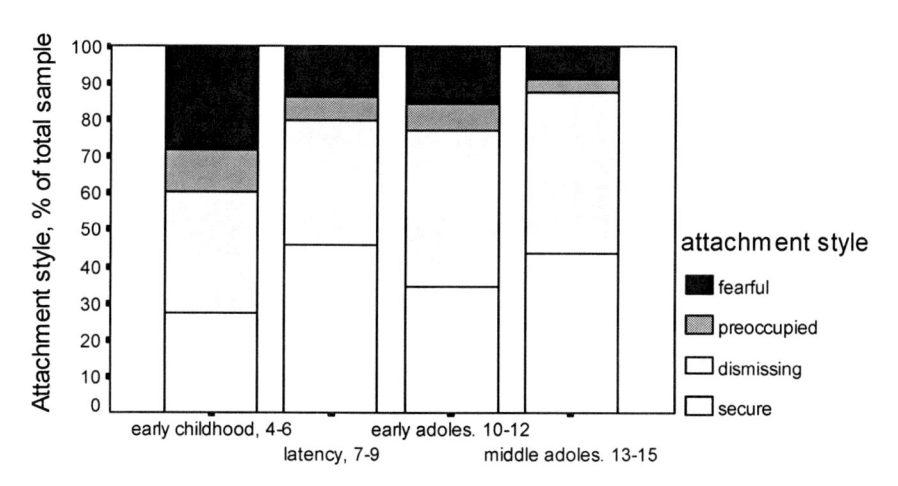

(a) Female

(b) Male

Figure 7.9 Attachment style as a percentage of each sample as a function of age when first evacuated.

In addition Figure 7.10 is a similar 100% plot for those males where the latency and early adolescent incidences have been pooled and compared with the control values. This highlights the large relative differences in the incidence of the Secure and Dismissing categories between those not evacuated and those evacuated: Secure percentages fall from 64% to 35% if evacuated, while Dismissing percentages rise from 28% to 49%, as mentioned earlier in this section ($\chi^2 = 15.3$, $p<.01$).

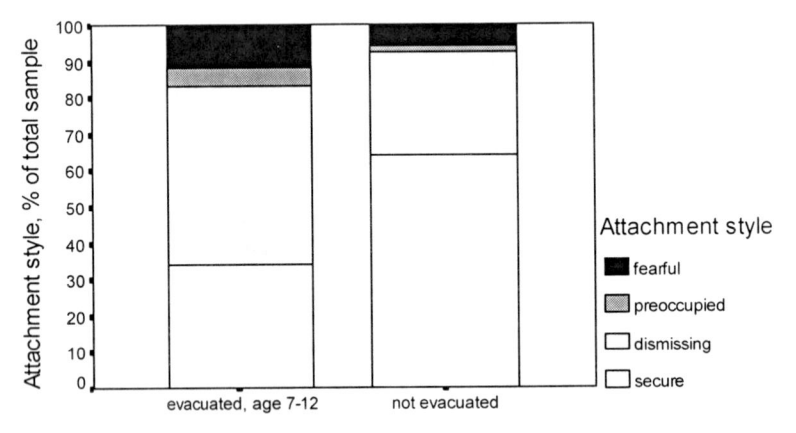

Figure 7.10 Attachment style as a percentage of each sample for those male respondents evacuated between 7-12 years of age and those not evacuated.

Summing up, the age at which respondents were first evacuated has influenced the incidence of respondents in the attachment categories. If evacuated at a young age, 4-6 years, respondents of both sexes are, on average, less secure in adult attachment terms, than those evacuated at 13-15 years or those who remained at home.

7.2.2.3.2 Care received during evacuation

Turning our attention to the second Evacuation Experience variable in Table 7.2 (a), Care received, it can be seen that only the results for the female samples exhibit any significant differences. As before we shall discuss the effects on each Adult Attachment Style variable in turn.

There is an increase in the incidence of the Secure style for both sexes with improving Care received during evacuation but only the result for females reaches significance, rising from 30% to 45%. These trends are illustrated in Figure 7.11, and once more the male percentages, even under Good Care received at 40%, do not approach the control value of 64%. The difference between these two last sample percentages is significant ($\chi^2 = 9.0$, p<.01).

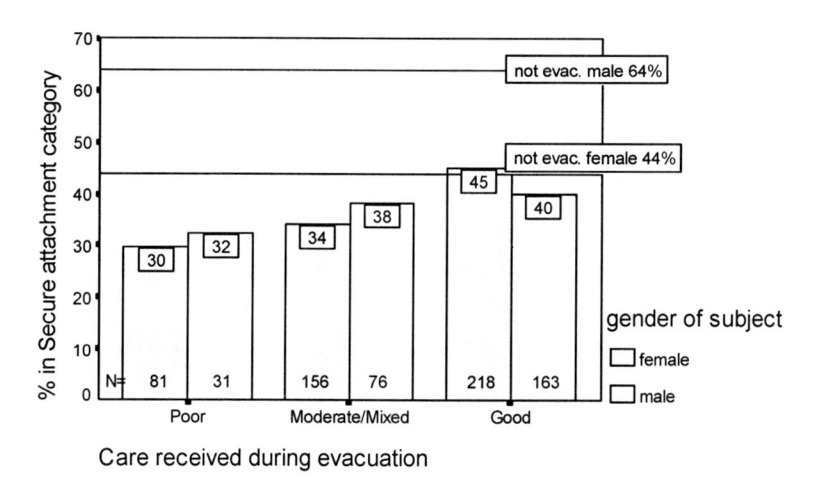

Figure 7.11 Incidence of Secure adult attachment category as a function of the Care received during evacuation.

There are no significant bivariate results for the Dismissing or Preoccupied variables listed in Table 7.2 (a), although there is a trend of reducing Preoccupied incidence for males with improving Care received which is not present in the female results. This difference has led to a significant interaction between Gender x Care received x Preoccupied (p=.045).

Table 7.2(a) shows there is a highly significant result for females in the Fearful category. With poor

Care received the incidence of females in the Fearful category is at a high level of 35%, dropping to only 8% when Good Care was received during evacuation, just below the level for those female respondents who were not evacuated, at 12%. The male sample shows the same trend but does not reach significance. These results have been plotted in Figure 7.12.

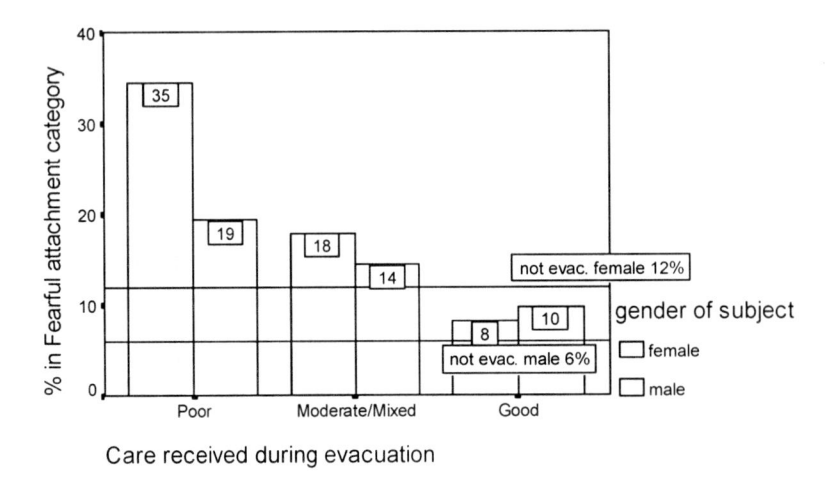

Figure 7.12 Incidence of Fearful adult attachment category as a function of the Care received during evacuation.

In an overall sense good Care received during evacuation is associated with a secure adult attachment style. Differences in attachment styles with Care received are most noticeable in the female sample; for example female respondents show almost twice the percentage incidence in the Fearful category compared to males when Care received was Poor, but this has fallen to a comparable value to males when Care received was Good.

7.2.2.3.3 Period away

Examination of the results under the third column in Table 7.2 (a), Period away, shows that there were no significant differences in percentages or scores or clear-cut trends for any of the outcome variables. Expected cell numbers were too small for male respondents in the Preoccupied category to carry out chi-square tests. The incidence for the Fearful category for females evacuated for a long period, greater than 2 years, was noticeably greater at 19% compared with values of 6% and 10% for shorter periods, and lay close to significance ($\chi(2) = 4.9$, $p=.09$).

It is perhaps surprising that no values were significantly different; however if we look back under the same Evacuation Experience variable in Table 5.3 (a) of Chapter 5 on mental health, there are no significant effects except that on Self-criticism. It would appear that the length of the evacuation period was of less importance in affecting the adult attachment, or mental health, of respondents than the age at which evacuation first took place and the care received during the period away.

7.2.2.3.4 Frequency of parental visits

Looking first at the effect of the Frequency of parental visits on the Secure category we can see that there are no significant differences. However the male results lie very close to significance ($\chi^2(4) = 9.1$, p=.06) and show that Secure percentages remained above 40% so long as visits were made by parents at least twice per year. These results have been plotted in Figure 7.13.

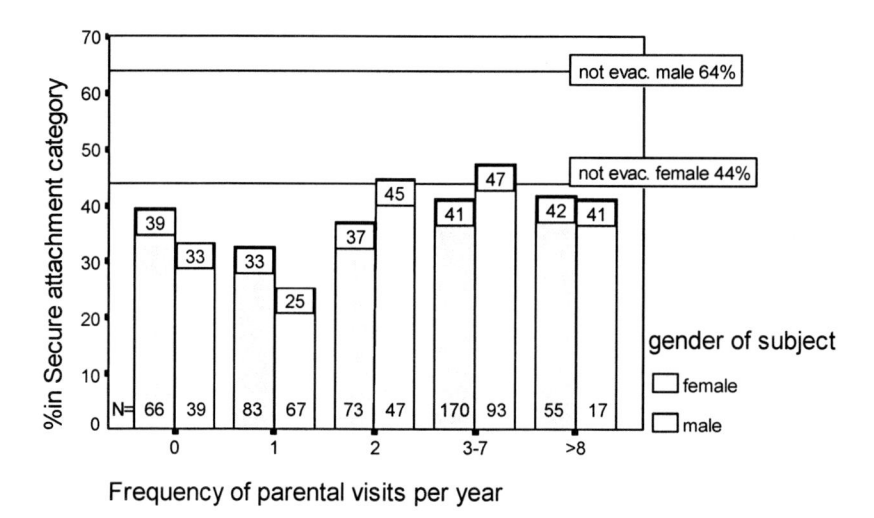

Figure 7.13 Incidence of Secure adult attachment category as a function of the number of visits made by parents per year.

The Dismissing and Preoccupied values do not show any significant effects. The percentages in the Fearful category for females do show significant differences, decreasing from a high level of 23%, when the frequency of visits was less than 1 per year, to 7% when visits were made >8 times per year. Although not significant, the male results show a similar trend. These values have been plotted in Figure 7.14. The reduction in this form of insecurity is reflected in the increase in the Secure category shown in Figure 7.13 when the frequency of visits increases.

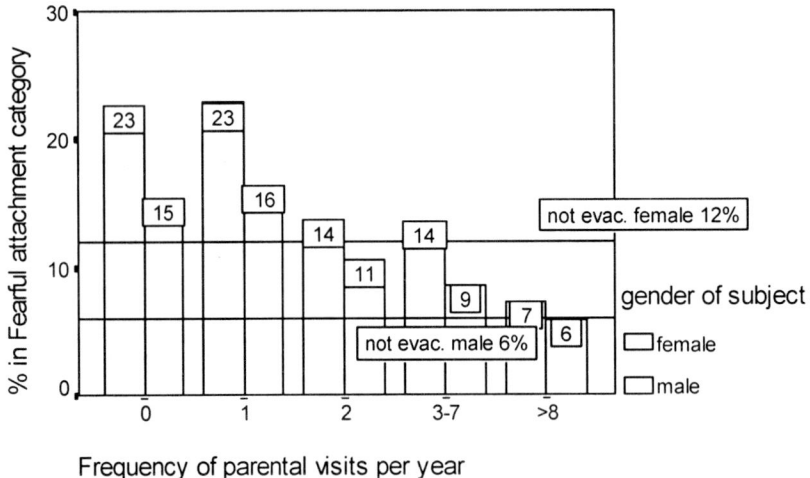

[Bar chart: % in Fearful attachment category vs Frequency of parental visits per year. Values shown: at 0 visits — 23 (female), 15 (male); at 1 visit — 23 (female), 16 (male); at 2 visits — 14 (female), 14 (male); at 3-7 visits — 11 (female), 9 (male); at >8 visits — 7 (female), 6 (male). Not evac. female 12%; not evac. male 6%.]

Figure 7.14 Incidence of Fearful adult attachment category as a function of the number of visits made by parents per year.

7.2.2.3.5 Number of billets

There are no significant effects or obvious trends for the effect of the Number of billets occupied on any of the Adult Attachment Style variables.

7.2.3 Summary

The main results for the long-term effects of evacuation on adult attachment are summarised below in Table 7.3, and these will be used as the basis for a discussion in the next section.

Table 7.3 Summary of the main results for the long-term effects of evacuation on adult attachment

---

1. Overall sample comparison between the sexes indicates a significant percentage increase for females in the Fearful category (Table 7.1).

2. Male respondents, taken as a whole, suffered a significant reduction in the percentage in the Secure category on evacuation, which was largely compensated by a significant increase in the Dismissing category (Table 7.1).

3. Females evacuated in early childhood had a significantly lower incidence of Secure attachment and a significantly higher incidence of Fearful attachment compared to those evacuated at an older age. Males showed the same trends in these attachment categories but values did not reach significance. The mean Secure incidence level of those male respondents evacuated in early childhood, latency and early adolescence, at 35%, lay significantly below the level of those not evacuated, at 64% (Table 7.2).

4. Male respondents evacuated at latency or early adolescence showed a high incidence in the Dismissing category, at 49%, which was significantly greater than that of the non-evacuated sample at 28%.

5. There is an increase in the incidence of the Secure style for both sexes with improving Care received during evacuation but only the female result reached significance, rising from 30% to 45%. Females also showed a significant decrease in the Fearful category, falling from 35% to 8%, with improved Care received; the male sample showed the same trends but values did not reach significance (Table 7.2).

6. Secure attachment percentages for male respondents remained above 40% so long as the Frequency of parental visits was at least twice per year. Females in the Fearful category showed a significant decrease from 23%, when Frequency of parental visits was less than 1 per year, to 7% when visits were made >8 times per year. Although not significant, the male results followed a similar trend (Table 7.2).

7.2.4 Discussion

In the Introduction to this chapter (Section 7.1) we raised the hypothesis that adult attachment patterns are developmental successors of those found in early childhood through the emergence of internal working models and the expectations these bring to the formation of adult interpersonal relationships (Shaver and Hazan, 1993; Rothbard and Shaver, 1991; Feeney and Noller, 1990). The present study can go some way to test this hypothesis in the sense that if it is true then we could expect to find that the varied experiences of respondents in childhood, due to their separation from parents whilst evacuated, will be associated with their adult attachment style in particular ways. The results given in Section 7.2.2 and summarised in Section 7.2.3, and discussed below, show that the evacuation experience is associated with respondents' adult attachment, and that these changes can be understood in terms of the expectations engendered by the internal working models developed in childhood.

The clearest indication that there is a connection between the evacuation experience and adult attachment is shown by the results related to Age at evacuation and Care received during evacuation. These show that if evacuated in early childhood, or if the care received was poor, then security of attachment in adulthood is reduced, both in relation to those evacuated at a later age or those who received improved care, or those who remained at home. This particularly applies to female respondents, but the trend is there for males too; in fact male respondents fail to reach the level of adult Secure attachment enjoyed by those who were not separated from their parents, even if evacuated in middle adolescence, or when the care received was good. This loss of security is reflected in an increase in the incidence of Fearful attachment for both sexes. This style of insecure attachment is characterised by a fear of intimacy and social avoidance (Bartholomew and Horowitz, 1991). There is a sense of unworthiness, or unlovability, combined with an expectation that others will be negatively disposed to oneself. By avoiding close involvement with others this style enables individuals to protect themselves against anticipated rejection by others. There is a clear resonance here with the conclusions of Serenius (1995) regarding the long-term effects on those young children evacuated from Finland to Sweden during the Second World War, where she believes her own difficulty, and that of many of her fellow evacuees, in finding a secure identity is related to the separation experience suffered in childhood (see Section 2.2). From our results there is also an indication that male respondents are prone to high levels of Dismissive attachment, particularly if evacuated in latency or early adolescence, compared to those who remained at home. Individuals in this category protect themselves against emotional pain and rejection by also avoiding close relationships and by maintaining a sense of independence, control and invulnerability

(Bartholomew and Horowitz, 1991). Many of these defensive strategies are covered by the categories and themes which arose from the grounded theory analysis of the Pilot Study (see Appendix 1).

It is surprising that both of the input variables, Period away and Number of billets, did not show any significant effects on the outcome variables of attachment and the three characteristics listed. This suggests that so long as evacuation did not take place at too young an age, and the care received was good, then more extended periods away could be tolerated without further loss of emotional security. This was dependent, however, on visits being made by parents at least 2-3 times per year.

The relationship between adult attachment styles and mental health was examined at the start of Section 7.2.2.1 when considering the overall results. From this examination it can be understood that the above trends to greater insecurity in adult attachment through evacuation can be associated with the mental health of respondents. For example there is a highly significant correlation between rating scores from the Fearful category and those of Self-criticism from the DEQ scale, and this is seen from the Pearson correlation coefficients listed below in Table 7.4.

Table 7.4 Pearson bivariate correlation coefficients between Self-criticism and the four Adult Attachment Style ratings

	Secure	Dismissing	Preoccupied	Fearful
Self-criticism	-.233	.165	.288	.432

N= 859. All significant, $p<.001$.

In this context Self-criticism was found to be the major predictor of Depression in the structural path diagrams given in Figures 5.33 and 5.34, and it will be remembered that evacuation in early childhood or with poor care is associated with high incidence levels for Depression (see Table 5.3). Comparison of these attachment and mental health results also suggests that the low incidence level of Depression enjoyed by male respondents evacuated in early adolescence, at 19% (comparable to those not evacuated) may be partly due to the defensive power of the Dismissing category since only 37% of this sample were in the Secure category compared to 64% in the sample who were not evacuated. Again the drop in the Secure percentages for females evacuated in early adolescence (see Table 7.2 (a)) may be related to similar anomalies seen in Chapter 5, where there were significant increases in the incidence of Clinical anxiety and Self-criticism scores for those evacuated at this age (10-12 years).

7.3 Long-term effect of upbringing on adult attachment

Following the same layout as that used in Chapter 5 on mental health we will consider here the effect of the four Upbringing variables on the Adult Attachment Styles as displayed in Figure 7.1, representing respondents' pathway through life. From the discussion of the theoretical background to adult attachment given in Chapter 2 it may be expected that there will be some associations between these early upbringing variables and the adult attachment styles. It will also be important to establish if the quality of nurture received during upbringing has had a moderating influence on the evacuation experience results and this will be examined in Section 7.4 which follows this present section.

7.3.1 Analysis

The Upbringing variables are those described in Section 3.2.2.1 of Chapter 3 and relate to the quality of nurture, divorce of parents, death of a parent and parental occupational class. The outcome variables used are the same as those described and employed in Section 7.2.1 of this present chapter, i.e. the four adult attachment styles as measured by the Bartholomew and Horowitz Relationship Questionnaire. Results were analysed in the same way as before with a total of 482 females and 315 males available.

7.3.2 Results

Results for the effect of upbringing on adult attachment style are given below in Table 7.5. Certain of the cells involved had expected counts below the accepted limits for chi-square analysis given in Chapter 3. Loglinear analysis showed only one significant interaction, between Gender x Nurture x Fearful, and this will be discussed in the relevant sub-section.

Table 7.5. Outcome variables for adult attachment as a function of gender and the four input variables of childhood upbringing

UPBRINGING

	Nurture Good enough Comfortless	Divorce of parents No Yes	Death of parents No Yes	Parental Class Middle Working
$N_F =$	292 53	292 26	292 68	138 344
$N_M =$	206 26	206 10	206 37	84 231

ADULT ATTACHMENT STYLES

	χ^2	χ^2	χ^2	χ^2
Secure				
Female	43% 23% 7.6**	43% 27% 2.5	43% 38% 0.5	36% 40% 0.6
Male	45% 23% 4.4*	cell too small	45% 32% 1.9	50% 39% 3.1
	(Figure 7.15)			
Dismissing				
Female	39% 38% 0.1	39% 38% 0.1	39% 29% 2.2	41% 36% 1.0
Male	40% 58% 3.0	cell too small	40% 51% 1.7	35% 44% 2.2
	(Figure 7.16)			
Preoccupied				
Female	cell too small	cell too small	8% 12% 1.3	8% 8% 0.0
Male	cell too small	cell too small	cell too small	8% 4% 1.9
Fearful				
Female	11% 30% 14.6***	cell too small	11% 21% 5.0*	15% 17% 0.1
Male	11% 12% 0.0	cell too small	cell too small	7% 13% 2.1
	(Figure 7.17)			

Chi-square tests have been carried out for this categorical data. Significance key: * p<.05, ** p<.01 and *** p<.001; all two-tailed.

The effect of each of the above four input variables associated with upbringing will be examined in turn in the following sections.

7.3.2.1 Nurture

Starting with the first column of Table 7.5, nurture in childhood has been divided into two categories, Good enough and Comfortless, following the selection procedure described in Chapter 3 on Methodology. Examination of the results shows that there has been a significant reduction for both sexes in the incidence of the Secure attachment style with deteriorating Nurture. These percentages have been plotted in Figure 7.15 and show clearly that both sexes have been affected to the same degree. The lower level of significance attached to the male sample in Table 7.5 is due to smaller respondent numbers, i.e. reduced power.

[Bar chart: % in Secure attachment category vs Quality of Nurture ('good enough' / comfortless), by gender. Values: female 43, male 45 ('good enough'); female 23, male 23 (comfortless). N= 292, 206, 53, 26.]

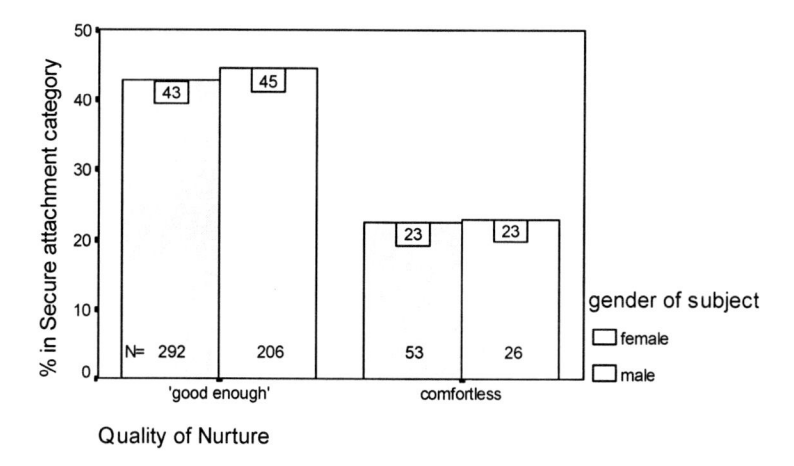

Figure 7.15 Incidence of Secure adult attachment category as a function of the quality of nurture received during upbringing.

The results for the Dismissing category are of interest in that females show no change, but males increase from 40% to 58% with poorer Nurture, a trend which lies very close to significance ($\chi^2(1) = 3.0$, $p = .08$). These percentages have been plotted in Figure 7.16.

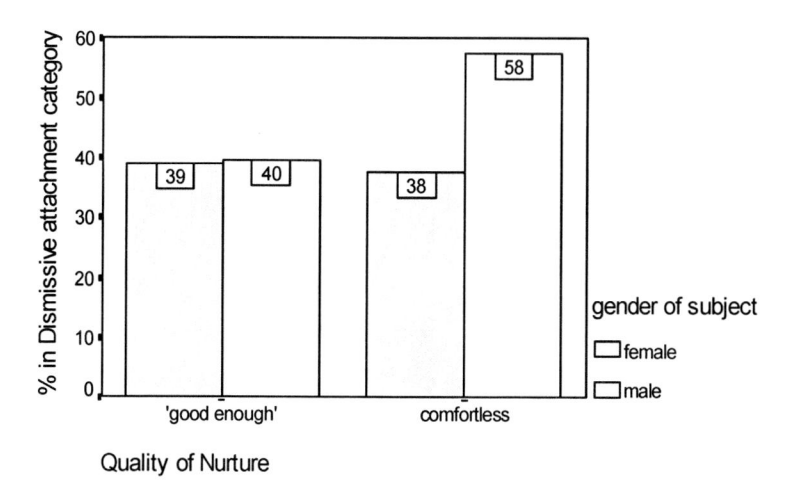

[Bar chart: % in Dismissive attachment category vs Quality of Nurture ('good enough' / comfortless), by gender. Values: female 39, male 40 ('good enough'); female 38, male 58 (comfortless).]

Figure 7.16 Incidence of Dismissing adult attachment category as a function of the quality of nurture received during upbringing.

Unfortunately the expected cell counts are too small in the Preoccupied category for chi-square tests to be made.

The Fearful category shows a highly significant increase for females with deteriorating Nurture but there is little change in the male sample. These differences between the sexes are shown in

Figure 7.17, and are significant in interaction terms (p=.042).

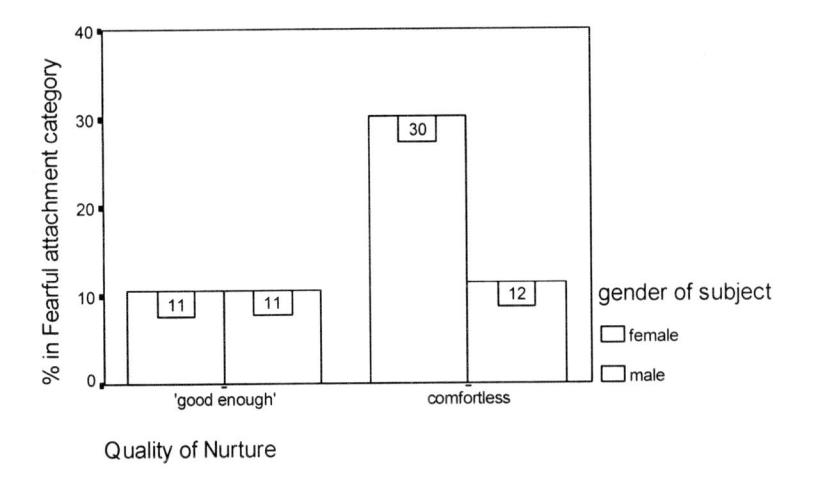

Figure 7.17 Incidence of Fearful adult attachment category as a function of the quality of nurture received during upbringing.

Again it is useful to plot the percentage incidences of the four adult attachment styles, as a proportion of the total samples, and these have been plotted for both sexes in Figure 7.18 (a) and (b) as a function of Nurture.

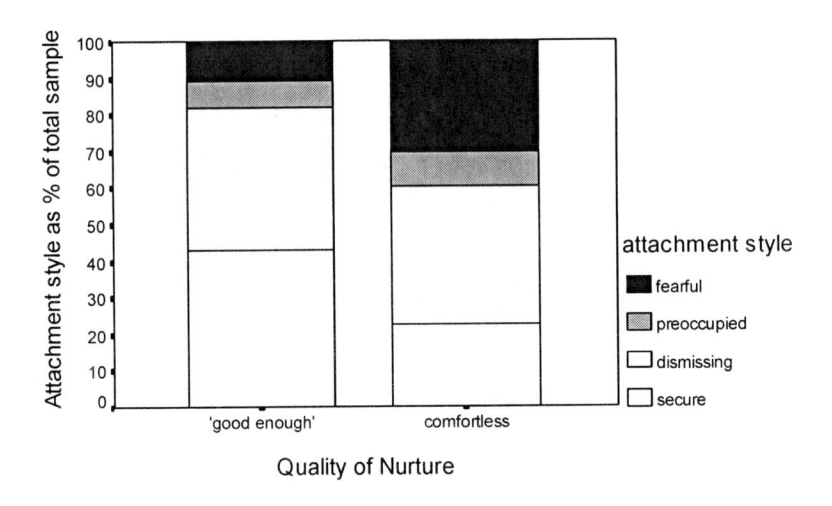

(a) Female

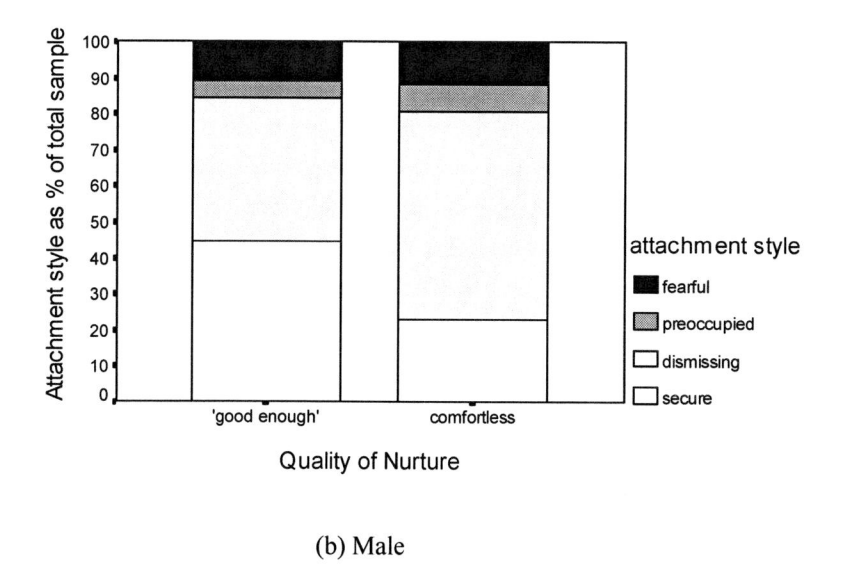

[Chart: Attachment style as % of total sample, by Quality of Nurture ('good enough' vs comfortless), with categories fearful, preoccupied, dismissing, secure]

(b) Male

Figure 7.18 Attachment style as a percentage of each sample as a function of the quality of nurture received in upbringing.

These two graphs show the proportional changes which have occurred in the attachment categories as a result of a deterioration in the quality of home nurture received in childhood. Apart from the reduction in Secure attachment which both samples have suffered equally, there is the obvious difference in how this loss has been 'reallocated' to the insecure categories. For females this has mainly resulted in a large increase in the Fearful percentage, and for males in the Dismissing percentage. This gives a clear distinction between the way the two sexes attempt to protect themselves against emotional pain and anticipated rejection by others in adulthood, as a result of poor nurture in childhood (cf Section 5.3 re mental health).

As discussed previously membership of the Fearful category is strongly related to the incidence of Depression ($\chi^2(1) = 36.2$, p<.001) while that of the Dismissing category is not ($\chi^2 = 2.4$, p =.10), so that female respondents are more liable to poor mental health through this defence mechanism. This difference in the incidence of depression between the sexes has been found and discussed in Chapter 5. From this adult attachment analysis it would seem that although respondents in both styles protect themselves by avoiding intimate relationships nevertheless those in the Fearful style have a need for dependence but are low in self-esteem. By contrast the Dismissing style requires the opposite: a detached or non-dependent attitude to others but with a relatively high level of self-sufficiency and self-confidence (see Bartholomew and Horowitz model of adult attachment, Figure 3.4).

7.3.2.2 Divorce or separation of parents

Most of the expected respondent numbers in those cells related to parents that had divorced or separated were too small for chi-square tests to be made using the accepted criteria. The only attachment style results which fell within the acceptable chi-square limits were for female respondents under the Secure and Dismissing categories (see Table 7.5). Neither was significant, but the Secure result does show a drop in Secure incidence from 43 to 27% with the divorce of parents ($\chi2(1) = 2.5$, p= .11).

It is unfortunate that the expected male respondent numbers in the cells which related to those whose parents divorced were so low since it would have been valuable to be able to compare the attachment results with those obtained for the outcome variables related to mental health in Chapter 5. These showed that male respondents were particularly affected by the divorce or separation of parents.

7.3.2.3 Death of parents

The only attachment style result of significance related to the death of a parent was for female respondents in the Fearful category which showed an increase from 11% to 21% with death of a parent. The equivalent case for male respondents was not tested due to a low expected cell size. It is interesting to see that whereas the incidence of female respondents in the Dismissing category reduces with death of a parent, that for males increases. Taken with the rise in the Fearful category for females it suggests the sexes are responding differently, on average, to the loss of a parent, as we discussed earlier for the effect of poor nurture.

7.3.2.4 Parental class

None of the attachment style results showed any significant effect of Parental class for either sex. However, the decrease in Secure attachment from 50% to 39% for male respondents in the Middle and Working classes lay close to significance ($\chi2(1) = 3.1$, p =.08). In Table 5.6 in Chapter 5 there were also no significant effects of Parental Class on mental health.

7.3.3 Summary

The main results for the long-term effects of upbringing on adult attachment are summarised below in Table 7.6, and these will be used as the basis for discussion in the next section.

Table 7.6 Summary of the main results for the long-term effects of upbringing on adult attachment styles

1. Both sexes show a significant and comparable decrease in the incidence of the Secure style with deteriorating Nurture. (Figure 7.15).

2. Male respondents only show an increase in the incidence of the Dismissing style with deteriorating Nurture. (Figure 7.16).

3. Female respondents only show a significant increase in the incidence of the Fearful style with deteriorating Nurture. (Figure 7.17).

4. Female respondents showed a significant increase in the incidence of the Fearful style with death of a parent; it was not possible to test the male sample due to a small cell size.

7.3.4 Discussion

The most apparent long-term effect found regarding a respondent's upbringing was due to the quality of nurture received in childhood. Both sexes suffered a significant reduction in percentages in the Secure category with a deterioration in the quality of home care. This percentage loss was 'redistributed' differently, on average, for the two sexes: females, alone, showed a highly significant increase in the Fearful category while males, alone, showed an increase in the Dismissing category.

When introducing, and later discussing, the earlier results in this chapter on the long-term effects of evacuation we demonstrated the association which exists between adult attachment style and the mental health of respondents. The above results regarding the effects of Nurture provide further evidence for this connection in that, again, a tendency was found for each sex to adopt a different style under conditions of comfortless care, in fact the same styles they each adopted when care during evacuation was poor. Females moved to the Fearful style, which requires a measure of dependence (Bartholomew & Horowitz, 1991) while males were more inclined to move away from dependent relationships and adopt a Dismissing style. This contrast in defensive mechanisms is very clearly illustrated by comparing Figures 7.16 and 7.17. As mentioned earlier, this may be one of the reasons why there is a difference in the incidence of depression between the sexes (O'Connor, Thorpe, Golding & Dunn, 1999), since the Dismissing option appears to provide good defence against mental health problems, whereas the Fearful style does not.

Unfortunately a number of the cells, particularly for males, were too small to carry out chi-square tests on the effect of parental divorce or death. In those cells which were above the expected frequency limits Females showed a reduction in the secure category with parental divorce, while male respondents showed a rather similar reduction in the same category with death of a parent. Females also showed an increase in percentages in the Fearful category with the death of a parent. Previous analyses in Chapter 5 on mental health had shown that males were rather more affected than females by both the divorce and death of parents; however these attachment results do not exhibit a complimentary tendency.

As we found earlier, when considering mental health, parental class has not significantly affected either the percentages in the four attachment styles or the mean scores of the three selected characteristics. Male respondents, however, do show a decrease in Secure attachment from the Middle to Working class which lies close to significance.

The overall impression given by the results in this section is that adult attachment has been affected by the quality of home nurture received, but has been rather less affected by parental divorce or death, or by the social class of the respondents' family in childhood. However these conclusions have to be treated with caution since, in many cases, cell sizes were small.

7.4 Long-term effect of the quality of home upbringing and care received during evacuation on adult attachment

In Sections 7.2 and 7.3 we have seen that the care received during evacuation, and the quality of nurture received in upbringing, have each affected the attachment style of respondents in adulthood. In this section these two input variables have been separated, as in Section 5.4 on mental health, to determine if the quality of nurture has moderated the way care received during evacuation has affected attachment style in adulthood.

7.4.1 Analysis

The input variables used are Quality of Nurture and Care received during evacuation, the same as those employed in Sections 7.2 and 7.3 and in the equivalent analysis in Section 5.4 of Chapter 5 on mental health. The outcome variables are the four adult attachment categories used before, derived from the Bartholomew & Horowitz (1991) Relationship Questionnaire. As before all cases were treated listwise in the computations, with a total of 317 female and 191 male respondents available. Pearson chi-square tests were made separately for each gender and Nurture category as a function of Care received for the outcome variables.

7.4.2 Results

The results listing the percentage incidences of adult attachment style as a function of home Nurture and Care received during evacuation are given below in Table 7.7. A number of the expected cell counts were too low for statistical analyses to be reliably made and these positions have been marked in the table. Loglinear analysis found no interactions between Nurture x Care received x Adult Attachment Styles for those samples with acceptable cell sizes.

Table 7.7 Outcome variables for adult attachment as a function of gender, the quality of childhood nurture and the care received during evacuation

	Nurture	Care received			χ^2
		poor	moderate	good	

ADULT ATTACHMENT STYLE

Secure

Female	'good enough'	27%a	38%ab	49%b	7.1*
	comfortless		cells too small		
			(Figure 7.19)		
Male	'good enough'	35%	39%	42%	0.3
	comfortless		cells too small		
			(Figure 7.20)		

Dismissing

Female	'good enough'	43%	45%	34%	2.9
	comfortless	21%	41%	59%	4.4
Male	'good enough'	29%	39%	46%	1.9
	comfortless		cells too small		

Preoccupied

Female	'good enough'	3%	7%	9%	1.6
	comfortless		cells too small		
Male	'good enough'		cells too small		
	comfortless		cells too small		

Fearful

Female	'good enough'	27%a	10%b	7%b	12.0**
	comfortless	43%a	41%a	6%b	6.9*
			(Figure 7.21)		
Male	'good enough'	24%	12%	10%	2.7
	comfortless		cells too small		

Chi-square tests have been carried out on this data. Significance key: * $p<.05$, ** $p<.01$ and *** $p<.001$; all two-tailed. Significance in the chi-square tests was followed by bivariate tests: Percentage values marked by different superscripts are significantly different at $p<.05$.

Looking first at the Secure attachment results it can be seen that the female 'good enough' Nurture percentages increase significantly with improving Care received during evacuation. Unfortunately certain expected cells were too small to carry out a chi-square test on the equivalent 'comfortless' Nurture sample. This also precludes making a loglinear analysis to test for interactions. Female Secure percentages have been plotted in Figure 7.19, where it can be seen that the effect of 'good enough' Nurture does not insure against the effects of poor Care received in evacuation. Secure attachment incidence only approaches the non-evacuated, or control, level of 44% if Care received during evacuation is moderate or good. Although the numbers of female respondents in the 'comfortless' Nurture cells are low (see N values in Figure 7.19), these results suggest that moderate or good Care received during evacuation does not, on average, overcome the effects of a 'comfortless' upbringing.

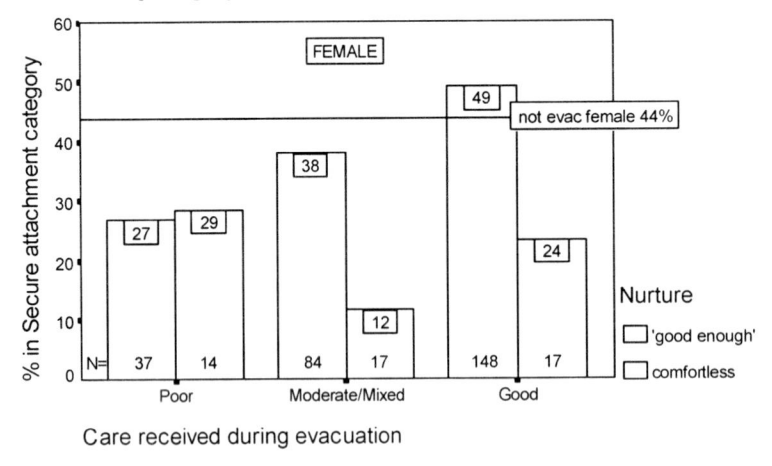

Figure 7.19 Incidence of Secure adult attachment category for female respondents as a function of the quality of home nurture and the care received during evacuation.

Male percentages have been plotted in Figure 7.20 and show a rather different trend; 'good enough' percentages do not rise so steeply with improving Care received, and even with good Care received, at 42%, they do not approach the non-evacuated level of 64%. However, when making these comparisons it should be remembered that the 'evacuated' samples are pooled for Age at evacuation. Again it would appear from the figure that good Care received during evacuation cannot overcome the effects of a 'comfortless' upbringing, although this needs to be treated with great caution as the cell numbers are so small.

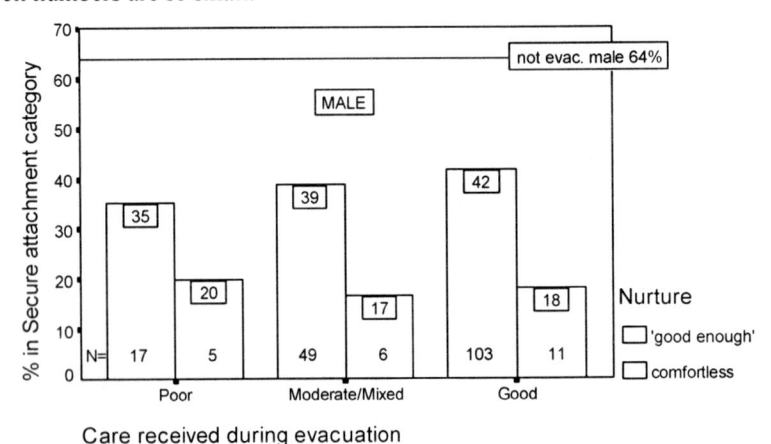

Figure 7.20 Incidence of Secure adult attachment category for male respondents as a function of the quality of home nurture and the care received during evacuation.

Female results in the Dismissing category do not reach significance, but they do point to some interesting differences across the attachment styles. There is a relatively high percentage level of 43% with 'good enough' Nurture plus poor Care received compared with that for 'comfortless' Nurture which gives a low level of 21%. What appears to be happening is that the relatively low incidence level in the equivalent Secure style, of 27-29% (see Figure 7.19), under poor Care received is being 'compensated' by a high level in the Dismissive category when Nurture is good, and a high level in the Fearful category when Nurture is 'comfortless', both at 43% of the total (see Table 7.7). Those females who have had a 'good enough' Nurture show a slight reduction in Dismissive incidence with improved Care received during evacuation, whereas those who have had a comfortless Nurture show a marked increase in incidence from 21% to 59%, with a concomitant sharp reduction in the Fearful category from 43% to 6% (see Table 7.7). Loglinear analysis showed that the 3-way interaction in these Dismissing results for females, i.e. Dismissing x Nurture x Care received, lay close to significance ($p = .051$). Male respondents show a rise in percentages in the dismissive category with improving Care received if Nurture was good, which was offset by a reduction in the equivalent Fearful category.

Percentages and expected and observed cell sizes in the Preoccupied category were too small to consider and added little to the overall patterns of adult attachment changes observed.

Female respondent samples showed significant reductions in percentages within the Fearful category for both levels of Nurture as Care received during evacuation improved, and this is clearly shown in Figure 7.21 (for N values see Figure 7.19). It is encouraging to see that if Care received was good the level of Fearful incidence was only 6%, even with comfortless Nurture; however, as mentioned above, the Dismissing level remains high at 59% for this sample. Results for male respondents in the Fearful category also showed a reduction in percentages with improving Care received if Nurture was good; the numbers in the cells for the equivalent 'comfortless' level of Nurture were too small to be reliable.

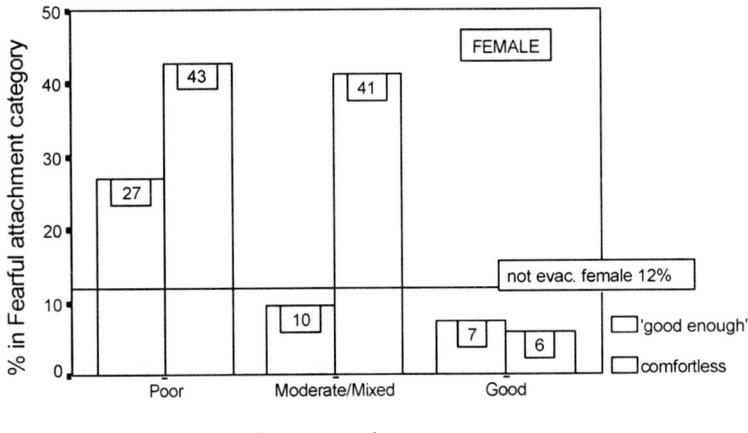

[Bar chart: % in Fearful attachment category vs Care received during evacuation (Poor, Moderate/Mixed, Good), FEMALE. 'good enough' bars: 27, 10, 7. comfortless bars: 43, 41, 6. not evac. female 12%]

Figure 7.21 Incidence of Fearful adult attachment category for female respondents as a function of the quality of home nurture and the care received during evacuation.

7.4.3 Summary

The main results for the long-term effects of the quality of home nurture and care received during evacuation on adult attachment are summarised below in Table 7.8, and these will be used as the basis for a discussion in the next section.

Table 7.8 Summary of the main results for the long-term effects of the quality of home nurture and care received during evacuation on adult attachment

---

1. For both female and male respondents 'good enough' Nurture did not insure against the effects of poor care received during evacuation in terms of a loss of secure attachment. Also for both sexes, moderate or good Care received during evacuation did not ameliorate the insecurity induced by comfortless Nurture (Figures 7.19 and 7.20).

2. Percentage incidence in the Dismissing category is high for female respondents who have received 'good enough' Nurture followed by poor Care received during evacuation, and this incidence reduces with improved Care received. The reverse occurs for the comfortless Nurture samples, where Dismissing incidence increases with improved Care received.

3. Female respondents showed significant reductions in percentages within the Fearful category for both levels of Nurture as the Care received during evacuation improved. This was particularly marked for the comfortless Nurture category, where incidence fell from 43% to 6% (Figure 7.21).

7.4.4 Discussion

As mentioned in Section 2.3.4 of Chapter 2 and in the Introduction to this chapter on adult attachment one of the questions which has been uppermost in the minds of researchers is the *degree* to which the quality of the relationship between young children and their parents defines their later adult attachment style (Ainsworth, 1967; Main & Cassidy, 1988; Grossman & Grossman, 1991; Kobak & Hazan, 1991; etc.). We have already seen in the results so far given in this chapter that the evacuation experience has influenced the adult attachment of respondents, and in this present section we have tried to focus down further by examining the effect on adult attachment of the interaction between the quality of home nurture in childhood and the quality of the care received during the evacuation period.

Within the limits of the analysis given in this section, which suffers from some small expected cell sizes, there are some interesting results. The interdependence of Nurture and Care received is most clearly, and reliably, seen in the results for female respondents in the Secure, Dismissing and Fearful adult attachment categories. It was found that good quality home nurture did not insure against the effects of poor care received during evacuation, nor did good care received overcome the insecurity engendered by a comfortless home upbringing. However, good care received during the evacuation experience did allow for a reasonable level of secure adult attachment to be achieved, comparable to those who remained at home, so long as the quality of home nurture was high. Fearful category percentages dropped sharply with improved care during evacuation irrespective of the quality of home nurture, but for those from a comfortless home background there remained a high residual insecurity in the Dismissing category even if the Care received while away from home was good.

Summing-up we can say, for those who were evacuated, security in adulthood is dependent on both good quality home nurture *and* good quality care being received while away from parents. If one or the other was missing then low levels of secure adult attachment were found.

7.5 Long-term effects of fathers' absence due to war service and of bombing on the incidence of adult attachment

In this section we will examine whether the absence of a father due to war service, or the aerial bombing of a respondents' home neighbourhood or home may have contributed to the adult attachment style of respondents.

7.5.1 Analysis

Following the procedure used in Section 5.5.1 in Chapter5 on mental health, the analysis is based directly on the presence or absence of a father due to war service and on three degrees of severity of bombing: no bombing, town or neighbourhood bombed, and family home bombed, for the situation when the respondent was present or absent from home during the event.

As before, all cases were treated listwise in the computations, with a total of 440 female and 292 male respondents available. Pearson chi-square tests were made separately for each gender as a function of the above categories for the incidence of adult attachment using the Bartholomew & Horowitz (1991) Relationship Questionnaire.

7.5.2 Results

Results for the effects of the absence of a father on war service and of bombing on the incidence of the four adult attachment styles and the three respondent characteristics are given below in Table 7.9.

Table 7.9. Outcome variables for adult attachment as a function of gender, bombing and the absence of a father due to war service

		Father				Bombing		
		At home	Absent		None	Nearby	Home bombed	
$N_F =$		351	89		140	230	99	
$N_M =$		226	66		85	181	49	

ADULT ATTACHMENT STYLE				χ^2	Respondent				χ^2
Secure									
	Female	40%	37%	0.3	Present	40%	44%	35%	1.1
					Absent	40%	37%	34%	0.5
	Male	46%	38%	1.5	Present	51%	38%	30%	4.4
					Absent	51%	43%	36%	2.0
Dismissing									
	Female	36%	42%	0.8	Present	36%	41%	42%	0.7
					Absent	37%	36%	36%	0.0
	Male	37%	52%	4.7*	Present	34%	44%	56%	4.2
					Absent	34%	42%	36%	1.3
Preoccupied									
	Female	7%	9%	0.5	Present	cell too small			
					Absent	9%	8%	9%	0.2
	Male	cell too small			Present	cell too small			
					Absent	cell too small			
Fearful									
	Female	17%	12%	0.9	Present	14%	11%	17%	0.8
					Absent	14%	19%	21%	1.9
	Male	12%	5%	3.3	Present	cell too small			
					Absent	12%	12%	18%	0.7

Chi-square tests have been carried out for this categorical data. Significance key: * $p<.05$, ** $p<.01$, *** $p<.001$; all two-tailed.

The effect of the two war-related moderating variables will be examined in turn in the following sections.

7.5.2.1 Fathers' absence

Only the Dismissive style for male respondents shows any significant effect of a father's absence, increasing from 37% to 52%, with a comparable fall in the Secure category. Female results show no discernible trends.

7.5.2.2 Effect of bombing

From Table 7.9 there are no significant effects of Bombing on the incidence of attachment styles. Both sexes show a trend to a reduced Secure incidence if their homes had been bombed, either when they were present or absent, and this was compensated by small rises in the Dismissive and Fearful percentages.

7.5.3 Summary

The results for the long-term effects of a father's absence due to war service and of bombing on adult attachment are summarised below in Table 7.10.

Table 7.10 Summary of the results for the long-term effect of a father's absence due to war service and to bombing on adult attachment style

---

1. The effect of a father's absence due to war service was found to increase the male Dismissive adult attachment percentage significantly.

2. Both sexes showed a trend to a reduced level of Secure attachment if their homes were bombed, when they were either present or absent, but these trends did not reach significance.

7.5.4 Discussion

The overall impression given by these results is that both the absence of a father, and the effects of bombing, have not substantially affected the distribution of respondents' adult attachment styles. There are certain minor trends, as listed above, but compared to the more robust effects of home nurture, age at evacuation and care received during evacuation the consequences are slight.

The fact that the mental health of respondents, particularly males, were significantly affected by the bombing of their homes in their absence (see Section 5.5.4 in Chapter 5 for a discussion on this), and that no comparable effects were reported in Table 7.9 for changes in the incidence of adult attachment, suggests that home bombing may not, of itself, lead to a greater incidence of insecurity but may predispose those who were already insecure, particularly those in the Preoccupied and

Fearful categories, to depression and clinical anxiety in later life.

7.6 The relationship between Occupational Class, Education level and Life Crises on adult attachment style

From the path diagram shown in Figure 7.1 we are here concerned with three life-course variables which may be related to adult attachment style. These life-course variables are Occupational Class, Education level and Life Crises. The analysis will be carried out in a similar manner to that described in Section 5.6.1 on mental health, although the direction of the relationships are not specified.

7.6.1 Analysis

As described in Section 5.6.1 Occupational Class is defined according to the Office of National Statistics User Guide (1996) and the category titles and their grading are listed in Section 5.6.1. In the present analysis, due to low numbers in Class1 this was pooled with Class 2 and likewise Class 5 was pooled with Class 4.

Educational level was defined as before, with regard simply to whether a respondent had or had not received any vocational or higher education, i.e. tertiary education. Life crises covered the following events in adulthood: Death of a spouse, Divorce or separation, Life-threatening illness of self or spouse, Long- term disability of self or spouse and Death of a son or daughter.

As before all cases were treated listwise in the computations with a total of 482 female and 315 male respondents available. Pearson chi-square tests were made separately for each gender as a function of the four adult attachment categories, and one-way ANOVA tests carried out on the scores from the three respondent characteristic rating scales.

7.6.2 Results

The results of this analysis are given below in Table 7.11 with a similar format to that used in previous tables. Tests by Loglinear analysis indicated a significant interaction for Gender x Life crises x Fearful and this will be considered in the relevant section.

Table 7.11 Outcome variables for adult attachment as a function of gender, occupational class, education level and life crises

LIFE COURSE

	Occupational Class 1/2	3	4/5		Education level Low	High		Life Crises No	Yes	
$N_F =$	89	192	201		273	107		240	247	
$N_M =$	147	128	40		157	71		214	101	

ADULT ATTACHMENT STYLE

				χ^2			χ^2			χ^2
Secure										
Female	42%	38%	39%	0.3	37%	41%	0.6	43%	34%	4.1*
Male	48%	38%	33%	4.9	45%	37%	1.3	43%	40%	0.4
Dismissing										
Female	31%	42%	53%	3.8	36%	37%	0.1	35%	39%	1.0
Male	39%	47%	33%	3.3	36%	51%	4.2*	41%	42%	0.1
Preoccupied										
Female	9%	6%	9%	1.7	9%	6%	1.3	8%	7%	0.1
Male	5%	5%	7%	0.5	5%	4%	0.1	5%	6%	0.2
Fearful										
Female	18%	14%	17%	1.1	18%	16%	0.3	14%	19%	2.5
Male	8%[a]	10%[a]	28%[b]	12.0**	14%	8%	1.4	11%	13%	0.3

Chi-square tests have been carried out for this categorical data. Significance key: * p<.05, ** p<.01, p<.001; all two-tailed. Significance on the chi-square tests was followed by bivariate tests: Percentage values for each gender marked by different superscripts are significantly different at p<.05.

7.6.2.1 Occupational Class

The results listed under Occupational Class show that only male respondents demonstrate any significant effects between class and attachment style. None of the results for females reached significance or showed any clear trends and this interaction in terms of gender was found to be significant by Loglinear analysis (p=.035). This difference between the sexes was also found in Table 5.13 of Chapter 5 when Occupational Class of respondents was examined as a function of the mental health variables, and was confirmed by the structural path model for females and males given in Figure 5.33 and Figure 5.34.

If we look more closely at the results it can be seen that for male respondents there is a reduction in percentages within the Secure category ($\chi^2(2) = 4.9$, p =.08) and that this is largely compensated by a highly significant increase in percentages within the Fearful category from 8% to 28% ($\chi^2(2) = 12.0$, p<.01). These changes are illustrated in Figure 7.22 where the four attachment style incidences for male respondents are shown stacked as a percentage of the total male sample.

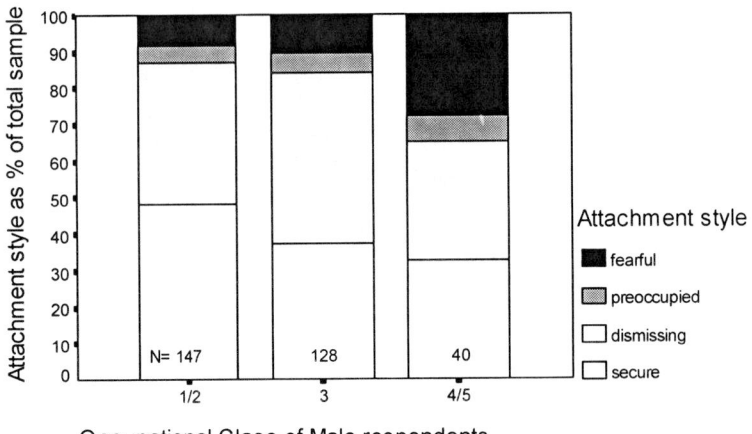

Figure 7.22 Attachment style as a percentage of the male sample as a function of Occupational Class.

7.6.2.2 Education level

The only significant result for the effects of Education level on attachment style is for male respondents, which shows a significant increase in the Dismissing category from 36% to 51% with higher education. This is compensated by a reduction in the Fearful and Secure categories. It is interesting to compare this with the only significant result between Education level and mental health variables in Table 5.13, which shows a reduction in Dependency for male respondents under the same conditions.

7.6.2.3 Life Crises

Only female respondents show any effects between Life Crises and adult attachment. There is a significant reduction in Secure incidence from 43% to 34% and this is compensated by an increase in both the Fearful and Dismissing categories with the advent of a life crisis or crises.

7.6.3 Summary

These results for the relationship between Occupational Class, Education level and Life Crises on attachment style and the three characteristics of respondents are summarised in Table 7.12 below.

Table 7.12 Summary of the results for the relationship between Occupational Class, Education level and Life Crises on attachment style and the three characteristics of respondents

1. Only male respondents demonstrate any significant effects between Occupational Class and Adult Attachment style. None of the results for females reached significance or showed any clear trends. For males there is a highly significant increase in percentages for the Fearful category from Class 1/2 to Class 4/5 and this is mainly compensated by a reduction in percentages within the Secure category.

2. Male respondents show a significant increase in the Dismissive style with the advent of Higher Education which is compensated by reductions in the Fearful and Secure categories.

3. Only female respondents show any effects between Life Crises and Adult Attachment. Secure incidence reduces significantly from 43% to 34% with the advent of Life Crises and this is compensated by an increase in both the Fearful and Dismisssive percentages.

7.6.4 Discussion

The fact that female respondents show no clear relationship between their occupational class and adult attachment styles, and that male respondents do, reflects the results for mental health given in Table 5.13 of Chapter 5 and the structural path diagrams given in Figures 5.33 and 5.34. It would seem that there is a dichotomy between the sexes in this respect, and that in the case of male respondents the relationship is *reactive*, i.e. the occupational class of male respondents is associated with their level of secure attachment. It was hoped to examine the *direction* of this relationship and its magnitude through a structural path analysis, but this was precluded by the high level of covariance existing between the attachment measures.

We have already commented on the rise in the Dismissing category for males with higher education and its association with a reduction in the Dependency score seen in Table 5.13 on mental health. The effects are significant but limited in degree, and do not seem to reflect the changes in attachment related to occupational class. This suggests that the relationship between occupational class, education level and adult attachment is a complex one, involving a range of life-course variables.

Only female respondents show any effects between crises in adult life and attachment, with a reduction in secure attachment as a result of such events. These effects are limited and do not reflect the robust results shown in Table 5.13 for mental health where both sexes are strongly affected by crises in adulthood. Unlike the equivalent relationship for mental health it would seem that attachment style and crises in adulthood are not reactive to the same extent, i.e. Life Crises do not lead to large changes in Adult Attachment Style, or vice versa. This suggests that insecure attachment, particularly of the Fearful or Preoccupied form, predisposes individuals to poor mental health, so that they are vulnerable to crises involving a loss of a close relationship.

7.7 General conclusions regarding adult attachment

As discussed in Section 2.3.4 in Chapter 2, from the basis of the theoretical and practical studies of infant and child attachment by workers such as Main et al.(1985), Erickson et al.(1985), Bretherton et al.(1990) and Grossman & Grossman (1991) and the relationship between such childhood attachment and adulthood (Waters et al., 2000a; Hamilton, 2000; Weinfield et al., 2000) it was predicted that adults who had experienced separation from their parents in childhood due to evacuation might exhibit the effects of that experience in their adult relationships. In terms of attachment theory such effects would be based on the working models of attachment generated in their formative years, and would include defences against rejection. In this context, wartime experience of separation from their parents has provided a unique and relatively controlled opportunity to examine such an hypothesis.

Two questions posed by researchers in the field of adult attachment relate to this present study. Rothbard and Shaver (1991) asked 'what proportion of the variance in adult attachment can be accounted for by experiences which occurred subsequent to the relationship between young children and their primary caregivers?'(p 65); and Henderson (1977) asked 'to what degree has a secure early childhood enabled respondents come to terms with, and accept, any past feelings of rejection or separation?'(p185). We cannot answer these questions in detail, or with conclusive prospective data, but we can say that the present results show that the evacuation experience, which for most occurred subsequent to a secure early childhood, is associated with adult attachment and so did account for part of the variance in that attachment. Also from the results given in Section 7.4, where the variables relating to the quality of home nurture and to the care received during evacuation have been separated, we can comment on the insurance provided by a secure early childhood.

Looking first at the overall effect of evacuation we saw that male respondents showed a large reduction in percentage in the Secure category from a high value of 64% down to 39%, and a compensating increase in the Dismissing category on evacuation. Females showed less of a difference in this respect, but by comparison the non-evacuated or control state incidence was rather less than that for males, at 44%. On breaking down the evacuation experience into its constituent parts we find that the most important input variables were Age at evacuation and Care received during evacuation. Both sexes showed that evacuation at a young age led to a reduction in the percentage in the secure category and an increase, particularly, in the percentage within the Fearful category. Those females evacuated in early adolescence showed a reduction in secure percentages compared to those evacuated in latency or in middle adolescence, in line with the same anomaly seen in the increased incidence of Clinical Anxiety and the mean score for Self-criticism in

Chapter 5 at this stage of child development. Secure category levels were found to rise for both sexes with improving Care received during evacuation, and this was compensated by a reduction in the Fearful category, particularly for females which dropped from 35% to 8%. By comparison the three other Evacuation Experience variables, Period away, Frequency of parental visits and the Number of billets, were found to have had less effect on adult attachment. Examination showed that so long as the period away did not exceed about 2 years, and parental visits were made at least twice per year, then effects assessed from the categorical analysis were slight.

As discussed earlier in Section 7.2.4 these results from the evacuation experience, particularly concerning the age at evacuation and the care received, provide evidence both for a modification to attachment styles, subsequent to early home childhood, and for the longevity of these modified attendant working models into late adulthood, a period of over 50 years. This is confirmed when we look at the effects of home nurture and its interaction with care received during evacuation. The quality of home nurture by itself was found to have a significant effect on the security of adult attachment for both sexes, but when the effect of Care received was deconstructed and examined as a function of both 'good enough' and 'comfortless' home nurture some interesting associations were found. A good, nurturant, home background did not insure against the insecurity engendered by poor care received during the evacuation period, and conversely a period of good care received during evacuation did not, on average, overcome the long-term attachment effects of a comfortless upbringing. Both of these results suggest that a sustained period of loving nurture and care throughout childhood and adolescence is the likely precursor of a secure adult attachment. Such results provide evidence that a significant part of the variance in adult attachment can be accounted for by 'experiences occurring subsequent to the relationship between young children and their primary caregivers' (Rothbard and Shaver, 1991) and help to answer Henderson's (1997) question 'to what degree has a secure early childhood enabled a respondent to come to terms with, and except, any past feelings of rejection or separation?'

Before leaving this discussion of the effects of home nurture and evacuation it is worth recalling that the loss of security resulting from comfortless nurture, or evacuation in early childhood, or due to poor care received, has, in general, had a different effect on the two sexes. There is a tendency for such feelings of insecurity and rejection to lead to an increase in the percentages of females in the Fearful category and to an increase of males in the Dismissing category. As discussed in Section 3.2.2.8 in Chapter3, when examining the Bartholomew and Horowitz model of adult attachment, and in Section 7.2.2.1.1 in this chapter when briefly considering the relationship between attachment styles and the mental health variables as a function of gender, these two insecure attachment styles differ in their association with dependency. The Fearful category is associated with a dependency on the 'other' and and a negative view of the self, whereas the Dismissing category is 'independent' with a positive view of the self. This is also reflected in the overall mental health results given in Table 5.1 in Chapter 5 where the mean score for Dependency on the DEQ scale is very significantly higher for females. A good example of the male predisposition towards a dismissive, or counter-dependent, form of defence is given in Figure 7.10 where the relative percentages of the four attachment styles have been plotted as a function of those first evacuated between the ages of 7 and 12 years and those who were not evacuated. Secure percentages fell from 64% to 35% while Dismissing percentages rose from 28% to 49%. Bearing in mind that the average period away during evacuation is just over 2 years, this means that the above age cohort will lie between the ages of 8 and 13 years at the middle of their evacuation period, i.e. from puberty to early adolescence.

Compared to the effects that Nurture, Age at evacuation and Care received during evacuation had on adult attachment the effects of the other variables concerned with upbringing were slight. The highly significant effects of divorce and death of a parent on the mental health of male respondents was not clearly replicated, but such results as there were pointed to the sexes again responding differently to this stress by females moving to the Fearful category and male respondents towards the Dismissing. Fathers' absence due to war also led to a significant move to the Dismissing category for male respondents. Although there were no comparable effects to those on mental health for male respondents absent from home during bombing there were nevertheless reductions in the Secure category for both sexes when homes had been bombed in their absence or when present. The fact that bombing, of itself, did not lead to a comparably robust effect on males suggests that it may predispose those who were already insecure to depression and clinical anxiety in later life, given proximal stressors.

If we now consider the life-course mediating variables it is interesting to see that only male respondents show any significant associations between occupational class and attachment style, in accord with the mental health results and the structural path models in Chapter 5 (Figures 5.33 and 5.34). The reduction in security with class number is compensated by a highly significant increase in the Fearful category from 8% to 28%. Again we are seeing the association between the Fearful category and the incidence of Depression, which increased from 5% to 50% between Classes 1 to 5 (Table 5.13). From a comparison with the structural path diagram for male respondents in Chapter 5 (Figure 5.34) it is reasonable to conclude that the direction of the path is *from* adult attachment style *to* Occupational class. Somewhat surprisingly, there are no similar associations for the influence of Education level, although males do show a significant rise from 36% to 51% in the Dismissing category with higher educational level which may be associated with a significant reduction in Dependency from the mental health results (Table 5.13). As we found in Chapter 5 for mental health so in adult attachment terms there is no clear relationship between Occupational class and Education level. Only females show any associations between Life crises and attachment style, with a significant reduction in security with one or more life crises. When this is compared to the robust results for the variables of mental health it would appear that unlike mental health adult attachment is not primarily reactive to life crises.

Summing up we can say that in answer to the questions raised at the start of this section we have found that the adult attachment of respondents has been affected by the details of the childhood evacuation experience, and that any insecurity engendered has, on average led to a different response between the sexes. Female respondents were more likely to move to a Fearful, dependent, style and males to a Dismissing, independent one. As expected the quality of home nurture also had an association for both sexes, but other upbringing variables and life course variables tested had very modest effects.

Since we have suggested from these results that modifications to the working models of attachment do occur as a result of young peoples' developmental experience up to middle adolescence, in our view Hazan and Shaver's (1994) original contention that attachment styles are relatively enduring characteristics does require some qualification. Bartholomew (1993) reminds us that Bowlby(1980) saw the formative period in the establishment of patterns of attachment as extending through adolescence, and Kobak (1994) comments that Bowlby also drew attention to the process of adapting working models to new situations, the 'updating and 'revising' of models. From the present study we are in agreement with Bowlby's (1973) belief that working models of attachment are gradually constructed out of experiences throughout infancy, childhood and adolescence, only then may they become relatively resistant to, but still not impervious to change. Here we have been able to show that the effects of separation from parents up to middle adolescence in childhood can still be seen in the adult attachment styles of respondents some 55 years later, albeit in a retrospective study.

This consistency of attachment was discussed earlier in Section 2.3.4, particularly in relation to the longitudinal studies of Waters et al.(2000a), Hamilton (2000) and Weinfield et al.(2000) up to early adulthood. From the review of such work in Section 2.3.4 it was hypothesised that associations would exist between the evacuation experience and adult attachment and that these would be dependent on any individual's experience in terms of age at evacuation, the care received and the degree to which parental attachment is maintained or lost, as well as the mediating effect of early family environment, as summarised in Table 3.10. In general terms this hypothesis has been confirmed by the results given in this chapter.

Chapter 8 Final conclusions of the study

This concluding chapter is in three sections: In the first the strengths and limitations of the survey design are discussed, in the second the major conclusions of the overall study are given for each of the outcome variables and in the third certain recommendations based on these conclusions are presented with proposals for future work.

8.1 Strengths and limitations of the survey

This retrospective quantitative study of the long-term effects of wartime evacuation has certain strengths and weaknesses which it is necessary to bear in mind before presenting the final conclusions. In its overall design it benefited from the qualitative pilot study which preceded it, which not only contributed to the conception of certain hypotheses based on the experience and perceptions of 16 individuals but also helped to provide some personal background detail which is lost in a quantitative study. Although the primary topic in the thesis is of evacuation per se, nevertheless such a large-scale movement of children away from their parents through this 'natural experiment' has allowed some conclusions to be drawn on a range of questions related to possible long-term effects of temporary childhood separation.

As mentioned in Section 3.1 the county of Kent was selected because many children were evacuated from the region yet because of the county's largely rural nature the level of bombing activity was modest compared to more urban areas. As a result any related confounding effects on the effects of evacuation, and so of temporary separation from parents, were likely to be minimised. In the sense that all children evacuated in England during World War 2 were billeted in rural areas, hopefully removed from enemy activity, the Kent children's' experience of evacuation would be similar to those from more urban areas. Nevertheless it may not be sensible to generalise certain conclusions to those from more urban areas, particularly where the bombing in the home neighbourhood was more intense.

In terms of recruitment participants were volunteers rather than being drawn from a random sample and this may have biased some results based on the evacuation experience, although the range of the evacuation experience variables sampled was found to be wide. One of the strengths of the survey is the relatively large number of respondents involved. As discussed in Section 3.1 the high initial response of 1118 volunteers who returned the completed questionnaire enabled a degree of valuable 'filtering' to take place so that only those 867 who were evacuated without their mothers and who were billeted in private foster homes were included. These individuals all responded to a range of short articles and notes placed in the libraries, school association newsletters and newspapers of Kent so that as a result individuals were not under any 'marketing' or financial pressure to respond, a factor which might have affected the distribution. No specific mention was made to the subject of evacuation per se, rather they were asked to contact the author if they lived as children in Kent during the war years and would be willing to participate in a survey of their perceptions and of any long-term effects of that period on their lives (see Appendix 2). By this means both evacuated and non-evacuated controls were recruited through the same invitation.

The success of this voluntary recruitment was demonstrated by the high return of completed questionnaires, at 76%, and the representative nature of both the evacuated and control samples in terms of the 1991 occupational class census distributions for Kent listed in Table 3.1. It was clear from the many letters received that the high return was largely due to a prevailing wish and willingness to talk about a period in childhood which, for many, had remained 'closed' for some 50 years. However, although total numbers were acceptable there is an imbalance in the female and male samples. Because of the smaller numbers in the male sample the statistical power of the tests made was less and this has affected some gender comparisons, and in a number of the bivariate tests male expected cell frequencies for chi-square tests did not meet the required criteria, particularly in the marital history and adult attachment analyses. For these reasons it would have been valuable to have had an increase in the male sample size. Respondent numbers for both sexes were, however, adequate for the multivariate CFA and SEM tests made.

The main limitation of the study is the fact that it is retrospective in design and this has been discussed under Section 3.2.2.1 in the methodology chapter, Chapter 3. Since the object was to examine any long-term effects, into older age, of an event which occurred some 50 years earlier in childhood, there was no alternative procedure available. Notwithstanding the evidence from both the 100 Sisters study by Bifulco et al.(1994) and the conclusions from the detailed review of retrospective studies made by Brewin et al. (1993), where both teams found that the unreliability of retrospective reports have been exaggerated, there remains a belief that such studies are often limited in reliability and validity. In the present survey possibly the greatest potential weakness lies in the recall of family life and upbringing required under question 1 of the questionnaire and also in recalling certain of the evacuation parameters and experiences for questions 3 and 4 (see Appendix 3). Although the descriptions of family life and the details of respondents' upbringing elicited from question 1 led to a valuable rated measure it might have been helpful to have supplemented this with a standardised measure such as the Parental Bonding Instrument (Parker, 1983) to aid comparisons between studies. In terms of the evacuation experience variables fortunately one of the more reliable parameters was Age at evacuation (see Section 3.2.2.2 on the way it was calculated) since it was found to be a critical evacuation experience variable, significantly associated with all the outcome variables. Both Period away and Number of billets are also reliably known as there is sufficient corroborating evidence in the questionnaire, but frequency of parental visits is less reliable since it is dependent on recall alone. Care received is the second most significant evacuation experience variable and is possibly the least reliable in that it is a recalled assessment based on the overall care received, often from multiple billets.

Unlike certain of the upbringing and evacuation experience variables the reliability of the mediating variables related to the war and the life course of respondents are unlikely to be affected by inaccurate or biased recall. However in this context the list of personal and family events used to define life crises is arbitrary and no comparison has been made with possible comparable definitions in the literature (see Table 3.3 in Section 3.2.2.4).

Theoretical and practical considerations regarding the strengths and limitations of the output variables have been discussed at some length in Sections 2.3. and 3.2.2. For mental health the inclusion of Blatt et al.'s (1976) Depressive Experiences Questionnaire has proved particularly valuable, not only in helping to elucidate the precursive tendencies to depressive states but also contributing to some understanding of the gender differences in this respect and their possible origins. Nevertheless it would have been beneficial to have included a standardised symptom questionnaire such as the General Health Questionnaire (Goldberg, 1978) to supplement the mental health measures and to aid more direct comparisons to be made between studies. Finally, concern was voiced in Section 3.2.2.8 about the different theoretical and practical bases for the concept of adult attachment. This is exemplified by the differences between the approach of Main et al. (1985) with the Adult Attachment Interview, largely based on participants' account of their upbringing and scored by raters, and the scales of Hazan & Shaver (1987) and Bartholomew & Horowitz (1991) based on adult relationships in which participants are asked to mark a Likert or forced-choice scale From the discussion in Section 3.2.2.8 it is likely that correlation between these different measures will be limited.

8.2 Major conclusions of the overall study

The main purpose of the study was to investigate the possible long-term effects of temporary separation from parents in childhood due to the exigencies of wartime evacuation. The design of this quantitative study was based on the conclusions of the earlier, qualitative pilot study where it was concluded by induction that the outcome of such an experience lay on a continuum between being a positive, life-enhancing experience to being a negative one with a legacy of emotional and relationship problems, dependent on the particular evacuation experience of an individual. This experience was believed to be adequately defined by five evacuation experience variables: Age at evacuation, Care received, Total period away, Frequency of parental visits and Number of billets occupied. To test this general hypothesis respondents' perceptions were first measured as a function of their evacuation experience, as described by these variables, so that later these perceptions could be compared and interpreted in terms of the chosen outcome measures of Mental health, Marital history and Adult attachment, again as a function of the same evacuation experience variables. In order to extend the value of this investigation by examining the relative impact of evacuation in the face of potential mediating and moderating influences certain upbringing and life-course variables were also include in the design. As a result of this approach it was possible to integrate developmental, psychoanalytic, social, personality and clinical elements into a lifespan approach to understand individuals over time.

In the five subsections which follow the major conclusions from the overall investigation will be given, both in terms of the initial design and including certain rather broader concepts which emerged from this natural experiment.

8.2.1 Respondents' perceptions of the effect of their evacuation experience on their development and adult lives

Following the analysis and results given in Chapter 4, based on the 7-item Perception scale developed for this study, it is clear that the dominant evacuation experience variables were found to be Age at evacuation and Care received, which were significantly associated with all the component items of the Perception scale except Anger with mother. Evacuation at a young age, or with poor care, led to a negative assessment of the developmental outcome of the experience, whereas evacuation in early or middle adolescence, or with good care, led to a positive assessment in terms of the Perception scale. Of the three remaining evacuation experience variables Frequency of parental visits was the most significant and was particularly associated with the perceived level of self-confidence achieved in life, also sociability and the quality of relationships, including the relationship with a respondents' mother on return from evacuation. Total Period away had, somewhat surprisingly, no statistical association with the perception scale items for females except for an increase in Anger with mother with increasing length of the evacuation period. Male respondents believed that their Overall development and their Outlook were associated with this variable, becoming poorer and narrower, respectively, as the period increased. In relation to the Number of billets there is only one significant association, for males only, with the Outlook item in the scale, in that the greater the number of billets occupied the broader a respondent's perceived horizons and interests were in adulthood.

The conclusions of this analysis are in broad agreement with the key hypothesis given in Table 3.12, based on the pilot study, that the evacuation experience is perceived at one extreme as a positive gain for development and at the other as an emotional legacy through life, and that such perceptions depend on the individual experience of evacuation, in particular the age at which it took place and the care received. It was hypothesised that all five evacuation experience variables would be significantly associated with the items in the Perception scale but the degree of association for Period away and Number of billets was low and in the case of Frequency of parental visits it was limited to certain items only.

In the following sections the major conclusions which relate to the four chosen outcome measures as a function of the same evacuation experience variables will be given, so that it will be possible to gauge to what degree respondents' perceptions are confirmed by these measures.

8.2.2 The effect of respondents' evacuation experience on their mental health in adulthood

At the start of the mental health analysis, and before possible associations with the evacuation variables had been examined in detail, two findings were made. The first of these showed that there were no significant differences in mental health between those who had, or had not been, evacuated and that this applied to both sexes. This is a somewhat surprising result in view of the significant effects found when the evacuation experience was later examined in detail. These detailed results showed that evacuation can have both a positive and negative outcome in developmental terms and it is the integration of these protective and risk-inducing effects which have led to this null result. The belief that evacuation can have both a positive and negative outcome was expressed by those taking part in the pilot study and was confirmed in this quantitative study by the way those same perceptions were associated with the evacuation experience variables, as discussed in the last section.

The second, equally clear-cut finding showed that there is a highly significant gender effect relating to the Incidence of Depression and to the mean scores of Dependency and Morbidity symptoms and that this applies to both the evacuated and non-evacuated samples; female respondents are at a greater risk of high values than males. Many workers have found this same gender imbalance in depressive disorders or symptoms and these results have been summarised by Goldberg & Huxley (1992). What is particularly interesting is that this present analysis suggest that a major part of the gender difference may be due to the greater propensity of females to Dependency, as defined by Blatt & Zuroff (1992), since the analysis in Section 5.2.2.1 shows that not only are they more prone to high Dependency levels but are more vulnerable to them in depressive terms. However, neither the univariate nor structural path analyses given in Chapter 5 demonstrate how these high female Dependency levels might arise. In this present study such levels are not significantly affected by either the upbringing or the the evacuation experience variables or the life-course variables as entered into the analyses. The results of the structural path (SEM) analyses for the two sexes showed that whereas 43% of the variance of Depression for males can be explained by the model in Section 5.7.3, based on those variables which were significantly associated with Depression in the univariate analysis, only 27% of the equivalent variance for females is explained. Bearing in mind too the measured 1.6 x increased incidence of depression for females found in this study this difference between the explained variance may not be environmental in origin. One explanation of this 'depressive' difference between the sexes would be that a major part of this accompanying form of dependency is innate, leading to a biological difference between the sexes in this respect. Some support for this is given by the work of Reiss et al. (1995) who found from the NEAD twin studies in the United States that the genetic and environmental variance components of separation anxiety were different in the sexes. Females were found to be biologically more affected with an innate variance component of 31-74% whereas males had a near-neglible innate variance component of 0-19%.

It is only when the evacuation experience is broken down and examined as a function of its five components that significant associations were found with the mental health variables. This may help to explain the somewhat equivocal nature of the conclusions on the effects of evacuation given by the Finnish studies of Räsänen (1992) and Lagnebro (1994, 2002) and also from the English surveys by Foster (2000) and Waugh (2001), as discussed in Section 2.2. In these instances samples were smaller and it was not possible to examine the evacuation experience in the same detail with complex multivariate analyses. This present study found that for both sexes increasing Age at evacuation and improving Care received were both associated with a reduction in the Incidence of Depression and Clinical Anxiety while the mean scores for Self-criticism and Morbidity symptoms were also reduced. Also an increase in Period away was found to be associated with an increase in Self-criticism. When these results are compared with the non-evacuated control samples some interesting trends were found. Male respondents evacuated after early adolescence benefit from a reduced Incidence of Depression in relation to controls, so long as the Care received was adequate, whereas females were not affected to the same extent, their levels remaining more constant with Age at evacuation. Both sexes show Clinical Anxiety incidences that are higher than controls if evacuated in early childhood, and these levels drop just below the control level in latency. In early adolescence female incidences rise significantly above the control level and become comparable to the level in early childhood, i.e. 4-6 years of age, and this anomaly is reflected in the same sharp rise in Self-criticism at this same age. Both these findings may be related to the separation from parents occurring soon after puberty, and in Figure 5.13 it was shown that it was only after about one years' separation that the anomalous increase in Self-criticism occurred. The possible influence of this has been discussed in Section 5.2.4 in relation to the work of Erikson (1968), Marcia (1980) and Paikoff & Brooks-Gunn (1991), where the importance of a close and effective parent-child relationship following menarche is emphasised for the achievement of a secure later identity.

Under the Upbringing variables the analysis included the simple dichotomous variable related to the quality of home nurture enjoyed, i.e. 'good enough' or 'comfortless'. This variable had a greater influence on adult mental health than the evacuation variables in the analyses made and this applied to both sexes. It was significantly associated with the Incidence of Depression and Clinical Anxiety and with the mean scores of Self-criticism in the univariate results and it also provided the highest loadings towards Depression in the structural path model, not directly but through the mediating variables of Self-criticism and Life Crises. When we look at the combined effects of home Nurture and the Care received during evacuation then the former is the stronger predictor. The effects are additive in terms of protection and risk, so that 'good enough' Nurture provided some emotional security during evacuation whereas 'comfortless' Nurture placed respondents at added risk, whatever the quality of Care received during the period of separation. These results relating to the interaction between Nurture and Care received during separation are in agreement with the evaluation made by Holmes (1993), when comparing the differences in the conclusions of Bowlby (1953) and Rutter (1982) regarding the effects of maternal deprivation. Holmes says: 'acute separation distress is probably less damaging and more complex than Bowlby first saw it... an important point comes from Hinde's rhesus monkey studies (Hinde & McGinnis, 1977) which showed the effects of separation depend on the mother-child relationship *before* the event: the more tense the relationship, the more damaging the separation.' (p.49). Both Holmes and Rutter believe it is not the separation itself which matters but its meaning and the context in which it occurs. These conclusions are in agreement with those of Brown et al. (1986) and Harris et al. (1990), discussed in Section 2.3.2, who in studies on the association of depression with childhood separation found evidence for the importance of both the quality of family care before separation and the subsequent quality of care received after separation. Results from this present study also reflect the findings of Harris et al. regarding the effect of age in that those under the age of six years were found to be at a much greater risk of depression, and any positive mediating effects of the subsequent care received was less. Harris et al. suggest that children of such an age may have particular problems mourning their loss due to the relative immaturity of their cognitive development; in terms of attachment theory this could be interpreted as a loss of attachment. Also under Upbringing it was somewhat surprising to find that it was only male respondents who were affected by the death of a parent or by parental divorce. These crises in their childhood were associated with a significant increase in the incidence of depression and morbidity symptoms in adulthood. This difference between the sexes has been provisionally explained by the fact that some 75% of the deaths were paternal and that divorce, when these respondents were young, usually meant loss of contact with a father.

Regarding the possible mediating effects of war there was one, rather surprising, finding that the bombing of respondents' home neighbourhood in their *absence* was associated with a significant increase in the Incidence of Clinical Anxiety. This also applied to the Incidence of Depression but for male respondents only; no such associations were found if they were at home during the bombing. These results provide some insight into the effect of direct wartime action on the emotional life of children, emphasising the importance of close family contact during such a time of great potential danger and loss. Absence appears to have internalised an increased degree of separation anxiety, associated with the possible physical loss of parents, so that it can surface again in adulthood when life course events occur which can be related to such feelings of personal loss and rejection.

In terms of the life course variables included in the analysis there was a marked difference between the sexes in the effect of Occupational Class on the Incidence of Depression. The incidence was high with no significant variation with class for females, whereas incidence values increased, with a high level of significance, from 5% to 50% from Class 1 to Class 5 for male respondents, which was also reflected in a significant increase in the mean number of Morbidity symptoms. This difference between the sexes was confirmed by the structural path models, with no significant paths present in the female model which related to Occupational Class. As a result no part of the variance of the Incidence of Depression for females can, in this study, be attributed to Occupational Class, contrary to the conclusion of Elmslie et al. (1999). The SEM model for male respondents showed a highly significant path from Care received during evacuation to Occupational Class, indicating that improving care during evacuation was associated with a higher Occupational Class in adulthood leading to a lower probability of Depression.

The occurrence of Life Crises had a highly significant effect for both sexes on the Incidence of Depression, Self-criticism and the number of Morbidity symptoms; the Incidence of Clinical Anxiety also increased, although only that for males reached significance. These results are in general agreement with those of Brown & Harris (1978) and Brown, Harris & Hepworth (1995), albeit for younger female samples, who found that the type of life events most likely to provoke depression or anxiety were those involving close relationships. In both structural path models for the sexes Life Crises was an important mediating variable between Nurture and the Incidence of Depression, and for males only there were also input paths from both Age at evacuation and Period Away. For Age at evacuation this was in the expected direction, i.e. evacuation at a young age led to a vulnerability to Depression via Life Crises, but the loading for Period Away was counter-intuitive, i.e. for male respondents increased length of time away gave some protection from the effect of life crises in adulthood. The male structural model also gives a clue as to how such an effect can arise: There is a significant level of positive correlation between Care received during evacuation and Period Away, so that separation from home under good care can develop a sense of self-reliance and independence, with the proviso that evacuation did not take place in early childhood. This is in agreement with the findings of the Perception analysis discussed in the last section, where the evacuation experience was perceived as 'life-enhancing' so long as the care received was good.

It is clear that the perception that evacuation may be a positive or negative experience in terms of developmental outcome is in general agreement with these findings and conclusions in relation to mental health. This is particularly the case when it comes to the important influence of both the age at which evacuation took place and the care received, which were also the two most influential evacuation variables in the perception analysis given in Chapter 4. Where the conclusions of the two analyses do differ is particularly in terms of gender. Whereas the perception results were broadly similar for the two sexes the history of mental health for the two gender samples was different. This difference could be summed up by saying that the female sample, overall, displayed a higher level of affective disorders, particularly for depression and morbidity, which were rather less affected by the details of the evacuation experience, whereas males had a more robust mental health overall but were more vulnerable to the vagaries of the experience if evacuated at a young age. But for those males evacuated in adolescence, who had received good care, there was a protective effect. It is suggested that this difference between the sexes is partly accounted for by the greater and possibly innate propensity for females to maintain dependent relationships which then makes them more vulnerable to the loss of those relationships, both as children and later in adulthood. This would be related to the way each sex responds to childhood separation in terms of attachment style.

8.2.3 The effect of respondents' evacuation experience on their marital history

In an analogous way to the results for mental health it was found that there was no overall effect of the occurrence or non-occurrence of evacuation on the marital history of respondents and it was only when the experience was examined in terms of the five evacuation experience variables that significant associations were found. So again such a finding lends support to the hypothesis that the evacuation experience is perceived by respondents as covering a wide range of emotional and developmental outcomes dependent on their evacuation experience, but when integrated overall for this sample yields a null response.

The three evacuation experience variables which were associated in the bivariate analyses with marital history in terms of divorce or separation were Age at evacuation for both sexes, and Care received and Frequency of parental visits for females only. In addition, in terms of the upbringing variables, the Quality of Nurture for both sexes and the Divorce of parents for females were significantly associated with marital history, while, in agreement with Diekmann & Engelhardt (1999), there was a lower association with Death of a parent compared with that of Divorce of a parent. Unfortunately there were insufficient male respondents whose parents had divorced to carry out a full comparative test. The most significant of these variables, that is Age at evacuation, Care received, Quality of Nurture and Divorce of parents were also entered in a multiple linear regression analysis using female respondents only. It was found that together they explained 44% of the variance of respondent Divorce. This figure may be compared with that of 14% if the Divorce of parents was entered alone. Such a comparison gives an indication of the influence of home nurture and family security in explaining such a major part of the variance. These results from both the bivariate and multivariate analyses generally support the conclusions from the research reviewed in Section 2.3.3 of Chapter 2 which found that the accepted generational association between parental divorce and the occurrence of offspring divorce is likely to be mediated by a number of factors which include important family and relationship components (Amato, 1996; O'Connor et al., 1999; Teachman, 2002). However in the literature there is clearly concern, expressed by Teachman and others, that so many workers have simply used the dichotomy 'parents divorced/not divorced' as the input variable, rather than attempting to define the mechanisms at work, however hard this may be to operationalise. This present study has shown that in the case of a childhood which includes temporary separation from parents it is the quality of home life plus certain parameters of the evacuation experience that together have contributed to the major share of the variance of respondent divorce, not the simple occurrence or non-occurrence of parental divorce.

The strength of the association for both sexes between Age at evacuation and the incidence of respondent Divorce is demonstrated by the highly significant bivariate results found in Table 6.2 (a), with levels from early childhood to middle adolescence dropping from 35% to 13% for females and 30% to 0% for males. This strength of association was further demonstrated by examining the numbers of both sexes who had experienced *multiple* divorces as a function of this evacuation variable. As discussed in Section 6.8 it was found that the percentage incidences for both sexes fell from about 10%, if evacuated between 4-6 years of age, to 0% if evacuated between 13-15 years of age. In terms of a 'dose-response' test of causality this would seem to indicate cause and effect (Rutter & Smith, 1995; Bifulco & Moran, 1998). It also supports the accounts from both Serenius (1995) and Lagnebro (1994) in relation to Finnish war children who both commented on the high divorce rates of those who had been evacuated at a young age. However, in terms of the positive effects of the evacuation experience the low incidence levels of divorce for those evacuated in the age range 13-15 years lie below those for the controls, where the divorce rate for females was 21% and males 14%. The large reduction for male respondents, i.e. from 14% to 0%, is interesting and may be compared with the evidence from the mental health results of a similar protection afforded to males in this age group in relation to the incidence of Depression and the level of Self-criticism.

For the incidence of divorce, in common with the mental health results, it was found that a secure and caring home background for females provided some degree of protection from the vagaries of the quality of the care received during evacuation. However, if nurture was 'comfortless' the incidence of divorce remained high and constant, around 35%, irrespective of the quality of care received during evacuation. Unfortunately the small cell sizes of the male sample precluded making a gender comparison.

In terms of the Life Course mediating variables there is a marked and interesting difference between the influence Occupational Class had on the incidence of depression and on divorce for male respondents. Whereas there was a highly significant association between Occupational Class and the incidence of Depression, with incidence rates rising from 5% to 50% across Classes 1 to 5, there was no such trend in Divorce which remained at an incidence of about 15% across the classes. Bearing in mind the correlation between the incidence of depression and divorce reported by O'Connor (1999), Goldberg & Huxley (1992) and others it was surprising to find that this mediating variable, Occupational Class, did not influence the incidence of divorce. The structural model given in Figure 5.34 in Chapter 5 for male respondents helps to explain why in that both Life Crises and Occupational Class load heavily on to Depression but there is no common path between Occupational Class and Life Crises. Since a major component of Life Crises in this mental health survey is the incidence of divorce it can be seen how this apparent anomaly arises: both Occupational Class and Divorce are mediating variables affecting Depression but are not linked in this model.

Although the analysis of the marital history of respondents was limited by the smaller size of the male sample, nevertheless there are indications that the two sexes may not always be responding to the exigencies of their childhood experience in a similar way. This was seen in the response to the Care received and, to a lesser extent, in the response to the Frequency of parental visits during evacuation. In each case the divorce rates of the female sample were significantly associated with these variables in the expected sense, but this did not apply to the male sample. It is possible that this difference may be related to the way the two samples responded to the evacuation experience in attachment terms, which will be considered in the next sub-section giving the conclusions from the adult attachment analysis. From the review of the literature given in Section 2.3.3 little attempt has been made to evaluate the possible childhood precursors of divorce as a function of gender, even though sample sizes were usually large (Pope & Mueller, 1999; O'Connor et al., 1999; Diekmann & Engelhardt, 1999).

In the sense that divorce is perceived as a negative outcome, and a stable marriage is seen in a positive light, then the results from the marital history analysis, like those for mental health, once again support respondents' perceptions of their evacuation experience in terms of the likely outcome. This is particularly the case for the influence of the age at which evacuation first took place, and in the case of females for the care received during evacuation, the two variables most strongly associated with these perceptions.

8.2.4 The effect of respondents' evacuation experience on their adult attachment style

A measure of adult attachment style was included in this study on the premise that adults who have experienced temporary separation from their parents, subsequent to home nurture in early childhood, may exhibit the effects of that experience in their adult relationships. This supposition was based both on the underlying theoretical constructs of attachment discussed in Section 2.3.4 and the associations found recently from longitudinal studies of attachment from childhood and into early adulthood (Waters et al., 2000a; Hamilton, 2000; Weinfield et al., 2000). In this context the separation anxiety engendered by evacuation has provided a unique and relatively controlled opportunity to test the level of continuity of working models of attachment over a life-span.

As far as the overall effect of evacuation was concerned male respondents showed a large reduction in the Secure category from 64% to 39% with a compensating increase in the Dismissing category on evacuation. Females showed less of a difference but by comparison the non-evacuated incidence was less than that for males, at 44%. In a similar manner to the results for both mental health and marital history it was found that when the overall experience was broken down into its components the two most significant input variables of evacuation were again Age at evacuation and Care received. Both sexes showed that evacuation at a young age led to a reduction in the percentage within the Secure category and an increase within the Fearful category. For those females evacuated in early adolescence there was a reduction in Secure percentages compared to those evacuated in latency or middle adolescence, which reflected the same anomaly found in the increased incidence of Clinical Anxiety and the mean score for Self-criticism at this stage of child development. The levels within the Secure and Fearful styles were also affected by the Care received during evacuation. Secure levels rose for both sexes with improving Care received and this was compensated by a reduction on the Fearful category, particularly for females. As found in the previous analyses the three remaining evacuation experience variables had less effect, except that both sexes showed a trend to higher levels of Fearful attachment if the frequency of parental visits fell below 2 or 3 per year.

These results from the experience of evacuation, concerning the age at which evacuation took place and the care received during the time of separation, provide evidence for both the influence of these two variables, subsequent to the home relationship with respondents' primary caregivers, and for the longevity of this influence throughout their lives in terms of working models of attachment. Further confirmation of this comes from looking at the effects of home nurture and its interaction with care received during evacuation. The quality of home nurture on its own was found to have a significant effect on the security of adult attachment for both sexes, but when the influence of these two evacuation variables was deconstructed it was found that a good, nurturant, home background did not fully insure against the insecurity engendered by poor foster care during the evacuation period. Conversely a period of good care received during evacuation did not overcome the insecurity engendered by a comfortless upbringing. These results emphasize the need for a sustained period of loving nurture and care throughout childhood and adolescence as the precursors of a secure adult attachment. They also provide evidence that some of the variance in adult attachment can be accounted for by 'experiences occurring subsequent to the relationship between young children and their caregivers', in answer to the question posed by Rothbard & Shaver (1991, p.65). It is also of relevance to these conclusions that of the 103 male respondents who reported both good home nurture *and* good care received during evacuation only 42% were in the Secure adult attachment category compared to 64% of those 52 respondents who had remained at home with their families in Kent throughout the war.

The insecurity engendered by the quality of home nurture or the evacuation experience has, in general terms, had a different effect on the the two sexes. There is a tendency for any such feelings of insecurity or rejection to lead to an increase in the percentage of females in the Fearful category and to an increase of males in the Dismissing category. As discussed in Section 3.2.2.8 in Chapter 3, when examining the Bartholomew & Horowitz model of adult attachment, these two insecure attachment styles differ in their association with dependency. The Fearful category is associated with a dependency on the 'other' and a negative view of the self, whereas the Dismissing category is 'independent' with a positive view of the self. These differences are also reflected in the their relationship to Factor 1, Dependency, of the DEQ analysis, illustrated in Figure 7.4. It is suggested that this movement to different insecure attachment styles contributes to the difference in levels of depression found between the sexes since it was shown in Figure 7.2 that those of both sexes in the Preoccupied and Fearful, dependent, categories are more than twice as likely to suffer depression as those in the Secure and Dismissing, independent, categories. In a recent review paper on the development of psychopathology from infancy to adulthood Fonagy (2003) expressed the opinion, based on work at the Menninger Clinic in Kansas which included use of the Bartholomew & Horowitz attachment measure that psychopathology may be inferred from the fact that 'at the extreme, fearful, end of the secure/fearful dimension there can be no effective strategy for interpersonal encounters because the attachment system is not there to sustain a consistent set of defences and so the capacity to arrive at representations of the motivational or epistemic mind state of the other, independent of those of the self, are profoundly compromised' (p.231).

By comparison with the effects of nurture those of the other variables concerned with upbringing, and also any possible effects of the war, were more minor. The highly significant associations found between the divorce or death of a parent and the mental health of male respondents were not reflected in the attachment results although there was a tendency, once more, for females to move to the Fearful category and for males to the Dismissing category. Fathers' absence due to war did lead to a significant move to the Dismissing category for male respondents. There were no comparable effects to those found for the mental health of respondents absent from home during bombing, and this suggests that the acute anxiety engendered may have predisposed those who were already insecure to clinical anxiety in later life, given proximal stressors.

As far as the life-course mediating variables were concerned it was only male respondents who showed any associations between Occupational class and attachment style, reflecting the mental health results and the linkages in the structural path models given in Chapter 5. The reduction in security from professional to working class was mirrored by a significant increase in the Fearful category, which can be associated with the large increase in the incidence of Depression found. No comparable associations were found for Education level for either sex. Only females showed any associations between Life crises and attachment style, with a significant reduction in security with one or more life crises. However, when this is compared with the robust associations found for mental health it would appear that unlike mental health adult attachment is not primarily reactive to any life crises, rather insecure attachment predisposes individuals to poor mental health, so that they are vulnerable to crises involving loss of a close relationship.

The main results of this study, and the conclusions which can be drawn from them, suggest that adult attachment styles are primarily associated with the quality of home nurture and the security engendered by that home background. Nevertheless the quality of the foster care received during evacuation does have a mediating effect: good care during evacuation has tended to ensure that the level of secure attachment achieved as a result of a nurturing early childhood is maintained through to adulthood, while poor care received during evacuation has led to a reduction in that level of security. There is also some difference between the sexes: While both sexes benefit from the positive effect of good care during evacuation following 'good enough' home nurture, this still leaves the proportion of secure male respondents in adulthood significantly below those who remained at home throughout the war. This discrepancy is of interest when taken in conjunction with the evidence from the mental health and marital history results which show there is no statistical difference in any of the five mental health variables, or for the incidence of divorce, between those who were, or were not evacuated. Bearing in mind also the very positive perceptions of those male respondents who received good care during evacuation this does suggest that attachment security is more vulnerable to the vicissitudes of the evacuation experience, and does not necessarily mirror these positive perceptions. This may be particularly so for the male sample with its propensity to move to the Dismisssive category, a style which was not found to be strongly associated with affective disorders or divorce and which might provide such individuals with a positive, if rather self-centred view of the benefits of their evacuation experience. There is a certain sad irony in the likelihood that the physical security provided by evacuation was not matched by emotional security, and that those who remained at home during the war, with reduced physical security, appear to have maintained a higher level of emotional security.

These conclusions do imply that the hypothesis which arose from the perceptions of respondents that the evacuation experience might have a positive or negative outcome on adult attachment dependent on the details of that experience, needs to be qualified. Certainly the security of adult attachment for females is associated with both the age at evacuation and the care received, and males show these same trends, but these effects are possibly not as robust as those seen for the outcome variables of mental health and marital history. In the case of adult attachment, possibly not surprisingly, the most significant variable is the quality of home nurture received. Nevertheless the results of this study have shown that modifications to the working models of attachment may occur as a result of young people's developmental experience up to middle adolescence, so that Hazan & Shaver's (1994) original contention that attachment styles are relatively enduring characteristics may require some qualification. However it is true that life crisis events subsequent to those of childhood development, as measured in this survey, did not seem to have had much effect on adult attachment. Bowlby (1980) saw the formation period in the pattern of attachment as extending through to adolescence and also drew attention to the process of adapting working models to new situations. This, albeit retrospective study, has shown that the effects of temporary separation from parents up to middle adolescence can still be seen in the adult attachment styles of respondents some 55 years after these events took place

8.3 Recommendations for future work and Food for thought

8.3.1 Recommendations for future work

The opportunities presented to replicate this study of the temporary separation of children from parents during a war are likely to be, fortunately, few and far between. It is a natural experiment based on a singular event involving large numbers of children under reasonably controlled conditions. Many children have suffered the ravages of war since World War 2 but it may prove difficult to carry out comparative surveys and to generalise from such results. Elders (1988) has warned of the particularities of cohort experiences in an historical context and the difficulty of disentangling developmental and historical effects. Perhaps of greater value would be to try and replicate and understand more fully some of the disparate findings from this study, some of which have a more general application in development psychology and certain recommendations are given below related to these findings. In this respect the lifetime experiences of this sample provided a particular advantage over those conducted with students or younger participants.

Initially it was surprising to find that the overall occurrence or non-occurrence of evacuation had little or no effect on the chosen outcome variables. However, the explanation was that this null result came about through the integration of a range of evacuation experiences, some positive and some negative, and this was effectively confirming the perceptions of respondents that the evacuation experience lay on a continuum between being a positive event, i.e. 'it made me', to being a negative one, 'it ruined my life'. When the experience was examined in detail the outcome variables of mental health, marital history and adult attachment were all significantly associated with the age at which evacuation took place. The youngest children, in the 4-6 year age range, were particularly vulnerable to the effects of evacuation, and this was largely independent of the period of time spent away, that is for periods in excess of about 6 months. As a recommendation for future research it would be valuable to try and obtain a more precise measure of this limiting period for young children and to determine how the risk function for affective disorders and adult insecure attachment varies in this intervening period depending on the quality of upbringing and the quality of foster care received. It is also important to try to understand, in terms of theoretical concepts of developmental psychology, what causes these children to be under much greater risk than those in latency, aged 7-9 years. Is this due to the limited stage of cognition reached in developmental terms or to an inability to retain attachment in absentia (Bowlby, 1973) or possibly to an inability to mourn as Harris (1988) has suggested? Another finding related to age at evacuation which requires replication and examination is that for female children, separated from their parents before menarche in the 10-12 age range. These children have been found to be predisposed to high levels of self-criticism and clinical anxiety in adulthood. Such vulnerability will depend on the quality and suitability of the foster care provided and no doubt also on contemporary mores which have altered so considerably over the past 50 years (Elder, 1998).

One of the more general and potentially valuable results of the study has been the highly significant difference found between the sexes for Dependency, from the DEQ scale of Blatt et al.(1976), and the fact that females are vulnerable to these high levels in terms of affective disorders, particularly depression. There is also the question of the origin of this level of Dependency which was not explained by the relevant structural model in this study. The hypothesis put forward that this difference is primarily biological in origin is based on the null model result and also on twin studies, but this needs to be considered in greater depth. The suggestion was also made that this difference between the sexes goes some way to explaining the greater vulnerability of females to depressive disorders, and again this requires further investigation. This factor, Dependency, in the form derived by Blatt et al. from their 66-item scale, also needs to be carefully evaluated in psychological terms and compared with other 'dependency' definitions and concepts (see Fairbairn, 1952; Birtchnell, 1984, 1988a).

The finding that a high percentage of the variance in the incidence of respondent divorce for females was explained not solely by the incidence of parental divorce but required the inclusion of the quality of a respondent's nurture plus the age and the care received during evacuation or separation, needs to be replicated. This may be impossible to operationalise in a similar manner to this present study but it should be possible to undertake a retrospective quantitative study based on the experiences of those who have been fostered at different ages and under different conditions by local agencies.

The study has demonstrated a link between temporary separation from parents in childhood and adult attachment, the two most significant variables being the age at which such separation took place and the quality of foster care received. In addition the quality of home nurture was found to be of significance. In general terms the sexes responded differently in that the insecurity engendered by negative childhood experiences had a divergent effect on the sexes. Females had a tendency to move to the Fearful insecure category while males moved to the Dismissive in adulthood. This has implications for their mental health in that the former was found to be associated with depression, clinical anxiety and morbidity while the latter, dismissive, style appeared to provide some defence against such an outcome. Clearly the findings linking these childhood factors to relationship insecurity in adulthood, as well as the differential gender effect, need to be replicated.

The study has benefited from keeping the sexes separate in that the analyses have demonstrated significant differences between the male and female responses to the evacuation experience and to upbringing in terms of mental health and adult attachment. There is sometimes an underlying assumption in developmental psychology that maintaining gender differentiation is unimportant but, looking back over a life-time, this study has shown this distinction is very important and needs to be retained in such developmental studies.

8.3.2 Food for thought

It is debatable how relevant the results and conclusions of this study may be for those who are concerned with the temporary separation of young children from their parents and their placement in foster care, such as family and child-care workers in the Social Services. However, within the context of the study, certain general lessons can be drawn, particularly in relation to age and the quality of care receved. These two variables of evacuation were found to be the most significant in terms of their association with the chosen variables of mental health, marital history and adult attachment. They have been shown to play a major part in determining the predisposition of respondents to depression, clinical anxiety, divorce and insecure adult attachment, all measured some 50 years after childhood. The wartime government had said that no children below the age of 5 years should be evacuated without their mothers, but some were as this sample confirms. What the study has shown, however, is that in order to mitigate the worst of the risk-inducing effects of such a temporary separation it would have been advisable to have raised the minimum age for unaccompanied children to at least 8 years. We have come a long way since those early wartime years, but the lessons are plain to see, for on average the younger children in this sample were shown to be emotionally more secure at home, notwithstanding the ravages of war. There is an additional concern here in that female children evacuated in the age range of 10-12 years have been shown to be at risk of clinical anxiety in adulthood and any possible emotional effects of puberty and the menarche were not taken into consideration in the selection of appropriate foster care.

As far as the care received during evacuation is concerned the government of the day has retrospectively received criticism from Parsons (1998) in his book 'I'll take that one' and from many others for the arbitrary manner in which children were billeted. The lessons are clear, the quality of care received was found to be a highly significant variable in mediating the effects of temporary separation from parents and even for some in mitigating the effects of a 'comfortless' upbringing. However it was a lottery, both insightful selection procedures and professional monitoring were virtually non-existent. Again we have come a long way since those days but these results bring home the importance of foster care selection and the monitoring of the care received.

By comparison with the effects of age and the care received it was surprising to find that the remaining variables of the evacuation experience, concerned with the total period away, the frequency of parental visits and the number of billets occupied, had only modest effects on the outcome variables. This suggests that once the 'die was cast' most of the older children accepted their situation and adapted to it as best they could, whatever their local circumstances. For the youngest children this was not an option and most were put at risk whatever the standard of care or the frequency of parental visits or the length of time away. Since the sample numbers of 4-6 year old children evacuated for less than one year was low it was only possible to make an estimate for the 'maximum' separation period which would have been acceptable without undue risk of affective disorders or loss of parental attachment. Examination of the fitted scatter plots for the incidence of depression and for the scores of self-criticism as a function of the period away suggested that a maximum of 6 months was possibly acceptable before the negative effects of this separation on the youngest children became evident and possibly irreversible. The fact that the frequency of parental visits had only modest associations with the outcome variables does suggest that however frequent such visits might have been it is the quality of such visits that matters. Many respondents commented on the inhospitality, or in some cases outright hostility, of foster parents towards visiting parents, providing an unsuitable venue and atmosphere for the maintenance of attachment. Ideally such visits would have needed to be of a reasonable duration and be free from the influence of foster parents. Even under the best possible conditions younger children, particularly, would still suffer the trauma of repeated separations, interpreted possibly as further rejections.

There are two other, unrelated, findings, which also provide food for thought. The first is that the only significant association with bombing, that for clinical anxiety, occurred for those of both sexes *absent* from home at the time their home neighbourhoods were attacked. These associations did *not* occur if respondents were *present* at the time of the raids, an important and practical commentary on the distinction between emotional and physical security, possibly something the government and senior civil servants failed to adequately consider. The second finding is that for many of those who were evacuated as older children, particularly boys, it was perceived to be a positive experience which broadened their minds, outlook and interests, and increased their self-confidence and led them to an interest in further education. These perceptions have been confirmed in this study and there is measured evidence for these beneficial effects in the reduction in the incidence of depression, the level of self-criticism and the incidence of divorce by comparison with those who had not been evacuated. Possibly this finding gives some encouragement to all those working with young people from deprived or urban backgrounds.

Finally there are potential policy implications from this survey with regard to the older age group studied. From the conclusions of the research it is clear that the general psychological health and resilience of such an older cohort is dependent on each individual's childhood history, on their adult attachment in terms of their ability to relate to others and on their individual situation, including the loss of partners or other primary attachment figures. This author believes that the conclusions of such research covering a lifespan have implications for those in the caring and clinical professions who are charged with the creation and implementation of policies designed to aid the accession to care services in old age, including the appropriate form of residential and clinical care which may be required.

APPENDIX 1. Summary of the project report: *Wartime evacuation: A pilot study of some effects using grounded theory* (Rusby, 1995).

This study was undertaken as a fourth-year undergraduate project in partial fulfilment of a degree in Psychology at the University of London (Rusby, 1995). Since it was a pilot study, with little detailed pre-knowledge of what variables or effects might be relevant, it was decided to use a 'contextual' or 'interpretative' approach. One such method, borrowed from sociology, is that of grounded theory first developed by Glaser and Strauss (1967). As they say:

'Grounded theory is an inductive, theory-discovery methodology that allows the researcher to develop a theoretical account of the general features of a topic while simultaneously grounding the account in empirical observations or data'.

In the present context it seemed to be a good instrument with which to try and make sense of the data from semi-structured interviews and thereby gain some understanding of both the more important evacuation variables and their associated outcome variables in adulthood, as a precursor of a possible quantitative study. For the purposes of this pilot study the research question was defined as being:

'Individuals' perceptions of the long-term effects of wartime evacuation on their lives and relationships'.

The majority of the individuals in the study had contributed their stories to an anthology of evacuation experiences edited by Joy Richardson entitled 'Children in Retreat' (1990), and she kindly arranged for the present author to contact them. All 16 of those interviewed came from Kent and the majority from the Medway towns on the Thames estuary. They were interviewed in their homes, 10 women and 6 men aged between 60 to 70 years, and Table A1.1 gives a summary of their evacuation details and experience. It can be seen that the distributions in age at evacuation, total period away and the care received were wide, as were their memories and perceptions of that time. Every effort was made during the interviews to cover the details of their upbringing prior to starting on the details of the evacuation itself. The post-evacuation period was also covered, particularly those aspects which might relate to any association between evacuation experiences and long-term effects, such as family relationships, including problems of fitting-back into the family, further development, physical and mental health and marital history. Considering the time lapse of over 50 years their average recall of events during evacuation appeared to be remarkably detailed, and many commented on how vivid their experiences still were to them. All interviews were recorded and the tapes transcribed, providing about 100,000 words available as data for the subsequent analysis by grounded theory.

Table A1.1 Summary of 16 interviewees' evacuation details

Interviewee	Home Town	Start of Evacuation Date	Age	Total period away, years	Evacuated to	No. of billets	Remarks
WOMEN:							
Mrs DG	Fulham,	Sept '39	13	4	Sussex	9	Very mixed quality billets. One good billet for 2 years. Detailed story with insight.
Mrs JA	Isle of	May '40	6	4	S. Wales	2	Happy first billet for 3 years, 'like family'. Poor. second billet. Responsible for 5-year old brother.
Mrs CG	Gravesend	Sept '39	9	2 3/4	Norfolk Devon	1 3	Somewhat traumatic experience. Became nervous child – fear of separation.
Mrs NF	Strood	Sept '39	14	2 1/2	Canterbury S. Wales	3 5	With mother for two years. A variety of billets, some good, some poor.
Mrs LF	Gillingham	May '40	10	2	S. Wales	1	Responsible for 5-year old brother. Very poor billet. Malnutrition. Reserved.
Mrs MS	Sevenoaks	May '44	9	1	Devon	1	Responsible for 7-year old sister. Good memories. Independence.
Mrs FC	Gillingham	Sept '39	14	3/4	Herne Bay	1	Came from very poor family. Very happy memories.
Mrs PW	Folkestone	Sept '39	8	3/4	S. Wales Gloucester	1 1	Two traumatic experiences. Deprivation.
Mrs MB	Beckenham	Sept '40	4	3/4	Bucks.	1	Evacuated with depressed mother. Very lonely time. Unhappy.
Mrs PE	Croydon	Sept '39	11	1/2	Berks	1	Private evacuation. Rigid regime but happy memories. 'Gained from it'. Love of literature.
MEN:							
Mr JN	Greenwich	Sept '39	7 1/2	5 1/2	Hastings S. Wales	4 11	Basically traumatic story - 3 hour interview. One good billet for final 9 months.
Mr JT	Dover	May '40	9	4 1/2	S. Wales	7	One good billet for 2 years, followed by six unhappy ones.
Mr FR	Sheerness	June '40	13	1 1/4	S. Wales	1	Came from very poor family. Father died in '30s. Happy memories – brought me out.
Mr WC	Chatham	Sept '39	15	1	Faversham S. Wales	2 1	Happy memories. 'Horizons broadened.
Mr RN	Gillingham	Sept '39	15	1	Faversham S. Wales	1 1	Came from very poor family. Father died in '34 (TB). Happy memories – 'Horizons' broadened'.
Mr CB	Beckenham	June '44	12	1/4	Somerset	2	With mother. Very happy memories. Love of natural history.

It is not intended to go through the analysis in detail, suffice it to say that the 16 tape transcriptions were examined, marked and coded in the recommended manner (Strauss and Corbin, 1990). Following this open-coding procedure connections were then made by 'axial coding' so that common themes were grouped together under labelled concepts, and these in turn were listed together under 'family' categories. This applied to concepts and categories derived from both the evacuation and post-evacuation stories, and a complete listing of these are given in Appendices 1 and 2 of the pilot study report (Rusby, 1995).

It soon became clear when analysing the transcribed data that the outcome of a period of evacuation was perceived by interviewees in different ways, leading to certain believed 'gains' and 'losses' in terms of subsequent development, interests and the ability to make secure relationships. In Appendix 2 of the pilot study there are 24 concept labels referring to a wide variety of positive outcomes under the category 'Gains in development' and 47 concept labels of negative outcomes under the category 'Emotional legacy'. Some of these are listed here:

'Gains in development' (+ve outcome)	'Emotional legacy' (-ve outcome)
'Saved us'	Solitariness
Self reliance	Holding back
Confidence	Emotional scars
Widened horizons	Unfinished business
Independence	'Spectators'
'Brought me out'	Unacknowledged anger
Positive gain	Guilt
Love of countryside	Dependency
Music	'Hard shell'
Boundaries set	Striving for identity
Love of books	Repressed memories
Survivability	Anger at parents
Breadth of experience	Aggressive
Achieving	Anxious
	Insecurity
	Superficial maturity
	Loner
	Controlling

From an examination of the different evacuation details and experiences of the 16 respondents (vide Table A1.1) it was possible to infer the likely input conditions which would have contributed to a perceived positive or negative outcome to evacuation. The histories of the majority of the interviewees who perceived that they had gained or lost from the experience fulfilled the following input conditions given below in Table A1.2.

Table A1.2 Input conditions on a dimension scale contributing to a perceived positive or negative outcome of the evacuation experience

Input conditions	Major property	Position on dimension scale for a perceived Positive	or Negative outcome
Evacuation organisation	Control	Well-monitored	Lax
Physical well-being	Care	Well cared for	Poorly cared for
Emotional experience	Security	Secure	Rejected
Parental contact	Frequency	Reasonably frequent	Infrequent
Age at evacuation	Years	Older	Younger
Length of evacuation	Years	Short	Long
Number of billets	Number	Small	Large
Sexual experience	Abuse	None	Abused
Cultural experience	Contrast	Beneficial	Not beneficial
Economic experience	Exploitation	None	Exploited

As a result of this grounded theory analysis it was hypothesised that it was these input conditions or variables which mainly contributed to an individual's evacuation experience and which determined the perceived outcome of that experience. Together with theoretical considerations from the developmental and mental health literature this led to the design of the present quantitative study and which is discussed in Chapter 2.

APPENDIX 2. Example of the note sent to secretaries of school associations in Kent for their use

A survey of the lives of war children from Kent
___

I have been contacted by Stuart Rusby, a psychologist doing research at Birkbeck College of London University, who is carrying out a survey of those who were children in Kent during the Second World War. He would like to contact any members of the Society, and any of their friends, who lived in Kent during the War years and who would be willing to participate in a survey of their perceptions of any long-term effects of that period on their lives.

The survey is being carried out by postal questionnaire, and any of you who would like to participate should contact him by leaving a telephone message on:
                    xxxxxxxxxx

requesting a copy of the questionnaire,

or by writing to:

        Stuart Rusby,
        Department of Psychology,
        Birkbeck College,
        University of London,
        Malet Street,
        London WC1E 7HX

Replies to the questionnaire can remain anonymous, but if you would be happy to be contacted after the main survey to follow up on certain themes in your life history then this can be indicated on the questionnaire. Also, for those who would like it, he will provide a summary of the main findings on the conclusion of the study.

APPENDIX 3.   Kent Survey Questionnaire

A Survey of the Lives of War Children from Kent

PHASE TWO - QUESTIONNAIRE

Stuart Rusby
Psychology Department
Birkbeck College
University of London

A survey of the lives of war children from Kent and South London

This questionnaire, which you have kindly agreed to answer, forms a major part of a study being undertaken in the Psychology Department of Birkbeck College at the University of London to survey the lives of those in Kent and South London who were children during the second World War. It follows a shorter pilot study made earlier in Kent.

The questionnaire appears long but you will see that about half the sections simply ask you to select an appropriate number on a rating scale for each item, and can be done fairly quickly. In fact it is best not to deliberate on this as your first thoughts are best! Nevertheless you may like to take a break, say at the end of section 9, and come back refreshed to finish it.

All replies will be treated as confidential, and no names will appear in any subsequent papers. Nowhere on the questionnaire are you asked to record your name and address, these will be filed separately and can only be traced by me using the reference number on the right-hand top corner of this page. If you wish to remain entirely anonymous then please just cut off this number.

Following this part of the survey I want briefly to interview a selected number of respondents in their homes. This will allow me to 'pick-up' on certain themes from an individual's life story, and discuss them with you in greater detail. If you are willing to be interviewed in this way please tick the box at the end of the questionnaire.

Since nobody has done this type of study before, little or nothing is known about the way in which war effects the children involved through social changes, or losses in the family relationships, including the effects of evacuation. It is our hope that by looking at your varied experiences as children during the war, some good some bad, and your life histories since, we will begin to see the ways in which these early experiences may have influenced your later lives. If they have, then the rersults of the study may have wider applications in the fields of child development and adult relationships.

If you would like me to send you a brief summary of the main conclusions from the survey then please tick the box at the end of the questionnaire.

Thank you for helping us in this way.

Stuart Rusby

WAR CHILD QUESTIONNAIRE

1. I would like you first to give some family details from your childhood, to 'set the scene' as it were:

    Are you male or female? ....

    Date and place of birth: ....

    Where were you brought up before the war?..

    ....

    Approximate dates of birth (and death) of any brothers and sisters:

    ....

Please give a brief description of your parents, and how you see your relationship with them in childhood and adolescence, including something on the way they brought you up. Mention also your family social situation when you were a child, and any family problems or crises at that time, including parental loss or divorce. Also any financial or employment difficulties your parents experienced during your early years.

2. From the diagrams below please select one numbered diagram in each case which best represents the closeness of your relations with your mother and father,

>in infancy, in childhood, during the war,
>immediately after the war, and in adulthood.

These degrees of closeness range from diagram No. 9 which represents an extremely close relationship to No. 1 where there was no communication or contact.

Write the chosen number in each case in the boxes after the diagrams.

	Chosen diagram No.	
Closeness to:	Mother	Father
In infancy		
In childhood		
During the war		
Immediately after the war		
In adulthood		

Were you evacuated in the war? Please tick box: YES ☐   NO ☐
If 'NO' then please go to Section 5.

3. Now follow some questions about your evacuation experiences. If you were evacuated on a second occasion please include this information as well:

	1st Evacuation	2nd Evacuation
When were you evacuated? (month/year)		
When did you return? (month/year)		
Where were you evacuated from?		
and to?		
How many billets were you in?		
How often did you see your parents?		

Did you have any brothers/sisters with you (give first names, age, and whether they were in the same or separate billets)? ....

Overall, how would you rate the care you received from your foster parents? Please tick the appropriate box.

Very Good   Good   Moderate   Poor   Very Poor   Mixed
☐   ☐   ☐   ☐   ☐   ☐

Please comment, if you wish, about the care or lack of care you received:

Were you ever physically, sexually or emotionally abused or exploited during the evacuation period? Please tick if so:

Physically	Sexually	Emotionally	Exploited as free labour
☐	☐	☐	☐

Please comment if you wish:

4. This section asks you to rate how you think the evacuation experience might have contributed to your development as an adult. If you tend to agree with the left-hand sentence then circle one of the left-hand numbers, 1-3. However if you tend to agree with its opposite, given in the right-hand sentence, then circle one of the right-hand numbers, 1-3, instead. If you believe the experience had no effect then circle the central number, 0. Please circle one number only on each line.

	Strongly agree	Moderately agree	Slightly agree	No effect	Slightly agree	Moderately agree	Strongly agree	
Overall - 'It made me'	3	2	1	0	1	2	3	'It ruined my life'
Confidence - 'It gave me confidence'	3	2	1	0	1	2	3	'It made me nervy and insecure'
Outlook - 'Evacuation narrowed my outlook on life'	3	2	1	0	1	2	3	'Evacuation broadened my horizons and interests'
In company - 'it helped me to come out of myself'	3	2	1	0	1	2	3	'It has made me something of a solitary person'

Effect on family - 'It has made me very protective of my family'	3	2	1	0	1	2	3	'It made me to let go of my children'
Anger with mother - 'Deep down it made me very angry with my mother'	3	2	1	0	1	2	3	'It drew me very close to my mother'
Unfinished business - 'It has left a dreadful urge .... to go back and put a name to the chapter'	3	2	1	0	1	2	3	'I did not feel a sudden loss on parting - there was no 'unfinished business''
Memories - 'I have difficulty recalling the memories of some events and foster parents in my evacuation'	3	2	1	0	1	2	3	'It is all very clear to me - as if it was yesterday'
A special people - 'We are an exclusive group - only those who were evacuated will understand'	3	2	1	0	1	2	3	'I do not feel different from others who were not evacuated'
Education - 'I lost out on my education'	3	2	1	0	1	2	3	'I gained in learning'

5. I would like you to give me some details of your home life during the war. If you were evacuated then please fill in what you can:

   Where was your family home(s) during the war?..

   Was your mother working?..

   When was your father at home and for how long? Give approximate dates......................

   ....

   What was his job(s)? (include any military service with approximate dates).....................

   ....

   ....

Did your family suffer any bombing, or other wartime crises? Give details: ....

....

....

If so, were you present?...

Did your family lose any immediate members during the war or did any suffer serious injury or

disabilities? If so, give details: ....

....

....

Please give a brief description of your home life during the war, including any events or crises which you feel may have affected your own development or relationship with your parents. If you were evacuated then give a brief description of your relationship with your parents and any problems of fitting in on your return:

6. Please give some details of your own adult life since the war:

    What training or study did you do after the war?

What work did you do? (with approximate dates)

What grade did you achieve? (with approximate salary) ....

What age did you marry? (if you did) and how old was your spouse? ....

Are you now (please tick):

Married ☐   Single ☐   Divorced ☐   Separated ☐   Widowed ☐

If married more than once please give brief details: ....

....

Age and sex of any sons and daughters: ....

Which, if any, live with you? ....

Where is your present home? (nearest town) ....

Where else have you lived since the war? (with approximate dates) ....

....

....

Have you ever been unemployed? Give brief details: ....

....

What age did you retire? (if you are retired) Was this early retirement or on medical advice? If so give details: ....

....

....

7. Here are four short paragraphs describing the way we relate to others. Please rate how well each description applies to you by putting a circle around one number in the scale beside each description:

	Fully applies						Does not apply
1. It is easy for me to become emotionally close to others. I am comfortable depending on others and having others depend on me. I don't worry about being alone or having others not accept me.	6	5	4	3	2	1	0
2. I am comfortable without close emotional relationships. It is very important for me to feel independent and self-sufficient, and I prefer not to depend on others, or have others depend on me.	6	5	4	3	2	1	0
3. I want to be completely emotionally intimate with others, but I often find that others are reluctant to get as close as I would like. I am uncomfortable being without close relationships, but I sometimes worry that others don't value me as much as I value them.	6	5	4	3	2	1	0
4. I am uncomfortable getting close to others. I want emotionally close relationships, but I find it difficult to trust others completely, or to depend on them. I worry that I will be hurt if I allow myself to become too close to others.	6	5	4	3	2	1	0

8. In this section if you tend to agree with the left-hand sentence then circle one of the left-hand numbers, 1-3. However if you tend to agree with its opposite, given in the right-hand sentence, then circle one of the right-hand numbers, 1-3, instead. Please circle one number only on each line.

	Strongly agree	Moderately agree	Slightly agree	Slightly agree	Moderately agree	Strongly agree	
Feelings - 'I like to express my feelings'	3	2	1	1	2	3	'I sit on my feelings'
Intimacy - 'I am capable of an intimate relationship'	3	2	1	1	2	3	'I do not want to relinquish myself'
Involvement - 'I find it easier to be an observer'	3	2	1	1	2	3	'I like to be fully involved'

Independence - 'I am fully self-sufficient'	3	2	1	1	2	3	'I am dependent on others'
Emotions - 'I readily show my emotions'	3	2	1	1	2	3	'My emotions are hidden under a hard shell'
Identity - I adjust, changing colour like a chameleon, not leaving any lasting impression'	3	2	1	1	2	3	'I feel a sense of continuity and stability, I know who I am'

9. Now follow 26 statements which refer to opinions regarding a number of social issues, about which some people agree and others disagree. Please mark each statement in the left-hand margin according to your level of agreement or disagreement as follows:

+1: slight support, agreement   -1: slight opposition, disagreement
+2: moderate support, agreement   -2: moderate opposition, disagreement
+3: strong support, agreement   -3: strong opposition, disagreement

____ 1. Obedience and respect for authority are the most important virtues children should learn.

____ 2. No weakness or difficulty can hold us back if we have enough will power.

____ 3. Science has its place but there are many important things that can never possibly be understood by the human mind.

____ 4. Human nature being what it is, there will always be war and conflict.

____ 5. Every person should have complete faith in some supernatural power whose decisions he or she obeys without question.

____ 6. When a person has a problem or worry it is best for him or her not to think about it, but to keep busy with more cheerful things.

____ 7. A person who has bad manners, habits and breeding can hardly expect to get along with decent people.

____ 8. What the young people need most is strict discipline, rugged determination, and the will to work and strive for family and country.

____ 9. Some people are born with an urge to jump from high places.

____ 10. Nowadays when so many different kinds of people move around and mix together so much, a person has to protect himself or herself especially carefully against catching an infection or disease from them.

____ 11. An insult to our honour should always be punished.

____ 12. Young people sometimes get rebellious ideas, but as they grow older they ought to get over them and settle down.

____ 13. What this country needs most, more than laws and political programmes, is a few courageous, tireless, devoted leaders in whom the people can put their faith.

____ 14. Sex crimes, like rape and attacks on children, deserve more than mere imprisonment; such criminals ought to be publicly whipped or worse.

____ 15. People can be divided into two distinct classes: the weak and the strong.

____ 16. There is hardly anything lower than a person who does not feel a great love, gratitude and respect for his or her parents.

____ 17. Some day it will probably be shown that astrology can explain a lot of things.

____ 18. Nowadays more and more people are prying into matters that should remain personal and private.

____ 19. Most of our social problems would be solved if we could somehow get rid of the immoral, crooked and feebleminded people.

____ 20. The wild sex life of the old Greeks and Romans was tame compared with some of the goings-on in this country, even in places where people might least expect it.

____ 21. If people would talk less and work more everybody would be better off.

____ 22. Most people don't realise how much our lives are controlled by plots hatched in secret places.

____ 23. Homosexual practice should not be condoned in our society.

____ 24. No sane, normal, decent person could ever think of hurting a close friend or relative.

____ 25. Familiarity breeds contempt.

____ 26. Everybody has a duty to contribute towards, or serve some caring organisation.

> Take a break?....

10. Listed below are a number of statements concerning personal characteristics. Read each item and decide whether you agree or disagree, and to what extent. If you strongly agree, circle 7; if you strongly disagree then circle 1; if you feel somewhere in between then circle anyone of the numbers between 1 and 7. The midpoint, if you are neutral or undecided, is 4.

		Strongly Disagree						Strongly Agree
1.	I set my personal goals and standards as high as possible	1	2	3	4	5	6	7
2.	Without support from others who are close to me, I would be helpless	1	2	3	4	5	6	7
3.	I tend to be satisfied with my current plans and goals, rather than striving for higher goals	1	2	3	4	5	6	7
4.	Sometimes I feel very big, and other times I feel very small.	1	2	3	4	5	6	7
5.	When I am closely involved with someone, I never feel jealous	1	2	3	4	5	6	7
6.	I urgently need things that only other people can provide.	1	2	3	4	5	6	7
7.	I often find that I don't live up to my own standards or ideals.	1	2	3	4	5	6	7
8.	I feel I am always making full use of my potential abilities.	1	2	3	4	5	6	7
9.	The lack of permanence in human relationships doesn't bother me.	1	2	3	4	5	6	7
10.	If I fail to live up to expectations, I feel unworthy.	1	2	3	4	5	6	7

		Strongly Disagree						Strongly Agree
		1	2	3	4	5	6	7
11.	Many times I feel helpless.	1	2	3	4	5	6	7
12.	I seldom worry about being criticised for things I have said or done.	1	2	3	4	5	6	7
13.	There is a considerable difference between how I am now and how I would like to be.	1	2	3	4	5	6	7
14.	I enjoy sharp competition with others.	1	2	3	4	5	6	7
15.	I feel I have many responsibilities which I must meet.	1	2	3	4	5	6	7
16.	There are times when I feel "empty" inside.	1	2	3	4	5	6	7
17.	I tend not to be satisfied with what I have.	1	2	3	4	5	6	7
18.	I don't care whether or not I live up to what other people expect of me.	1	2	3	4	5	6	7
19.	I become frightened when I am alone.	1	2	3	4	5	6	7
20.	I would feel like I'd be losing an important part of myself if I lost a very close friend.	1	2	3	4	5	6	7
21.	People will accept me no matter how many mistakes I have made.	1	2	3	4	5	6	7
22.	I have difficulty breaking off a relationship that is making me unhappy.	1	2	3	4	5	6	7
23.	I often think about the danger of losing someone who is close to me.	1	2	3	4	5	6	7
24.	Other people have high expectations of me.	1	2	3	4	5	6	7
25.	When I am with others, I tend to devalue or "undersell" myself.	1	2	3	4	5	6	7
26.	I am not very concerned with how other people respond to me.	1	2	3	4	5	6	7

		Strongly Disagree						Strongly Agree
27.	No matter how close a relationship between two people is, there is always a large amount of uncertainty and conflict.	1	2	3	4	5	6	7
28.	I am very sensitive to others for signs of rejection.	1	2	3	4	5	6	7
29.	It's important for my family that I succeed.	1	2	3	4	5	6	7
30.	Often, I feel I have disappointed others.	1	2	3	4	5	6	7
31.	If someone makes me angry, I let him (or her) know how I feel.	1	2	3	4	5	6	7
32.	I constantly try, and very often go out of my way, to please or help people I am close to.	1	2	3	4	5	6	7
33.	I have many inner resources (abilities, strengths).	1	2	3	4	5	6	7
34.	I find it very difficult to say "No" to the requests of friends.	1	2	3	4	5	6	7
35.	I never really feel secure in a close relationship.	1	2	3	4	5	6	7
36.	The way I feel about myself frequently varies: there are times when I feel extremely good about myself and other times when I see only the bad in me and feel like a total failure.	1	2	3	4	5	6	7
37.	Often, I feel threatened by change.	1	2	3	4	5	6	7
38.	Even if the person who is closest to me were to leave, I could still "go it alone".	1	2	3	4	5	6	7
39.	One must continually work to gain love from another person: that is, love has to be earned.	1	2	3	4	5	6	7
40.	I am very sensitive to the effects my words or actions have on the feelings of other people.	1	2	3	4	5	6	7
41.	I often blame myself for things I have done or said to someone.	1	2	3	4	5	6	7
42.	I am a very independent person.	1	2	3	4	5	6	7

		Strongly Disagree						Strongly Agree
43.	I often feel guilty.	1	2	3	4	5	6	7
44.	I think of myself as a very complex person, one who has "many sides".	1	2	3	4	5	6	7
45.	I worry a lot about offending or hurting someone who is close to me.	1	2	3	4	5	6	7
46.	Anger frightens me.	1	2	3	4	5	6	7
47.	It is not "who you are", but "what you have accomplished" that counts.	1	2	3	4	5	6	7
48.	I feel good about myself whether I succeed or fail.	1	2	3	4	5	6	7
49.	I can easily put my own feelings and problems aside, and devote my complete attention to the feelings and problems of someone else.	1	2	3	4	5	6	7
50.	If someone I cared about became angry with me, I would feel threatened that he (she) might leave me.	1	2	3	4	5	6	7
51.	I feel uncomfortable when I am given important responsibilities.	1	2	3	4	5	6	7
52.	After a fight with a friend, I must make amends as soon as possible.	1	2	3	4	5	6	7
53.	I have a difficult time accepting weaknesses in myself.	1	2	3	4	5	6	7
54.	It is more important that I enjoy my work than it is for me to have my work approved.	1	2	3	4	5	6	7
55.	After an argument, I feel very lonely.	1	2	3	4	5	6	7
56.	In my relationships with others, I am very concerned about what they can give to me.	1	2	3	4	5	6	7
57.	I rarely think about my family.	1	2	3	4	5	6	7

		Strongly Disagree						Strongly Agree
58.	Very frequently, my feelings toward someone close to me vary: there are times when I feel completely angry and other times when I feel all-loving towards that person.	1	2	3	4	5	6	7
59.	What I do and say has a very strong impact on those around me.	1	2	3	4	5	6	7
60.	I sometimes feel that I am "special".	1	2	3	4	5	6	7
61.	I grew up in an extremely close family.	1	2	3	4	5	6	7
62.	I am very satisfied with myself and my accomplishments.	1	2	3	4	5	6	7
63.	I want many things from someone I am close to.	1	2	3	4	5	6	7
64.	I tend to be very critical of myself.	1	2	3	4	5	6	7
65.	Being alone doesn't bother me at all.	1	2	3	4	5	6	7
66.	I very frequently compare myself to standards or goals.	1	2	3	4	5	6	7

11. Here are 3 comments made about marriage. If you are or have been married or are widowed please just circle the most appropriate numbers in each case:

	Strongly Disagree						Strongly Agree
'It was like a rebirth'.	1	2	3	4	5	6	7
'It gave me the nourishment I lacked'.	1	2	3	4	5	6	7
'I came home at last, a secure base'.	1	2	3	4	5	6	7

12 Have you ever suffered from any of the following? Please tick in the box if so:

- ☐ Depression
- ☐ Clinical Anxiety
- ☐ Eating disorders
- ☐ Nervous breakdown
- ☐ Alcohol Abuse
- ☐ Drug Abuse
- ☐ Sleep disruption
- ☐ Attempted suicide
- ☐ Severe or long-lasting headaches
- ☐ Extreme fatigue
- ☐ Severe irritability
- ☐ Phobias or irrational fears
- ☐ Fear of sickness, injury or death
- ☐ Recurring nightmares related to the family or to experiences in the war
- ☐ Avoidance behaviour (places, people, food, animals etc.)
- ☐ Extreme loneliness
- ☐ Feelings of unreality ('not quite being there')
- ☐ Asthma

If you have please give brief details and dates, including any relevant family or other crises which you believe may have contributed to the condition:

13. Have you ever suffered from any major illnesses, or had any major medical treatments or operations? Include heart attacks and strokes. Please give brief details and approximate dates:

14. Please list your past and present main interests and club/society memberships, with some brief background detail and dates. Include voluntary work, sports activities and any local council or political work:

15. Please comment on any connections you see between your wartime experiences and your later personal development, relationships, interests etc.

16. What main life events, transitions or crises have had the greatest effect on you since the war? In what way and why?

17. Finally something about your present relationships:

   1. Do you have any intimate, confiding relationship(s) in which you can express your feelings freely and without self consciousness and from which you gain a sense of security and place? Such a relationship could be provided by your spouse or partner, close friend or relative. If so, please give their first name, approximate age and whether they are related to you:

5. Do you have any relationship(s) where you believe continuing and extensive assistance would be provided to help you, should you ever need it, irrespective of mutual affection? If so, please give the first name(s) and approximate age of any such family members or other who you are assured would care for you in this way. Please say if they are related to you:

6. Do you have access to someone, professional or not, who can provide you with emotional support and guidance, particularly in a crisis, and so help you formulate and carry through some line of action? If so, please say if they are a professional worker, minister of religion or a friend/relative:

This is the end of the questionnaire. As I said on the introductory page, if you would be willing to be briefly interviewed in your home to 'follow-up' on certain themes from your life history then please tick this box: ☐

And if you would like me to send you a brief summary of what we have learned from the survey then please tick this box: ☐

Please make use of the enclosed stamped addressed envelope to return the questionnaire.

Again, may I thank you for your interest and the time you have given to this survey.

Stuart Rusby

References

Ainsworth, M.D.S. (1967). *Infancy in Uganda: Infant care and the growth of attachment.* Baltimore: John Hopkins University Press.

Ainsworth, M.D.S. (1982). Attachment: Retrospect and prospect. In C.M. Parkes and J. Stevenson-Hinde (Eds.): *The Place of Attachment in Human Behaviour.* London: Tavistock.

Ainsworth, M.D.S., Blehar, M., Waters, E. & Wall, S. (1978). *Patterns of attachment: Assessed in the Strange Situation and at home.* Hillsdale, NJ: Erlbaum.

Alt, C. (1991). Stichproben und Repräsentativität der Survey-Daten. (Sample and representativity of the survey). In: H. Bertram (Ed.), *Die Familie in Wesdeutschland: Stabilitat und Wandel familialer Lebensformen.* Opladen: Leske und Budrich.

Amato, P.R. (1988). Long-term implications of parental divorce for adult self-concept. *Journal of Family issues,* **9**, 201-213.

Amato, P.R. (1996). Explaining the intergenerational transmission of divorce. *Journal of Marriage and the Family,* **58**, 628-640.

Amato, P.R. (2001). Children of divorce in the 1990s: An update of the Amato and Keith (1991) meta-analysis. *Journal of Family Psychology,* **15**, 355-370.

Amato, P.R. & Booth, A. (1991). Consequences of parental divorce for adult well-being. *Social Forces,* **69**, 895-914.

Amato, P.R. & Keith, B. (1991). Parental divorce and the well-being of children: A meta-analysis. *Psychological Bulletin,* **110**, 26-46.

Bartholomew, K. (1993). From childhood to adult relationships: Attachment theory and research. In: S. Duck (Ed.), *Understanding relationship processes: 2. Learning about relationships.* London: Sage.

Bartholomew, K. & Horowitz, L.M. (1991). Attachment styles among young adults: A test of a four-category model. *Journal of Personality and Social Psychology,* **61**, 226-244.

Beck, A.T., Ward, C.H., Mendelsohn, M., Mock, J. & Erbaugh, J. (1961). An inventory for measuring depression. *Archives of General Psychiatry,* **4**, 892-898.

Beckwith, L., Cohen, S.E. & Hamilton, C.E. (1999). Maternal sensitivity during infancy and subsequent life events related to attachment representation at early adulthood. *Developmental Psychology,* **3**, 693-700.

Bemporad, J.R., & Romano, S. (1993). Childhood experience and adult depression: A review of studies. *American Journal of Psychoanalysis,* **53**(A), 301-315.

Bentler, P.M. (1980). Multivariate analysis with latent variables: Causal modelling. *Annual Review of Psychology,* **31**, 419-456.

Bentler, P.M. (1988). Causal modelling via structural equation systems. In: J.R. Nesselroade & R.B. Cattell (Eds), *Handbook of Multivariate experimental psychology*. New York: Plenum.

Bentler, P.M. (1992). On the fit of models to covariances and methodology. *Psychological Bulletin,* **112,** 400-404.

Bentler, P.M. (1993). *EQS/Windows User's Guide: Version 4.* BMDP Statistical Software: Los Angeles.

Bentler, P.M. (1995). *EQS Structural Equations Program Manual.* Encino, CA: Multivariate Software Inc.

Bifulco, A., Brown, G.W. & Harris, T.O. (1987). Loss of parent, lack of parental care and adult psychiatric disorder: the Islington study. *Journal of Affective disorder*, **12**, 115-128.

Bifulco, A., Harris, T.O. & Brown, G.W. (1992). Mourning or early inadequate care? Re-examining the relationship of maternal loss in childhood with adult depression and anxiety. *Development and Psychopathology*, **4**, 433-449.

Bifulco, A., Brown, G.W. & Harris, T.O. (1994). Childhood Experience of Care and Abuse (CECA): a retrospective interview measure'. *Journal of Child Psychology and Psychiatry*, **35**, 1419-1435.

Bifulco, A., Brown, G.W., Lillie, A. & Jarvis, J. (1997). Memories of neglect and abuse: corroboration in a series of sisters. *Journal of Child Psychology and Psychiatry*, **38**, 365-374.

Bifulco, A. Moran, P. (1998). *Wednesday's Child.* London: Routledge.

Billings, A., Cronkite, R.C. & Moos, R.H. (1983). Social-environmental factors in unipolar depression: Comparisons of depressed patients and nondepressed controls. *Journal of Abnormal Psychology,* **92**, 119-133.

Billings, A., Cronkite, R.C. & Moos, R.H. (1983). Social-environmental factors in unipolar depression: Comparisons of depressed patients and nondepressed controls. *Journal of Abnormal Psychology,* **92**, 119-133.

Birtchnell, J. (1970). Depression in relation to early and recent parent death. *British Journal of Psychiatry*, **116**, 299-306.

Birtchnell, J. (1984). Dependence and its relationship to depression. *British Journal of Medical Psychology,* **57**, 212-225.

Birtchnell, J. (1988a). Defining dependence. *British Journal of Medical Psychology,* **61**, 111-123.

Birtchnell, J. (1988b). Depression and family relationships. *British Journal of Psychiatry*, **153**, 758-769.

Birtchnell, J. & Kennard, J. (1984). How do experiences of the early separated and the early bereaved differ and to what extent do such differences effect outcome? *Social Psychiatry*, **19**(4), 163-171.

Blatt, S.J., D'Affitti, J.P., & Quinlan, D.M. (1976). Experiences of depression in normal young adults. *Journal of Abnormal Psychiatry*, **85**, 383-389.

Blatt, S.J. & Zuroff, D.C. (1992). Interpersonal relatedness and self-definition: two prototypes of depression. *Clinical Psychology Review*, **12**, 527-562.

Blatt, S.J., Chevron, E., Quinlan, D.M., Schaffer, C. & Wein, S. (1992). *The assessment of qualitative and structural dimensions of object representations.* Unpublished research manual, Yale University.

Blatt, S.J., Zohar, A.H., Quinlan, D.M., Zuroff, D.C., & Mongrain, M. (1997). Subscales within the Dependency factor of the Depressive Experiences Questionnaire. *Journal of Personality Assessment*, **64**, 319-339.

Bowlby, J. (1946). *Forty-four juvenile thieves: their characters and home life*. London: Bailliere, Tindall and Cox.

Bowlby, (1953). *Child care and the growth of love*. London: Harmondsworth.

Bowlby, J. (1960). Symposium on 'psychoanalysis and ethology': II. Ethology and the development of object relations. *International Journal of Psychoanalysis,* **41**, 313-317.

Bowlby, J. (1961). Separation Anxiety: A critical review of the literature. *Journal of Child Psychology and Psychiatry*, **1**, 251-269.

Bowlby, J. (1969). *Attachment and Loss: Vol. 1, Attachment*. London: Hogarth Press.

Bowlby, J. (1973). *Attachment and Loss: Vol. 2, Separation*. London: Hogarth Press.

Bowlby, J. (1980). *Attachment and Loss: Vol. 3, Loss, sadness and depression*. London: Hogarth Press.

Bowlby, J. (1982). *Attachment and Loss: Vol.1, Attachment* (2nd Ed.). New York: Basic Books

Bowlby, J. (1988). *A Secure Base: Clinical Applications of Attachment Theory*. London: Routledge.

Box, G.E.P. (1954). Some theorems on quadratic forms applied in the study of analysis of variance problems: 1. Effect of inequality of variance in the one-way classification. *Annals of Mathematical Statistics*, **25**, 290-302.

Bretherton, I. & Waters, E. (1985). *Growing Points of Attachment Theory and Research.* Monographs of the Society for Research in Child Development, vol. 50 (1-2), serial No. 209. Chicago: University of Chicago Press.

Brewin, C.R., Andrews, B. & Gotlib, I.H. (1993). Psychopathology and early experience: a reappraisal of retrospective reports. *Psychological Bulletin*, **113**, 82-98.

Brown, H. (1985). *People, Groups and Society.* Milton Keynes: Open University Press.

Brown, G.W. & Harris, T. (1978). *Social origins of depression: A study of psychiatric disorder in women*. London: Tavistock.

Brown, G.W., Harris, T. & Bifulco, A. (1986). Long-term effects of early loss of parent. In: M. Rutter et al (Eds.), *Depression in young people: Clinical and Developmental Perspectives* (pp. 251-296). New York: Guilford Press.

Brown, G.W., Harris, T. & Hepworth, C. (1995). Loss, humiliation and entrapment among women developing depression: a patient and non-patient comparison. *Psychological Medicine*, **25**, 7-21.

Bumpass, L.L., & Sweet, J.A. (1972). Differentials in marital stability: 1970. *American Sociological Review*, **37**, 754-766.

Bumpass, L.L., Martin, T.C. & Sweet, J.A. (1991). The impact of family background and early marital factors on marital disruption. *Journal of Family Issues*, **12**, 22-42.

Burt, C. (1940). The incidence of neurotic symptoms among evacuated school children. *Brit. J. Educ. Psychology*, **10**, 8-15.

Burt, C. (1941). The billeting of evacuated children. *Brit. J. Educ. Psychology*, **11**, 85-97.

Burt, C. (1943). War neurosis in British children. *Nervous Child*, II, **4**, 324-344.

Byrne, B.M. (1994). *Structural equation modelling with EQS and EQS for Windows.* Thousand Oaks, CA: Sage.

Carey-Trefzer, C.J. (1949). The results of a clinical study of war-damaged children who attended the Child Guidance Clinic, The Hospital for Sick Children, Great Ormond Street, London. *Journal of Mental Science*, **95**, 535-559.

Carp, F.M.. (1991). *Lives of career women: Approaches to work, marriage, children.* New York: Insight Books.

Chevron, E.S., Quinlan, D.M. & Blatt, S.J. (1978). Sex Roles and Gender Differences in the experience of Depression. *Journal of Abnormal Psychology*, **87**, 680-683.

Coffman, S., Levitt, M.J., & Guacci-Franco, N. (1993). Mother's stress and close relationships; Correlates with infant health status. *Pediatric Nursing*, **19**, 135-142.

Cohen, J. (1960). A coefficient of agreement for nominal scales. *Educational and Psychological Measurement*, **10**, 37-46.

Cohen, J. (1988). *Statistical power analysis for the behavioural sciences (2nd. ed.).* New York: Academic Press

Crowell, J.A. (1990). *Current Relationship Interview.* Unpublished manuscript, State University of New York at Stony Brook.

Crowell, J.A. & Treboux, D. (1995). A review of adult attachment measures: Implications for theory and research. *Social Development*, **4**, 294-327.

Davies, S. (1996). Personal communication.

Davies, S. (1997). The long-term psychological effects of World War 2. The Psychologist, August, 1997.

Diekmann, A. & Engelhardt, H. (1999). The social inheritance of divorce: The effects of parent's family type in post-war Germany. *American Sociological Review*, **64**, 783-793.

Eaves, L.J., Silberg, J.L., Meyer, J.M., Maes, H.H., Simonoff, E., Pickles, A., Rutter, M., Neale, M.C., Reynolds, C.A., Erikson, M.T., Heath, A.C., Loeber, R., Truett, K.R., & Hewitt, J.K. (1997). Genetics and developmental psychopathology: 2. The main effects of genes and environment on behavioural problems in the Virginia Twin Study of Adolescent Behavioural Development. *Journal of Child Psychology and Psychiatry*, **38**, 965-980.

Emslie, C., Hunt, K. & Macintyre, S. (1999). Gender differences in minor morbidity among full time employees of a British university. *Journal of Epidemiology and Community Health,* **53**, 465-475

Erikson, E.H. (1968). *Identity: Youth and Crisis.* New York: Norton.

Erickson, M.F., Sroufe, L.A. & Egeland, B. (1985). The relationship between quality of attachment and behaviour problems in preschool in a high risk sample. In: I. Bretherton & E. Waters (Eds.), *Growing points of attachment theory and research.* Monographs of the Society for Research in Child Development, 50 (1-2, Serial No. 209), 147-186.

Fairbairn, W.R.D. (1952). *Psychoanalytic Studies of the Personality.* London: Routledge.

Faravelli, C., Sachetti, E., Ambonetti, A., Conte, G., Pallanti, S. & Vita, A. (1986). Early life events and affective disorder revisited. *British Journal of Psychiatry*, **148**, 288-295.

Feeney, J.C. & Noller, P. (1990). Attachment style as a predictor of adult romantic relationships. *Journal of Personality and Social Psychology*, **58**, 281-291.

Fonagy, P. (2003). The development of psychopathology from infancy to adulthood: The mysterious unfolding of disturbance in time. *Infant Mental Health Journal*, **24**(3), 212-239.

Fornell, C. (1982). *A second generation of multivariate analysis: Vol. 1. Methods.* New York: Praeger.

Foster, D. (2000). *The evacuation of British children during World War 2 : A preliminary investigation into long-term effects.* Thesis submitted as part fulfilment of a Doctorate in Clinical Psychology, University College, London.

Freud, S. (1905). Three essays on Sexuality. In: *The Complete Psychological Works of Sigmund Freud.* London: Hogarth Press.

Freud, S. (1926). Inhibitions, Symptoms and Anxiety. In: *The Complete Psychological Works of Sigmund Freud.* London: Hogarth Press.

Freud, A. & Burlingham, D.T. (1944). *Infants without families and Reports on the Hampstead Nurseries, 1939-45.* London: Hogarth Press.

Frosh, S. (1991). *Identity Crisis.* London: Macmillan.

Furukawa, T.A., Oguna, A., Hirai, T., Fujihara, S., Kitamura, T., & Takahashi, K. (1999). Early parental separation experiences among patients with bipolar disorder and major depression: A case control study. *Journal of Affective Disorders*, **52**(1-3), 85-91.

George, C., Kaplan, N. & Main, M. (1984). *Adult Attachment Interview*. Unpublished protocol, Department of Psychology, University of California, Berkeley.

Glaser, B. & Strauss, A. (1967). *The discovery of grounded theory.* Chicago: Aldine.

Glass, G.V. & Stanley, J.C. (1970). *Statistical Methods in Education and Psychology.* New Jersey: Prentice-Hall.

Glenn, N. & Kramer, K.B. (1985). The psychological well-being of adult children of divorce. *Journal of Marriage and the Family*, **47**, 905-912.

Goldberg, D. (1978). *Manual of the General Health Questionnaire.* Windsor: NFER Nelson.

Goldberg, D. & Huxley, P. (1992). Common mental disorders. London: Routledge.

Grossman, K.E. & Grossman, K. (1991). Attachment quality as an organiser of emotional and behavioural responses in a longitudinal perspective. In: C.M. Parkes, J. Stevenson-Hinde & P. Morris (Eds.), *Attachment across the life cycle* (pp. 93-114). London: Tavistock/Routledge.

Gunn, D. (1995). Personal communication.

Guntrip, H. (1973). *Psychoananalytic Theory, Therapy and the Self.* New York: Basic Books.

Hamilton, C.E. (2000). Continuity and discontinuity of attachment from infancy through adolescence. *Child Development*, **71**, 690-694.

Harlow, H. (1958). The nature of love. *American Psychologist*, **13**, 673-685

Harris, T., Brown, G.W. & Bifulco, A. (1986). Loss of a parent in childhood and adult psychiatric disorder: The role of lack of adequate parental care. *Psychological Medicine*, **16**, 641-659.

Harris, T.O. (1988). Psychosocial vulnerability to depression. In: S. Henderson & G. Burrows (Eds.), *Handbook of Social Psychiatry*. Amsterdam: Elsevier.

Harris, T., Brown, G.W. & Bifulco, A. (1990). Loss of a parent in childhood and adult psychiatric disorder: a tentative overall model. *Development and Psychopathology*, **2**, 311-328.

Hayward, P. (1997). *Children in Exile.* Dover: Buckland.

Hazan, C. & Shaver, P.R. (1987). Romantic love conceptualised as an attachment process. *Journal of Personality and Social Psychology*, **52**(3), 511-524.

Hazan, C. & Shaver, P.R. (1994). Attachment as an organisational framework for research on close relationships. *Psychological Inquiry*, **5**, 1-22.

Henderson, S. (1977).The social network, support and neurosis, the function of attachments in adult life. *British Journal of Psychiatry*, **131**, 185-191.

Henirch, C.C., Blatt, S.J., Kuperminc, G.P., Zohar, A. & Leadbeater, B.J. (2001). Levels of interpersonal concerns and social functioning in early adolescent boys and girls. *Journal of Personality Assessment*, **76**(1), 48-67.

Holmes, J. (1993). *John Bowlby and Attachment Theory*. London: Routledge.

Howell, D.C. (1992). *Statistical Methods for Psychology*. Belmont, CA: Duxbury.

Infrasca, R. (2003). Childhood adversities and adult depression: an experimental study on childhood depressogenic markers. *Journal of Affective Disorders,* **76**, 103-111.

Isaacs, S., Brown, S.C. & Thouless, R.H. (1941). (Eds.). *The Cambridge Evacuation Survey*. London: Methuen.

Kaplan, N. (1987). *Individual differences in six-year-olds' thoughts about separation: Predicted from attachment to mother at age one*. Doctoral Dissertation, University of California at Berkeley.

Kaplan, D. (1990). Evaluating and modifying covariance structure models: A review and recommendation. *Multivariate Behavioural Research,* 25(2), 137-155.

Kessler, R.C., Davis, C.G., & Kendler, K.S. (1997). Childhood adversity and adult psychiatric disorder in the US National Comorbidity Survey. *Psychological Medicine*, 27(5), 1101-1119.

Klein, M. (1934). On Criminality. In M. Klein et al.: *Developments in Psychoanalysis*. London: Hogarth.

Kleinfeld, J. & Bloom, J. (1977). Boarding schools: Effects on the mental health of Eskimo adolescents. American Journal of Psychiatry, 1977, **134**(4), 411-417.

Kobak, R. & Hazan, C. (1991). Attachment in marriage: Effects of security and accuracy of working models. *Journal of Personality and Social Psychology*, 60, 861-869.

Kobak, R. (1994). Adult attachment: A personality relationship construct? Commentary in C. Hazan & P.R. Shaver target article: Attachment as an organisational framework for research on close relationships. *Psychological Inquiry*, **5**, 1-79.

Kulka, R.A. & Weingaarten, H. (1979). The long-term effects of parental divorce in childhood on adult adjustment. *Journal of Social Issues*, 35, 50-78.

Lagnebro, L. (1994). *Finska krigsbarn (Finnish Warchildren)*. Doctoral thesis for Umea University, Sweden.

Lagnebro, L. (2002). Personal communication.

Laing, R.D. (1965). *The Divided Self*. London: Penguin.

Langer, J.A. (2001). *Developing and testing a model of depression: Gender, dependency, self-criticism and mutuality*. Doctoral Thesis for the University of Minnesota.

Lee, S.-Y., Poon, W.-Y. & Bentler, P.M. (1994). Covariance and correlation structure analyses with continuous and polytomous variables. In: T.W. Anderson, K.-T. Fang & I. Olkin (Eds.), *Multivariate Analysis and its Applications: Vol. 24*. Hayward, CA: Institute of Mathematical Statistics.

Levine, H. (1960). Robust tests for the equality of variance. In: I. Olkin (Ed), *Contributions to probability and statistics*. Palo Alto, CA: Stanford University Press

Levine, L., Tuber, S., Slade, A. & Ward, M.J. (1991). Mother's mental representations and their relationship to mother-infant attachment. *Bulletin of the Meninger Clinic*, 55, 454-469.

Levinger, G. (1976). A socio-psychological perspective on marital dissolution. *Journal of Social Issues*, **52**, 21-47.

Levinson, D.J. & Huffman, P.E. (1955). Traditional family ideology and its relation to personality. *Journal of Personality*, **23**, 251-273.

Levy, K.N., & Blatt, S. J. (1993). *Attachment style and mental representation in young adults.* Unpublished manuscript.

Lorenz, K. (1952). *King Solomon's Ring*. London: Methuen.

Maccoby, E.E. (1980). *Social development - Psychological growth and the parent-child relationship.* New York: Harcourt Brace Jovanovich.

Main, M. (2001). The organised categories of infant, child and adult attachment: Flexible v. Inflexible attention under attachment-related stress. *Journal of the American Psychoanalytic Association,* **48**, 1055-1096.

Main, M. & Cassidy, J (1988). Categories of response to reunion with the parent at age 6: Predictable from infant attachment classifications and stable over a 1-month period. *Developmental Psychology*, **24**, 415-426.

Main, M., Kaplan, N. & Cassidy, J. (1985). Security in infancy, childhood and adulthood: A move to the level of representation. In: I. Bretherton & E.Waters (Eds.), *Growing Points of Attachment Theory and Research.* Monographs of the Society for Research in Child Development. vol.50 (1-2), serial No. 209.Chicago: University of Chicago Press.

Marcia, J.E. (1980). Identity in adolescence. In: J. Adelson (Ed.), *Handbook of Adolescent Psychiatry.* New York: Wiley.

Mueller, R.O. (1996). *Basic principles of structural equation modelling.* New York: Springer.

National Centre for Health Statistics. (1998). *Sample design, sampling weights, imputation and variance estimates in the 1995 National Survey of Family Growth.* Washington, DC: U.S. Government Printing Office.

Norušis, M.J. (1993). SPSS for Windows, Release 6. Chicago: SPSS Inc.

O'Connor, T.G. Thorpe, K. Golding, J. & Dunn, J. (1999). Parental divorce and adjustment in adulthood: findings from a community sample. *Journal of child psychology and psychiatry*, **40**, 777-789.

Odlum, D. (1948). The psychological effects of war on British children. *Schweizer-Archiv-fuer-Neurlogie-und-Psychiatrie*, **61**, 406-407.

Office for National Statistics, (1998). *Simplified list of Social Class based on Occupation.* ONC: Fareham.

Padley, R. & Cole, M. (1940). *Evacuation Survey: A report of the Fabian Society.* London: Routledge.

Paikoff, R. and Brooks-Gunn, J. (1991). Do Parent-child relationships change during puberty? *Psychological Bulletin,* **110**, 47-67.

Parker, G. (1982). Early environment. In: E.S. Paykel (Ed.). *Handbook of Affective Disorders.* Edinburgh: Churchill Livingstone.

Parker, G. (1983). Parental affectionless control as an antecedent to adult depression. *Archives of General Psychiatry*, **134**, 138-147.

Parsons, M.L. (1998). *I'll take that one: Dispelling the myths of civilian evacuation, 1939-1945.* Peterborough: Beckett Karlson.

Perris, C., Holmgren, S., von Knorring, L. & Perris, H. (1986). Parental loss by death in the early childhood of depressed patients and of their healthy siblings. *British Journal of Psychiatry*, **148**, 165-169.

Pettigrew, T.F. (1958). Personality and socio-cultural factors in intergroup attitudes: a cross-national comparison. *Journal of Conflict Resolution*, **2**, 29-42.

Pope, H. & Mueller, C.W. (1976). The intergenerational transmission of marital instability; Comparisons by race and sex. *Journal of Family Issues*, **32**, 49-66.

Quinton, D. (1989). Adult consequences of early parental loss: Quality of care matters more than the loss itself. *British Medical Journal*, **299**, 694-695.

Radloff, L.S. (1977). The CES-D Scale: A self-report Depression scale for research in the general population. *Applied Psychological Measurement*, **1**, 385-401.

Rank, O. (1924). *The Trauma of Birth*. London: Kegan Paul.

Räsänen, E. (1992). Excessive life changes during childhood and their effects on mental and physical health in adulthood. *Acta Paedopsychiatrica*, **55**, 19-24.

Reiss, D., Hetherington, E.M., Plomin, R., Howe, G.W., Simmens, S.J., Henderson, S.H., O'Connor, T.J., Bussell, D., Anderson, E.R. & Law, T. (1995). Genetic questions for environmental studies: Differential parenting and psychopathology in adolescence. *Archives of General Psychiatry*, **52**, 925-936.

Richardson, J. (1990). *Children in retreat*. Sawd Publications.

Robertson, J. (1953). Some responses of young children to the loss of maternal care. *Nursing Care*, **49**, 382-386.

Robertson, J. & Bowlby, J. (1952). Responses of young children to separation from their mothers. *Courrant Centre Internationale Enfance*, **2**, 131-142.

Roffey, J. (1997). Personal communication

Rokeach, M. (1960). *The open and closed mind.* New York: Basic Books.

Roskies, E. & Carrier, S. (1994). Marriage and children for professional women: Asset or liability? In: G.W. Keita & J.J. Hurrell (Eds.), *Job stress in a changing workforce: Investigating gender, diversity and family issues* (pp. 269-282). Washington, DC: American Psychological Association.

Rothbard, J.C. & Shaver, P.R. (1991). *Attachment styles and the quality and importance of attachment to parents.* Unpublished manuscript, State University of New York at Buffalo.

Rothbard, J. C. & Shaver, P.R. (1994). Continuity of Attachment across the life span. In: M.B. Sperling & W.H. Berman (Eds.), *Attachment in Adults: Clinical and Developmental Perspectives* (pp.31-71). New York: Guilford Press.

Roy, A. (1978). Vulnerability factors and depression in women. *British Journal of Psychiatry*, **133**, 106-110.

Roy, A. (1981). Role of past loss in depression. *Archives of General Psychiatry*, **38**, 301-302.

Rusby, J.S.M. (1995). *Wartime evacuation: a pilot study of some effects using grounded theory.* Project report submitted as partial fulfilment for the degree of Bachelor of Science in Psychology, Birbeck College, University of London.

Rutter, M. (1972). *Maternal deprivation reassessed.* London: Harmondsworth.

Rutter,M. (1977). Isle of Wight studies, 1964-1974. *Annual Progress in Child Psychiatry*, 1977, 359-392.

Rutter, M. (1980). *Changing youth in a changing society: Patterns of adolescent development and disorder.* Cambridge, M.A.: Harvard University Press.

Rutter, M. (1982). *Maternal deprivation reassessed (Second edition).* London: Harmondsworth.

Rutter, M. (1994). Family discord and conduct disorder: Cause, consequence or correlate. *Journal of Family Psychology, 8,* 170-186.

Rutter, M. & Smith, D. (1995). (Eds.) *Psychosocial disorders in young people. Time trends and their causes.* Chichester:Wiley.

Scheffé, H.A. (1959). *The analysis of variance.* New York: Wiley.

Serenius, M. (1995). The silent cry: A Finnish child during World War 2 and 50 years later. *International forum of Psychoanalysis (Stockholm)*, **4**, 35-47.

Serenius, M. (1996). Personal communication.

Shaver, P.R. & Hazan, C. (1993). Adult romantic attachment: Theory and evidence. In: D. Perlman & W. Jones (Eds.), *Advances in personal relationships* (Vol. 4, pp. 29-70). London: Jessica Kingsley.

Strange, A. & Main, M. (1985). Attachment and parent-child discourse patterns. Paper presented at the biennial meeting of the Society for Research in Child Development, Toronto.

Strauss, A. & Corbin, J. (1990). *Basics of qualitative research: grounded theory procedures and techniques.* London: Sage.

Tabachnick, B.G. & Fidell, L.S. (1996). Using Multivariate Statistics, 3rd Edition. New York: Harper Collins.

Takeuchi, H., Hiroe, T., Kanai, T., Morinobu, S., Kitamura, T., Takahashi, K., & Furukawa, T.A. (2002). Childhood parental separation experiences and depressive symptomatology in acute major depression. *Psychiatry and Clinical Neurosciences*, **53**, 215-219.

Teachman, J.D. (1982). Methodological issues in the analysis of family formation and dissolution. *Journal of Marriage and the Family*, **44**, 1037-53.

Teachman, J.D. (2002). Childhood living arrangements and the intergenerational transmission of divorce. *Journal of Marriage and the Family*, **64**, 717-729.

Tennant, C., Hurry, J. & Bebbington, P. (1980). Parent-child separations during childhood: Their relation to adult psychiatric morbidity and to psychiatric referral: preliminary findings. *Acta Psychiatrica Scandinavica (Symposium)*, **31**, 324-331.

Tennant, C., Hurry, J. & Bebbington, P. (1982). The relation of childhood separation experiences to adult depressive and anxiety states. *British Journal of Psychiatry*, **141**, 475-482.

Tennant, C. (1988). Parental loss in childhood: Its effect in adult life. *Archives of General Psychiatry*, **45**, 1045-1050.

Tinbergen, N. (1953). *The Study of Instinct.* Oxford: Clarendon Press.

Titmus, R.M. (1950). *Problems of Social Policy.* HM Stationery Office, London.

Tizard, B. & Hodges, J. (1978). The effect of early institutional rearing on the development of eight-year-old children. *Journal of Child Psychology and Psychiatry,* **19**, 99-118.

Tweed, L. Schoenbach, V., George, L. & Blazer, D. (1989). The effects of childhood parental death and divorce on six-month history of anxiety disorders. *British Journal of Psychiatry*, **154**, 823-828.

Vaughn, B. & Egeland, B. (1979). Individual differences in infant-mother attachment at twelve and eighteen months. *Child Development*, **50**, 971-975.

Waters, E., Merrick, S., Treboux, D., Crowell, J. & Albersheim, L. (2000a). Attachment security in infancy and early adulthood: A twenty-year longitudinal study. *Child Development*, **71**, 684-689.

Waters, E., Weinfield, N.S. & Hamilton, C.E. (2000b). The stability of attachment security from infancy to adolescence and early adulthood: General discussion. *Child Development*, **71**, 703-706.

Waugh, M. (2001). *The long-term sequelae of childhood experiences during World War 2.* Thesis submitted as part fulfilment of a Doctorate in Clinical Psychology, University College, London.

Weinfield, N.S., Sroufe, L.A. & Egeland, B. (2000). Attachment from infancy to early adulthood in a high-risk sample: Continuity, discontinuity and their correlates. *Child Development*, **71**, 695-702.

Weissman, M.M & Olfson, M.(1995). Depression in women: Implications for health care research.

Science, **269**, 799-801.

Wicks, B. (1988). *No time to say goodbye.* London: Bloomsbury.

Wing, J.K., Cooper, J.E. & Sartorius, N. (1974). *The Measurement and Classification of Psychiatric Symptoms: An instruction manual for the Present State Examination and CATEGO Programme.* London: Cambridge University Press.

Winnicott, D.W. (1965). *The Maturational Process and the Facilitating Environment.* London: Hogarth.

Wolf, K.M. 1945. Evacuation of children in wartime. In A. Freud, H. Hartmann & E. Kris (Eds.), *The Psychoanalytic study of the child, Vol.1*

Wolfinger, N. (1999). Trends in the intergenerational transmission of divorce. *Demography*, **36**, 415-420.

Women's Group on Public Welfare. (1943). *Our towns: A close up.* Oxford University Press.

Zahner, G.E.P. & Murphy, M. (1989). Loss in childhood: Anxiety in adulthood. *Comprehensive Psychiatry*, **30**, 553-563.

Zung, W.W. (1965). Self-rating Depression Scale. *Archives of General Psychiatry*, **12**, 63-70.

Printed in the United Kingdom
by Lightning Source UK Ltd.
132182UK00001BA/12/P